Praise for

# The Other Slavery

"*The Other Slavery* is a necessary work that occupies a loaded historical landscape . . . [Reséndez's] evidence speaks for itself, and the horrors
quietly pile up . . . Even if you know some of the embarrassing details
(Native Americans only legally became citizens of their own country in
1924), *The Other Slavery*'s understated just-the-facts reportage will likely
surprise you. It's a study in the abuse of power that lays bare a shameful
history, and suggests a clear, chilling line to our present."    — NPR

"Reséndez corrects a blind spot in our understanding of North American history and illuminates mechanisms by which present-day versions
of the practice endure."    — *The New Yorker*

"It is not often that a single work of history can change the course of an
entire field and upset the received notions and received knowledge of
the generations, but that is exactly what *The Other Slavery* does . . . [Re-
séndez] shows a masterful grasp of the history and an astonishing
command of archival material in not a few languages . . . Carefully re-
searched and compelling . . . This book is, arguably, one of the most profound contributions to North American history published since Patricia
Nelson Limerick's *Legacy of Conquest* and Richard White's *The Middle
Ground*."    — *Los Angeles Times*

"[A] long-awaited and important book . . . No other book before has so
thoroughly related the broad history of Indian slavery in the Americas,
and not just its facts but the very reason it has been overlooked."

— *San Francisco Chronicle*

# *The* OTHER Slavery

### *The* UNCOVERED STORY *of* INDIAN ENSLAVEMENT *in* AMERICA

## Andrés Reséndez

MARINER BOOKS
HOUGHTON MIFFLIN HARCOURT
BOSTON • NEW YORK

First Mariner Books edition 2017
Copyright © 2016 by Andrés Reséndez

For information about permission to reproduce selections from this book,
write to trade.permissions@hmhco.com or to Permissions, Houghton Mifflin Harcourt
Publishing Company, 3 Park Avenue, 19th Floor, New York, New York 10016.

www.hmhco.com

*Library of Congress Cataloging-in-Publication Data*
Names: Reséndez, Andrés.
Title: The other slavery : the uncovered story of Indian enslavement
in America / Andrés Reséndez.
Other titles: Uncovered story of Indian enslavement in America
Description: Boston : Houghton Mifflin Harcourt, [2016]
Includes bibliographical references and index.
Identifiers: LCCN 2015037557 | ISBN 9780547640983 (hardcover)
ISBN 9780544602670 (ebook) | ISBN 9780544947108 (pbk.)
Subjects: LCSH: Indian slaves — United States — History. | Slave trade —
United States — History. | Indians, Treatment of — United States — History. |
Indians of North America — History. | Slavery — United States — History. |
Indian slaves — North America — History. | Indians, Treatment of —
North America — History. | Slave trade — North America — History. |
Slavery — North America—History.
Classification: LCC E98.S6 R47 2016 | DDC 306.3/620973 — dc23
LC record available at http://lccn.loc.gov/2015037557

Book design by Chrissy Kurpeski
Maps and charts by Mapping Specialists, Ltd.

Printed in the United States of America
DOC 10 9 8 7 6 5 4 3
4500690208

*To my family in California, Mexico, and Finland*

# *Contents*

# List of Illustrations

# List of Maps

*All commissioned maps rendered by*
*Mapping Specialists, Ltd., Fitchburg, Wisconsin.*

# List of Appendixes

# The Other Slavery

# Introduction

THE VERY WORD "slavery" brings to mind African bodies stuffed in the hold of a ship or white-aproned maids bustling in an antebellum home. Textbooks, memoirs, and movies continuously reinforce the notion that slaves were black Africans imported into the New World. We may be aware that in the long sweep of history, peoples other than Africans have been held in bondage—a practice that continues today as millions of Asians, hundreds of thousands of Latin Americans, and thousands of Europeans can readily attest. But we still seem unable to escape our historical myopia.[1]

Consider the debate at the conclusion of the U.S.-Mexican War of 1846–1848. The United States had just acquired Texas, New Mexico, Arizona, California, Nevada, Utah, more than half of Colorado, and parts of Wyoming and Kansas. The question facing the country was whether slavery should be allowed in this vast territorial haul. By slavery, of course, politicians of that era meant *African* slavery. But the adjective was wholly unnecessary, as everyone in the United States knew who the slaves were. Therefore it came as a revelation to many easterners making their way across the continent that there were also Indian slaves, entrapped in a distinct brand of bondage that was even older in the New World, perpetrated by colonial Spain and inherited by Mexico. With the

Treaty of Guadalupe Hidalgo at the end of the war, this other slavery became a part of Americans' existence.[2]

California may have entered the Union as a "free-soil" state, but American settlers soon discovered that the buying and selling of Indians was a common practice there. As early as 1846, the first American commander of San Francisco acknowledged that "certain persons have been and still are imprisoning and holding to service Indians against their will" and warned the general public that "the Indian population must not be regarded in the light of slaves." His pleas went unheeded. The first California legislature passed the Indian Act of 1850, which authorized the arrest of "vagrant" Natives who could then be "hired out" to the highest bidder. This act also enabled white persons to go before a justice of the peace to obtain Indian children "for indenture." According to one scholarly estimate, this act may have affected as many as twenty thousand California Indians, including four thousand children kidnapped from their parents and employed primarily as domestic servants and farm laborers.[3]

Americans learned about this other slavery one state at a time. In New Mexico, James S. Calhoun, the first Indian agent of the territory, could not hide his amazement at the sophistication of the Indian slave market. "The value of the captives depends upon age, sex, beauty, and usefulness," wrote Calhoun. "Good looking females, not having passed the 'sear and yellow leaf,' are valued from $50 to $150 each; males, as they may be useful, one-half less, never more." Calhoun met many of these slaves and wrote pithy notes about them: "Refugio Picaros, about twelve years of age, taken from a rancho near Santiago, State of Durango, Mexico two years ago by Comanches, who immediately sold him to the Apaches, and with them he lived and roamed . . . until January last [1850], when he was bought by José Francisco Lucero, a New Mexican residing at the Moro." "Teodora Martel, ten or twelve years of age, was taken from the service of José Alvarado near Saltillo, Mexico by Apaches two years ago, and has remained the greater portion of the time on the west side of the Rio del Norte."[4]

Americans settling the West did more than become familiar with this other type of bondage. They became part of the system. Mormon settlers arrived in Utah in the 1840s looking for a promised land, only to discover that Indians and Mexicans had already turned the Great Basin into a slaving ground. The area was like a gigantic moonscape of bleached sand, salt flats, and mountain ranges inhabited by small bands no larger than extended families. Early travelers to the West did not hide their contempt for these "digger Indians," who lacked both horses and weapons. These vulnerable Paiutes, as they were known, had become easy prey for other, mounted Indians. Brigham Young and his followers, after establishing themselves in the area, became the most obvious outlet for these captives. Hesitant at first, the Mormons required some encouragement from slavers, who tortured children with knives or hot irons to call attention to their trade and elicit sympathy from potential buyers or threatened to kill any child who went unpurchased. Brigham Young's son-in-law Charles Decker witnessed the execution of an Indian girl before he agreed to exchange his gun for another captive. In the end, the Mormons became buyers and even found a way to rationalize their participation in this human market. "Buy up the Lamanite [Indian] children," Brigham Young counseled his brethren in the town of Parowan, "and educate them and teach them the gospel, so that many generations would not pass ere they should become a white and delightsome people." This was the same logic Spanish conquistadors had used in the sixteenth century to justify the acquisition of Indian slaves.[5]

The beginnings of this other slavery are lost in the mists of time. Native peoples such as the Zapotecs, Mayas, and Aztecs took captives to use as sacrificial victims; the Iroquois waged campaigns called "mourning wars" on neighboring groups to avenge and replace their dead; and Indians in the Pacific Northwest included male and female slaves as part of the goods sent by the groom to his bride's family to finalize marriages among the elite. Native Americans had enslaved each other for millennia, but with the arrival of Europeans, practices of captivity originally embedded in specific cultural contexts became commodified, expanded in unexpected ways, and came to resemble the kinds of human trafficking that are recognizable to us today.[6]

The earliest European explorers began this process by taking indigenous slaves. Columbus's very first business venture in the New World consisted of sending four caravels loaded to capacity with 550 Natives back to Europe, to be auctioned off in the markets of the Mediterranean. Others followed in the Admiral's lead. The English, French, Dutch, and Portuguese all became important participants in the Indian slave trade. Spain, however, by virtue of the large and densely populated colonies it ruled, became the dominant slaving power. Indeed, Spain was to Indian slavery what Portugal and later England were to African slavery.

Ironically, Spain was the first imperial power to formally discuss and recognize the humanity of Indians. In the early 1500s, the Spanish monarchs prohibited Indian slavery except in special cases, and after 1542 they banned the practice altogether. Unlike African slavery, which remained legal and firmly sustained by racial prejudice and the struggle against Islam, the enslavement of Native Americans was against the law. Yet this categorical prohibition did not stop generations of determined conquistadors and colonists from taking Native slaves on a planetary scale, from the Eastern Seaboard of the United States to the tip of South America, and from the Canary Islands to the Philippines. The fact that this other slavery had to be carried out clandestinely made it even more insidious. It is a tale of good intentions gone badly astray.[7]

When I began researching this book, one number was of particular interest to me: how many Indian slaves had there been in the Americas since the time of Columbus? My initial belief was that Indian slavery had been somewhat marginal. Even if the traffic of Indians had flourished during the early colonial period, it must have gone into deep decline once African slaves and paid workers became available in sufficient numbers. Along with most other historians, I assumed that the real story of exploitation in the New World involved the twelve million Africans carried off across the Atlantic. But as I kept collecting sources on Indian slavery in Spanish, Mexican, and U.S. archives, I began to see things differently. Indian slavery never went away, but rather coexisted with African slavery from the sixteenth all the way through the late nineteenth century. This realization made me ponder more seriously the question of visibility. Because African slavery was legal, its victims are easy to spot in the historical record. They were taxed on their entry into ports and appear on bills of sale, wills, and other documents.

Because these slaves had to cross the Atlantic Ocean, they were scrupulously — one could even say obsessively — counted along the way. The final tally of 12.5 million enslaved Africans matters greatly because it has shaped our perception of African slavery in fundamental ways. Whenever we read about a slave market in Virginia, a slaving raid into the interior of Angola, or a community of runaways in Brazil, we are well aware that all these events were part of a vast system spanning the Atlantic world and involving millions of victims.[8]

Indian slavery is different. Until quite recently, we did not have even a ballpark estimate of the number of Natives held in bondage. Since Indian slavery was largely illegal, its victims toiled, quite literally, in dark corners and behind locked doors, giving us the impression that they were fewer than they actually were. Because Indian slaves did not have to cross an ocean, no ship manifests or port records exist, but only vague references to slaving raids. Yet in spite of the clandestine and invisible nature of Indian slavery and the impossibility of counting Indian slaves accurately, we possess a sizeable and continuous paper trail. Historians working on all regions of the New World have found traces of the traffic of Indian slaves in judicial proceedings, official inquiries, and casual mentions of raids and Indian captives in letters and assorted documents. Considered in isolation, a couple of hundred Indians here and there do not seem to amount to much. But once we contemplate the breathtaking geographic scope of this traffic and consider its full chronological sweep, the numbers are astounding. If we were to add up all the Indian slaves taken in the New World from the time of Columbus to the end of the nineteenth century, the figure would run somewhere between 2.5 and 5 million slaves (appendix 1).[9]

Such large numbers of enslaved Indians not only approximate the African tragedy in sheer scale but also reveal an even more catastrophic result in relative terms. Without question, both Africans and Indians lost incommensurably. Yet broad comparisons between the two slaveries — still incipient and subject to revision — can provide some useful context. At the height of the transatlantic slave trade, West Africa suffered a population decline of about twenty percent, as it went from about twenty-five million in 1700 to roughly twenty million by 1820.

During this time, some six million Africans were shipped to the New World, and at least two million died in raids and wars related to the traffic of slaves. In absolute numbers, this human loss was tremendous. But in relative terms, indigenous peoples of the New World experienced an even more catastrophic decline in the sixteenth and seventeenth centuries. In the Caribbean basin, along the Gulf coast, and across large regions of northern Mexico and the American Southwest, Native populations were reduced by seventy, eighty, or even ninety percent through a combination of warfare, famine, epidemics, and slavery. Biology gets much of the blame for this collapse, but as we shall see, it is impossible to disentangle the effects of slavery and epidemics. In fact, a synergistic relationship existed between the two: slaving raids spread germs and caused deaths; deceased slaves needed to be replaced, and thus their deaths spurred additional raids.[10]

Beyond the question of numbers, I became intrigued by some of the unique features of Indian enslavement. For instance, in stark contrast to the African slave trade, which consisted primarily of adult males, the majority of Indian slaves were actually women and children. In this way, the two slaveries seem like mirror images. Indian slave prices from such diverse regions as southern Chile, New Mexico, and the Caribbean reveal a premium paid for women and children over adult males. As noted by the New Mexico Indian agent James Calhoun, Indian women could be worth up to fifty or sixty percent more than males. What explains this significant and persistent price premium? Sexual exploitation and women's reproductive capabilities are part of the answer. In this regard, Indian slavery constitutes an obvious antecedent to the sex traffic that occurs today. But there were other reasons too. In nomadic Indian societies, men specialized in activities less useful to European colonists, such as hunting and fishing, than women, whose traditional roles included weaving, food gathering, and child rearing. Some early sources also indicate that women were considered better suited to domestic service, as they were thought to be less threatening in the home environment. And just as masters wanted docile women, they also showed a clear preference for children. Children were more adaptable than grown-ups, learned languages more easily, and in the fullness of time could even identify with their captors. Indeed, one of the most striking features of this form of bondage is that Indian slaves could eventually become part of the dominant society. Unlike those caught up in African slavery, which was a legally defined institution passed down from one generation to the next, Indian slaves could become menials, or servants, and with some luck attain some independence and a higher status even in the course of one life span (see chapter 2).

Another fascinating feature of the traffic of Natives has to do with the involvement of the Indians themselves. As noted earlier, prior to European contact Native Americans practiced various forms of captivity and enslavement. With the arrival of Europeans, they naturally began offering captives to the newcomers. At first Indians occupied a subordinate position in the emerging regional networks of enslavement, serving as guides, informants, intermediaries, guards, and sometimes junior partners, generally dependent on the Europeans' markets and slaving networks. Europeans had the upper hand because of their superior war technology — specifically, horses and firearms — which allowed them to prey on Indian societies almost at will. What started as a European-controlled enterprise, however, gradually passed into the hands of Native Americans. As Indians acquired horses and weapons of their own, they became independent providers. By the eighteenth and nineteenth centuries, powerful equestrian societies had taken control of much of the traffic. In the Southwest, the Comanches and Utes became regional suppliers of slaves to other Indians as well as to the Spaniards, Mexicans, and Americans. The Apaches, who had early on been among the greatest victims of enslavement, transformed themselves into successful slavers. In colonial times, Apaches had been hunted down and marched in chains to the silver mines of Chihuahua. But as Spanish authority crumbled in the 1810s and the mining economy fell apart during the Mexican era, the Apaches turned the tables on their erstwhile masters. They raided Mexican communities, took captives, and sold them in the United States.[11]

So persistent and widespread was Indian slavery that ending it proved nearly impossible. The Spanish crown prohibited Native bondage under all circumstances in 1542, but the traffic continued. More than a century later, in the waning decades of the seventeenth century, the Spanish monarchs launched an empire-wide campaign to free all Indian slaves. But this precocious crusade also fell short of what increasingly appeared to be an unattainable goal. In the early nineteenth century, Mexico proscribed all forms of bondage and extended citizenship to the Indians. Yet Indian slavery persisted. One of the most revealing aspects of this other slavery is that since it had no legal basis, it was never formally abolished like African slavery. After the Civil War, the U.S. Congress passed the Thirteenth Amendment prohibiting both "slavery" and "involuntary servitude." Although the inclusion of the latter term opened the possibility of the liberation of all Indians held in bondage, in the end the U.S. Supreme Court opted for a narrow interpretation of the Thirteenth and Fourteenth Amendments that focused on African Americans and generally excluded Indians. It would require the involvement of Congress, President Andrew Johnson, and some of the most dedicated abolitionists and colorful figures of the post–Civil War era to bring some relief to a people who had long been subjected to one of the worst forms of bondage. Even so, the other slavery continued through the end of the nineteenth century and in some remote areas well into the twentieth century. Disguised as debt peonage, which stretched the limits of accepted labor institutions and even posed as legal work, this other slavery was the direct forerunner of the forms of bondage practiced today.

The more I learned, the more I became convinced that the other slavery had been a defining aspect of North American societies. And yet it has been almost completely erased from our historical memory. At last count, there were more than fifteen thousand books on African slavery, whereas only a couple of dozen specialized monographs were devoted to Indian slavery. To be sure, scholars of Latin America have broached the topic of labor coercion in considerable detail. But such work is often subdivided under various rubrics such as *encomiendas* (grants of Indians given to meritorious Spanish overlords) and *repartimientos* (compulsory labor drafts to which Indians were subjected), which are generally distinguished from outright enslavement. The end result is a failure to grasp the common threads running through all these institutions and gain a better appreciation of their combined scope. The consequences are plainly visible today. Whenever the conversation turns to slavery, people typically imagine black slaves. Hardly ever does anyone think of Indians. It is as if each group fits into a neat historical package: Africans were enslaved, and Indians either died off or were dispossessed and confined to reservations.

Such an oversimplification is troublesome, because Indian slavery actually explains a great deal about the shared history of Mexico and the United States and casts new light on even familiar events. If we want to find answers to such varied questions as why the Pueblo Indians launched a massive rebellion in 1680 and drove the Spaniards out of New Mexico; why the Comanches and Utes became so dominant in large areas of the West; why the Apache chief Geronimo hated Mexicans so much; why article 11 of the Treaty of Guadalupe Hidalgo prohibited Americans from purchasing "Mexican captives held by the savage tribes"; why California, Utah, and New Mexico legalized Indian slavery, disguising it as servitude or debt peonage; or why so many Navajos appear in New Mexico's baptismal records in the aftermath of Colonel Kit Carson's Navajo campaign of 1863–1864, we have to come to terms with the reality of this other slavery. Anyone who reads about the history of northern Mexico or the American Southwest will invariably run into indigenous rebellions prompted by exploitation, raids on Indian communities, and labor coercion. And yet it remains hard to see the forest for the trees. Lacking a sense of the overarching system of enslavement, it is impossible to put such scattered and localized practices in their proper places, just as it would be extremely difficult to make sense of the kidnappings or intertribal warfare of West Africa without reference to the transatlantic slave trade. With *The Other Slavery,* I hope to provide a broad but detailed portrait of the system of Native enslavement that loomed over North America for four centuries and is a key missing piece of this continental history.

Before embarking on this exploration, I feel compelled to issue two caveats. First, this book does not offer a running history of Indian slavery in the Western Hemisphere. Such a gargantuan task—the equivalent of writing the history of African slavery in the New World—could not be accomplished in twenty or even fifty volumes. Instead, I focus on some areas that experienced intense slaving. Thus the story begins in the Caribbean, continues through central and northern Mexico, and ends in the American Southwest—with occasional glimpses of the larger context. And even within this restricted geography, I limit myself to examining moments when the evidence is particularly abundant or when the traffic of Indians underwent significant change.

The second caveat concerns the definition of Indian slavery. Who exactly counts as an Indian slave? The honest answer is that no simple definition is possible. Although some scholars of African slavery have attempted to specify the defining qualities of the "peculiar institution," such an exercise is very difficult to complete when confronted with the extremely variable labor practices to which Native Americans were subjected. Initially, Indian slavery was legal, and therefore the victims of this traffic were clearly labeled as slaves in the documentation. But after the Spanish crown prohibited the enslavement of Indians, owners resorted to a variety of labor arrangements, terms, and subterfuges—such as encomiendas, repartimientos, convict leasing, and debt peonage—to get around the law. Although these forms of labor are impossible to fit into a simple definition, they generally shared four traits that made them akin to enslavement: forcible removal of the victims from one place to another, inability to leave the workplace, violence or threat of violence to compel them to work, and nominal or no pay. Like a deadly virus, Indian slavery mutated into these strains and became extraordinarily resistant through the centuries.

In this book, therefore, I use the phrase "the other slavery" in the double sense that it targeted Native Americans rather than Africans and that it involved a range of forms of captivity and coercion. Some scholars may object to this broad usage, which glosses over conventional labor distinctions, but my reasons are threefold. First, since masters and officials devised these newfangled terms and practices to retain control of Native Americans when formal enslavement was no longer possible, it makes sense to lump them together in recognition of their ultimate purpose, which was to forcibly extract labor from Natives. Kaleidoscopic labor categories have long prevented us from assessing the labor system as a whole and making fundamental distinctions between voluntary and coerced work. Second, these labor practices may have seemed quite distinct to officials and masters at the time, and continue to seem so to researchers today, but they were decidedly less so to the victims themselves, who experienced the everyday reality of labor coercion with little or no compensation — whether on account of debt, because they had allegedly committed a crime, or for some other circumstance. The third reason is that a similar multiplicity of coercive arrangements is still prevalent today in what is often called "the new slavery." There is no single institution or business model in the contemporary trafficking of humans; instead, there are several related practices adapted to different regions of the world and types of trade, such as sex trafficking or child labor. And even though these modern forms of bondage cannot be neatly defined or reduced to fit into a single all-encompassing definition, they are no less real. It was no different with the other slavery.[12]

# 1

## *Caribbean Debacle*

INDIAN SLAVERY POSES a fundamental demographic puzzle. The first Europeans in the New World found a thriving archipelago: islands large and small covered by lush vegetation, teeming with insects and birds, and alive with humans. The Caribbean was "a beehive of people," wrote Bartolomé de Las Casas, the most well known of the region's early chroniclers, who accompanied several expeditions of discovery. "As we saw with our own eyes," he added, "all of these islands were densely populated with natives called Indians." The people who greeted Columbus were indeed plentiful. Modern scholars have proposed wildly varying population estimates for the Caribbean, ranging from one hundred thousand to ten million. But while the initial population is debatable, no one doubts the cataclysmic collapse that followed. By the 1550s, a mere sixty years, or two generations, after contact, the Natives so memorably described by Columbus as "affectionate and without malice" and having "very straight legs and no bellies" had ceased to exist as a people, and many Caribbean islands became eerie uninhabited paradises.[1]

As every schoolchild knows, epidemic disease was a major reason for this devastation. Europeans introduced pathogens to which the Natives had little or no resistance, triggering "virgin soil" epidemics. It was like "dropping lighted matches into tinder," wrote Alfred W. Crosby in his pioneering work on the depopulation of early America. Measles, malaria, yellow fever, influenza, and above all smallpox ravaged the indigenous population in deadly bouts that spread across the islands. Surely some Indians succumbed in pitched battles against the white intruders, who, after all, possessed superior steel weapons and unmatched mobility with their horses. But by far the Spaniards' most devastating weapon was germs.[2]

And yet there is a profound disconnection between this biological explanation and what sixteenth-century Europeans reported. Bartolomé de Las Casas, who arrived in the New World in 1502, averred that greed was the reason Christians "murdered on such a vast scale," killing "anyone and everyone who has shown the slightest sign of resistance," and subjecting "all males to the harshest and most iniquitous and brutal slavery that man has ever devised for oppressing his fellow-men, treating them, in fact, worse than animals." It is true that Las Casas was a passionate defender of Indian rights and therefore had every reason to dwell on Spanish brutality. But we do not have to take his word for it. Early chroniclers, crown officials, and settlers all understood the extinction of the Indians as a result of warfare, enslavement, famine, and overwork, as well as disease. King Ferdinand of Spain — no Indian champion and probably the most well-informed individual of that era — believed that so many Natives died in the early years because, lacking beasts of burden, the Spaniards "had forced the Indians to carry excessive loads until they broke them down."[3]

Early sources do not mention smallpox until 1518, a full twenty-six years after Columbus first arrived in the Caribbean. This was no oversight. Sixteenth-century Spaniards were quite familiar with smallpox's symptoms and lived in constant fear of diseases of any kind. They were keenly aware, for example, that having sex with Indian women could cause *el mal de las búas* (literally, "the illness of the pustules," or syphilis), which afflicted several of Columbus's mariners and spread throughout Italy and Spain immediately on their return. As early as 1493, colonists in the Caribbean also reported an illness that affected both Indians and Spaniards and was characterized by high fevers, body aches, and prostration — clinical signs that point perhaps to swine flu. Influenza is usually benign, although it is capable of mutating into deadlier forms resulting in pandemics. The famous "Spanish flu" pandemic of 1918, which wreaked havoc around the world, is only one example. Early Caribbean sources do not describe an influenza pandemic, but merely an influenza-like disease of some concern. There is no mention of smallpox or any other clear episode of mass death among the Natives until a quarter of a century after Columbus's first voyage. Of course, it is impossible to rule out entirely the possibility of major outbreaks that went unreported, but the documentation suggests that the worst epidemics did not affect the New World immediately.[4]

The late arrival of smallpox actually makes perfect sense. Smallpox was endemic in the Old World, which means that the overwhelming majority of Europeans were exposed to the virus in childhood, resulting in one of two outcomes: death or recovery and lifelong immunity. Thus the likelihood of a ship carrying an infected passenger was low. And even if this were to happen, the voyage from Spain to the Caribbean in the sixteenth century lasted five or six weeks, a sufficiently long time in which any infected person would die along the way or become immune (and no longer contagious). There were only two ways for the virus to survive such a long passage. One was for a vessel to carry both a person already infected and a susceptible host who contracted the illness en route and lived long enough to disembark in the Caribbean. The odds of this happening were minuscule — around two percent according to a back-of-the-envelope calculation by the demographer Massimo Livi Bacci. The second possibility was that an infected passenger left behind the live virus in scabs that fell off his body. Since smallpox has now been eliminated from the face of the earth except in some labs, no one really knows how long the virus could have survived outside the body under the conditions of a sixteenth-century sailing vessel. But even if the virus had remained active aboard a Spanish ship that reached the New World, it would still have had to find its way into a suitable host. In short, far from strange, a delayed onset of smallpox in the New World is precisely what we would expect.[5]

Well before smallpox was first detected in the Caribbean, the Native islanders found themselves on a path to extinction. "La Isla Española," the island now shared by Haiti and the Dominican Republic, was the first home of Europeans in the New World. It is a very large landmass, about the size of South Carolina, which at the time of contact was dotted with as many as five or six hundred Indian villages — an extreme dispersion that would have militated against the spread of disease. Typically, these were small settlements of a few extended families, except for a handful of communities that had a thousand people or more — no Aztec or Inca cities, but substantial villages nonetheless. Friar Las Casas put Española's total population at "more than three million," but given the island's carrying capacity, the archaeological remains, and early Spanish population counts, a more realistic number would be perhaps two or three hundred thousand. By 1508, however, that figure had fallen to 60,000; by 1514 it stood at merely 26,000, according to a fairly comprehensive census (no longer guesswork); and by 1517 the number had plunged to just 11,000. In other words, one year before Europeans began reporting smallpox, Española's Indian population had dwindled to five percent or less of what it had been in 1492. Clearly, the Native islanders were well on their way to a total demographic collapse when smallpox appeared to deliver the coup de grâce.[6]

When we think of the early Caribbean, we imagine mass death caused by pathogens attacking an immunologically defenseless population. But as the case of Española indicates, this image has been deduced rather than having been directly observed. It began to take shape only fifty or sixty years ago when a group of demographers and historians proposed very high population estimates for pre-contact America. Since there was no way to count the Indian population of any area of the hemisphere in 1492, these "High Counters," as they came to be known, derived their estimates by indirect methods, such as taking the earliest population censuses of the Spanish era and multiplying them by a factor of ten or more to work their way back to 1492, or using fragmentary population numbers for a small region and applying the same death rate to much larger geographic areas. Needless to say, such methodologies proved controversial, although their eye-popping numbers circulated widely. And, of course, these numbers raised questions about the causes of the massive decline that followed. Could Spaniards with rusty swords and cumbersome harquebuses have killed so many Indians? In the Caribbean, for example, fewer than ten thousand Europeans would have had to dispose of an Indian population that was a thousand times larger (assuming a High Counters' estimate of ten million). To their credit, the original High Counters in the 1960s and 1970s acknowledged that the decline had occurred for multiple reasons, ranging from warfare and exploitation to epidemics. But their successors emphasized epidemics, which gradually became the overriding and most logical explanation of the Indians' cataclysmic demise.[7]

A more recent consensus is now emerging that revises down the High Counters' numbers. But smaller population numbers for pre-contact America do not make the decline any less dramatic. More modest initial numbers do, however, have a bearing on the possible causes of the Indians' subsequent demise. While it is hard to fathom each Spaniard killing one thousand Indians with anything other than germs, it is much easier to imagine each conquistador, possessing superior technology and motivated by greed, subduing thirty Indians, who ultimately perished through a combination of warfare, exploitation, famine, and exposure to new diseases. We may never know how many Natives died solely because of illness and how many perished due to human intervention. But if I had to hazard a guess using the available written sources, it would be that between 1492 and 1550, a nexus of slavery, overwork, and famine killed more Indians in the Caribbean than smallpox, influenza, and malaria. And among these human factors, slavery has emerged as a major killer.[8]

## The Admiral's First Scheme

The Spanish crown never intended to commit genocide or perpetrate the wholesale enslavement of the Native inhabitants of the Caribbean. These outcomes were entirely contrary to Christian morality and to Spain's most basic economic and imperial interests. Yet a handful of individual decisions, human nature, and the archipelago's geography led to just such a Dantean scenario. Christopher Columbus's life offers us entrée into this tragic chain of decisions and circumstances.

Columbus was a visionary mariner, but he was also a businessman, a role that has not attracted the same level of attention in the literature. Born to a family of weavers and merchants from Genoa, he spent his whole life in the company of people who turned a profit by buying and selling. When he conceived his extraordinary project of reaching the East by sailing west, he patiently negotiated with various European courts, insisting on terms that often became sticking points and deal breakers. We can see what a hard-nosed negotiator Columbus was in the famous Capitulations of Santa Fe, the agreement he signed with King Ferdinand and Queen Isabella in April 1492. Although he did request titles and honors for the rest of his life, which he could then bequeath to his heirs and successors for all eternity, he placed two commercial clauses at the heart of the contract. First, Columbus requested one-tenth of "all the merchandise, whether pearls, precious stones, gold, silver, spices, and any other marketable goods of any kind, name, or manner that can be bought or bartered." Evidently, at the time of the negotiations, Columbus was still thinking about spices, silks, and other products from the Orient. But the inclusive formulation of merchandise "of any kind, name, or manner" would have important repercussions for his New World enterprises. Columbus was also able to extract a second concession in the form of an option—which functioned in much the same way as a present-day stock option—whereby he would be able to invest one-eighth of the total cost of fitting out all present and future expeditions and in return receive an additional one-eighth, or 12.5 percent, of the profits reaped by such ventures. These two clauses meant that Columbus—a single individual—would be able to control close to one-quarter of the overall trade between the Spanish empire and the Orient.[9]

Columbus's first voyage to the New World was successful, and his return to Spain in the spring of 1493 was triumphal. On his way to Barcelona, where Ferdinand and Isabella were holding court, Columbus received an encouraging letter from his sponsors, addressing him with the full titles promised: "To Don Cristóbal Colón, our Admiral of the Ocean Sea, Viceroy and Governor of the Islands that he discovered in the Indies." On his arrival, the entire court and city came out to greet him, "and the crowds could not fit in the streets." The next day Ferdinand and Isabella received the Admiral at the Alcázar warmly but with great solemnity. The Catholic monarchs rose from their thrones when Columbus approached. And when he knelt down to kiss the hands of his benefactors, they gave him the greatest accolade, reserved only for a handful of grandees: they made him rise and requested a chair so that he could be seated in their presence. The Admiral of the Ocean Sea then regaled Ferdinand and Isabella with tales of his voyage and all the marvelous things he had seen. He presented his patrons with some forty tropical birds, which had "the most brilliant plumage"; strange jewels made out of gold; and the six Indians who had survived the passage. As one of Columbus's principal biographers has observed, "Never again would he know such glory, receive such praise, enjoy such favor from his Sovereigns." Between celebrations and toasts, the monarchs approved a second and much larger expedition: not just three smallish caravels as before, but a fleet of seventeen ships; not just a few sailing families and convicts from Palos and Moguer, but a contingent of fifteen hundred colonists from all over the Iberian Peninsula transported by professional naval crews. It is hard to imagine the excitement during the summer of 1493 as preparations for that journey proceeded at full tilt. Great promise lay beyond the horizon. And Columbus could only congratulate himself for having insisted on very favorable terms for a venture that had once seemed like a harebrained scheme but was now likely to be a marvelous, and potentially very lucrative, reality.[10]

The fleet first sailed to the Lesser Antilles, passing the southern coast of Puerto Rico before reaching Española. Columbus had visited Española on his earlier voyage, and one of his captains had traded for gold with the Indians there. So the second time around, the Spaniards surveyed the island's north coast quite carefully, asking the Natives about the source of the metal. The locals said that the gold was in the mountainous interior, in a region called Cibao, in what is now the Dominican Republic. Although encouraged by the presence of the yellow metal, the explorers quickly discovered that panning the riverbeds and mining the alluvial placers of Cibao would require time and considerable labor.[11]

The voyagers also looked for plants. A few sackfuls of cloves, nutmeg, or saffron would sell at outrageous prices in Europe and thus could help

This fifth-century Roman mappamundi divides the earth into five zones: two frozen bands at the poles, a torrid region by the equator (believed to be occupied by an ocean), and two temperate zones. According to subsequent Christian writers, in the aftermath of the great Flood humans adapted to these climatic regions and thus came to acquire widely different physical and mental traits.

offset the costs of the fleet. The exotic and varied Caribbean vegetation fooled the explorers at every turn. Columbus thought he saw rhubarb and cinnamon, but none of these prized substances existed in the Caribbean. Chile pepper was the only spice to be had, and even though capsicum would in time transform the cuisines of the world, from South Asian curries and Sichuan stir-fries to Hungarian *paprikás*, it commanded little attention and no market value at the time. All in all, the colonists' findings were paltry: some gold but no spices or silks, nor any of the other legendary products from the Orient. And in the meantime, the costs of their journey were mounting.[12]

All along the Admiral had been extremely observant of the Native islanders — men, women, and children who went about completely naked, or nearly so, and who often painted themselves from head to toe in red and black. In Columbus's journal and letters, we can find many passages about how plentiful, well proportioned, docile, and alert the Caribbean Indians were. His comments seem innocuous. However, we need to understand his observations in the context of what he expected to find, as historian Nicolás Wey Gómez has recently reminded us. The explorer and his contemporaries subscribed to very old and deeply held notions that linked latitude with character. In this view, belts of latitude wrapped around the earth and corresponded with specific human traits. The inhabitants of the "cold zone" in northern Europe, for instance, tended to be audacious but "of lesser prudence," while those of the "hot zone," such as sub-Saharan Africans, were intelligent but "weaker and less spirited." Such ideas about latitude and character, which harked back to Aristotle and Ptolemy and ran through biblical and medieval authors all the way to Columbus, justified a clear human hierarchy. As luck would have it, the inhabitants of the temperate zone — roughly extending across the Mediterranean — possessed a perfect balance of strength and prudence, which gave them dominion over the peoples who inhabited other latitudes. The Greeks and Romans had shown as much with their conquests, and Portugal's more recent exploits in western Africa had confirmed this natural hierarchy.[13]

Had Columbus's pilots pointed their compasses due west from the coast of Spain, they would have landed somewhere on the Chesapeake Bay just south of modern-day Washington, D.C. Instead, the Admiral went to the Caribbean because, as he put it, "under that parallel of the world [close to the equator] more gold and things of value are found." A prominent cosmographer of the Spanish court elaborated on the same idea. "All good things come from very hot regions whose inhabitants are black or dark brown," Jaume Ferrer de Blanes wrote in a letter to Columbus, "and therefore in my judgment, until Your Lordship meets such peoples, You shall fail to find an abundance of such things."[14]

By journeying to a part of the world where the sun's rays were strong, Columbus anticipated finding dark-skinned peoples. On his first voyage, he wrote in his journal that the Indians were "the color of the Canary Islanders, neither black nor white," and that their hair was not curly but "straight and as coarse as horsehair"—thus they occupied an intermediate position between whites and blacks, an observation that was in line with Columbus's expectations, because the newly discovered lands lay roughly on the same parallel as the Canary Islands. During the second and third voyages, the Admiral traveled farther and farther south, approaching the equator, but the Natives' pigmentation did not darken. Columbus and other early explorers were at a loss to explain why the Indians were not "black as in Guinea," though the sun was strong and the heat was sometimes unbearable in those parts. Regardless of their skin color, Columbus knew these peoples were intelligent but "weaker and less spirited" than Europeans, making them especially suitable as slaves. It is in the context of these assumptions, widely shared by Europeans of the Age of Discovery, that we must understand Columbus's entries about the "docility" and "ingenuity" of the Indians, as well as his earliest slaving proposals.[15]

Columbus captured perhaps two dozen Indians during his first voyage. Strictly speaking, these were not slaves but "showpieces" intended as proof of his discovery. The Admiral also hoped that these Indians would learn Spanish and serve as translators on subsequent expeditions. Some of them came from Cuba's north coast, close to a natural port that Columbus named Puerto Mares. On November 12, 1492, while his ships surveyed the port and river, six Indians in a canoe paddled to the side of one of the caravels to trade. Five Native men climbed up and were easily imprisoned on the Admiral's orders (the Indian who remained in the canoe narrowly escaped). As they were not enough to suit his needs, Columbus sent some of his men ashore to catch more Natives, "and they brought me seven head of women between young old, and three children. I did this because the men would behave themselves better in Spain having women from their homeland than they would without them." Later that night, another canoe approached the *Santa María*, this time containing a man of about forty-five years of age, whose wife and three children had been captured earlier in the day. He begged the Europeans to take him as well, and the Admiral obliged.[16]

On the way home, Columbus had occasion to observe his captives in close quarters and to reaffirm his preconceptions about their "tameness" and "ingenuity," so characteristic of peoples in the hot regions. "They began to understand us, and we them, whether by words or by signs," Columbus would later write of these first captives, "and these have been of great service to us." The return ocean passage also afforded him time to develop his economic plans, which included the wholesale export of Native slaves. In his very first letter after his return, addressed to the royal comptroller, Luis de Santángel, he promised gold, spices, cotton, and "as many slaves as Their Majesties order to make, from among those who are idolaters." The Admiral's plan to ship Natives to Europe was quite understandable given his ideas about the nature of the Indians, his anxieties about making his discovery economically viable, and the one-tenth of the proceeds of the sale of these captives that he would pocket according to the terms of the capitulations.[17]

Columbus had a model in mind. Ten years before his great voyage of discovery, he had sailed along the coast of Guinea and visited São Jorge da Mina, the first European fortress and trading post in sub-Saharan Africa. The Portuguese had built the fort one or two years before Columbus's visit in order to protect their claim to the trade on what is now the coast of Ghana. Unannounced, a fleet of very large ships known as *urcas*, or hulks, had appeared on that coast loaded with bricks, roof tiles, building tools, and scores of masons and carpenters. While Portuguese diplomats overcame the reluctance of the local ruler and the soldiers made room for the fort by bribing African families to move out of their houses and off their plots, the masons worked around the clock. They completed a tower and the outer wall of São Jorge da Mina in a record twenty days, amid rising tensions. At the time of Columbus's visit, the fort was new, and the resident merchants conducted a diversified trade, mostly in gold dust but also in copper, ivory, salt, and slaves. São Jorge da Mina was still far from becoming one of the most important slaving depots of West Africa — the infamous Elmina, as it was known in later centuries, a corruption of the original Portuguese name, where the slaves bound for the New World were kept before crossing the Atlantic. But even in its early days, Columbus could observe how a European stronghold on another continent could thrive by trading a variety of products, including humans.[18]

There is little doubt that the Admiral of the Ocean Sea intended to turn the Caribbean into another Guinea. Early in his second voyage to America, Columbus sent dozens of Carib Indians back to Spain with the first returning ships. Accompanying them was a candid letter to Ferdinand and Isabella: "May Your Highnesses judge whether they ought to be captured, for I believe we could take many of the males every year and an infinite number of women." The Admiral treaded lightly before touting the quality of the merchandise. "May you also believe that one of them would be worth more than three black slaves from Guinea in strength and ingenuity, as you will gather from those I am shipping out now." Columbus's optimistic appraisal of the Indian slaves had a clear intention. Ten days later, he wrote again to the Catholic monarchs, explaining that his stores of wine and wheat were running low. Requesting more caravels loaded with provisions, he proposed, "We could pay for all of that with slaves from among these cannibals, a people very savage and suitable for the purpose, and well made, and of very good intelligence."[19]

Columbus's shipments would continue. A year later, in February 1495, he sent 550 Indians from Española crammed into four caravels bound for the slave market of southern Spain, his largest shipment thus far. Michele da Cuneo, a childhood friend who returned to Europe at this time, wrote an unusually explicit letter about his experiences in the New World. Among other things he reported that his old friend had given him as a present "a beautiful Carib girl [bellisima Camballa] who was brought to my cabin . . . and seeing her completely naked as is their custom, the desire to have her came over me." About the slaves with whom he traveled, Cuneo wrote that about 1,600 captives had been brought to the docks but only 550 of them — "the best males and females" — could be loaded. The rest were distributed among the Europeans who stayed behind or were turned loose. The caravels were filled to capacity. The conditions were extreme. During the passage, approximately 200 Natives perished "because they were not used to the cold weather," Cuneo wrote, "and we cast their bodies into the sea." Of the remaining Indians, half were ill and very weak when they finally arrived in Spain. With this voyage, Columbus inaugurated the Middle Passage, complete with the overcrowding and high mortality rates commonly associated with African slavery.[20]

The Admiral's enslavement plans reached their zenith in 1495–1496. "Under the protection of the Holy Trinity, from here [the Caribbean] we can send all the slaves needed," Columbus insisted yet again to Ferdinand and Isabella, "and if the information that I possess is correct, we could sell four thousand slaves who will be worth at the very least twenty *cuentos* [20 million *maravedís*, or ten times the total cost of Columbus's first voyage]." It was a remarkable proposal considering that so many Natives would have to be transported to Spain in thirty or forty shiploads. But the payoff would be enormous even if the Admiral's calculations were only half-correct.[21]

Left to his own devices, the great discoverer would have turned the Caribbean into another Guinea. Yet two factors steered the Columbian experiment in a different direction. First, the Spanish monarchs opposed the enslavement of the Natives of America. When the first load of slaves arrived, in the spring of 1495, Ferdinand and Isabella initially approved their sale. "About the Indians who came on the caravels," they wrote to the man in Seville who oversaw the affairs of the New World, Bishop Juan Rodríguez de Fonseca, "it seems to us that they would be more easily sold in Andalusia than in other parts." But only four days later, the Spanish sovereigns wrote again countermanding their previous order and urging Bishop Fonseca to stop immediately the sale of Indians "until we know whether we can sell them or not." Ferdinand and Isabella needed time to wrestle with the legal, theological, and moral implications of the transactions.[22]

Slavery was a venerable institution in Spain (and throughout the Mediterranean world). Anyone visiting Seville, Valencia, Barcelona, or any other Iberian city in the fifteenth century would have come in contact with a variety of slaves. Many of these people were Muslims who had lived in Spain for centuries and who had been seized as prisoners during the Reconquista, the Christian campaigns to retake the peninsula.

Other captives came from the eastern edges of Christendom — Greeks, Bulgarians, Russians, Tartars, Circassians, and others traded by Mediterranean merchants. More recently, Spaniards had introduced the Native inhabitants of the Canary Islands, known as *guanches,* and the Portuguese had sold Africans from the west coast of Africa. But regardless of the provenance and circumstances of these captives, they had to go through the same procedure before they could be sold legally. First, they appeared before a Spanish official, who took the depositions of the captors and — crucially — the captives to determine whether they were in fact "enemies of the Catholic church and of the crown" who had been taken in a "good" or "just" war. As a practical matter, this was merely a formality, as officials seldom blocked the sale of captives. But clearly this bureaucratic practice reflected a deeply ingrained Iberian and, more generally, western European belief that proper slaves had to be non-Christian enemies taken not in slaving raids but in wars formally declared by popes and kings. Muslim jihadists clearly fit the bill. But not so — or at least less clearly so — others who regularly appeared shackled in the Spanish slave markets. For example, some masters were troubled or uneasy about acquiring Orthodox Christian Greeks as slaves.[23]

Therefore the question before the Catholic monarchs was whether the Natives of the New World met this legal standard of "enemy" and thus constituted an enslaveable people. Ferdinand and Isabella appointed a committee of lawyers and theologians to help them reach a final determination. This body deliberated for an astonishing five years. The case must have been difficult in the extreme: the Indians of the New World were not Muslims, and they were not waging an offensive war against Spain; instead it was the other way around. Unfortunately, the committee's final report is now lost, so we do not know what arguments were advanced for and against the enslavement of the Indians or why the committee deliberated for so long.[24]

During those five years, however, the monarchs' reluctance to enslave Natives intensified. In particular, Queen Isabella emerged as an early champion of Indian rights. As Columbus kept insisting on his plans of enslavement and his men continued to ship Indian slaves in one guise or another, Isabella became exasperated. All along she had been extremely

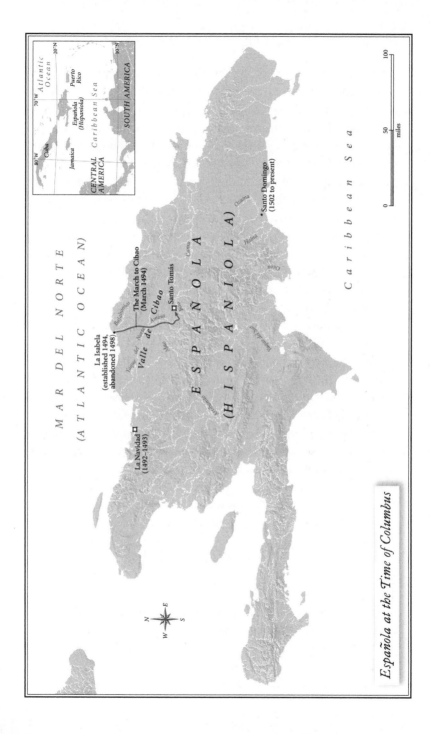

MAR DEL NORTE
(ATLANTIC OCEAN)

La Navidad □
(1492–1493)

La Isabela
(established 1494,
abandoned 1498)

The March to Cibao
(March 1494)

Valle de Cibao

ESPAÑOLA

(HISPANIOLA)

Santo Tomás □

Santo Domingo
(1502 to present)

Caribbean Sea

*Españ_ola at the Time of Columbus*

CUBA
Jamaica
Española
(Hispaniola)
Puerto Rico
Atlantic Ocean
CENTRAL
AMERICA
Caribbean Sea
SOUTH AMERICA

0    50    100
miles

supportive of the Admiral. But by 1499, when she learned of the arrival of yet more Indians, she famously exploded: "Who is this Columbus who dares to give out my vassals as slaves?" Isabella and Ferdinand freed many Indians and, astonishingly, mandated that many of them be returned to the New World. We know that in the summer of 1500, a group of Indians was asked whether they wanted to go back. With the exception of one old man who was too sick to travel and a little girl who wished to remain in Spain, all of the others chose to make the perilous voyage to the Caribbean.[25]

The opposition of the Catholic monarchs was a serious blow to Columbus's plans for a transatlantic Indian slave trade. But the most important limiting factor was the economic development of the Caribbean. European colonists slowly realized that the lush archipelago was nowhere near the East or the Spice Islands but nonetheless possessed valuable natural resources. To extract these riches, many laborers were needed. Columbus himself explained it better than anyone else in a *memorial* (historical account) in which he reflected on his lifelong accomplishments. He wrote that he "would have sent many Indians to Castile, and they would have been sold, and they would have become instructed in our Holy Faith and our customs, and then they would have returned to their lands to teach the others." Yet according to the Admiral, they stayed in the Caribbean because "the Indians of Española were and are *the greatest wealth of the island,* because they are the ones who dig, and harvest, and collect the bread and other supplies, and gather the gold from the mines, and do all the work of men and beasts alike."[26]

## The Greatest Wealth

The Spaniards did not so much discover the gold of Española as they were led to it by the Indians. The colonists saw the Natives of the north coast wearing shiny "leaves" dangling from their earlobes and nostrils. The islanders were in the habit of picking up small pieces of gold and beating them into thin strips or leaves. Using signs, the visitors questioned the Natives about where they had procured this gold, to which they responded in kind by pointing to the mountainous interior and saying "Cibao."[27]

Columbus dispatched a group of some thirty men under the command of Alonso de Ojeda, a "young and courageous nobleman" (and future slaver), into the promising mountains. Indian guides gladly led the way. From the coastal plain, the party ascended a mountain range that gave way to a broad interior valley and then a second range (the Cordillera Central), which was Cibao proper. Large rivers crisscrossed the foothills of this range. The indigenous escorts were the first to demonstrate how to collect the gold. "They dug a hole in the river sand about the depth of an arm, merely scooping the sand out of this trough with the right and left hands," wrote one chronicler, "and then they extracted the grains of gold, which they afterwards presented to the Spaniards." The chronicler, Pietro Martire d'Anghiera (Peter Martyr), an Italian nobleman attached to the Spanish court, remarked that many of the grains were the size of peas or garbanzo beans and affirmed that in Old Castile he had seen an ingot procured by Ojeda that was "as large as a man's fist ... and to my great admiration I handled it and tested its weight." The Indians evidently placed some value on gold and used it to make ornaments. But the interest shown by the strangers was on a different scale altogether. Gold seemed to be an obsession with them.[28]

The young nobleman Ojeda reported that in two weeks, he had found more than fifty streams and rivers that contained gold and that the gold-bearing places were so numerous "that a man could not name them all." An elated Columbus investigated for himself. Wishing to impress the Indians, he organized a second and much larger group, consisting of "all the gentlemen and about four hundred foot soldiers." Proceeding in military formation, these men carried banners and upon their approach to Indian villages fired guns and blew trumpet fanfares. We can only guess what the people of Cibao thought of these theatrics. The martial display must have worked on some level, because the Natives received the strangers "as though they had come from the sky."[29]

The Spaniards had come to stay. They chose a promontory by a riverbank to build a fortified post they called Santo Tomás, because just like the doubting saint, they had to see in order to believe. This was the first of a number of fortifications, smelters, mining camps, and placer operations built throughout the foothills and interior valley in the next few years. By 1496 the settlers were firmly in control of Cibao, and by the turn of the sixteenth century the gold region of Española had already become the mainstay of the Spanish presence in the New World.

Gold was not the only valuable product on the island. Española was a gateway and resupply center for expeditions bound for other parts of the New World. Entrepreneurial colonists made money by selling pigs or cattle to the passing ships. Other Europeans came to control the trade in dyewood collected on the southwest coast and the pearls arriving from Venezuela. Still others found their fortune in sugarcane, operating the very first sugar plantations in the New World. More than any other enterprise, however, the gold mines determined the economy of Española and the entire archipelago and dictated how the Spaniards went about procuring labor.[30]

The goldfields of Cibao were not the most dangerous places for the Indians to work. For sheer horror and attrition rates, the "pearl coast" was worse. Indian divers there spent agonizing days making repeated descents of up to fifty feet, while holding their breath for a minute or more. Few Natives could endure these brutal conditions for long. Although the goldfields of Cibao were not as lethal, they affected the largest number of Indians in the entire circum-Caribbean region. Looking at the placid environment of modern Cibao, one cannot imagine that it was once the pulsating heart of the colonial enterprise. Today there are ranches and green pastures with lazy cows, humble houses where ordinary people struggle to make ends meet, and scenic spots where wealthy Dominicans have built their vacation homes. But five hundred years ago, it was the site of the first gold rush in the Americas.

Columbus's initial attempt to squeeze the gold out of Española consisted simply of requesting that all the Indians of Cibao who were fourteen years of age or older provide enough gold dust to fill a hawkbell — a few grams — as tribute every three months. (Hawkbells, used in falconry in Europe, were brought to the New World as trade goods.) "All prudent and learned readers will immediately recognize the justice of this tribute, and the violence, fear, and death that its imposition necessitated," warned Bartolomé de Las Casas. Although some caciques (chiefs) made halfhearted efforts to meet the Spanish quota, this method of obtaining gold failed completely. Most Indians did everything they could to avoid the tribute, including hiding away in the mountains or fleeing Cibao altogether. After three collection periods,

This contemporary drawing captures the three tasks involved in panning for gold. Though crude, the tools shown here were quite effective and are still used by present-day gold seekers.

the Indians had provided only 200 pesos' worth of gold out of an anticipated 60,000. Clearly, if the Spaniards wanted gold from Española, they would have to get it themselves.[31]

Spanish miners and prospectors flocked to the streams, savannas, and mountains of Cibao. Although flecks of gold could be found all over the region, only certain areas contained enough gold to make extraction profitable. An early colonist, Gonzalo Fernández de Oviedo, tried his hand at gold panning and left the most detailed portrayal of these activities.[32]

Each Spaniard arrived with his *cuadrilla,* or team of Indians. In most cases, the "miner" was merely a colonist with no knowledge of metals or mining techniques. Once he settled on a place — probably chosen after a mixture of hearsay, intuition, and preliminary digging and sampling — he had his Indians clear a square trench of about eight by eight feet. Sandy beaches along the rivers were ideal, but many alluvial placers were in wooded areas, known as *arcabucos,* or along hillsides that required the removal of large rocks and trees. Once the Indians completed this preparatory work, they dug the cleared area to a depth of about twice the length of a worker's palm setting aside the removed sand and earth. They dug with simple tools, even with sticks and their bare hands in the early years. This was strenuous labor, but easier than the next step.

The same "digging" Indians or other members of the cuadrilla transported the piles of dirt to the nearest stream. An average-size trench produced more than six thousand pounds of dirt mixed with the tiniest fragments of gold. The Indians carried this dirt on their bare backs, in loads weighing three to four *arrobas,* about sixty to ninety pounds. These were very heavy burdens considering the slender build of most of the bearers. The work proceeded ceaselessly all day. Instead of using valuable beasts of burden, the Spaniards compelled Natives to do all the hauling; horses and mules were devoted to the tasks of conquest and pacification. The Indians were even forced to carry their Christian masters in hammocks. As a result, they developed "huge sores on their shoulders and backs as happens with animals made to carry excessive loads," commented Friar Las Casas, who arrived in Española right at the time of the gold rush, "and this is not to mention the floggings, beatings, thrashings, punches, curses, and countless other vexations and cruelties to which they were routinely subjected and to which no chronicle could ever do justice."

By the water, a third group of "washing" Indians—usually women, because this work was less physical—received the cargo. Standing in the stream with the water up to her knees, each woman held a large wooden pan called a *batea*. "She grabs the *batea* by its two handles," wrote Oviedo, "and moves it from one side to the other with great skill and art, allowing just enough water to rush in as the earth dissolves and the sand is washed away." With some luck, after sifting thousands of pounds of earth, the woman would find "whatever God wishes to give in a day"—a few grains of gold—in the bottom of the *batea*.[33]

Each cuadrilla consisted of at most a few dozen laborers. The smallest had only five: two diggers, two carriers, and one washer. Yet put together, all these teams made Cibao a veritable anthill. In promising areas, the competition was fierce. When a miner struck gold, others immediately flocked there. To prevent rivals from setting up next to him, he would "invite someone whom he wishes to help and chooses as a neighbor" to move in first. Even though Columbus and his family attempted to limit the number of Spaniards going to the gold region, the number of cuadrillas grew steadily in the late 1490s and early 1500s. During the first decade of the sixteenth century, the heyday of gold production in Española, the island may have yielded around two thousand pounds of gold per year. It is possible to imagine an enormous ingot of that weight, but it is much harder to comprehend the madness of some of the Spanish owners—one of whom became notorious for throwing parties in which the saltshakers were full of gold dust—or to grasp the suffering of some three or four thousand able-bodied Indians—perhaps as many as ten thousand—toiling daily in the gold mines of Cibao to make such opulence possible for the colonists.[34]

Like any other rush, the gold rush of Española was chaotic and destructive. "Take the most advantage, because you do not know how long it will last" was a saying that circulated among the early miners. This bit of wisdom applied not only to the amount of gold one could extract but also to the number of Indians one could command. Columbus's initial proposals for enslavement fit perfectly with the labor needs. The first slaves working in the mines were islanders who had rebelled during the 1490s and whom the Spaniards had defeated and captured. The end of these rebellions, coupled with Queen Isabella's insistence that the Indians were free, threw a monkey wrench into his plans and brought to the fore the problem of keeping the mines supplied with workers.[35]

The man who had to address the vexing problem of forcing Indians to work in the mines without enslaving them outright was Nicolás de Ovando, the highest political authority in Española during the gold rush years. At the time of his appointment, Ovando was already fifty years old, an advanced age in the sixteenth century for someone who had to travel to the New World to impose his will on strong-minded conquistadors and indomitable Indians. Yet Ovando more than compensated for his age with tremendous energy, loyalty to the crown, and experience. His native Extremadura was a frontier area where Ovando had participated in the civil wars of the 1470s and 1480s and witnessed the final stages of the Reconquista.[36]

The Catholic monarchs dispatched the aging Ovando to the Caribbean to restore order to a colonial experiment that had fallen into complete disarray. Columbus had attempted to monopolize the wealth of Española, igniting a rebellion by Spanish soldiers who had long mistrusted their commander and now found themselves shut out of the gold mines. Sending Ovando to the island in April 1502, with almost absolute power and at the head of 30 ships and 2,500 colonists, by far the largest expedition up to that time, was the crown's boldest attempt to restore stability. As King Ferdinand reminded Diego Columbus, the Admiral's son, "We sent him [Ovando] to that island because of the bad mistakes committed by your father while discharging the office that you currently have; the island was all up in arms, lost, and yielding no benefit whatsoever."[37]

Ovando's view of the Indians — quite similar to his perception of Muslims — was that they had to be treated firmly but not necessarily as enemies or animals. The deeply religious governor may have been a hardened frontiersman, but he was not a heartless slaver. For instance, after visiting the war-torn town of Alcántara, Spain, in 1496, his initial efforts were directed toward building a new convent and church as a way to revive communal life. In addition to his faith, weighing heavily on his plans for the Natives of America was Ovando's close relationship with Queen Isabella, who at that time remained a most determined and powerful defender of Indian rights. Ovando, on the basis of past experience and religious conviction, intended to grant the beleaguered islanders a measure of relief in the face of the headlong gold rush and scramble for Indian laborers. Yet his governorship illustrates the most salient feature of the crown's early dealings with the Indians: good intentions gone terribly wrong.[38]

Ovando's most important initiative was to distribute the Natives of the island to various *encomenderos,* or grantees. In effect, each Spanish grantee was "given" or "entrusted with" a cacique and his people, making sure in return that they were introduced to the mysteries of Christianity. The contract drawn up at the start of each distribution of Indians read: "You are hereby entrusted with the cacique *fulano* [so and so] and one hundred Indians, so you can make use of them in your ranches and mines and teach them the things of our holy Catholic faith."[39]

Known indistinctly by the two relevant Spanish words *repartimiento* (from the verb *repartir,* to distribute) and *encomienda* (from *encomendar,* to entrust), this institution amounted to an extraordinary bridge between two vastly different historical realities. In feudal Spain, lords had wielded great power over the peasants who lived on their lands. They had the right to receive tribute from the peasants in exchange for protection. To be sure, there were significant differences between the feudal world of medieval Europe and the encomienda system proposed for Española. But at least to some degree, Spanish conquistadors could style themselves as lords of the New World. Interestingly, the encomienda was not entirely alien to the islanders. The Taíno people of the Caribbean were organized in stratified societies, with paramount caciques exercising control over lesser caciques and ordinary Indians. These caciques regularly extracted tribute in products and labor from their dependents. It was not a tremendous stretch, therefore, for the islanders to understand the encomienda as an extension of their own system, except that now the ultimate beneficiaries were no longer the caciques but the encomenderos.

Ovando did not intend the encomiendas to become a disguise for slavery. He carefully regulated these arrangements, spelling out mutual rights and obligations. To prevent sexual predation, for example, Ovando insisted that prospective encomenderos had to be married, preferably with their wives present on the island. Before receiving an encomienda, each grantee had to understand the limits of his authority. He did not *own* the Indians in any sense of the word and therefore could not sell them or rent them out. In fact, the Indians would continue to live in their own villages under their caciques and by their own rules. The encomendero did have a right to require labor from the Indians given to him, and he was naturally eager to send them to the mines. But he had to pay each Indian 1 gold peso per year — an absurdly low wage that distinguished encomienda Indians from slaves. The Indians would work in the mines only for a limited period, known as the *demora,* which was initially set at six months a year. If the encomendero failed to abide by these terms, Governor Ovando could take away his encomienda and award it to someone else, a powerful lever in a cutthroat world in which only some Europeans had encomiendas and all others clamored for them.

Ovando's intention to protect the Indians is also evident in the fact that he did not distribute all the Natives of Española. The governor allowed some caciques to continue to live on their own, free and apart from the Spanish colonial world. These were Natives who had shown the greatest loyalty to Spain and had made the greatest strides in becoming Hispanicized. One of these fortunate caciques was known to the Spaniards as "the doctor" because "he was the one who knew the most of them all." Another one went by the name Diego Colón because the Admiral had raised him like his own son Diego, taking the boy back to Spain after his first voyage. Diego Colón spoke Spanish fluently and was well known to all the early colonists. Others included a cacique known as Alonso de Cáceres, who lived in Governor Ovando's household for some time; Francisco, who had been raised by Franciscan friars in a newly established monastery; and Masupa Otex, whose *cacicazgo* (chiefdom) incongruously lay in the heart of the gold region. By allowing these caciques and their people to live without Spanish interference, the governor wished to show that Indians were responsible neighbors and upstanding vassals of the empire, entirely capable of charting their own destiny.[40]

Unfortunately, reality overwhelmed Ovando's careful plans. Dispersed in five or six hundred small villages, the islanders became easy prey for Spaniards determined to succeed at all costs. Some conquistadors simply enslaved the islanders illegally. Encomienda owners also found ways to get around the restrictions and safeguards. Instead of keeping the Indians in the mines for only six months, they compelled them to stay longer. In fact, being sent to the goldfields amounted to something close to a death sentence. According to one source, "Out of every hundred Indians who go only seventy come back, and in the worst cases out of three hundred only thirty return alive." In their haste to obtain gold, the encomenderos pushed the Indians beyond the limits of survival. "The greed of men is insatiable," commented Gonzalo Fernández de Oviedo. "Some owners gave excessive work to the Indians, and others provided them with too little food." Contemporaries spoke of *quebrantamiento,* the breaking down of the body, turning laborers into walking cadavers stripped of the will to continue living. Such merciless exploitation was compounded by the constant shifts from one encomendero to another, "one more covetous than the previous one." The encomiendas were granted at Ovando's pleasure and lasted three years or less. Thus owners had an incentive to get the most out of their Indians, even if that meant passing on famished and exhausted workers to the next encomendero, who repeated the cycle of exploitation with renewed vigor.[41]

The misery also extended to the Indians who stayed behind in the villages: the elderly, children, pregnant women, and others who were somehow unsuitable for the arduous work in the mines. With all the able-bodied adults gone, they could not raise enough food for

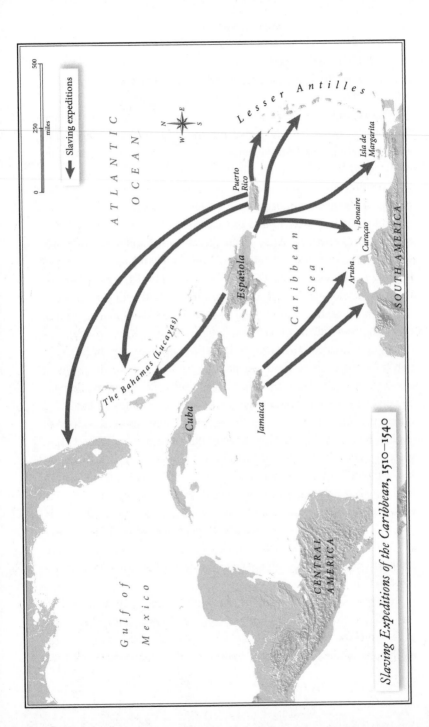

Slaving Expeditions of the Caribbean, 1510–1540

themselves, let alone for the scores of men and women returning from the goldfields. Widespread famines affected the island during Ovando's years, and what little food existed was sent to the gold mines. Even the Indian villages given a pass by Governor Ovando failed. "They are improvident, especially about food," one observer wrote about these communities. "If they have a lot of meat or fish, they eat them day and night without anticipating the future and realizing that tomorrow they will not have anything." Prior to contact, these Indians had enjoyed a seemingly carefree lifestyle. But the harsh colonial demands rendered their traditional practices untenable and their survival impossible.[42]

Despite Ovando's well-intentioned administration, the gold rush wiped out the island's population. The mines destroyed the Taínos working there and in the process doomed those left behind in the villages. Caciques who had ruled over hundreds of individuals saw their dependents shrink to a handful of survivors after ten years of unrelenting work. Las Casas was one of the 2,500 colonists who had arrived in Española with Governor Ovando, and he had received an encomienda in the goldfields of Cibao, where he observed the cataclysmic decline of the Indians. He believed that three million Indians had died in just a few years. "Who of those born in future generations will believe this? I myself who am writing this and saw it and know most about it can hardly believe that such was possible." Another knowledgeable contemporary writing a few years later, Pietro Martire d'Anghiera, expressed the same idea. "Let us be strictly truthful and add that the craze for gold was the cause of their destruction," he wrote to the pope, "for these people who were accustomed as soon as they had sown their fields to play, dance, and sing, and chase rabbits, were set mercilessly to work." By 1508–1509 the surviving islanders could no longer sustain the gold production of Cibao, let alone raise food, build towns for the Spaniards, and do all the other work required of them. Ovando himself, realizing the depth of the crisis and the failure of his policies, proposed a dramatic and far-reaching solution: bring Indian slaves from the surrounding islands to work in the gold mines and other endeavors of Española. A new chapter in the sad history of the early Caribbean had begun.[43]

## *Los Armadores*

In the early years of the sixteenth century, Puerto Real and Puerto de Plata were two drab ports on the north shore of Española. Everything seemed modest and temporary: a couple of muddy streets, thatched huts with one or two stone houses, half-built churches that lacked even stone crosses. These communities were dangerously exposed to the tropical storms and hurricanes that sometimes roared through the Caribbean basin. Yet as the Indians of Española became scarce, Puerto Real and Puerto de Plata came alive. Local residents and wealthy colonists pooled their resources, chartered or bought dilapidated boats, hired disheveled crews, and launched their merchant vessels across the Caribbean Sea. They were known as *los armadores* (shipowners), an appellation that seems much too grand when compared with their counterparts in Seville, who were at the same time launching armadas across the Atlantic and around the world.[44]

The northern shore of Española opened up to the green-blue waters of the Caribbean and to dozens of islands that were large enough to sustain Native populations but small enough that the people could not hide from Spanish slavers. Even the Caribbean geography seemed ideal for the trafficking of Indians. Directly to the east were the Lesser Antilles, a cluster of islands in the shape of an arc, inhabited by Carib Indians and reaching all the way to South America. The Caribs refused to submit to the Spaniards or even negotiate. The Spaniards regarded them as fierce, physically strong, and very dangerous because they used arrowheads dipped in a poisonous substance made from shrubs and plants. One observer noted that "those who are wounded with this poison die in writhing pain, throwing up, biting their own hands, and beside themselves on account of the great pain." But the practice of the Caribs that stood out most in the collective European mind was cannibalism. Columbus was the first to make invidious distinctions between the friendly Indians of the large islands and the cannibals of the Lesser Antilles, and indeed we owe the term "cannibal" to the Admiral's conflation of the term "Caniba" — an appellation for the fierce peoples of the eastern Caribbean — with their custom of eating human flesh. Eventually, the term was applied to all man-eating peoples.[45]

North of Española lay the Bahamas. The Spaniards called them *las islas lucayas* but also knew them as *las islas inútiles* (the useless islands) because they did not possess gold, pearls, or any other marketable products. The only "goods" that could be derived from them were Indians. Opinions varied about the nature of the Lucayo Indians, their degree of civilization, and whether or not they were cannibals. But there was a broad consensus among the Spaniards of Española that the Lucayos had to be removed from a place where there was nothing of value and transported to other islands where their work was badly needed. Since the life of these Natives was oriented toward the sea, many of them ended their days in the pearl fisheries — "the most infernal and insane life of our time," according to a knowledgeable sixteenth-century witness.[46]

Beyond the Lesser Antilles and the Bahamas, Spanish mariners caught glimpses of coastal Florida and the shores of Central America, Colombia, and Venezuela. This was the edge of their known world. Some of these lands were thought to be inhabited by giants. Indeed, the islands of Aruba, Curaçao, and Bonaire, off the coast of Venezuela, were called *las islas de los gigantes*. The belief in these giants arose partly from the chivalric romances that were popular among the conquistadors, but also from the very real fact that Natives in some of these areas were considerably taller than sixteenth-century Spaniards. Whether they were real giants or merely tall, these Indians were highly prized by Europeans.[47]

The first step for anyone wishing to launch a slaving expedition was to obtain a license. Clandestine slaving was possible, but because captives needed to be certified by crown officials before their legal sale in the markets of Española or Puerto Rico, it was best to get a license. Although King Ferdinand and Queen Isabella had prohibited the enslavement of Indians in 1500, their order was followed by what appeared to them to be three judicious exceptions. In 1503 the crown authorized the enslavement of Indians who were cannibals — cannibalism being an especially nefarious practice that marked those who engaged in this practice as somehow less than human. In 1504 the monarchy also allowed the capture of Indians taken in "just wars," extending to the New World the doctrine that had long justified the impressment and bondage of enemies in Europe. And in 1506 the monarchs permitted the colonists to "ransom" Indians who were enslaved by other Indians and whom the Spaniards could then keep as slaves—the logic being that ransomed Indians would at least become Christianized and their souls would be saved. Governor Ovando and his successors were able to issue licenses by taking advantage of these exceptions. Of the three, they most often used cannibalism to legitimize their raids. Scholars have argued that early Spaniards had perverse incentives to exaggerate, sensationalize, and even fabricate stories of man-eating Indians, given the legal context. Contemporaries also recognized as much. A Spanish judge concluded in 1518 that many *armadores* were "taking Indians from Barbados, the gigantes, and elsewhere who are not Caribs nor proper to be slaves." But as with other canards, there was a kernel of truth in this one: cannibalism was real in some quarters of the Caribbean and elsewhere in the New World.[48]

Slave traffickers prowled the Caribbean in the 1510s and 1520s, greatly expanding Europeans' geographic knowledge. Juan Ponce de León, the discoverer of Florida—often depicted as a deluded explorer bent on finding the Fountain of Youth—was in fact deeply involved in the early Caribbean slave trade, sponsoring slaving voyages to the Bahamas and opening Florida to the trade. In fact, the royal patent confirming Ponce de León's discovery of the "island" of Florida allowed him to "wage war and seize disobedient Indians and carry them away for slaves." Similarly, the Spaniard who first laid claim to the coast of South Carolina, Lucas Vázquez de Ayllón, a man of "great learning and gravity" deferentially addressed as *el licenciado*, was a prime mover in the slave trade. (The term *licenciado* refers to someone who holds a university degree, usually a lawyer.) We often think of these men simply as "discoverers," when in reality considerable overlap existed between discoverers and slavers.[49]

Somewhat counterintuitively, the dispersion of Natives across the Caribbean greatly facilitated the task of capturing and transporting them. Villagers living in small communities on self-contained and exposed islands had little chance to hide from the intruders or to repel unexpected attacks. Slave raiders formed compact groups of around fifty or sixty men. They arrived quietly on their ships; waited until nighttime, "when the Indians were secure in their mats"; and descended on the Natives, setting their thatched huts on fire, killing anyone who resisted, and capturing all others irrespective of age or gender. Once the initial ambush was over, the slavers often had to pursue the Indians who had escaped, unleashing their mastiffs or running the Natives down with their horses. If there were many captives, the slavers took the trouble of building temporary holding pens by the beach, close to where their ships were moored, while horsemen combed the island. The attackers literally carried off entire populations, leaving empty islands in their wake.[50]

The Indians were then loaded on the ships, packed into the space belowdecks. The scene in the hold of a slaving ship was infernal. Lack of air, poor provisioning, and the relentless tropical heat magnified the slaves' suffering to the highest degree. "The Indians could not move," wrote a young man from Milan named Girolamo Benzoní, "and there they lay like animals amid their vomits and feces. When the sea was calm and the ship could not move, sometimes there was no water for these poor people. Broken down by the heat, the bad smell, and the discomforts, they died miserably down there." Unlike the Middle Passage, which required a month of travel, slaving voyages in the Caribbean lasted only a few days. Yet the mortality rates of these short passages surpassed those of transatlantic voyages. Friar Las Casas reported that "it was never the case that a ship carrying three or four hundred people did not have to throw overboard one hundred or one hundred and fifty bodies out of lack of food and water" — making for a mortality rate of twenty-five to fifty percent. Although it is tempting to disregard this claim as another of Las Casas's exaggerations, sources confirm his mortality estimates. Vázquez de Ayllón's slaving expeditions were among the most notorious for their poor provisioning and very high mortality rates, which cut deeply into his profits and caused untold human suffering and senseless death.[51]

Spanish slavers did not win every time. In particular, the Natives of the Lesser Antilles were able to fend off raids and occasionally even go on the offensive, surprising lonely ships and Spanish strongholds. In 1513 about one thousand Caribs attacked the Spanish settlements of Puerto Rico, killing many colonists. Ponce de León blundered when he led a retaliatory slaving raid on the island of Guadalupe in 1515, which ended in total disaster: twenty Spaniards were wounded, and five died. The Indians found themselves at a tremendous technological disadvantage. Indian arrowheads made of fish bones could not penetrate the chain mail armor of the Spaniards, and Indian canoes, though they could easily outmaneuver a caravel, had no chance in a long-distance chase. Nevertheless, the Natives were occasionally able to prevail against the Europeans.[52]

In general, however, small crews of European slavers operating from dilapidated ships proved tremendously effective in subduing and capturing Indians across the Caribbean. Slaving licenses issued by crown authorities reveal just how responsive these crews were to market opportunities. The number of licenses grew steadily from 1514 through 1517, the years when the Taínos of Española were no longer available in sufficient numbers to satisfy the Spaniards' demand for gold. There was a sudden drop in licenses in 1518, followed by an extraordinary spike in 1519. It is not difficult to explain these changes. A smallpox epidemic ravaged the Caribbean archipelago in 1518, curtailing the traffickers' activities. The following year, slavers worked harder than ever before to replenish the dead or dying Indian workforce of the large Caribbean islands, launching more slaving raids than in all the previous years combined and spreading desolation and death to the Bahamas, the Lesser Antilles, and parts of the mainland (see appendix 2). We can only imagine the grim circumstances of the Caribbean islanders who had to endure the alarming epidemic that took the lives of family members and neighbors, causing widespread dislocation and famine and tremendous hardship. And just when the worst seemed to be subsiding, Indian slavers appeared on the horizon, ready to stuff them into the holds of their ships and take them to the goldfields of Española or the pearl banks off the coast of Venezuela. The Bahamas became almost entirely depopulated. Las Casas estimated the number of Lucayos captured at forty thousand, while a slave trafficker put the figure at "only" fifteen thousand. Regardless of the actual number, no Lucayo communities remained in the Bahamas except as bands of refugees. By 1520 *armadores* like Vázquez de Ayllón were forced to bypass the Bahamian archipelago altogether and venture on to Florida and beyond to find human prey.[53]

The shorthand version of the history of the Americas posits that virgin soil epidemics were at the root of the demographic devastation that ensued. However, an exclusively biological explanation is at odds with much of the documentation of that era and runs contrary to the observed adaptability of humans. In the long sweep of history, human populations have survived virgin soil epidemics. The most well-known case is the Black Death. Possibly originating in China and spreading along the Silk Road, this epidemic arrived in Europe during the second half of the fourteenth century, when devastating outbreaks wiped out perhaps one-third of the continent's inhabitants. It is hard to overstate the fear, suffering, and dislocation caused by the Black Death. But its aftermath shows the resilience of human populations. Europe's losses lingered until the early decades of the fifteenth century, but then the population made a stunning demographic comeback. Men and women kept marrying, enjoyed higher standards of living, and had more children, boosting birthrates all across the continent. The recovery was powerful and long lasting. By the middle of the sixteenth century, all major European regions had reached or surpassed their pre-plague populations. Indeed, we can think of Europe's colonization of the New World as an extension of this remarkable demographic rebound.[54]

Left to their own devices, the Native peoples of the Caribbean would have limited their exposure to illness, coping like many other human populations before and after them. We will never know how many Indians actually died of disease alone. But even if one-third, or two-thirds, of the Caribbean islanders had died of influenza, typhus, malaria, and smallpox, they would have been able to stem the decline and, in the fullness of time, rebound demographically. In fact, some Indian populations of the New World did just that. But unlike fourteenth-century Europeans, the Natives of the Caribbean were not left to their own devices. In the wake of the epidemics, slavers appeared on the horizon.[55]

# 2

## *Good Intentions*

THE SPANISH MONARCHY may have been bureaucratic, tortuous, and frequently complicit in the enslavement of Indians, but it was also capable of embracing a good cause. In the wake of the demographic debacle of the Caribbean, a group of activists gathered around the Spanish court to stem the tide of further disaster in the early 1540s. The most visible figure among them was Friar Bartolomé de Las Casas. One of his favorite tactics consisted of scandalizing court members by reading aloud from a manuscript that he would go on to publish a decade later under the title *Brevísima relación de la destrucción de las Indias* (A short account of the devastation of the Indies). University students today still learn about the gory details of Spain's conquest from this book.

With the king's backing, these activists introduced a sweeping new legal code for the Americas, intended to improve the lives of Indians. Airily known as the New Laws, this legislation attempted to achieve nothing less than a new beginning, a new compact with the Natives of the New World. The New Laws of 1542 prohibited the granting of new encomiendas, forbade colonists to compel Natives to carry loads against their will, and prevented Spaniards from forcing Indians to dive for pearls. They were also quite explicit about Indian slavery. Indians were "free vassals," the code affirmed, "so from here on, no Indian can be made into a slave *under any circumstance* including wars, rebellions, or when ransomed from other Indians." Spaniards who had long relied on Indian laborers were in shock, and even later commentators were somewhat confused about the extent of this legislation. Yet there was no ambiguity in the laws themselves, which absolutely prohibited any further enslavement of Indians, closing the few loopholes in previous legislation that had led to the Caribbean disaster.[1]

One might assume that, though well-meaning, the New Laws were utterly unenforceable. Historians have long noted that they did not stop the enslavement of Indians, and this is undoubtedly true. Centuries after 1542, Spaniards continued to hold Natives in bondage. But even though the laws failed in this regard, they did shape the contours of this institution to a remarkable extent. Owners found themselves perennially at risk of losing their indigenous slaves. Important colonial officials complicit in the traffic of Natives had to worry about royal investigations. And the Indians themselves learned that they were free vassals of the Spanish king. In fact, there is no better evidence for the enduring importance of the New Laws than the lawsuits initiated by Indians all over the empire in an attempt to claim their freedom. If the laws did not matter, why bother? Clearly, Natives cared enough to take their masters to court, even at tremendous personal costs.[2]

A brief comparison with the legal framework of slavery in the United States will reinforce this point. In the antebellum South, black slaves possessed no legal standing. They were barred from southern courtrooms, which were populated by white judges, lawyers, and witnesses — the majority of whom were slaveholders. Laws specifically prevented persons of color, whether free or slave, to testify, except in the rarest of cases. Ironically, slaves were frequently the objects of litigation — for example, buyers sued sellers over slaves' physical or moral defects or sought compensation for slaves injured by overseers. Yet the slaves themselves could not act legally. A white master could mistreat or even kill a slave, and as long as there were no white witnesses, he could not be brought to justice. As the former slave Harriet Jacobs famously wrote in her autobiographical account, a slave woman has "no shadow of law to protect her from insult, from violence, or even from death." The notion that a slave could sue his or her master to attain freedom would have been laughable to most southerners during the first half of the nineteenth century.[3]

Spain's slaves lived under an entirely different legal regime. The New Laws not only affirmed that Indians were free vassals but also instructed the *audiencias,* or high courts, of the New World to "put special care in the good treatment and conservation of the Indians," to remain informed of any abuses committed against Indians, and "to act quickly and without delaying maliciously as has happened in the past." Because the Spanish legal system was open to Indians, a class of specialized lawyers that became known as *procuradores generales de indios* served to represent them. These procuradores assisted indigenous clients in building their cases and navigating the Spanish bureaucracy. In stark contrast to the black slaves of the antebellum South, Indians could rely on these lawyers for at least some representation in the Spanish legal system.[4]

To be sure, sedentary Indians living in large cities had a great deal more access to the law than nomadic peoples from peripheral areas. And even those who lived in cities could not always rely on the letter of the law. Daily interactions between slaves, masters, and judges generated legal cultures that could deviate substantially from a strict interpretation of the law. Indians may have been "free vassals" in the eyes of the law, but Spanish masters resorted to slight changes in terminology, gray areas, and subtle reinterpretations to continue to hold Indians in bondage. Still, the larger point remains true: the legal regimes under which African and Indian slaves operated were vastly different. The title of this book, *The Other Slavery,* is meant to draw a contrast between African and Indian slaves that was ultimately rooted in the law.[5]

## The Indians of Spain

To understand how the law shaped the lives of Indian slaves, we need to begin in Spain. During the first half of the sixteenth century, upwards of 2,500 Natives were shipped to the Iberian Peninsula and spent years there toiling in obscurity. Locked up in houses and shops in various towns and cities in southern and western Spain, they would have died without leaving a trace had it not been for the New Laws of 1542, which specifically required all Spaniards already in possession of Indians to show their legitimate titles of ownership and if they did not have them, to liberate their slaves at once. By all accounts, the Spanish king Charles I was very serious about enforcing this provision. Immediately after the promulgation of the code, he directed royal officials to make inquiries and look for Natives held in bondage improperly.[6]

The man most directly responsible for carrying out this effort was the licenciado Gregorio López. He had been part of the small cabal that in 1541–1542 had pushed for the pro-Indian legislation and in 1543 was appointed to Spain's powerful Council of the Indies. His first year as councilor was a veritable baptism of fire. He spent his time compiling a list of owners of Indian slaves in Seville, gathering information about these Natives, and initiating no less than sixteen lawsuits. He had to deal with irate slaveholders and decide the fates not only of Natives who won their cases but also, more dramatically, of those who lost. López could not have been more different from Las Casas in temperament and method. The licenciado had never set foot in the New World. He was married to a cousin of Francisco Pizarro, the conqueror of Peru. He was a legal scholar who felt more comfortable poring over the minutiae of legal cases than making grand pronouncements in public. Yet López, in his own quiet way, became the best hope for the enslaved Indians of Spain.[7]

The archives in Seville contain more than a hundred cases of Natives who had the courage to partner with Spanish attorneys and officials to sue their masters. These cases were sixteenth-century courtroom dramas featuring not faceless "Indian slaves," as I have called them thus far, but highly motivated human beings, such as Gaspar, María, and Beatriz (whose stories are presented later in this chapter), pitted against owners who were just as motivated to hold on to what they regarded as their property. No Indian slaves wrote detailed accounts of their lives comparable to the works penned by African or African American slaves, such as Olaudah Equiano's *Interesting Narrative* (1789), Frederick Douglass's *Narrative* (1845), and Harriet Jacobs's *Incidents in the Life of a Slave Girl* (1861). Nonetheless, these court cases are powerful examples of how Natives, even after they had been forcibly moved halfway around the world, were capable of adapting, making a place for themselves, and fighting to regain their freedom.[8]

Who were these Indians? They hailed from the areas colonized by Spain, first Española and the other Caribbean islands, then coastal Mexico, Florida, and Venezuela, as well as elsewhere. The most striking observation about them is that a majority were women and children. When we think of the Middle Passage, we immediately imagine adult African males. This image is based on fact. Of all the Africans carried to North America from the sixteenth through the eighteenth century, males outnumbered females by a ratio approaching two to one, and they were overwhelmingly adults.[9]

The "reverse Middle Passage," from America to Spain, was just the opposite: the slave traffic consisted mostly of children, with a good contingent of women and a mere sprinkling of men. The main reason was that Indians going to Europe were intended for work in homes, not on plantations, and European heads of household largely regarded children and women as better suited than men for domestic service. Children were more adaptable than adults, learned new languages quickly, and they could be trained and molded with greater ease. Women were less threatening than men and could be sexually exploited. These preferences had enduring demographic consequences. Most slaves held in Italian and Spanish households in the fourteenth, fifteenth, and sixteenth centuries — whether Slavs, Tartars, Greeks, Russians, or Africans — were women. Females comprised an astonishing eighty percent or more of the slaves living in Genoa and Venice, the two leading slave-owning cities in Italy. The situation was similar in the Iberian Peninsula. Contrary to what one might expect, women accounted for a majority of the African slaves in cities such as Granada and Lisbon.[10]

Thus it is no wonder that Europeans would also demand women and children from the New World. Slave prices in the Caribbean already implied such preferences. Women were easily the most expensive of all Indian slaves. On average, adult Native women in Santo Domingo or Havana cost sixty percent more than adult males. Girls were next, followed by boys in the middle of the price range, then full-grown men, who were considerably cheaper (see appendix 3). It is difficult to know exactly what determined these prices. One possibility is that the supply of women and minors was less abundant due to restrictions on their capture and enslavement. But the most likely explanation is simply that the demand for women and children was much greater. Indeed, scattered price information indicates that the premium for Indian women and children spanned the entire hemisphere, from southern Chile to northern Mexico, and endured from the sixteenth through the nineteenth century.[11]

Indian women and children were carried to Europe primarily because customers wanted them. Additionally, the well-intentioned but ultimately deleterious royal policies regarding Indian slavery played a role. As we have seen, the Spanish crown originally prohibited Indian slavery except in a handful of cases (cannibalism, ransomed Indians, and slaves obtained in "just wars") but closed those loopholes in 1542 with the passage of the New Laws. As a result, Spaniards who wished to transport Indians to Europe had to demonstrate that they were taking legitimate slaves—branded and bearing the appropriate documentation from the time when slavery was legal—or were accompanied by "willing" Native travelers. Faced with these circumstances, traffickers went to great lengths to procure "willing" Indians, particularly children, who were more easily tricked and manipulated than adults. Years later, when these Indians appeared in court and recounted their lives, they often began with how they had been taken to Spain by "deception" and "trickery" when they were twelve or thirteen years old. Some enslaved children may have been even younger. Since Native children did not come with birth certificates, traffickers determined age by height, by the presence of pubic hair, and, undoubtedly, by the need to comply with regulations that prohibited the enslavement of children below age twelve.[12]

Once these Indians were in Spain, their lives revolved around the master's house. Occasionally they accompanied their masters on errands or were sent out of the house to fetch water, food, or some other necessity. For the most part, however, they were confined to the home, where their chores were never-ending. They swept floors, prepared food, looked after children, and worked in the master's trade. On duty at all hours of the day and night, they watched as the days turned into months and years. The major milestones in their lives occurred when they were transferred from one master to the next. In return for their ceaseless work, they received no compensation except room and board.

The case of a slave named Gaspar illuminates this situation. Gaspar was thirteen when a Spanish merchant found him in Española and "by means of trickery" took him to Seville. For the next twenty-one years, he served in various households around the Spanish port. In 1559, when he was in his early thirties, he finally ran away. He drifted in the city, eking out a living for more than a month, until, quite by chance, his master spotted him in the Plaza de San Francisco. Rather than risk public scandal or a violent altercation, the master prudently called a guard (police officer), who in turn approached Gaspar. Instead of returning the slave to his master, however, the guard took him to the municipal jail, where the local authorities launched an investigation.[13]

As a child, immediately after disembarking in Seville, Gaspar had been sold for 36 ducats to a family of tailors and weavers. The bill of sale describes him as a thirteen-year-old "obtained in a just war" who was "not a drunkard or a thief or an escapist" and who had "no public or private illnesses," all stock phrases that appeared in contracts involving slaves of all races and ethnicities. In his new home, he joined two Indian women who were already working there. The three Natives spent their days under the watchful eye of Ana Sánchez, the matriarch of the family. In addition to doing chores around the house, Gaspar was given some weaving to do, which enabled him to become skilled in this trade.

After thirteen years of service, Gaspar was transferred to a new household. The occasion was the marriage of one of Ana Sánchez's daughters: Gaspar was part of the dowry. Giving slaves as a dowry was a common practice in early modern Spain and a clever way for parents to shield a newlywed daughter from the increased workload of setting up a household, tending to a husband, and starting a family. For Gaspar this move was only the first in a series of transfers over the next few years. Ana Sánchez's intention was to give each of her children a turn with him. After staying with her daughter for some time, Gaspar was transferred to the household of Luis Álvarez, the matriarch's son. From the surviving documentation, it is not possible to determine how long Gaspar remained with the daughter, when he came to Luis Álvarez, or why he also spent time in other households working as a weaver. Years later Gaspar declared in court that all along the person who had remained truly in control of his life was Ana Sánchez.

Complicating all of these moves was Gaspar's wife. Ana Sánchez had consented to his marriage to Elvira, a free Indian woman working in her household as a weaver. Gaspar and Elvira probably occupied a room in the house and were able to stay together even when Gaspar was temporarily rented out to other weavers. But in 1559 Ana Sánchez sold Gaspar to a sixty-year-old man named Bartolomé Vallejo. The new owner refused to accommodate the Indian couple. He took Gaspar away from Seville and kept him as his personal servant during a lengthy stay in the Spanish court. A few days after Gaspar and his master returned to Seville, the slave fled from the elderly Vallejo.

Gaspar's story reveals that slaves could improve their condition with the passage of time. He started out as an Indian boy from Española who had been deceived and victimized by a slave trader. Once in Spain, he acquired a trade, became an asset to his masters, got married, and expected to be treated with the considerations due to a loyal and valuable servant. And yet, as Gaspar discovered, slaves could lose this hard-earned social esteem in an instant. After being sold to Bartolomé Vallejo and working for him for some time, Gaspar decided to risk everything by becoming a fugitive of the law.

The basic justification of slavery invoked by theologians and officials was that Indians like Gaspar were better off in Christian homes than in their own state of *naturaleza,* or nature, a term that conjured up images of barbarity and heathenism. Even as an exploited underclass, the argument went, slaves had the opportunity to save their souls and acquire the rudiments of civilization. Indians did become Europeanized during their long years of bondage in the Old World, but this acquisition of Western culture came at a tremendous cost. Gaspar's story leaves no doubt that even the most well-intentioned masters participated in a system that produced degradation, exploitation, and bitter resentment.[14]

The story of María, an Indian woman from Mexico City, reveals that women faced a different set of circumstances. María had a relationship with a Spanish merchant of clothes and jewels named Juan Marquez. Although we have few details about their life together in Mexico City, it is certain that they were not married. Years later María's brother Pedro testified simply that Marquez "had a carnal relationship with my sister. And from this relationship they had three children, two girls and one boy." Regardless of the precise nature of the relationship, Juan Marquez regarded María as his partner and recognized their three mestizo children—Catalina, Luisa, and Juan—as his own. They lived in Mexico for some years before moving to Spain, where they settled in Ciudad Rodrigo, a small town in Old Castile with an imposing castle, a cathedral, and a massive outer wall. María's brother Pedro, by all accounts a very resourceful man, came along as well.[15]

In one sense, Juan Marquez defied the social conventions of a small Spanish town by establishing a household with five Mexican Indians. But in another respect, these Natives fit into the preexisting social grid. María was perceived as Juan Marquez's concubine and the children as *criados* (children who were not members of the family but were raised in a household and given room and board in exchange for doing menial jobs). Pedro's status must have been the most difficult to pin down. The people of Ciudad Rodrigo were familiar with African and Indian slaves, who could usually be identified by the brands on their faces. Yet Pedro had no visible brand. And when curious neighbors would ask if the Indian man was a slave, Juan Marquez would reply emphatically that Pedro "was not his slave or anyone else's but a free man." Most Spaniards familiar with the Marquez household knew that Pedro and María were not "wild," or nomadic, Indians caught in raids and sold in slave markets in the Caribbean, but rather "city" Indians who had always been free.

The Indians' situation in Ciudad Rodrigo deteriorated steadily. First, Juan Marquez decided to take a Spanish wife. Marriage to a European was more appropriate for a successful merchant. He married an assertive woman named Isabel de Herrera. Her arrival in the Marquez household reduced María's status to that of a concubine/servant and drastically reconfigured the lines of authority. When Isabel de Herrera was later asked in court if "during the time she had lived and spoken with Juan Marquez, her husband, she had ever heard that María and the children were free," she said no. From her testimony, one can also gather that there was no love lost between Isabel and María. Relations between wives and live-in concubines were normally contentious throughout the Mediterranean world, and this was no exception. Although Isabel de Herrera was keen on asserting her authority over the Indians in her household, Juan Marquez continued to treat the children well and to protect their mother. When María died sometime in the early 1540s, it was up to Pedro to defend his freedom and that of his nieces and nephew.[16]

The final demotion of Pedro and the children occurred when Juan Marquez fell ill during a business trip. In the throes of death, the merchant wrote his last will and testament, leaving everything to Isabel de Herrera. Marquez died a few days later, and his wife embarked on a long-contemplated reorganization of the household. She immediately sold Pedro for 10,000 *maravedís* and put the children up for sale, not concerned if that meant splitting them up among separate households. Pedro fought back. Suddenly treated as a slave, he sought out a *fiscal* (attorney) and sued Isabel de Herrera to recover his freedom, stop the sale of the children, and keep the family together. Pedro's lawsuit was successful; he recovered his freedom and obtained custody of the children. The journey of Pedro and his family from free Indians to slaves and back to free exemplifies both the uncertain status of Indians in the mid-sixteenth century and the legal options available to them.[17]

## Fighting for Their Freedom

For indigenous men and women who seldom stepped outside the house, the thought of initiating legal proceedings and making formal statements in front of lawyers, judges, and owners must have been daunting. Yet the demands of public appearances paled in comparison with their private ordeals. The minute the lawsuit was filed, their relationship with their master turned decidedly hostile. Since slaves had nowhere else to go, they generally continued to live under the same roof with their masters during their trials, which could last for months or even years, giving masters ample opportunities to punish, torture, or somehow make their slaves desist. So routinely did masters beat their petitioning slaves or hide them away in rural properties beyond the arm of the law that the legal document informing them that they had been sued included a clause warning them against such retaliation. Thus Indian slaves had the chance to become free, but only at the risk of anguish and bodily harm. They also faced the very real possibility of losing in court, and in that case their efforts and suffering would have earned them nothing but their masters' eternal hatred.

The multigenerational saga of Beatriz and her children is a good example of the workings of the Spanish legal system, as well as the incredible tenacity of both masters and slaves. Described as "a short, thin woman with a missing upper tooth," Beatriz arrived in Spain when she was fourteen but already carrying a baby named Simón. Both were given to an up-and-coming resident of the town of Carmona named Juan Cansino as part of his wife's dowry in 1534 and remained in his household for twenty-four years. During this time, the relationship between master and slaves evolved and became quite contentious. First, Cansino sold off Simón against Beatriz's will after he discovered that the little boy had stolen from him. Cansino then mistreated Beatriz, who bore four more children by unidentified men. All four remained in Cansino's house as slaves.[18]

A turning point in their relationship occurred around 1556 when Beatriz's oldest daughter, Catalina, a feisty seventeen-year-old, repeatedly tried to escape, urging the others to do the same. Juan Cansino, who had become a wealthy merchant and alderman of the town of Carmona, could not tolerate this challenge. He sent Catalina to a nearby barber, "right next to the meat shop," who branded her on the face with a hot iron. During the trial, Cansino declared that Catalina had become incorrigible, "always trying to escape and having stolen a money purse, a silver chain, jewels, cheese, wool, wine, and whatever else she and her mother could get." Shortly after the branding of Catalina, Beatriz and her daughter began to speak out about being *indias* (Indians) and having the right to be free. They had heard that some Indians living in the neighboring city of Seville had successfully sued for their freedom.

In the spring of 1558, after twenty-four years of service, Beatriz fled

Cansino's house. Leaving her children behind, she made her way to Seville, where she remained for five months, meeting with lawyers and officials. With the help of the *procurador general de indios* Francisco Sarmiento, Beatriz gathered witnesses and prepared her case. When everything was ready at the end of September, Juan Cansino was summoned to Seville to answer the charges lodged against him by his slave Beatriz.

The case could not have been more straightforward. If Beatriz could prove that she had come from the Spanish Indies (meaning all of Spain's overseas colonies, including Mexico), Cansino would have to set her free according to the provisions of the New Laws. For the same reason, Beatriz's children would also go free. The judges were at first sympathetic when Beatriz claimed she was from Mexico. They even noted that the plaintiff had "every appearance of someone from the Indies." But when they asked Beatriz if she could speak the Mexican language (Nahuatl), she said that she could not. Beatriz and Sarmiento presented their witnesses, all of whom lived in the immediate neighborhood of Juan Cansino's household: a widow from just up the street, the butcher's wife, a shoemaker named Diego Gómez. They all affirmed that Beatriz spoke "a strange tongue" and declared that she was an Indian from Mexico. Beatriz's star witness was a blind Indian named Juan Vázquez who claimed to have known Beatriz for thirteen years. His testimony, almost poetic, has come down to us, recorded in the third person: "Even though this witness could not see the said Beatriz, he knew it was her because of the words they have exchanged . . . and the witness believes that she is a native from Malacata because he is from New Spain and understands the tongue of Malacata and it is the same that Beatriz speaks, and he has never heard anything contrary to this."[19]

Indians taken to Spain when they were very young often could not speak Native languages or remember much about their homelands. So slave owners' most common strategy consisted of asserting that their slaves had not come from the Spanish Indies but from the *Portuguese* Indies (Portuguese colonies) — Brazil, northern and western Africa, and parts of Asia — where the enslavement of Natives was legal. Juan Cansino took precisely this tack. He declared that "he had always believed

Beatriz to be an *alarabe* [Arab from northern or western Africa] because she often said that she was the daughter of a Moor." Cansino's cunning lawyer went on to subject Beatriz to a battery of leading questions: What types of fabrics existed in her homeland? Had she seen camels, elephants, tigers, or lions? Were there spices such as ginger, pepper, cinnamon, or cloves? His obvious intention was to exploit Beatriz's gullibility and lack of knowledge. Cansino's lawyer also seized on the assertion that Beatriz was from "Malacata." He demonstrated that no such place existed in the Americas but posited that in all likelihood, the witness was referring to the Malagueta Coast of Africa, where the famous malagueta pepper came from. Cansino's lawyer called several witnesses, including a mariner from Lisbon, Luis Calaforte, who, after swearing in front of a crucifix, stated that he had sailed many times the coast of Africa and was entirely certain that Malagueta was a stretch of coast below São Tomé in the Portuguese Indies.

Meanwhile, Beatriz and Juan Vázquez insisted that she came from "Malacata" in New Spain (Mexico), while other witnesses pointed to other places. A woman named Catalina Hernández, who claimed to be Beatriz's cousin, testified that "from her father's side Beatriz was from Margarita [which she maintained was close to Lima, Peru] and from her mother's side she was from Puerto Rico, such that from both sides she comes from His Majesty's Indies." Sarmiento called a witness named Francisco de Vega, who had traveled widely in the New World and had encountered many slaves from the Portuguese Indies. He cautiously expressed the opinion that Beatriz "struck him as someone from the Spanish Indies." With these divergent and lukewarm testimonies, it was impossible for Beatriz to win her case. We can only imagine what the consequences for her were when she was returned to Cansino.

But the fight was not over. Thirteen years after the first trial, in 1572, Beatriz's oldest daughter, Catalina, sued Cansino again. By then Beatriz had died a slave, Catalina was in her early thirties and had a ten-year-old daughter of her own, and Juan Cansino was an elderly patriarch and slave owner. His son Fernando Cansino had taken over as alderman of Carmona.

Through all the years, Catalina's feistiness had remained intact. During the spring of 1572, she spoke with lawyers and officials, including Francisco Sarmiento, who was still *procurador general de indios*. Catalina told them that her mother had been "a woman with little understanding who got drunk on most days" — in other words, who was too addled to prepare a good case. This time, Catalina left nothing to chance. She assembled a long list of witnesses and made sure that their testimonies were consistent. They all declared that Beatriz had come from Mexico, and therefore her children and grandchildren had to go free immediately.

On this occasion, Cansino's strategy consisted of questioning Catalina's witnesses' credibility. The witnesses included Africans, Indians, and some impoverished residents of Carmona, but no Spaniards from Old Christian families. (Purity of blood was a major concern at this time. "Old Christians" referred to Spaniards who had not intermarried with Muslims or Indians.) One of these witnesses was a former slave named Isabel Navarra, who was immediately discounted by Cansino's side as "a person belonging to a lowly race with no fixed opinions and who is untrustworthy because she is a *morisca* who descends from Moors." Another witness was an Indian and former slave from Mexico named Mariana, who was immediately dismissed by the slave-owning side: "She is an Indian and as such would lie in order to favor Catalina, and, as an Indian, she is a lowly person with no fixed opinions and to whom one should not give credit." When Fernando Cansino learned that these two were going to testify on Catalina's behalf, he "confronted and insulted them" and used threats to dissuade them from testifying. Both sides fought tenaciously, but more than forty years after Beatriz's arrival in Spain, the witnesses' memories were fading and the information about Beatriz's origins had been mostly lost. The judges found that "Francisco Sarmiento, on behalf of the said Indians, could not prove his demand and intention." The final verdict reads, "We therefore must absolve Juan Cansino Aragonés . . . admonishing him to treat his slaves well." Under this ruling, Catalina, her brothers and sisters, and her ten-year-old daughter would remain slaves. Within two years, however, the Council of the Indies overturned the ruling and set Catalina and her family free.

Notwithstanding the legal experiences of Beatriz and Catalina, the evidence indicates that the majority of Indian litigants won their cases. The archives in Seville contain several documents that attest to these legal victories: "royal order addressed to the justices of these kingdoms and of the Indies granting freedom to the Indian Magdalena who had been a slave of Esteban Vicente from the town of Medina del Campo"; "order against Juan de Jaén, priest of Fregenal, about setting the Indian that he had as a slave free"; and "order to Catalina de Olvera, resident of Santa Olalla, about granting freedom to the Indian Inés who she had as a slave," among many others. Contextual information contained in some of these judicial proceedings similarly strengthens this conclusion. For example, when Beatriz sued Juan Cansino in the fall of 1558, one of the judges asked her pointedly "why she had not attained her freedom at the same time that the other Indians of Seville" had, clearly implying that most other Indians had already been freed.[20]

The greatest legal victory was probably achieved by two Indians who sued none other than Nuño de Guzmán, one of the most influential and ruthless conquistadors in all of Mexico. In the late 1520s and early 1530s, Guzmán's power rivaled that of even Hernán Cortés. He served as governor of the provinces of Pánuco and Nueva Galicia and presided over the first Audiencia of Mexico. Yet in 1549, two slaves he had brought back to Spain, Pedro and Luisa, had the audacity to sue him. What is more, Pedro and Luisa also demanded 3,000 *maravedís* for every year each of them had served since their arrival in Spain in 1539. For someone like Guzmán, under whose watch ten thousand Indians from Pánuco and Nueva Galicia had been sold into slavery, the loss of the legal battle with these two lowly slaves whom he had raised in his home must have been infuriating. But there was little he could do. Through his lawyer, Guzmán sought to reduce the cash award, arguing that "the service provided by the said Pedro and Luisa, and of any other Indian, amounts to very little as they are useful only for minor tasks of little substance, and the work that they perform is not even sufficient to pay for the food and dress and shoes that the said Guzmán has given them."[21]

The New Laws did not end Indian slavery in Spain, but they did initiate the gradual eradication of this peculiar institution in the Iberian

Peninsula. After 1542 it became public knowledge that the king of Spain had freed the Indians of the Americas. Word about Indians suing their masters and scoring legal victories spread quickly. By the 1550s, Indian slaves living in small Spanish towns were well aware that they were entitled to their freedom. Among Spanish owners, the possession of Indian slaves increasingly became an embarrassment and a brazen violation of the law. More tangibly, owners faced greater difficulty in selling their Indians at full price. Indian slaves continued to be exchanged in Spain during the second half of the sixteenth century and even into the early decades of the seventeenth century, but the number of transactions declined steadily until they disappeared almost completely.[22]

## The Slaves of Early Mexico

The Spanish crown also attempted to end Indian slavery in the New World, but the situation could not have been more different there. Indian slaves constituted a major pillar of the societies and economies of the Americas. In Mexico their importance was evident from the very beginning. No sooner had Hernán Cortés landed on the Gulf of Mexico coast near the site of modern Veracruz in 1519 than he began to anticipate that the lands that he was about to enter would include "many heathen Indians who would wage war on the Spaniards." Cortés requested permission from the crown to subdue such groups by force and distribute the vanquished Natives as slaves, "as it is customary to do in the lands of the infidels, and it is a very just thing to do."[23]

Cortés's breathtaking ascent to the Valley of Mexico and eventual conquest of the Aztec empire put millions of Indians nominally under the control of a few thousand Spaniards. Enslaving all of these Natives would have been both impossible and impractical. Instead, Cortés and his men imported the encomienda system from the Caribbean. "The Spaniards went from conquest to conquest, subjecting the land," explained one friar, "and after each town was taken, a Spaniard would ask Cortés to grant it to him and he then received it as an *encomienda*." In the Caribbean, the encomienda had failed to protect the Natives from colonists bent on extracting gold. The encomienda of central Mexico was less insidious. The Indians there were agriculturalists who had long been accustomed to paying tribute. They continued to transfer a portion of their crops and other products to the Spanish encomendero. In return, the Natives remained in their towns and villages and retained a great deal of autonomy. Although abuse was rife, the encomienda of central Mexico was not tantamount to slavery.[24]

But Spanish conquerors also acquired slaves, tens of thousands of them. Many were taken from among those who resisted conquest. They were called *esclavos de guerra,* or war slaves. According to one of Cortés's soldiers who later wrote an eyewitness account, before entering an Indian town Spaniards requested its inhabitants to submit peacefully, "and if they did not come in peace but wished to give us war, we would make them slaves; and we carried with us an iron brand like this one to mark their faces."[25]

The crown authorized Cortés and his soldiers to keep these Indians as long as the conquerors paid the corresponding taxes. Treasury accounts thus offer a few clues about the scope of slave taking in early Mexico. For the period between January 1521 and May 1522 — that is, a few months before and after the fall of Tenochtitlán — Spaniards paid taxes on around eight thousand slaves taken just in the Aztec capital and its immediate surroundings. Thousands more flowed from Oaxaca, Michoacán, Tututepec, and as far away as Guatemala as these Indian kingdoms were brought into the Spanish fold. "So great was the haste to make slaves in different parts," commented Friar Toribio de Benavente (also known as Motolinía) some years later, "that they were brought into Mexico City in great flocks, like sheep, so they could be branded easily."[26]

Besides the slaves taken in military campaigns, Spaniards also purchased Indians who had already been enslaved by other Indians and were regularly offered in markets and streets. They were called *esclavos de rescate,* or ransomed slaves. To distinguish these slaves from those taken in war, the Spaniards used a different type of brand, also applied on the face.

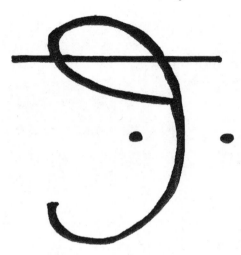

The brand used for "war slaves" resembled the letter *g*, for *guerra* (war). Slaves were usually branded on the cheek or forehead.

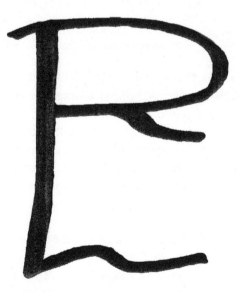

The brand used for "ransomed slaves" resembled the letter *r*, for *rescate* (ransom).

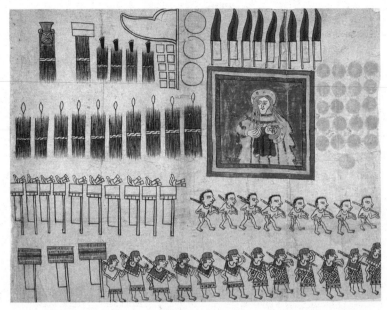

Along with textiles and feathers, Spanish encomenderos occasionally requested Indians as tribute. In 1529 Nuño de Guzmán received eight males and twelve women, all tethered by the neck, from the people of Huejotzinco, as shown in this page from an account book.

Slavery had been practiced in Mexico since time immemorial. Pre-contact Indians had sold their children or even themselves into slavery because they had no food. Many Indians had been sold into slavery by other Indians as punishment for robbery, rape, or other crimes. Some war slaves were set aside for public sacrifices and ritual cannibalism. Some towns even had holding pens where men and women were fattened before the festivities. All of these pre-contact forms of bondage operated in specific cultural contexts. But as Brett Rushforth has recently argued, they were close enough to what Europeans understood as slavery that they persisted into the post-contact period. This was certainly the case in central Mexico, where Spaniards acquired Indians in *tianguis*, open-air markets, for decades after conquest. In the 1520s, these slaves were so plentiful that their average price was only 2 pesos, far less than the price of a horse or cow. Spaniards typically traded small items such as a knife or piece of cloth in exchange for these human beings. As for their number, we do not have the slightest indication, as these transactions were private and went untaxed.[27]

Sixteenth-century Spaniards gave widely different estimates of the overall number of Indian slaves. Las Casas reported that by the middle of the century, more than three million slaves had been made in Mexico, Central America, and Venezuela. The Franciscan friar Toribio de Benavente (who considered Las Casas a "turbulent, injurious, and prejudicial man") estimated the number of slaves taken in the different provinces of Mexico up to 1555 to be less than two hundred thousand and possibly not even one hundred thousand. It is clear that even at the low end of this range, Indian slaves had become a major portion of Mexico's workforce.[28]

The urgent need for slaves became evident during Mexico's gold rush in the 1520s. At first Spanish overlords sent their encomienda Indians to the mines, but the Natives resisted this breach of the original encomienda terms. Moreover, after the Caribbean experience, the crown expressly forbade the use of encomienda Indians for mining. Therefore mine owners had to resort to Indian and African slaves organized in work gangs known as cuadrillas.

Notarial documents give us fleeting glimpses of this ruthlessly exploitative world. Fernando Alonso, an ironsmith from Mexico City, and a rancher named Nicolás López de Palacios Rubio formed a partnership to develop a mine in Michoacán. The ironsmith was to contribute crowbars and assorted tools to the operation, along with one hundred Indian slaves — "up to two hundred if possible" — while the rancher agreed to feed these workers for a year. Workers like these became an integral part of the mines where they toiled. They settled down around the mines and performed specialized tasks. In fact, much of the value of a mine was derived from the labor attached to it. As the notarial documents show, all sales of mines included the mine's slaves. For instance, Pedro González Nájera sold his stake in a mine in Oaxaca in the summer of 1528 and was able to get 600 pesos for it, largely because it had "one hundred slaves taken in a good war and skilled in the work of the mines." Interestingly, these laborers were both males and females. A 1525 contract between

Pedro de Villalobos and Álvaro Maldonado stipulated that each partner would supply fifty Indian slaves "between men and women." The sale of one mine involved "sixty Indian slaves, half males and half females," and another included a clause that allowed the new owner of the mine to select "fifty Indian slaves, 30 males and 20 females, and all aged thirty years or younger."[29]

Along with the Indians were a handful of African slaves who performed specialized tasks. Immediately after conquest, Indian slaves were abundant and cheap, while African slaves were rare and expensive. Thus the cuadrilla of Pedro de Sepúlveda and Martín Sánchez in 1528 consisted of twenty Indian slaves along with four Africans who operated a blacksmith shop to make crowbars. Tellingly, one of the provisions of their contract was that should the four black slaves die or run away, both partners would absorb the loss. As the century progressed, the share of African slaves in the cuadrillas increased, but Indians continued to make up the majority of slaves.[30]

As in many other things, the ubiquitous Cortés led the way in mining. After toppling the Aztec empire, he turned his formidable energy and resources to this enterprise. As is evident from notarial documents, mining was not just a matter of digging holes in the ground. It also required a large number of workers, all of whom needed to be fed, clothed, and supplied with tools. Cortés was in the best position to invest in mining because he owned the largest encomiendas in all of Mexico. On November 20, 1536, the celebrated Spanish leader acquired one-fourth of a mine called Mina Rica de la Albarrada in Sultepec, along with twenty Indian slaves of both sexes. Later in the day, he paid 10,000 pesos for another fourth of Mina Rica de la Albarrada, which also came with "a certain number of Indian slaves and their tools." And before the day was over, he disbursed 6,230 pesos to acquire yet another nearby mine, which came with seventy Indian slaves. Altogether, he spent more than 20,000 pesos and acquired between one hundred and two hundred Indian slaves in a single day. Ultimately, not only was Cortés the richest man in Mexico, he was also the largest owner of Indian slaves. And wherever Cortés led, others followed.[31]

# A New Regime

Mexico's economic promise lay in the extraction of gold and silver based on Indian labor. Yet across the Atlantic, Spanish reformers wished to do away with both encomiendas and Indian slaves. The struggle between reformers and slave owners had been brewing for decades, but things finally came to a head in 1539 when King Charles I ordered the Audiencia of Mexico to free all Indians held in bondage. Spanish colonists and officials in Mexico were stunned. After days of heated discussions, the audiencia wrote back to the monarch imploring him to reconsider. Along with their petition, they included questionnaires filled out by some of the oldest and most respected colonists, who had answered leading questions that sometimes ran half a page or more. For example: "Do you know that when Hernán Cortés first came to Mexico, he found a Spaniard named Jerónimo de Aguilar who had been shipwrecked before and had been held as a slave by the Indians for many years in a land called Yucatán?" "Do you know that the Indians of Mexico have had and continue to have many slaves in their power, and that they ordinarily buy them and sell them peacefully in their *tianguis*?" Questions such as these were intended to show that Indians had enslaved other Indians long before the Spaniards arrived. Other questions were meant to draw attention to the beneficial effects of the institution, including the following: "Do you know that the Indians of the outlying areas are idolaters and eat human flesh?" "Do you know that the slaves held by the Indians of Mexico are well treated and are being instructed in our Holy Catholic Faith?" The last section of the questionnaire touched on economic matters: "Do you know that in Mexico there are not enough workers and slaves are needed to extract gold and silver and grow food and other things . . . and [that] if His Majesty were to free the slaves this land would be lost and such a great and rich kingdom as Mexico would become depopulated?" In spite of the audiencia's objections, Charles reaffirmed his previous order and went on to promulgate the New Laws of 1542, thus prohibiting new encomiendas and abolishing Indian slavery in all cases.[32]

In Spain the New Laws produced discontent, but in the Spanish colonies they caused outright rebellion. In Peru a group of colonists murdered the official sent from Spain to enforce the laws and then decapitated him. For a time it seemed that Peru might even break away from the empire. Spanish slave owners in Mexico were no less determined. As in Peru, the Spanish crown did not entrust the execution of these unpopular laws to Spanish authorities in Mexico, but instead sent a high-ranking officer directly from Spain. Francisco Tello de Sandoval, a member of the Spanish Inquisition and the Council of the Indies, crossed the Atlantic Ocean, disembarked in Veracruz, and made his way to the viceregal capital of Mexico City, all the while sensing the tremendous opposition to the New Laws. When he entered the city in 1544, he saw that some local officials were wearing mourning garb to greet him. As he met with the highest civil and religious authorities, the economy came to a standstill pending the outcome of these meetings. Tello de Sandoval could well have suffered the same fate as his Peruvian counterpart, but after much pleading by Mexican slave owners, and perhaps sensing a fatal end to his tour of duty, the Spanish envoy agreed to suspend the New Laws until he received further instructions from the king. Charles and the members of the Council of the Indies considered the situation and eventually consented to the granting of more encomiendas. It was a major victory for slave owners. Encomiendas remained in existence for another century and a half, affecting tens of thousands of Indians. Other provisions of the New Laws were not suspended, however, and the crown continued to press for the abolition of Indian slavery in the New World.[33]

Thus a new regime emerged in the 1540s and 1550s, a regime in which Indians were legally free but remained enslaved through slight reinterpretations, changes in nomenclature, and practices meant to get around the New Laws. All over the Americas, the other slavery took shape as Spaniards struggled to implement the laws. Two opposing camps came into existence. On one side were the ardent reformers led by Las Casas, who advocated for a broad, categorical, and literal interpretation of the provision that abolished Indian slavery without any exceptions or qualifications. On the other side stood officials and clergymen who

The war of the mountaintops, as depicted twenty years after the event in a manuscript painting known as the *Codex Telleriano-Remensis*. The top left square shows the year "ten house," or 1541. Below is a dead conquistador identified as Pedro de Alvarado. He was nicknamed "Tonatiuh" (the Sun) because of his striking red hair, thus his body is appropriately linked to a little sun. Below the corpse is a naked warrior standing on a mountaintop, surrounded by a stream. He is shooting arrows at a Spaniard below.

understood that abolition was a noble goal but insisted on certain exceptions and limitations to make it viable. The two camps tried to resolve their differences at a high-level council held in Mexico City in December 1546. It was attended by Tello de Sandoval, Viceroy Antonio de Mendoza, and the highest religious authorities in Mexico, including none other than Friar Las Casas, who at the time was serving as bishop of Chiapas. The stakes were enormous. Bishop Las Casas and his allies pressed for an unconditional and immediate liberation of all Indian slaves, while Viceroy Mendoza and other officials resolutely avoided making any pronouncements on the subject. When Las Casas expressed his displeasure at the lack of resolution, the viceroy reportedly said that "he wished to remain silent on the matter because of *reasons of state.*"[34]

Viceroy Mendoza's reasons for circumspection are obvious. Just six years earlier, Mexico had suffered its first massive Indian insurrection. What had started as isolated attacks on Spanish ranches in the coastal plains of western Mexico had grown into a major anti-Christian movement in 1540–1542, eventually involving fifteen thousand rebels who nearly dislodged the Spanish presence all along the Pacific coast. The Spaniards called it *la guerra de los peñoles,* the war of the mountaintops, because the rebels took up fortified positions in the mountains. It was also called the Mixtón War. Scores of Spaniards lost their lives in this upheaval, among them Pedro de Alvarado, Cortés's main captain (military leader) and reputedly the most daring and capable of all the conquistadors. Only a massive offensive organized in Mexico City involving thirty thousand Indian allies and led personally by Mendoza finally succeeded in quelling the rebellion.[35]

Spanish colonists took at least 4,700 slaves during this bloody war. Moreover, in 1543 they sent a petition to the king asking for encomiendas in perpetuity along a three-hundred-mile stretch of coastal plain between Compostela and Culiacán. They also requested permission to undertake *entradas* (exploring expeditions) and to enslave nomadic Indians who had been sympathetic to the rebels. These Spaniards were not about to agree to a royal order abolishing Indian slavery "under any circumstance including wars [and] rebellions." Members of the Audiencia of Mexico wrote as much to the king in the spring of 1545. The only way to induce settlers to fight against the Indians was with the promise of spoils of war, they argued. How could the land be pacified and the Spanish settlers mobilized without the inducement of taking slaves? This became a major quandary as the entire northern region of Mexico burst into open rebellion during the second half of the sixteenth century.[36]

Other doubts about the application of the New Laws revolved around the new silver discoveries. In September 1546, Spanish prospectors climbed a promontory crowned by a semicircular rock formation that would become the mine of Zacatecas. For two years, it was unclear whether this venture would be different from many other fleeting strikes. But the discovery of the *veta grande* (large vein) finally turned this promontory in the middle of the desert into a major pole of attraction. By 1550 Zacatecas had taken its place as the brightest star in a new constellation of mines that included Guanajuato, Chalchihuites, Avino, Sombrerete, and others.[37]

Workers were urgently needed at all of these mines, and the New Laws were a stumbling block. All along King Charles had been committed to abolishing all forms of Indian enslavement. But when it came to protecting the silver that had started flowing into the royal coffers, he and, above all, his son and successor, Prince Philip, were willing to find a compromise. In 1552 Philip drafted a remarkable plan aimed at reconciling the New Laws with the empire's needs. Indian slavery would be abolished, and the Indians working in the mines would be set free. To prevent disruptions in the production of silver, however, the officials freeing the slaves would explain to them that although they were no longer subject to servitude of any kind, "they would still be required to work for their sustenance, and, if they did not wish to work, they would be compelled to do so as long as they were paid." In this way, unemployed or "lazy" Indians would be rounded up and distributed to the miners in exchange for a nominal wage. Only the elderly and the ill would be spared. Philip's proposal had far-reaching consequences. During his long reign as king of Spain (1556–1598), this system of remunerated but compulsory work and the distribution of Indians known as *repartimiento de indios,* or simply *repartimiento,* became widely used. The Indians were free, but they were still compelled to work.[38]

Since the New Laws had been introduced in Spain in 1542, no legal procedure had been in place in Mexico to allow Indians to sue for their freedom. Finally, in 1550, a new viceroy, Don Luis de Velasco (1550–1564), arrived in Mexico City bearing pointed instructions about liberating the Indians. He was an affable man, perhaps genuinely concerned about the Indians' condition. In the spring of 1551, Velasco appointed as procurador a respected lawyer named Bartolomé Melgarejo, who held a position at the Royal and Pontifical University of Mexico. Melgarejo's vast new duties included publicizing the abolitionist provision of the New Laws, assisting Indians in their lawsuits, liberating all Indian minors held as slaves, and making sure that freed Indians who had been brought from distant places such as Yucatán or Guatemala be restored to their communities. All of this made for a tall order, but the learned Melgarejo seemed up to the task.[39]

First and most important, Melgarejo had to decide whether to adopt a literal interpretation of the abolition of Indian slavery "under any circumstance" and without exceptions or qualifications, as Bishop Las Casas wanted, or to opt for the more nuanced and practical approach favored by many mine owners and officials. As Melgarejo began his deliberations, he felt the need to write a letter to the Spanish king laying out his position. Ever the university professor, Melgarejo was drawn to fine distinctions and complex reasoning involving divine and human law. After his opening remarks, the procurador concluded that "some Indians had been made into slaves properly and justly while others had not." He thus took the side of the pragmatists. Rather than pushing for a blanket abolition of Indian slavery, he spent years considering each case on its own merits.[40]

In one decade, Melgarejo freed 3,150 Indian slaves, a small fraction of the 100,000 or more of them in Mexico at the time. The trial transcripts are missing (or at least have not been found), so all we know about the trials comes from the reports written by the procurador himself. Still, it is possible to glean some sense of how they progressed. First, since Melgarejo believed that some slaves were justly made and others were not, he insisted on lengthy proceedings to get to the bottom of each case. Whereas on the island of Española, the procurador had granted freedom automatically to all petitioners, in Mexico Indian slaves faced long and arduous legal fights and therefore had strong incentives to settle their cases. Especially in the early years, trials could last a year or longer, during which time many of the slaves either died, fled, or found an accommodation with their masters or some other individuals. Slaves often dropped their lawsuits after agreeing to serve their masters for a few more years, while receiving token salaries. In this sense, they remained "in deposit" with their former masters under conditions that could not have been much different from slavery.[41]

It is also evident that Melgarejo bowed to political pressure in some of his decisions. For example, many lawsuits were initiated by Indians from western Mexico who had been captured during the Mixtón War. Because that uprising had been so serious, the Audiencia of Mexico had declared legal the enslavement of the former rebels, who numbered in the thousands. Melgarejo had the authority to overrule the audiencia, but in the end he went along with its decision and refused to liberate any petitioners involved in that war.[42]

Perhaps the greatest challenge to Mexican authorities was what to do with the Indians working in the mines. They had been reluctant to liberate these Indians out of fear of disrupting the colonial economy. According to an account provided by a member of the Audiencia of Mexico in 1550, when Indians toiling in the nearby mines of Taxco, Zultepec, and Zumpango arrived in Mexico City to request their freedom, they were ordinarily returned to their owners if they had brands on their faces. The brands were considered sufficient proof of their servile status. "And the most common outcome, is that the owner gets his slave back and the case ends there and the Indian continues as before if not worse because he infuriated his master."[43]

Indians who worked in distant mines on the frontier were even more disadvantaged because they had to travel great distances to Mexico City to appeal for their freedom. Occasionally the crown sent *visitadores,* or inspectors, to the mines, in which case the Indians could present their petitions to the inspectors. In 1550 Hernando Martínez de la Marcha made the rounds of several mines. A man of great energy and strong opinions, Martínez de la Marcha traveled through western

Mexico almost continuously for a year, sometimes on horseback and other times on a litter carried by Indians—a mode of transportation that raised some eyebrows. Undaunted, the *visitador* wrote reports about the unsettled conditions of the frontier and the convenience of making Indian slaves. When mine workers approached him to request their freedom, far from liberating them, he admonished them to obey their masters.[44]

In spite of the crown's insistence, New World liberations were few and extremely difficult to accomplish. The specific application of the New Laws in the various colonies differed, but the results were much the same. In Venezuela, for example, the laws, and specifically the prohibition against Indian slavery, were made public but not enforced. Slave raids continued in Cubagua and Margarita even though royal officials were well aware that such activities were strictly forbidden. Colonists in Venezuela generally refused to give up their Indian slaves and insisted that the brand on a slave's face was sufficient title and reason to keep him or her in bondage. They also retained the service of a class of Indians known as *naborías,* who were indigenous servants attached to them for life. The only difference between naborías and outright slaves was that naborías could not be legally bought and sold.[45]

In contrast, in Central America an uncompromising and vigorous royal official named Alonso López de Cerrato embarked on blanket liberations of Indian slaves. Next to Bartolomé de Las Casas, Cerrato ranks as the most ardent champion of Indian liberty of the sixteenth century. As president of the Audiencia of Central America, Judge Cerrato prosecuted slave takers, criticized officials who "preferred to make friends with the colonists rather than applying the New Laws," and refused to make invidious distinctions among Indians to justify the enslavement of some of them, as happened in Mexico. Cerrato's vigorous reforms ended formal Indian slavery in Central America, restricted the use of naborías, and regulated the use of Indians as *tamemes,* or load bearers. But even these victories proved temporary. Cerrato acquired a reputation of being an overzealous crown official and died in 1555 largely repudiated by his fellow colonists. After his passing, subsequent officials reversed some of his policies. The naborías returned, Indian load bearers proliferated, and many Indians, though technically free, were compelled to render "personal services" to the Spanish colonists under various guises.[46]

All over Spanish America, Indian slave owners and colonial authorities devised subtle changes in terminology and newfangled labor institutions to comply with the law in form but not in substance. Frontier captains no longer took "Indian slaves," but only "rebels" or "criminals" who were formally tried and convicted; forced to serve out sentences of five, ten, or twenty years; and sold to the highest bidder. Colonists in Venezuela and the Caribbean resorted to naborías, while those in Central America continued to receive "personal services" throughout the sixteenth century. Ranchers in northern Mexico relied on encomiendas that, unlike those of central Mexico, often amounted to cyclical enslavement as they gathered their "entrusted" Indians at gunpoint and forced them to work during planting and harvesting time. Miners in many parts of the New World relied on the repartimiento system, in which Indians received token salaries but were otherwise compelled to work. In short, Spaniards adapted Indian slavery to fit the new legal environment, and thus it became the other slavery.[47]

# 3

## The Trafficker and His Network

THROUGHOUT THE HEMISPHERE, Spaniards chanced upon Indian villages or nomadic bands and snatched a woman or a couple of children to make a tidy profit. While constant, these spur-of-the-moment kidnappings were narrow in scope. The real slavers, the individuals who truly benefited from trafficking humans, operated on a much larger scale. They planned their expeditions carefully, procured investors and funds for weapons and provisions, hired agents to sell the slaves in mines and other enterprises, and — because Indian slavery was illegal — made sure to exploit loopholes and elicit plenty of official protection. Frontier captains were ideally suited for this line of work, as the empire expanded prodigiously during the sixteenth century. For them, slavery was no sideline to warfare or marginal activity born out of the chaos of conquest. It was first and foremost a business involving investors, soldiers, agents, and powerful officials.

Perhaps no one understood this better than Luis de Carvajal y de la Cueva, a frontier captain who had occasion to operate in Africa and America and to deal in both black and Indian slaves. His activities give us a rare opportunity to compare the slave trade on two continents. Carvajal was more colorful and baffling than many fictional characters. Born to a Jewish family in 1537, he spent his early years dodging the long arm of the Inquisition. Many years earlier, in 1492, the Spanish monarchy had expelled all Jews from the empire, forcing them either to convert to Christianity or to leave. At least one hundred thousand Jews left Spain. The majority went to neighboring Portugal, but this solution proved only temporary, as the Portuguese crown issued its own decree of expulsion in 1496. Already uprooted once, many Jewish families stayed in Portugal in spite of the risks. They remained close to the border between Spain and Portugal, a liminal area known as *la raya de Portugal* (the line of Portugal), in case they needed to cross into Spain if pursued by the Portuguese, then cross back into Portugal if run out by the Spanish. Straddling the border became a common survival strategy for many practicing Jews.[1]

Luis de Carvajal spent his earliest years negotiating these turbulent waters in the town of Mogadouro, on the Portuguese side. But when the Portuguese Inquisition began investigating neighbors and friends of the Carvajals, Luis was promptly shipped back to Spain — ostensibly to further his education, but more likely to steer him away from trouble, as Samuel Temkin's recent biography shows. Just seven or eight at the time, Luis would go on to spend six years in the household of the Count of Benavente, where he perfected his Spanish and surely acquired a solid Catholic education. After the danger had passed, one of his uncles, a larger-than-life figure named Duarte de León, personally journeyed to Benavente to bring Carvajal back to Portugal — this time to Lisbon — and to a new start in life. At fourteen Luis had reached what in the sixteenth century was considered a working age.[2]

Duarte de León was a very prominent merchant. Even though he was a "New Christian" — that is, a Jew who had recently converted to Christianity — or possibly a crypto-Jew, still practicing his faith secretly, his business contacts reached up to the highest levels of the Portuguese court. Duarte de León served the king as a slave broker. In the 1550s, the Portuguese crown was in the habit of auctioning off to well-heeled individuals monopoly rights to such crucial Portuguese outposts in Africa as the coast of Guinea, the fort of São Jorge da Mina, and the island of São Tomé. Several of these bidders were New Christians whose finances were undiminished by their forced conversions and who appreciated the religious freedom of Portugal's overseas colonies. Duarte de León acquired the trading rights to "the Rivers of Guinea and the Cape Verde Islands," but there was only so much he could do from Lisbon. To profit from his concession, he needed agents in Africa—a business network.[3]

Carvajal was fourteen or fifteen when he started working for his uncle in the Cape Verde Islands. Even for someone like him, who had seen slaves in Portugal, the experience of Cape Verde must have been eye-opening. Located four hundred miles from the westernmost tip of Africa, the archipelago was remote and forbidding. Winds from the southern Sahara blew all the way to these ten islands and five islets, sweeping them barren. Only Fogo and Santiago received much rain. The principal "product" of these islands was evident on arrival. Santiago, where Carvajal established himself, had a total population of around 13,400. Of these, 11,700, or nearly ninety percent, were African slaves forcibly transported from the mainland. Some of these slaves toiled on a few scraggly plantations, but most of them merely waited to be resold. The island was like a gigantic holding pen.[4]

Cape Verde's specialty was supplying African slaves to Spanish America. Because the Spaniards possessed no slaving ports of their own in western Africa, they had to rely on the Portuguese to obtain black slaves. Cape Verde was ideal for this purpose. The archipelago lay in the same latitude as the Spanish Caribbean and was four hundred miles closer to it than the African coast. As in all forms of commerce, time was of the essence. But this was particularly so in a business in which the length of the passage determined the survival rate. Every additional day of travel represented more dead slaves and lost profits. By virtue of being the part of Africa closest to Spanish America, the Cape Verde Islands developed as the preeminent reexport center for slaves.[5]

In 1551 the young Luis de Carvajal started his work in Cape Verde as a "trading agent." Eight years later, he was appointed "royal treasurer of the assets of those who died or became absent from the islands of Santiago and Fogo." Considering that Cape Verde lay two thousand miles from Portugal, that deaths and disappearances were common, and that on average every Portuguese residing on the islands of Santiago and

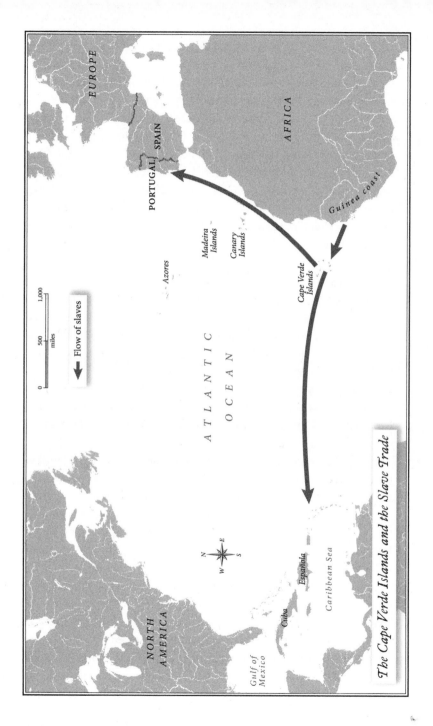

The Cape Verde Islands and the Slave Trade

EUROPE

AFRICA

PORTUGAL

SPAIN

Guinea coast

Madeira Islands

Canary Islands

Azores

Cape Verde Islands

ATLANTIC OCEAN

NORTH AMERICA

Gulf of Mexico

Cuba

Española

Caribbean Sea

Flow of slaves

0    500    1,000
      miles

Fogo possessed nine or ten slaves, this appointment gave Carvajal considerable access to unclaimed slaves.[6]

However, Carvajal's commercial success owed less to his business acumen than to his membership in a family trading syndicate spanning Portugal, the African coast, and the Cape Verde Islands. The head of the syndicate was Duarte de León, who owned the trading rights to "the Rivers of Guinea and the Cape Verde Islands." From his headquarters in Lisbon, he negotiated slave contracts and oversaw all operations. Duarte's brother, Francisco Jorge de León, was in charge of the coast of Guinea. He was posted in the minuscule village of São Domingos, at the end of a river that brought more slaves from the interior of Guinea than any other. Completing this triangular network was Carvajal in Cape Verde. As a trading agent in a slave reexport center, he was principally concerned with selling slaves to captains headed to the New World. He could purchase these slaves locally or even procure them from deceased slave owners or those who had gone missing. But Carvajal's chief advantage over his competitors was his ability to get slaves directly from the source in São Domingos. In other words, Carvajal could always undersell all the other slave merchants because his uncle Francisco Jorge de León controlled the cheapest and most abundant source of slaves on the coast of Guinea.[7]

Carvajal may have lived out his whole life on the African islands had it not been for the arrival of a fantastic business opportunity. In the early 1560s, the Portuguese and Spanish monarchies began negotiating a major slave contract. Cape Verde was to supply eight thousand slaves over a period of four years at a price of about 100 ducats apiece. The king of Portugal sent a representative to Seville to settle the last remaining details. It is probable that Duarte de León needed representation for the negotiation in Seville, and what better choice for such a task than his own nephew, who had grown up in Spain, could conduct himself as a Spanish gentleman, and had ample experience in the slaving business. In 1564 Carvajal traveled first to Lisbon, where he stayed briefly, and then to Seville, where he remained for two years as negotiations first stalled and finally broke down. The two Iberian monarchies could not agree on a price. It must have been a major setback for Duarte de León's syndicate, but by then the former agent of Cape Verde was already dreaming of new ventures and his own network in the New World.[8]

## Pánuco Slaves

Carvajal traveled to Mexico in the summer of 1567 as a man of means and enterprise. He took his own ship, carried a full load of wine, and transported several passengers, including high-ranking officials. He settled in the province of Pánuco, a marshy area on the Gulf of Mexico to the south of Texas. A province that was well populated and easily accessible by land and sea, Pánuco had been an active slaving ground for decades. Early Spanish colonists were delighted to learn that the Natives of the area did not have "universal lords" like the Aztecs and Tarascans, but "individual chiefs," and that they waged war "as if they were Italian city-states" and took captives from one another.[9]

Faced with these propitious circumstances, settlers began acquiring Natives as early as the 1520s and selling them to the slave traffickers of the Caribbean. Pánuco initially funneled many slaves to the goldfields of Cuba and Española. This trade flourished especially under the energetic governorship of Nuño de Guzmán, who issued licenses to all Spanish residents "so each of them could take twenty or thirty slaves." Guzmán also fitted out his own ships, which he loaded with Pánuco Indians to trade for cattle from the islands. The first bishop of Mexico, Friar Juan de Zumárraga, estimated that by 1529 "around nine or ten thousand branded Indians from Pánuco had been traded for animals." This barter was so brisk that Pánuco experienced what some scholars refer to as an "ungulate explosion." Northeastern Mexico amassed the largest cattle herds in sixteenth-century North America and paved the way for the ranching empire that would flourish in Texas in later centuries.[10]

By the time Carvajal arrived in Pánuco in 1567, the local traffickers were no longer selling slaves in the Caribbean. The development of silver mines in central and northern Mexico in the 1540s and 1550s had completely transformed the slave trade. Pánuco merchants had reoriented their business away from Cuba and Española and toward the

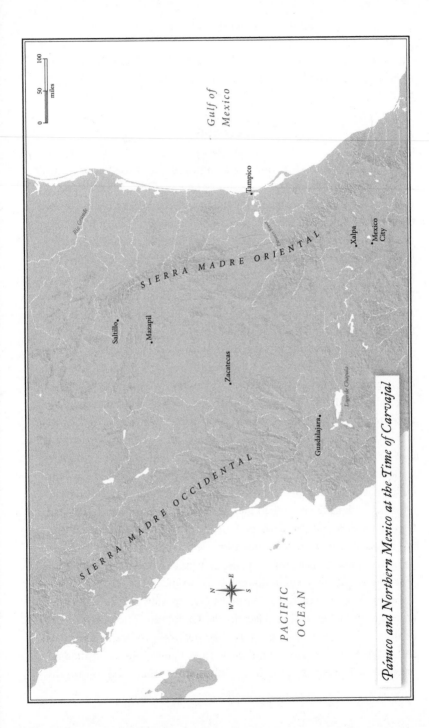

Pánuco and Northern Mexico at the Time of Carvajal

interior of Mexico, organizing caravans and pioneering new land routes to principal mining centers there. When Carvajal arrived, he simply adapted to the system of enslavement already in place.

The most insightful testimonies about the workings of the Pánuco slave trade come not from indigenous victims but from a band of English pirates who washed up on the Gulf coast in October 1568. The Englishmen hacked at the brambles and bushes that tore their clothes and assaulted their bodies. They made their way through thickets of grass that grew taller than a man "so we could scarce see one another," recalled one of the men, Miles Phillips. As the days passed and the pangs of hunger increased, their morale plummeted. The pirates disagreed about how best to save themselves and went their separate ways. What had once been a contingent of 114 men splintered into several smaller groups, reducing their ability to resist Indian attacks or capture by Spanish authorities. Phillips cast his lot with a group that chose to travel south along the coast hoping to find a town that would take pity on them.[11]

These raggedy Englishmen were themselves slavers. A year earlier, they had arrived in Plymouth, England, to sign up for what must have seemed an exceptionally promising expedition. Queen Elizabeth, along with thirty merchants from London, had invested heavily in the venture. John Hawkins, a legendary privateer on his third slaving voyage, took command of the fleet, accompanied by "M. Francis Drake, afterward knight." The ships headed first to Cape Verde and the coast of Guinea, where they procured "very near the number of 500 Negroes," and then crossed the Atlantic and lurked in the Caribbean and the Gulf of Mexico in search of buyers. Problems arose when the pirates became overconfident and entered Mexico's principal port of Veracruz, where they were hemmed in by a Spanish fleet. The ensuing battle resulted in the loss of all but two of the English ships. Hawkins and Drake were lucky to escape on these vessels, scampering north along the coast but carrying too many passengers and too few provisions. Hawkins decided to put ashore more than one hundred men with the promise that "the next year he would either come himself, or else send to fetch them home."[12]

For eight days, Miles Phillips's abandoned group managed well enough. According to him, the men were "feeble, faint and weak," but they resolutely walked along the coast, braving "a kind of fly, which the Spaniards called mosquitoes . . . [that] would suck one's blood marvelously." The pirates also ran into a group of "Chichimecas," as Phillips called them, using the generic term applied to the hunter-gatherer societies of northern Mexico. In his opinion, they were "very ugly and terrible to behold" on account of their very long hair, "even down to their knees," and because "they also colour their faces green, yellow and blue." At first the Indians attacked the Englishmen — mistaking them for Spaniards — "shooting off their arrows as thick as hail." But once they became aware of the strangers' desperate circumstances, they showed remarkable restraint, making the castaways sit down while they went through the pirates' belongings. The nomadic Indians took some colorful articles of clothing ("those that were appareled in black they did not meddle withal") and then left without harming them.[13]

The pirates' good fortune ran out when they approached the Pánuco River. Not having tasted water in six days, they rushed to the stream and drank in great gulps. They were resting still when they saw Spanish horsemen riding up and down the river on the opposite bank. Phillips saw the Spaniards dismount, step into canoes, and begin crossing the river, their horses tied by the reins and swimming behind. "And being come over to that side of the river where we were," he wrote, "they saddled their horses and came very fiercely running at us." The pirates had no choice but to submit peacefully. With only two or three rusty swords in their possession, it would have been futile to resist; flight was entirely out of the question. They crossed the river in the Spanish canoes in groups of four and made their way to the nearby town of Tampico.[14]

The Englishmen's lives were now in the hands of none other than Luis de Carvajal. The former Cape Verde agent had been in the port of Tampico for only a few months. He had bought a cattle ranch near town, and being a man of wealth, he also had purchased the appointment of *alcalde ordinario*, or lower magistrate. At the time, the town had a resident population of about 40 Europeans and 150 Indians. It was Carvajal who had received news of the English pirates roaming on the Pánuco coast and had organized the troop of Spanish horsemen who had spotted the castaways on the river.

When the prisoners filed into town, Carvajal interrogated them, "showing himself very severe," and threatened to hang them on the spot. After demanding the scant money and valuables they carried, he had the Englishmen locked up in the public jail — "a little house much like a hogsty" — in a space so small that the men nearly smothered one another. And when they asked for a surgeon (doctor) to treat their wounds, they were told, according to Phillips, that "we should have none other surgeon than the hangman, which should sufficiently heal us of all our griefs."[15]

The pirates remained in this condition for three days. On the fourth day, Phillips and the others sensed that many Spaniards and Indians had massed outside the building. The captives feared the worst. When the doors opened, they filed out of the cell, crying to God for mercy. Waiting outside were several guards and a man with newly made leather halters. Uncertainty and the ever present fear of immediate and painful death were key to the psychology of enslavement. "With those halters," Phillips wrote, "they bound our arms behind us, and so coupling two and two together, they commanded us to march on through the town, and so along the country from place to place towards the city of Mexico, which is distant the space of ninety leagues [270 miles]." From the hot and humid coastal plains of Pánuco, the captors marched the English pirates in the very fashion and along the very routes that innumerable Indian slaves had followed through towns and ranches, paraded and showcased for the benefit of potential buyers. Had the prisoners been "Chichimecas," they would have already been sold along the way. But since they were Englishmen, they were destined for Mexico City.[16]

Driving the caravan were two Spaniards and "a great number of Indians warding on either side with bows and arrows, lest we should escape." This method for transporting captives by tethering them in lines was common throughout northern Mexico and bore more than a passing resemblance to African "coffles," caravans of shackled slaves. One of the Spanish guards was an old man whose task was to procure provisions. He went ahead of the moving body to warn the authorities in the next town and make preparations. Always short on resources, he had to rely on charity to feed and clothe the prisoners and attend to their medical needs. The other Spaniard was young and "a very cruel caitiff," according to Phillips's account. He was responsible for preventing escape and for driving the column on schedule. He carried a javelin, "and when our men with very feebleness and faintness were not able to go so fast as he required them, he would take his javelin in both his hands, and strike them with the same between the neck and the shoulders so violently, that he would strike them down." The driver would then say aloud, *"Marchad, marchad Ingleses perros, Luteranos, enemigos de Dios* or *[M]arch, march on you English dogs, Lutherans, enemies to God."*[17]

When the column entered Mexico City, men and women came out to see them. Many were sizing up the English captives, already thinking how much to offer for them. For six months, the prisoners remained in a hospital on the outskirts of the city. "We were courteously used," Phillips observed philosophically, adding that they received visits from gentlemen and gentlewomen from the city, who gave them "suckets [sweets] and marmalades, and that very liberally."[18]

At last the viceroy of Mexico ordered that the men be transferred to certain "houses of correction" in Texcoco, also on the outskirts of Mexico City, "which is like to Bridewell here in London," the young Englishman wrote, referring to the notorious English workhouse for paupers and criminals. Indians were routinely marched to these houses of correction and "sold for slaves, some for ten years, and some for twelve." Phillips's heart sank to the ground: "It was no small grief unto us when we understood that we should be carried thither and be used as slaves, we had rather be put to death."[19]

Spanish gentlemen and ladies gathered at a garden in Texcoco belonging to the viceroy in order to choose their English slaves. "Happy was he that could get soonest one of us," Phillips observed. Each new owner simply took his or her slave home, clothed him, and put him to work in whatever was needed, "which was for the most part to attend upon them at the table, and to be as their chamberlains, and to wait upon them when they went abroad." Like the liveried Africans who waited on their wealthy masters around Mexico City, these Englishmen represented conspicuous consumption, meant to be displayed to houseguests and on outings. Ordinary Indian slaves would not have fared so well.[20]

Some of the English prisoners were sent to work in the silver mines, but there too they received favorable treatment, as they became "overseers of the negroes and Indians that laboured there." Some of them remained in the mines for three or four years and, in a strange twist of fate, became rich.[21]

The experiences of Miles Phillips and the others differed in important respects from those of Indian slaves, but they were still subjected to the slavers' methods. They traveled from Pánuco in a coffle, were sold in the slave markets of Texcoco, worked in the mines, and witnessed the living conditions of Indian men and women in bondage.

## The Chichimec Wars

Carvajal's involvement with the English pirates was momentous, but his greatest challenge by far had less to do with raggedy Europeans than with Indians. Carvajal's arrival in Pánuco in 1567 coincided with a major escalation of the war against the nomads of northern Mexico. The Spanish push into the silver-rich lands of Zacatecas, Guanajuato, Durango, Mazapil, and others had triggered early skirmishes that grew into a no-holds-barred struggle known as the Chichimec Wars. At the time of Carvajal's arrival, the *tierra de guerra,* or war zone, encompassed an enormous arc that stretched from the Pacific to the Atlantic coast. Although Mexico City and its immediate surroundings remained eerily quiescent, Spanish colonists and Indian allies who ventured into the north found constant danger. They lived in a patchwork of newly founded silver mines, cattle ranches, supporting settlements, and a few roads. The rest was Indian ground, and the violence was ever present. Carvajal's chosen town, Tampico, lay right on the edge of the war zone. To the north began the lands of the Chichimecs. All one had to do was cross the Pánuco River to run into roaming Indians like the ones the English pirates had encountered in the fall of 1568. The Chichimec Wars were all too real in Tampico. An English visitor recounted that during his brief stay there in 1572, Indian raiders killed fourteen Spaniards who had ventured just to the outskirts to gather salt.[22]

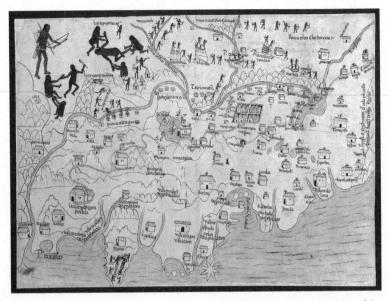

This 1550 map of what is now western Mexico reveals the violence and mayhem of the Chichimec Wars. Spanish towns and settlements are surrounded by Indians who are carrying bows and arrows, attacking colonists, and taking captives.

When we try to imagine this conflict, it is tempting to fall back on the imagery of America's nineteenth-century frontier, where white settlers confronted equestrian Indian societies such as the Comanches and Utes that possessed firearms. Yet sixteenth-century Spaniards faced a very different challenge. The Chichimecs overwhelmingly moved on foot, and they fought strictly with bows and arrows. Before engaging in combat, they took off all their clothes and taunted the Spaniards, who were attired in heavy coats and chain mail. They were each armed with only a bow and four or five arrows, which they could deliver with lethal speed and precision. Many a Spanish colonist was pierced while desperately fiddling with his flintlock harquebus, priming horn, and firing hammer. Capture was frightful. "Regardless of whether it is male or female," wrote an Augustinian friar who had lived among Guamares and Guachichiles and was otherwise quite sympathetic to the nomads, "the first thing they do is remove the top of the head, taking off all the skin and leaving the skull clean just like one takes a friar's tonsure." Although scalping was usually fatal, the friar met a Spaniard who had been scalped years before and, in a different incident, a woman "who survived many days." The Chichimecs were also known for impaling their victims, cutting off their arms and legs while they were still alive, and removing their tendons, which were used for tying arrowheads to shafts. Reports of robberies, killings, abductions—all manner of atrocities—poured into Mexico City as the entire Chichimec arc burst into flames.[23]

The man held most responsible for doing something about the raging conflict was Viceroy Martín Enríquez de Almanza. Like Carvajal, Enríquez was a newcomer to the New World. In fact, he had traveled on the very fleet that had interrupted John Hawkins's brazen trading mission in Veracruz in 1568, and he had participated in the fierce battle that had resulted in the sinking of all but two of the English ships. Enríquez's order to attack the pirates had been risky, but it had paid off in the end. Enríquez had been pleased to learn a few days later that some of the Englishmen who had escaped from Veracruz had been apprehended by the energetic alcalde of Tampico. Thus an early bond was formed between Enríquez and Carvajal, both of whom were firm believers in decisive action.[24]

Once in Mexico City, Viceroy Enríquez turned his attention to the war in the north. He convened a high-level council in 1569 in which the three main religious orders and other clergymen and lawyers would decide whether the war against the Chichimecs might be considered "just." This was hardly an arcane legal exercise, but rather an official ruling that would determine whether Indians taken in the war could be legally enslaved. Most of the councilors sided with the viceroy in calling it a *guerra a fuego y a sangre,* or war by fire and blood, the designation that would permit the Spaniards to kill and enslave their Indian enemies. Only the Dominican friars went against the general opinion by arguing with undeniable logic that the Spaniards, not the Indians, were the true aggressors, and therefore that the war could not be considered "just" nor could the Chichimecs be enslaved.[25]

Strictly speaking, Viceroy Enríquez could not grant a free hand to the Spaniards on the frontier, as such a policy would be in violation of the New Laws of 1542. The Spanish king was the only one who could grant a general exception to the accepted regulations prohibiting the enslavement of Indians. So the practical Enríquez steered a middle course by calling it a war by fire and blood, but with limitations and euphemisms: Chichimec women and children could not be taken, captured adult males had to be tried and found guilty of a crime before "their service" could be sold, and they could not be enslaved in perpetuity, but only "held in deposit" for a specified number of years ranging from six to twenty. From a narrow legal perspective, these Indians would not be slaves, but rather convicts serving out their sentences. In an atmosphere of patent alarm over the nomads' assertiveness, however, the viceroy's middle course drew sharp criticism. The archbishop of Mexico, Pedro Moya de Contreras, was one of the viceroy's most notable critics. He believed that assigning Indians to the soldiers who defeated them was a necessary reward for frontier service; that the wars in the north would be endless if Indian women and children could not be enslaved; and that no Spanish colonist would go to war if he had to go through the trouble of gathering information to determine the guilt of every Indian he captured. The archbishop's views reflected a common opinion among colonists and ranchers.[26]

The legal debate would rage for years, but for the time being the viceroy had enough support to wage his war. Throughout the *zona de guerra* (war zone), he named captains to punish robberies and murders and to keep the Chichimecs at bay. In Pánuco he bestowed this title on Carvajal. The former agent of Cape Verde was now the viceroy's right-hand man in northeastern Mexico. Viceroy Enríquez's orders to Carvajal spelled out in astonishing detail the parameters of his slaving activities. Captain Carvajal was to punish the rebellious Indians by executing the ringleaders and "doing justice in the manner of war." As for other Indians found guilty of crimes, "their service should be sold for ten years," with the exception "that no Indian under the age of twelve can be sold in service." Carvajal soon demonstrated an uncommon talent for these endeavors. When he and his men caught up with offending Chichimecs, they carried out their orders to the letter, surrounding the Indians, killing the leader, and taking about thirty captives, "whom he [Carvajal] punished in accordance with his commission."[27]

By 1576 more than six thousand Chichimec Indians had been re-duced to slavery and were living in central Mexico, according to the conservative estimate of a crown official. Carvajal was now a full part-ner in the system of enslavement. It was a vast system that began with the Spanish king—even if only because he tolerated or overlooked the practice—passed through the viceroy and his advisers in Mexico City, and extended to the governors, captains, soldiers, and Indian allies who carried out the raids. It was not too different from the system Carvajal had known in Cape Verde. There too it had begun at the top, with the Portuguese granting trading privileges for portions of western Africa, which royal contractors and agents had proceeded to exploit. The main difference was that whereas in Africa the actual catching of slaves had been done by other Africans, in northern Mexico Spanish or mestizo captains did much of the capturing. Even that would change, however, as the slave trade in the New World evolved and passed largely into In-dian hands.[28]

Like any other slaving system, the one in northern Mexico boiled down to pesos. The expeditions into Chichimec lands were expen-sive undertakings that required up-front outlays of cash. Each soldier needed to pay for horses, weapons, protective gear, and provisions. Ex-perienced Indian fighters estimated that a soldier could not equip him-self adequately for less than 1,000 pesos. Yet the crown generally paid a yearly salary of only 350 pesos (which was increased to 450 pesos after 1581). So the first thing a captain had to do in order to attract soldiers and volunteers was to assure them that the campaign would yield Indian captives. Without being offered a chance to capture Natives, few would risk life or horse. Time and again, Carvajal faced this fundamental eco-nomic reality. On one occasion in the early 1580s when he was gathering men to put down an Indian rebellion in the Sierra Gorda, his volunteers became discouraged because they anticipated that the rebels would ne-gotiate a truce at their approach. The Chichimecs were crafty, and this was a favored tactic. In that case, the men would be left with no captives, and their provisions and other expenditures would be wasted. Would Carvajal pay the soldiers out of his own pocket? To overcome their reluctance, Carvajal reportedly placed his hands on a crucifix and told the men that "he swore by the Gospels that even if the rebellious Indians came in peace he would imprison them in such a way that for every ten Indians that came [in peace], five would remain in the land and the other five he would distribute to the soldiers."[29]

In short, punitive expeditions into the Chichimec frontier were economic enterprises. Investors offered loans or equipment to the volunteers, who would repay them through the sale of captives at the end of the campaign. Detailed records of such financial arrangements are rare, but the unhappy end of soldier Gaspar de Ribera gives us a glimpse. Ribera served under Captain Francisco Cano near the mines of Mazapil in the vicinity of Pánuco. In October 1569, Ribera and his companions cornered a group of Chichimecs in a cave not far from the silver mines. But as Ribera stepped up to the entrance, an arrow flew straight into his left eye, and another lodged in his head, killing him almost instantly. When Captain Cano settled Ribera's estate, he discovered that Ribera was in partnership with a widow from Mazapil named Constanza de Andrada. This redoubtable frontier woman had advanced horses and arms to the soldier in exchange for half of his share of the spoils. During the campaign, Ribera had earned two Guachichil Indians, a girl of twelve and a woman of twenty-five. The captain felt compelled to honor the terms of Ribera's agreement with Andrada. So he sold the Indians to the highest bidder — 70 pesos for the two — and transferred half of the proceeds to the widow. The arrangement between Ribera and Andrada makes painfully clear how the expeditions functioned as investment vehicles and why soldiers were so keen on taking captives.[30]

Carvajal established himself as an able frontier captain, rounding up English pirates, subduing rebellious Indians, and blazing new trails. And as he made himself the master of Pánuco, his ambition grew. With the full backing of the viceroy, Captain Carvajal traveled to Spain in the summer of 1578 to ask for a royal contract. It took him about ten months of lobbying at the court of Philip II, but the results were spectacular. Carvajal was named governor and captain general of the New

Kingdom of León, the largest kingdom north of New Spain (Mexico).[31] It comprised a gigantic quadrangle measuring two hundred leagues (more than six hundred miles) north to south and another two hundred leagues east to west, encompassing all of the modern states of Tamaulipas (Pánuco), Nuevo León, and Coahuila; almost all of Zacatecas and Durango; and portions of San Luis Potosí, Nayarit, Sinaloa, Chihuahua, Texas, and New Mexico. Captain Carvajal was already an integral part of the slaving system of northern Mexico. With this appointment, he would have tremendous autonomy to profit from the traffic of Indians, and even the opportunity to create his own slaving system.

## Zenith and Downfall of a Slaver

Catching a slaver in the archival record is no mean task. Indian traffickers were influential, smart, and secretive, and they always had justifications for what they did. Many of their activities involved labor coercion but were legal. For example, according to the terms of his royal contract, Governor Carvajal had the power to "distribute" Indians in encomiendas to worthy colonists. Whereas in central Mexico the encomienda did not amount to enslavement, as Indians continued to live in their communities subject to their own authorities and simply paid tribute to their Spanish overlords, in the north it was tantamount to slavery, albeit with some peculiar features. Encomienda owners in the north were assigned bands of hunter-gatherers who, unlike the agriculturalists of central Mexico, had little to give but their labor. To profit from their encomiendas, encomenderos had to hunt down their "entrusted" Indians, transport them (often at gunpoint) to an estate, and make them work during planting or harvesting time without pay before releasing them again. This system of cyclical enslavement became widespread and quite characteristic of the encomiendas of Nuevo León. Granting nomadic peoples in encomiendas under these conditions was abusive, but it was entirely legal and well within Carvajal's powers.[32]

Some of Carvajal's other activities also fell into an extensive gray area. A good example is his foray into the Rio Grande delta in 1585–1586. At that time, the mouth of the Rio Grande was a remote region seldom visited by Spaniards that lay more than one hundred miles from their closest settlement. The governor said that he went there looking for a suitable place to establish a fort and to locate a silver-laden ship that had reportedly capsized there. As the Spaniards were exploring the area, "a great quantity of Carib Indian thieves" came out of the marshes and attacked them, according to Carvajal's affidavit. His use of the loaded term "Carib," conjuring images of cannibalism, anticipates the tenor of his entire report. "And even though we required the Indians to come back in peace telling them that they would suffer no harm," Carvajal explains further, "they continued to throw arrows at us with undiminished courage, and I took some of these Indians with their women and children."[33]

Governor Carvajal had the power to apprehend Indians who had committed crimes and to sell their service to the highest bidder. In theory he was adhering to a protocol for waging war on the Chichimecs that had been vigorously discussed and painstakingly negotiated in Mexico City. But the particulars of the case lay bare Carvajal's methods. First, most of the captives were women and children. Second, Carvajal chose not to determine their guilt in the Rio Grande delta, where they were caught, but instead marched them about 125 miles to the newly founded town of León (present-day Cerralvo), where he finally had them tried in March 1586. To be sure, the governor appointed a lawyer to defend the Indians, but the proceedings were a mere formality. Although some of the males confessed to having committed murder, the evidence was circumstantial at best for the women and children. Carvajal himself summarized the case against the Indians this way: "These Indians had made arrowheads from iron nails and pieces of swords and knives, and these and other objects may have come from Flemish caravels and clearly point to their crimes." In fact, these people lived in a region so distant from any Spanish settlements that it was absurd to pin any crimes on them. Yet officials in Mexico City estimated that Carvajal's raids on the Rio Grande delta yielded upwards of two thousand Indians.[34]

One of the Indians captured at the mouth of the Rio Grande was a thirteen-year-old boy who was given the Christian name Francisco. He had several stripes (tattoos) on his lips and chin. A long line ran from the top of his forehead to the tip of his nose, and there were smaller lines around his eyes. Francisco had been condemned to fifteen years of service and assigned to Governor Carvajal, who then transferred the boy to his nephew, Luis de Carvajal, known as "el Mozo," meaning "the Younger." El Mozo had explored and settled Pánuco with his famous uncle and evidently served as his agent. As a "merchant of the mines and other parts," el Mozo's occupation included the selling of Indians. He transported Francisco from León all the way to the mine of Zacualpan, in central Mexico, where he sold the boy for 120 pesos to a miner named Alonso de Nava. Exactly how the governor and his nephew split the money remains unknown.[35]

Even more revealing is Governor Carvajal's pacification campaign in the Sierra Gorda. In 1583 he gathered thirty or forty volunteers — "including some of the most delinquent and shady individuals that can be found in these parts," as they would later be described to the king of Spain — to travel to the Sierra Gorda by way of Cuzcatlán. The Sierra Gorda was an extremely rugged region between Pánuco and Mexico City where many Indian groups had taken refuge and established strongholds. At the appearance of the Spanish force, the Indians immediately sent envoys and sued for peace. Governor Carvajal apparently played his part with consummate skill. He received the Indians warmly, begging them to send messengers to other rebels so everyone could receive "authority canes" (canes given to indigenous leaders to recognize their high standing) and take part in the agreement. The governor also insisted that women and children had to be present so that they could be baptized. The Indians themselves constructed an *enramada,* a makeshift church with branches, and arranged an adjacent area with a baptismal font. Everything was set for Sunday, January 8, 1584. At the eleventh hour, the priest refused to go through with the ceremony. He understood that he would be serving as bait for the Indians, and he reportedly said that it was wrong to deceive God. But it was too late. As the action was later reported to the Spanish king, "More than five hundred Indians between men and women came happily and in peace asking to be baptized, and he [Carvajal] had them manacled and initiated proceedings against them, and condemned eight of them to certain sentences and all others without a single exception were given ten or twelve or fourteen years of service, and they were distributed to the soldiers separating wives from husbands and children from parents."[36]

By virtue of his appointment as governor and captain general of the New Kingdom of León, Carvajal assumed a position that was in many ways analogous to the one his uncle Duarte de León had occupied as royal contractor of "the Rivers of Guinea and the Cape Verde Islands." Both possessed trading monopolies granted by their respective crowns, both relied on family members to build their networks of agents, and both exploited the availability of human slaves to create wealth. Uncle and nephew developed comparable systems in Africa and America. The notion of a trafficker and his slave network may seem simplistic, but it is crucial to understand the reality of Indian slavery not as a residue of colonial wars or a transitional phase until African slaves arrived in the New World in sufficient numbers, but as an established network with staying power in which a host of individuals, from imperial bureaucrats down to miners, governors, frontier captains, and Indian allies, had a stake.

Carvajal's downfall occurred with the intrigue and precision of a Shakespearean play. His activities in Pánuco in the 1570s had unfolded at a time when he had enjoyed the support of Viceroy Enríquez. But when he became governor of Nuevo León in the following decade, he operated in a more hostile political environment that culminated in a major crackdown against Indian slavery. What had been acceptable to one viceroy was entirely out of the question to his successor. During the colonial era, periods of harsh treatment of frontier Indians were often followed by attempts at reform. Evidently Carvajal was caught in one of those cycles.

Yet Carvajal's fall from grace did not occur solely because of his slaving. In the course of his career, he had made powerful enemies willing to use any means at their disposal to stop his ascent. And indeed they found a very powerful lever. When Carvajal was named governor of the New Kingdom of León in 1579, he had been allowed to take one hundred colonists and additional soldiers from Spain to Mexico. Ordinarily, royal officials at the powerful House of Trade (the agency in charge of Spain's overseas exploration and colonization) in Seville reviewed the backgrounds of all colonists bound for the New World to make sure they were not New Christians, who were barred from traveling to the Americas. But in this particular contract, Carvajal was allowed to choose his own passengers and make his own inquiries. It was up to the governor—and not zealous crown officials—to determine who could accompany him, as long as he made sure they were "clean persons and not of the forbidden to go to those lands." In fact, a majority of the two hundred colonists who eventually signed up with Carvajal (there is no explanation for the discrepancy between this number and the number allowed by his contract) hailed from *la raya de Portugal*. Many of them were New Christians and crypto-Jews who viewed their journey to the New World as a unique chance to leave Iberia and its religious strictures behind. Moreover, among the passengers were several members of Carvajal's family, including his sister and her husband, along with their children. One of these children was Luis de Carvajal, whose sobriquet "el Mozo" (the Younger) distinguished him from the governor, who came to be known as "el Viejo" (the Elder). The evidence suggests that Governor Carvajal himself was a Catholic but his immediate family was not.[37]

All of this would come to haunt Carvajal. The first one to be denounced as a practicing Jew and tried by the Mexican Inquisition was the governor's niece. At first she refused to speak, but when she was forced to undress and lie on the torture rack, she could not hold back. When the ropes were tightened with the first turn of the ratchet, Doña Isabel implicated her mother, father, and brother; after the second turn, amid great screams of pain, she exposed all of her relatives as practicing Jews. The governor's sister was also tortured. It took as many as five turns of the ratchet to break her down, but she too implicated her entire family.[38]

Yet the most damaging testimony was that of Luis de Carvajal el Mozo, the governor's nephew and designated successor to the governorship of Nuevo León. El Mozo had traveled to the New World when he was thirteen. Together with his uncle, he had explored Pánuco and helped establish settlements there. A close bond had developed between uncle and nephew, so close that one night when el Mozo had gotten lost in Pánuco and remained — as he put it — "thirsty and disarmed in the land of the Chichimeca enemies and fearful of a horrible death," the governor had organized an all-out night rescue. When el Mozo was found, he reported, "the happiness and joy of my uncle and those who had stayed behind was great."[39]

El Mozo's parents were both practicing Jews, but they had refrained from telling him during his childhood — a practice that was common among crypto-Jewish families to avoid being accidentally denounced. Once in Mexico, however, when el Mozo discovered that he was Jewish, his devotion grew fierce. While in Pánuco, he constantly studied the Bible "and learned much while alone in the wilderness." During his comings and goings as an itinerant merchant and while selling Indian slaves, he came in contact with a remarkable network of crypto-Jews. He also wrote a secret diary, signing it "Joseph Lumbroso" (Joseph the Enlightened). This process of religious self-discovery took a toll on el Mozo's relationship with his Catholic uncle. At one point in his diary, the younger Carvajal referred to his older kinsman as "that miserable blind man [blind to Judaism] who was governor of that province." El Mozo also resented his uncle's attempts to "marry off the poor orphans, my sisters, or at least bring them into contact with Gentile soldiers or captains." The Mexican Inquisition found el Mozo's activities disturbing and aroused the inquisitors' suspicions about what Governor Carvajal may have known about the religious beliefs of his closest family members.[40]

Out of respect for his high investiture, they did not subject Governor Carvajal to the rack or to any other form of torture. Although they concluded that he was a Catholic and not a Jew, they found him guilty of being "an abettor and concealer of heretics." In the course of his life, Carvajal had been a trading agent in Cape Verde, a frontier captain in Pánuco, and a slaver in the New Kingdom of León. He must have killed, maimed, and sold into bondage innumerable Africans and Indians. Yet the Inquisition condemned Carvajal for one of the most magnanimous and courageous decisions of his life: offering passage to many New Christians and crypto-Jews who faced uncertain lives in the Iberian Peninsula. Carvajal was banished from Mexico for six years for this transgression. It was a light sentence considering that his nephew, nieces, and sister would eventually be garroted and burned at the stake. Still, Carvajal would not see the light of day again. From his cell at the Inquisition, he was transferred to an ordinary jail to answer to the charges of Indian slavery.

Carvajal was merely one of several frontier captains who fought in the Chichimec Wars. His peers included the likes of Doctor Francisco de Sande, later nicknamed "Doctor Sangre" (Doctor Blood), who served in various slaving grounds, including northern Mexico, the Philippines, Guatemala, and Colombia; and Don Gonzalo de Las Casas, another memorable man of action, as well as the author of a courageous exposé of the enslavement of Indians. Mounted on large horses, carrying lances, and wearing padded cotton armor, buckskin jackets, and heavy boots, these frontier commanders may seem quaint to us. But they were surprisingly modern in one respect: they were all entrepreneurs faced with the logistics and financial burdens of outfitting expeditions into remote regions. Captains had to deal with partners, investors, and soldiers, all of whom were primarily concerned with turning a profit.[41]

Their slave-taking enterprise was neither a residue of colonial wars nor a transitional phase until sufficient numbers of African slaves arrived in the New World. Rather it was a *system,* one with extraordinary staying power recalled fifty years after Carvajal's inquisitorial tribulations by Alonso de León, another notable frontiersman and the first chronicler of the New Kingdom of León: "In those days, we did not consider anyone a man until he had journeyed to the Indian *rancherías,* whether friends or enemies, and seized some children from their mothers to sell; and there was no other way to sustain ourselves or open new trails without tremendous difficulties."[42]

# 4

## *The Pull of Silver*

THE CALIFORNIA GOLD rush transformed the western United States. Within one decade of James W. Marshall's discovery of a few flecks of gold in a ditch in 1848, some three hundred thousand migrants had moved to California. These Chinese, Italian, German, Chilean, and other newcomers turned the remote and picturesque Mexican outpost of San Francisco into a bustling port. They also fanned out into the Sierra Nevada to build cabins, divert rivers, and pan for the yellow metal. This is a familiar story of long journeys, ethnic conflict, broken dreams, and explosive growth.[1]

Yet the California gold rush was neither the largest metal-induced rush of North America nor the most transformative. By any measure, that title belongs to the earlier Mexican silver boom. In terms of duration, for instance, the California gold rush was like a hurricane. Gold production skyrocketed in 1849 but peaked as early as 1852, only four years after the start of the rush, and declined markedly thereafter. For all practical purposes, the rush was over by 1865, lasting less than twenty years. The use of pressurized water to wash down entire hillsides—a process known as hydraulic mining—kept gold production from declining even faster than it did. By contrast, Mexico's silver boom started in the 1520s and grew through the sixteenth and early seventeenth centuries, reaching a plateau at the end of this period. Remarkably, it gained

The very royal-looking Spanish peso was made of almost pure silver. Minted in the Iberian Peninsula as well as in Mexico City, Lima, Potosí, and smaller towns in the New World, the peso was in demand throughout the world. The largest consumer of silver during the colonial era was China.

a second wind in the late seventeenth century and kept increasing during the eighteenth century, not attaining its high-water mark until the first decade of the nineteenth century — almost three centuries after the boom had begun. By then silver was the principal way in which empires and nations around the world stored their wealth, and the Spanish peso had emerged as the first global currency, used throughout the Americas, Europe, and Asia, where it was often countersigned (authenticated by the treasury or other monetary authorities) and employed in everyday transactions. It remained legal tender in the United States until 1856.[2]

Not only did the Mexican silver boom last longer than the California gold rush, but it was more extensive. The gold rush was confined largely to the northeastern quadrant of the state, with a few additional mines sprinkled along its border with Oregon and in southern California. Prior to the gold rush, there had been small strikes in the southern Appalachians (North Carolina, South Carolina, Tennessee, and Georgia), and after the California discoveries, new goldfields emerged in some of the Rocky Mountain territories. Mexico's centuries-long silver boom surpassed these gold strikes in both geographic scope and sheer density. Historians usually refer to the mines of *northern* Mexico, but in

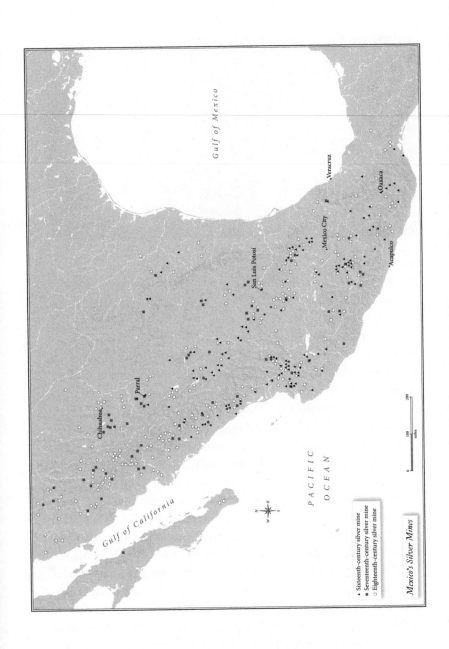

Mexico's Silver Mines

Gulf of Mexico

PACIFIC
OCEAN

Gulf of California

Veracruz
Oaxaca
Mexico City
Acapulco
San Luis Potosi
Parral
Chihuahua

▲ Sixteenth-century silver mine
■ Seventeenth-century silver mine
○ Eighteenth-century silver mine

0   100   200
      miles

truth the silver boom started in southern and central Mexico. Present-day tourists driving from Mexico City to Acapulco still stop at Taxco (1534), a silver town that Hernán Cortés himself developed. Taxco was part of a cluster of mines in southern Mexico that included Sultepec (1530), Amatepec (1531), Zacualpan (circa 1540), Zumpango (1531), and others. Only gradually did prospectors venture north into the lands of the Chichimecs, along the Pacific coast and up into the escarpments of the Sierra Madre Occidental. They had to bring in Indians from central Mexico as workers and overcome other tremendous logistical problems, but they succeeded in establishing a string of mines throughout western Mexico. After this initial push, prospectors crossed the Sierra Madre, proceeding on to the central plateau, where they founded some of the richest mines in the world, including Zacatecas (1546) and Guanajuato (1548). But even these mines were not sufficient. Spaniards next explored the present-day states of Durango and Chihuahua, as well as parts of northeastern Mexico. Altogether, they founded more than 400 mines (143 in the sixteenth century, 65 in the seventeenth century, and 225 in the eighteenth century) scattered throughout much of Mexico, from the semitropical regions of the south to the deserts of Chihuahua, and from the Pacific to the Atlantic coast.[3]

Given its longer duration and more extensive geography, it is no wonder that Mexico's silver boom produced roughly twelve times as much metal as the nineteenth-century gold rushes in the United States — 44.2 million kilograms (48,722 tons) of silver compared with 3.7 million kilograms (4,078 tons) of gold (see appendix 4). This massive production is even more impressive considering the work and danger involved. The gold of California lay in placers, or surface deposits of sand and gravel, which had resulted from mountains eroding and yielding nuggets or flecks of gold, which collected at lower elevations along hillsides and in streams. Mining these bits of precious metal required a great deal of superficial digging, carrying, and washing. As we saw earlier in the Caribbean, that could be very hard work, but it was not nearly as daunting or dangerous as mining silver. Instead of lying in open-air deposits, the silver had to be extracted from deep underground. The main shaft in the mines of San Luis Potosí was 250 yards long, and that in the Valenciana mine in Guanajuato plunged 635 yards down. When this shaft was completed around 1810, it was considered the deepest man-made shaft in the world. Digging to such depths required an untold amount of work, and yet this was only the beginning of a long, involved process that required bringing the ore to the surface (frequently on the backs of humans), crushing the rocks into a fine powder, and mixing that powder with toxic substances such as lead and mercury.[4]

If the silver boom had occurred in the nineteenth century, Mexico would have become a worldwide magnet, like California. In an era of newspapers, steamboats, and widespread transoceanic travel, there is little doubt that the great Mexican silver mines would have lured immigrants from all quarters of the globe. But because the boom predated these communication and transportation conveniences and unfolded at a time when the Spanish monarchy prohibited all foreigners from going to the silver districts, Mexico had to make do with its own human resources. Whereas California attracted three hundred thousand people, colonial Mexico had to satisfy a hugely greater labor demand with no access to volunteers from the rest of the world.

## Parral

There is hardly a better place than Parral to explore the pull of silver. Today Parral is a scraggly town in southern Chihuahua, trying to cope with the closure of its mine after more than three and a half centuries of uninterrupted production and attempting to weather a drug-related wave of violence that has engulfed much of the state in recent years. Amazingly, it is succeeding by reinventing itself as a tourist destination. Visitors can witness a reenactment of the final earthly moments of the legendary revolutionary leader Pancho Villa, whose car was riddled with bullets at a Parral intersection. Tourists are also encouraged to spend time at the Palacio de Alvarado, a sumptuous late-nineteenth-century house that belonged to a mining baron. But the main attraction is the mine itself. Accompanied by a guide, one can descend into the bowels of the hill overlooking Parral and then wander through an elaborate gallery of tunnels that were excavated beginning in the seventeenth century.

In colonial times, Parral was neither the largest nor the most productive silver mine in Mexico. It was certainly a major operation compared with dozens of flash-in-the-pan silver strikes, but it produced less silver than Zacatecas, Guanajuato, Pachuca, and possibly some other mines. And yet Parral had a profound influence on northern Mexico's environment, economy, and human populations. Like Española's gold mines—which may not have employed more than five thousand workers but were still responsible for a vortex of enslavement and death across the Caribbean basin—Parral became a hub of exploitation, its spokes extending far and wide throughout the region and even around the world.[5]

It all began in the summer of 1631, when a peripatetic ensign named Juan Rangel de Biesma conducted diggings in a hill that he called "La Negrita," probably in reference to the gray-black color of the rocks there. Rangel de Biesma had only recently moved into the region and was a complete novice in the mining business. Less than a year earlier, he had relocated from his native Culiacán, on the Pacific coast, with his sister, who had married an encomendero from the Parral area. The thirty-year-old took up residence with the young couple at an estate that happened to be barely two miles away from the hill. Perhaps merely to give him something to do, Rangel de Biesma was put in charge of a team of Indian servants whose job was prospecting for silver. For decades Spaniards had been searching the area, but wars with the Indians, the dense scrub oak, the lack of servants, and simple bad luck had conspired to prevent them from discovering the enormous treasure buried in that hill.[6]

Rangel de Biesma and his team cleared an area close to the top and found that it was completely studded with black rocks. As far as anyone could tell, the vein was enormous, and the silver concentration was remarkable. Typically, miners were happy when they found ore containing one or two marcos per quintal (1 marco equals 230 grams, or a little over 8 ounces, and 1 quintal in colonial Mexico equaled 46 kilograms, or about 100 pounds). The samples from La Negrita reached *seven* marcos per quintal. This was the discovery of a lifetime. Not since the strike of Zacatecas more than eighty years earlier had anyone stumbled on such a massive silver deposit.[7]

No single individual, not even one in partnership with a powerful encomendero, could work the site by himself. So Rangel de Biesma invited family, friends, and neighbors, who claimed mining rights in adjacent areas. Word spread quickly beyond this small circle, and miners from other regions began pouring into the hill, bringing with them teams of black slaves and Indian servants. La Negrita soon came to resemble a giant anthill, with workers crawling around it, clearing scrub oak, digging tunnels, and carrying ore. By the start of 1632, just six months after the initial discovery, four hundred Europeans and as many as eight hundred "people of service" had settled by the hill. Those were heady years, when the riches of La Negrita seemed inexhaustible. As one enthusiastic miner put it, "The entire hill is made up of silver."[8]

Over the next decade, Parral's population continued to grow by leaps and bounds, surpassing 5,000 in 1635 and 8,500 by 1640. An entire city mushroomed at the base of the hill. Urban centers in Spanish America were usually arranged in a characteristic checkerboard grid, departing from a central plaza with a church on one side and a government building on the other. Yet Parral sprouted helter-skelter. The town's houses — initially no more than leather tents resembling Indian tepees — were crowded as close to the hill as possible. With the passage of time, these temporary quarters turned into more permanent *jacales,* adobe structures surrounded by corrals and vegetable plots. Parral's eastern end was the only section that resembled a real city. A vacant square lot grandly known as *la plaza del real* was surrounded by the sturdiest houses, a church, and the principal stores. Francisco de Lima, one of Parral's foremost merchants, owned an entire block of houses opposite the plaza, where he sold overpriced clothes, basic foodstuffs, and, occasionally, Indian slaves brought from New Mexico. The captives were auctioned off right in the plaza. In comparison to present-day cities, Parral's 8,500 inhabitants may not sound like much, but in the seventeenth century it was the largest town north of the Tropic of Cancer in the Americas. And nowhere else in what is now northern Mexico, the

United States, or Canada were there more Indians or a larger concentration of African slaves living in a single place.[9]

Finding silver at Parral was not nearly as difficult as securing the human power to get it out of the ground. Miners were initially attracted by the superficial outcroppings of the metal at the top of La Negrita. But once these easy pickings were depleted, they had to dig tunnels following the veins wherever they led — usually down. Already by the 1650s, the shafts plunged 250 feet underground. A nearby mine known as San Diego de Minas Nuevas was even deeper. The principal shaft of that mine went down 420 feet, more than the length of a football field. The effort needed to make these tunnels is hard to imagine. Workers dug with simple picks, wedges, moils (metal points), and crowbars, toiling from sunrise to sunset. (Explosives were not introduced until the early eighteenth century.) Some of the tools weighed thirty or forty pounds. Merely lifting them was difficult, let alone wielding them for twelve hours or more a day. In addition to being taxing in the extreme, the work was dangerous. Diggers regularly fell into the shafts or were crushed by collapsing sections of the mine. Many more lives were lost to the floating dust laced with sharp silica. Workers could not help but breathe in these particles, which became lodged in their lungs, causing scar tissue and decay. The unmistakable symptoms of such damage were fits of coughing, shortness of breath, chest pains, and vomiting. Silicosis could develop within a year and would gradually build up over five to ten years, causing severe scarring of the lungs, low blood oxygen levels, and ultimately death.[10]

Digging the shafts was a major undertaking, but it was only the start of the operation. Unlike much of the gold of the Caribbean, which could be collected as flecks or nuggets, silver was mostly embedded in the rock and combined with other substances. This geological reality added immensely to the work that was necessary to extract it. In Parral, as in many other silver mines throughout Mexico, Indians and black slaves carried the ore to the surface. Carrying leather bags full of rocks, they had to crawl through low passages and ascend by means of notched pine logs, or "chicken ladders." Since the carrier's hands were occupied holding the ladder, the heavy bag — which could weigh between 225 and 350 pounds — dangled perilously from his forehead and was propped against

Workers continued to carry heavy bags of ore on their backs well into the twentieth century. An American engineer toured Mexico in 1905 and took this photograph while visiting the famous mines of Guanajuato.

his back. Ore carriers were generally referred to as *tenateros,* a name derived from the Nahuatl word *tenatl,* a fiber or leather bag. Needless to say, the danger of slipping or falling was constant.[11]

Once the ore reached the surface, it was transported by carts pulled by mules to any of dozens of estates devoted to processing the ore. In 1633 there were already twenty-two ore-processing estates, known as *haciendas de beneficio,* in the region. Each of them was a world unto itself. The main work took place on a central patio, where one could see heaps of ore and crews crushing rock and isolating the silver. Most of the haciendas in Parral used the smelting method. After crushing the ore into coarse gravel, workers shoveled it into blast furnaces and combined it with molten lead. The idea was to use gravity to separate the silver from the rock, as the heavier silver-lead alloy sank to the bottom, while the lighter waste product, known as "slag," rose to the top and was raked away. Although this was the most common method of processing ore in Parral, it was not the most efficient.

A few of the haciendas used the "patio process," which resulted in a higher yield of silver. In this case, the ore was crushed to a fine powder, spread on a courtyard or patio, and sprinkled with mercury. Water was added to allow the heavier metals to sink to the bottom of this sludge. In Parral the worst job consisted of walking in shackles over this toxic mud in order to mix it thoroughly. This job invariably resulted in serious health problems, as the poisonous metal would enter the body through the pores and seep into the cartilage in the joints. Miners ordinarily purchased convicts who were serving out their sentences to perform this dreadful task at the *morteros* (mortars), where the ore was crushed and processed. The last step of the patio process was to heat the amalgam in order to vaporize the mercury and water and leave only the silver behind. Workers involved in this step absorbed the mercury vapors through their mucous membranes, which generally caused uncontrollable shaking of the limbs and death in as little as two or three years.[12]

Security was no afterthought at these ore-processing haciendas. Workers were frequently monitored during their shifts. Moreover, the patios were completely enclosed by single-story buildings that included a chapel, stables for the draft animals, a granary, a storage room for the ore and silver, a main house, and living quarters for the servants and slaves, many of whom were kept locked up or chained at night. To be sure, not everyone was compelled to work at Parral. As we shall see, there were many salaried Indians, as well as mestizos who worked alongside forced or semi-forced Indians, blacks, and mulattoes. But compulsion was very much a part of the mix.[13]

The work required to dig the shafts and tunnels; carry the ore to the surface; crush it completely; mix it with lead, mercury, and other reagents; and recover the silver was prodigious. And that is not even counting the demands on surrounding businesses, such as livestock ranches, timber camps, salt pits, and *carboneras* (charcoal-producing fields), that supplied the mines with various essential products and required yet more workers. It is no wonder that mine owners complained about the lack of laborers, often claiming that this was the main limiting factor in the production of silver. As early as 1572, the viceroy of Mexico, Martín Enríquez de Almanza, a capable administrator with personal knowledge of the mines of northern Mexico, wrote to the king of Spain and presented the owners' quandary in a remarkably lucid manner: "For the mine owners the key is to have workers, and the [black] slaves are not enough. I have already written to Your Majesty about the importance of sending Indians to the mines and paying good wages to them. Many of them go on their own accord and earn enough to eat well. But the natives are lazy by nature and do not persevere in any kind of work unless they are compelled. Without a direct order from Your Majesty I do not dare to give Indians to the miners because it is a practice that is forbidden, although it would be very suitable."[14]

Mine owners went to extraordinary lengths to procure workers. To get a sense of Parral's gravitational pull, all one has to do is consider its population. Of the 8,500 residents in 1640, about 1,000 were African or mulatto slaves. It was easily the largest concentration of African slaves anywhere in northern Mexico. About half of them had been born in the New World and were Hispanicized. The other half had been imported directly from Africa. They came primarily from Angola — a major slaving region in western Africa in the seventeenth and eighteenth centuries — as well as from the Congo and as far away as Mozambique, in eastern Africa. They had been conveyed through the interior of Africa, across the Atlantic, from Veracruz to Mexico City, and finally along the royal roads leading to the silver districts of northern Mexico. Hispanicized or not, these slaves were greatly valued by Parral owners. They were dependable, sometimes already possessed mining skills, and, since they came from such remote lands, could not run away and easily find refuge in the local population. From the standpoint of the owners, African slaves had only one major drawback: they were extremely expensive. The going rate for a healthy African or mulatto slave in Parral ranged from 400 to 500 pesos (with men commanding somewhat higher prices than women, thus suggesting that black slaves were employed primarily in mine-related activities). To put things in perspective, a black slave cost as much as three to five Indian slaves. Bishop Alonso de la Mota y

Escobar observed that in the mines of Zacatecas, "the most difficult job is to dig up the metal and bring it to the surface, because the mines are very deep. And it is the Indians who do this job and not the black slaves because it is known from past experience that African slaves get swollen and are afflicted by a thousand illnesses because of the great cold and humidity of the mines." Bishop Mota y Escobar's medical reasoning may have been off the mark, but his observation that black slaves were generally used for aboveground tasks makes perfect sense economically. In effect, their high price restricted the tasks to which they were assigned.[15]

There were also "Chinese" slaves in Parral. ("Chinese" was a blanket term used for all Asian people.) Although they were never numerous, their presence revealed a network of enslavement that operated across the Pacific Ocean. Nicolás de Tolentino, for example, originally came from the Indian subcontinent; he is variously identified as being "from the Malabar coast" or "of Bengali caste." When he was twelve years of age, Nicolás was sold on the coast of India to a Spanish officer who took him to the Philippines. Once in Manila, Nicolás changed hands until he was acquired by an Augustinian friar named Joseph Duque, who kept him for some years. In 1658 Fray (Friar) Duque made the decision to ship Nicolás across the Pacific, entrusting him to a broker who was to sell him in Mexico. At the port of Acapulco, Nicolás was acquired by an encomendero, resold to a captain from Cuernavaca, and finally transported to Mexico City and on to the northern frontier. When he finally reached Parral at age twenty-eight, Nicolás had been the object of a string of transactions throughout most of his life, having traveled immense distances and experienced bondage with masters from widely different cultures. Like their African counterparts, Asian slaves were extremely expensive. When Nicolás was first sold on the coast of India, the Spanish officer paid 50 pesos for him. By the time he reached Acapulco, he was sold for 380 pesos, and in Parral he commanded no less than 700 pesos. His very presence in this northern mining center, along with that of other men and women hailing from other remote locales, is indicative of the tremendous power of the local miners and their extreme need for laborers. But fetching such high prices, Africans and Asians could only be a partial solution to this vexing problem.[16]

The sheer number of Indians at Parral, speaking different languages and engaged in all aspects of the silver economy, was as impressive as the sight of Africans and Asians. Indians came from all quarters. We may be inclined to think of Parral as a Spanish or mestizo mining center, but its majority population was in fact indigenous. By 1640 fully 5,500, or almost two out of every three residents of Parral, were Indians. They could be found all around the town, some as squatters or servants living directly on La Negrita, others locked up at the ore-processing haciendas, and many more scattered at the base of the hill and throughout the mining district. Indians from some regions became so numerous that they formed their own neighborhoods. One section of town, for example, was known as the "Yaqui neighborhood" for the predominance of Yaqui Indians from Sonora living there.[17]

The most privileged Indians came to Parral of their own volition to work for wages. Perhaps 2,000 of the 5,500 Indians were in this situation. They hailed from more densely populated areas, especially central Mexico, or from more established mining areas. Lured by the glint of silver, they had taken their chances by venturing into the Chichimec frontier and accepting dangerous jobs at Parral that they performed for interminable hours. For their troubles, they were compensated with real salaries and, "far more important," as Bishop Mota y Escobar perceptively wrote, "with silver ore that they got to keep and which they call among themselves *pepena*." Indeed, after doing their daily work, free Indians were permitted to collect any silver-encrusted rocks they wanted. They could then sell this valuable ore in the black market or attempt to refine it into pure silver on their own. The *pepena* system existed in many mines throughout Mexico and shows that mine owners were willing to offer extraordinary concessions to attract workers.[18]

Impressed by the ubiquity of salaries and *pepenas*, some historians have hailed these silver mines as the vanguard of the free wage system in colonial Mexico. Already by the late sixteenth century, free wage earners outnumbered forced workers in some mines. More recent studies have revealed a sobering reality, however. While salaried workers did indeed account for a significant percentage of the workforce in many mines — including thirty-six percent of all Indians in Parral — these workers did not replace coerced laborers, but rather coexisted with them. One reason is that mine owners never fully embraced a labor system that essentially allowed workers to plunder the mines. From the owners' perspective, the incentives were completely wrong. Free workers hid the richest ores in order to claim them later as part of their *pepenas*. They were also prone to drift from mine to mine in search of better conditions. If they felt the ore was not rich enough or heard about a more promising strike down the road, they had no compunction about packing up at a moment's notice and leaving behind unfinished jobs. Mine owners therefore regarded salaried work not as an ideal form of labor, but as a necessary evil and a first step toward acquiring a more pliable and stable workforce.[19]

One strategy to achieve this goal involved advancing wages in pesos or specie (silver coins) to free workers. Since food, clothes, and many other necessities were outrageously expensive in Parral (and often because of gambling and drinking habits), workers frequently incurred debts. In principle these were free individuals who had temporarily fallen on hard times. But the reality was more ominous. Unable to repay their debts, these workers could not leave the mines until they closed their accounts. We may think of debt peonage as a phenomenon of great haciendas in the years leading up to the Mexican Revolution. Yet two centuries earlier, indebted servants and peons proliferated in Parral. One miner's account book, for example, shows that out of the twelve Indians in his labor gang, seven of them were in debt. From such scattered evidence, it is not possible to draw general conclusions about the overall level of indebtedness in Parral and the level of coercion used to get workers to pay. But it is clear that many indebted workers were considered part of the mines' inventories and more or less permanently attached to them. For instance, when Parral owners put a mine up for sale, they specifically listed the number of indebted workers. Evidently the existence of such workers was a major consideration for prospective buyers.[20]

Notwithstanding the free or supposedly free workers, some 3,000 of Parral's 5,500 Indians consisted of forced laborers under the encomienda and repartimiento systems. There were relatively few encomienda Indians directly involved in Parral's mining economy, as they were mostly set aside for agricultural and ranching activities. The majority of forced workers in the mines and ore-processing haciendas came from neighboring communities and missions as part of the extensive repartimiento system of forced labor. The system was set in motion when owners requested workers from colonial authorities, specifying the number of Indians needed and the type of work to which they would be assigned. Governors and local authorities would then work out the number of Indian workers (both male and female) that each community and mission was required to contribute to meet these requests. It goes without saying that failure to provide sufficient workers would result in significant repercussions. And, as it is easy to imagine, the actual drafting of these Indians was a process fraught with abuse that could lead to violence. The fact that local officials were regularly admonished to exercise great caution while acquiring repartimiento Indians suggests that things could easily get out of hand. For their part, Indians had every reason to resist. They were forced to abandon their families and leave their animals and fields unattended. They had to travel twenty, fifty, or even a hundred miles to the mines. And although in theory their work stint could not last more than six weeks, in reality it could be much longer. Repartimiento Indians were supposed to receive compensation, but their wages were woefully inadequate, and they were often paid in clothes rather than cash. Indians considered the repartimiento system a major inconvenience at best and tantamount to periodic enslavement at worst. Parral's explosive growth in the 1630s and 1640s, as well as the mine owners' great need for workers, meant that repartimiento Indians came from a large catchment area and experienced longer and more arduous tours of duty.[21]

By the late 1640s, the strain of the mines on surrounding Native communities and missions had become so great that the Indians started to revolt. The colonial archives of Parral include no less than 225 files on "seditions," "uprisings," and full-scale "rebellions" from 1633 to 1789. The Indians resented the repartimientos, epidemics, and other problems that stemmed directly or indirectly from the furious expansion of the silver economy. No historian has delved fully into these files, but even a partial examination of the records for the seventeenth century reveals that Parral's prodigious growth disrupted Indian life within a radius of two to three hundred miles. The wave of indigenous unrest reached a high point in the 1650s, when the Tarahumaras, Conchos, and others turned defiant and rendered labor relations extremely volatile. At the same time, Parral experienced a significant population decline. By 1640 the town had 8,500 residents, but by the 1650s that number had dropped to around 5,000. Parral's demographic decline was clearly linked to the wave of indigenous rebellions all around it, but the precise causal chain remains murky. The most likely explanation is that Parral's easy silver had been exhausted by the late 1640s, and therefore a higher level of exploitation was required to extract the remaining silver, which in turn prompted the Indians to revolt. However, it is also plausible that the rebellions around Parral made the recruitment of Indian workers even more difficult, resulting in fewer people in Parral and less silver.[22]

Regardless of the exact sequence of events, mine owners ultimately addressed the problem of insufficient workers by bringing Indians to Parral from even farther away. Indian slaves had been present there since the mines' inception. In 1640 there were about 500 of them, or about ten percent of the indigenous workforce. But after the wave of Indian rebellions in the 1650s, miners were forced to rely more and more on these slaves. As we have seen, frontier captains were in the habit of waging war on the "barbarous" or "errant" nations, accusing them of a variety of crimes, and convicting captives to five, ten, or twenty years of forced labor. Technically these were not slaves but criminals serving out their sentences. Yet such technicalities were lost on those who were captured in raids, stuffed into carts, transported over long distances, and sold to the highest bidder in Parral's central plaza. Hundreds of Indians came from the provinces of Sonora and Sinaloa. These coastal Natives were hunted down and transported with great difficulty across the Sierra Madre Occidental to Parral. Other slaves came from the large desert region to the east of Parral, where various bands of Indians vaguely known as Tobosos both enslaved other Indians and were themselves victims of slaving raids. The largest stream of Indian captives pouring into Parral came from the northernmost reaches of the Spanish empire.[23]

## New Mexico's Mining Connections

The conquest of New Mexico is often presented as an incomprehensible story of Spanish cruelty and wanton destruction. In 1598 Juan de Oñate arrived there with his men and in short order took possession of this kingdom. Oñate apportioned Indians who submitted peacefully in encomiendas, but he reserved a far worse fate for those who resisted. To this day, New Mexicans recall Oñate's exemplary punishment of the Indians of Acoma after they revolted: all males over age twenty-five had one foot cut off. In this rendering, Oñate appears as a royal envoy mindlessly expanding the bounds of the empire. Hidden from view, however, are all the mining connections. In truth, Oñate went to New Mexico first and foremost as a mining baron. His father, Cristóbal de Oñate, had been one of the founders of the silver mines of Zacatecas and therefore was one of the richest individuals in all of Mexico. Juan de Oñate himself was born and raised in Zacatecas and knew all there was to know about silver mining. His stated purpose in going to New Mexico was to open new lands to Christianity. But his far more practical reason, as we shall see, was to prospect for precious metals and obtain Indian laborers.[24]

For a start, Oñate's expedition was part of a mining rush that was already spilling into New Mexico. At least since the 1580s, mine owners, labor recruiters, and Indian traffickers from northern Mexico had attempted to tap into New Mexico's population. Little information survives about these early entradas. Entrepreneurs engaged in trafficking Indians were understandably secretive, but the few extant sources are quite revealing. One young soldier named Diego Pérez de Luxán enlisted in a 1582–1583 expedition into New Mexico and kept a diary of his experiences. He casually described how the party ran into a *jacal* (hut) along the Conchos River that was very far from any Indian or Spanish settlement. (The Conchos is a tributary of the Rio Grande just south of New Mexico.) This structure, he explained, had been built by a party of slavers the previous year to keep its human quarry. Pérez de Luxán knew all of this because he himself was a slaver. Indeed, the following year our diarist returned to New Mexico to conduct additional raids.

We would never have known about these activities had Pérez de Luxán not repented of his youthful mistakes later in life, denounced the "unjust wars" waged against the Indians, and accepted the position of *protector y defensor de los indios* in the mining district of Santa Bárbara, a thriving slave market close to the hill that would later give rise to Parral.[25]

Another example of an early slaving raid into New Mexico was the one led by Gaspar Castaño de Sosa, the lieutenant governor of the New Kingdom of León who took charge of the province after Governor Luis de Carvajal was forced to leave. Castaño de Sosa remained in the town of Almadén with around sixty Spanish colonists until 1590. His position became untenable not only on account of the dwindling silver around Almadén but also because of the hostility of two successive viceroys. To escape possible prosecution, as well as to explore another kingdom, Castaño de Sosa conceived the fantastically bold plan of relocating his entire township from Nuevo León to New Mexico. It was the first — albeit unauthorized — European attempt to settle New Mexico permanently.[26]

Consisting of hardened settlers uninhibited by the presence of churchmen or royal officials, Castaño de Sosa's party spent much of 1590 traversing the parched lands of northern Coahuila, venturing up the Pecos River, and eventually reaching the territory of the Pueblo Indians, more than twelve hundred miles from Mexico City and one of the most inaccessible corners of the empire at the time. The viceroy then in charge of New Spain, Luis de Velasco II, dispatched a captain and forty soldiers to this unimaginably remote locale to capture the renegades and bring them to Mexico City in chains. As the members of this second party made their way to New Mexico, they began gathering depositions from some of the Nuevo León settlers who had refused to go with Castaño de Sosa, as well as some of the men who did accompany him but were apprehended by the soldiers near the Rio Grande. The proceedings — close to eighty pages of testimonies and confessions — detail some of Castaño de Sosa's slaving activities. One prominent colonist named Diego Ramírez Barrionuevo, for instance, stated that Castaño de Sosa and his soldiers had taken "many pieces of Indian men and women all of whom were sentenced to service, and taken out of their land and environment, and sold away in other parts." From such depositions one can only conclude that slave taking had become a significant economic activity in the northernmost reaches of the Spanish empire.[27]

Oñate's 1598 expedition was the latest bid to integrate the kingdom of New Mexico into the expanding silver economy of northern Mexico. As it turned out, Oñate did not find any gold or silver there, but he did find that the number of Indians living in *pueblos,* or towns, was remarkable. New Mexico contained the largest number of sedentary Indians north of central Mexico. These Pueblo Indians, as they came to be known, were surrounded by several nomadic groups with whom they traded. Governor Oñate immediately parceled out the pueblos as encomiendas. He was ruthless toward Indians who refused to submit to his authority, but he was also an entrepreneur; his punishments usually tended to be utilitarian in nature. For example, quite apart from the few dozen Indians from Acoma whose feet were amputated, Oñate and his captain sentenced all Acoma males between the ages of twelve and twenty-five and all females over age twelve to twenty years of personal servitude. Hundreds of Indians were thus divvied up among the earliest Spanish colonists of New Mexico.[28]

There is little information about the fate of these early Pueblo captives, but two points are worth emphasizing. First, they were expensive. Oñate's nephew and subsidiary captain, Vicente de Zaldívar, received dozens of Acoma Indians. But according to Zaldívar's deposition, sixty of them subsequently ran away. Zaldívar estimated his losses at more than 10,000 pesos, which works out to a little more than 160 pesos per slave. This sum of money is greater than the value of a stone house in Mexico City or Oñate's yearly salary as governor. Second, even though these slaves were potentially very valuable, in order to turn them into real money, one had to transport them out of New Mexico and sell them in more southerly markets, where small pieces of silver and other forms of liquid payment were in circulation. According to Oñate, at least forty-five Spanish soldiers and officers, "in anger at not finding bars of silver on the ground right away," left New Mexico, taking slaves with them. Even Oñate and his nephew Zaldívar were accused of transporting slaves all the way to Mexico City (although they were later acquitted of this charge). Traffickers had to set aside wagons to transport the slaves and had to go through the trouble and expense of feeding them for months along the way. They did it because they knew that in the end, they would still make a profit.[29]

Governor Oñate set an enduring precedent in this line of business. A long list of New Mexican governors, right up to the Pueblo Revolt of 1680 (see chapter 6), were not only tolerant or complicit in the trafficking of Indians, but they were directly and actively involved in this human trade. Instances of seventeenth-century officials implicated in the traffic of New Mexican Indian slaves are too numerous to recount here. However, a few vignettes point to some of the milestones in the development of the Indian slave trade. Governor Juan de Eulate (1618–1625), for example, was the first to issue *vales,* or small pieces of paper authorizing the bearer to seize an "orphaned" girl or boy. "And once they get their vales," one witness recalled, "the soldiers go to the pueblos and take the orphans and keep them in their homes as if they were black slaves." One friar averred that such children were treated as if they were "yearling calves or colts," while another resident observed that often they were not orphans at all, but children forcibly taken away from their parents. At the end of his term, Governor Eulate traveled to Mexico City, where he was arrested for illegally transporting Indians out of New Mexico.[30]

Governor Felipe Sotelo Osorio (1625–1629) spearheaded the use of Indian auxiliaries to conduct slaving raids. This innovation was fully on display when a group of Vaquero Apaches entered the Spanish town of Santa Fe asking to see "the Mother of God." The object of the Indians' curiosity was the statue of the Virgin Mary known as *La Conquistadora,* which had been brought from Spain in 1625. They were led into a crude chapel that harbored the figure, which was carved of solid willow and adorned with a crimson garment covered with golden leaves in arabesque. The leader of the visiting Indians, an elderly man, was so impressed that, "speaking with great devotion," he declared his intention to become a Christian. What occurred next, however, was hardly edifying. After the Vaquero Apaches departed, Governor Sotelo Osorio "sent for a gutsy Indian captain," a declared enemy of the visitors, and commanded him and his posse to "bring back whomever they could catch." They did as they were told, overtaking the Indians; killing the elderly chief, who was still wearing a rosary around his neck; and bringing a number of captives back to Santa Fe. As one friar summed up this sad episode, the Vaquero Apaches had been on the brink of converting, "but the Devil had recourse to one of his wiles, choosing as his instrument the greed of our governor."[31]

Governor Luis de Rosas (1637–1641) experimented with the use of slaves *within* New Mexico to manufacture goods for export to Parral. He set up an *obraje,* or textile sweatshop, in Santa Fe, where he kept some thirty Indians locked up. These Indians, seized in "unjust wars," according to one resident, made stockings and other woolen items and painted *mantas* (cloths) with charcoal. Governor Rosas was a hands-on owner; he could be frequently found at the shop covered with charcoal, "and one could tell him apart from the Indians only by his fine clothes." Working conditions in *obrajes* all over Mexico ranged from bad to appalling, and those in New Mexico were no different. Although some of Governor Rosas's Indians died of starvation, the governor had the good business sense to replace them by expanding the Spaniards' war with the Apaches and Utes. By calling for unprovoked attacks on the Indians, Governor Rosas initiated a cycle of reprisals and counter-reprisals that resulted in ideal conditions for obtaining Indian workers, some of whom ended their days in his textile shop.[32]

We have seen that the demand for Indian slaves increased markedly in the wake of the Indian rebellions around Parral in the 1650s. Governor Juan Manso (1656–1659) rose to the occasion. This frontier entrepreneur took his predecessors' policies to the next logical level by issuing a "definitive death sentence against the entire Apache nation and others of the same ilk." In other words, he declared open season on all Apaches and their allies. At the same time, Governor Manso devised a legal framework to bypass the crown's prohibition against Indian slavery. He gave out certificates that entitled the bearers to keep Apaches "in deposit"—not as slaves—for a specified number of years. "The Apaches have been irreducible enemies of our Catholic faith and of all Christians of this kingdom," read one of these certificates signed in Santa Fe on October 12, 1658, "and by virtue of this sentence they may be taken out of this kingdom [New Mexico] and kept in deposit for a period of fifteen years starting on the day when they reach twelve years of age, and at no time would they be able to come back to this kingdom." This particular certificate was issued for Sebastián, a seven-year-old boy with big black eyes and a face scarred by smallpox.[33]

We can get a good sense of Parral's gravitational pull on New Mexico in Governor Bernardo López de Mendizábal's frantic preparations as he readied nine wagons for departure for the mining center in the fall of 1659. As an incoming governor eager to profit from his position of authority, Mendizábal first dispatched a squadron to bring back "heathen Indians" to sell. They collected about seventy Natives. Governor Mendizábal also sent orders to six pueblos in the Salinas area "to carry salt on their shoulders and on their own animals" for a distance of up to thirty leagues (ninety miles) without pay. A captain left a vivid description of Mendizábal's exertions in a letter worth quoting at length:

> This sending of salt to El Parral by the governor is injurious, Sir, because, to equip his wagons with some degree of safety, he forthwith sent his *alcaldes mayores* [higher magistrates] (who are people of ordinary sorts, only concerned with promoting their own interests), to some of the pueblos to take away from the natives their grass mats, which were the only beds they had, giving them nothing in exchange. From others they took their buckskins and their *tecoas* (which are pieces of dressed leather that they use for footwear). The *alcaldes* use these things to cover their wagons. We have evidence that in the pueblo of Taos alone, they took forty buckskins without any pay whatsoever.[34]

Clearly by the 1650s, the kingdom of New Mexico had become little more than a supply center for Parral.

From the preceding examples and many others, it is possible to reconstruct the overall trajectory of the traffic of Natives from New Mexico. The earliest Spanish settlers began by enslaving Pueblo Indians. But they quickly discovered that keeping Pueblos as slaves was counterproductive, as this bred discontent among the Natives on which Spaniards depended for their very sustenance. Although the occasional enslavement of Pueblos continued throughout the seventeenth century, the colonists gradually redirected their slaving activities to Apaches and Utes. The Spaniards injected themselves into the struggles between different *rancherías* (local bands) and exploited intergroup antagonisms to facilitate the supply of slaves, as Governor Sotelo Osorio did with the "gutsy Indian captain."[35]

Although New Mexican governors played the leading role in developing the slave trade and controlling the lion's share of the proceeds, private entrepreneurs also gained a foothold in the business. Colonists who owned encomiendas were able to extract unpaid labor from their Pueblo Indians and, as one witness admitted, occasionally send some of them away "to be sold as slaves in New Spain, as was the practice." Spanish settlers without encomiendas were at a clear disadvantage concerning the commercial opportunities of the silver economy. But they could still acquire Indian captives/servants, whom they could sell in more southerly markets or keep in New Mexico to produce export goods. From the start, New Mexican colonists possessed an extraordinarily high number of servants. Already in 1630 Santa Fe's minuscule white population of about 250 held around 700 servants and slaves; that is, every white man, woman, and child residing in the capital possessed between two and three Native servants on average. These Indians, Pueblos as well as Plains Indians acquired through slave raids, toiled in sweatshops or private homes weaving and decorating textiles, preparing hides, and harvesting pine nuts.[36]

The growing number of New Mexican Indians in Parral can be gleaned from baptismal records, which contain entries such as these: "Inés, baptized on April 16, 1671, Indian girl from New Mexico of unknown parents, *criada* of Ensign Lorenzo Samaniego"; and "Antonia, baptized on May 7, 1674, Apache girl of unknown parents from the hacienda of Captain Andrés del Hierro." Even though parish records refer to them as *criadas* (servants) rather than *esclavas* (slaves), everyone in Parral knew that they had been acquired in public auctions at the main plaza. The number of New Mexican slaves sent to Parral increased in the 1650s, continued to expand in the 1660s, and reached record numbers in the 1670s (see appendix 5).[37]

By 1679 so many Indians were flowing out of New Mexico that the bishop of Durango launched a formal investigation into this burgeoning business. Bishop Bartolomé García de Escañuela undertook this inquest less out of a sense of moral or religious duty than out of concern about the church's declining revenues. Ordinarily, the faithful of Nueva Vizcaya — a province that included the modern states of Chihuahua, Durango, Sonora, and Sinaloa — had to pay a yearly tithe to the bishopric of ten percent of their animals and crops. But ranchers all over this region discovered that they were able to reduce their herds — and consequently their tax liabilities — by trading tithe-bearing animals for Indian slaves, who were tax-free. In effect, the acquisition of Indians amounted to a tax shelter, and the amount of the sheltered revenue was large enough that the tithes of the bishopric of Durango were declining. As Bishop Escañuela toured his enormous ecclesiastical district, he interviewed merchants and slave traffickers from New Mexico to learn more about the human traffic. One outspoken young man named Antonio García explained that no merchant could leave New Mexico on his own because the Indians around El Paso del Norte were at war with the Spaniards, "so when the governor sends his Indians and his merchandise to this bishopric of Nueva Vizcaya, he invites everyone to come together in a convoy." García himself had joined the convoy in the fall of 1678. On that occasion, he had taken three Indian girls and had received fifteen or sixteen mares for each of them. He was a small merchant compared with one of his traveling companions, who had exchanged his human cargo for more than a thousand cows. The consequences of this trafficking were not long in coming. In the summer of 1680, the Indians of New Mexico launched a massive rebellion, which, as we will see in chapter 6, was motivated to a large extent by the growing Indian slave trade.[38]

Beyond northern Mexico, coerced Indian labor played a fundamental role in the mining economies of Central America, the Caribbean, Colombia, Venezuela, the Andean region, and Brazil. Yet the specific arrangements varied from place to place. Unlike Mexico's silver economy, scattered in multiple mining centers, the enormous mine of Potosí dwarfed all others in the Andes. To satisfy the labor needs of this "mountain of silver," Spanish authorities instituted a gargantuan system of draft labor known as the *mita,* which required that more than two hundred Indian communities spanning a large area in modern-day Peru and Bolivia send one-seventh of their adult population to work in the mines of Potosí, Huancavelica, and Cailloma. In any given year, ten thousand Indians or more had to take their turns working in the mines. This state-directed system began in 1573 and remained in operation for 250 years. Other mines of Latin America, such as the gold and diamond fields of Brazil and the emerald mines of Colombia, depended more on itinerant prospectors and private forms of labor. But even though the degree of state involvement and the scale of these operations varied from place to place, they all relied on labor arrangements that ran the gamut from clear slave labor (African, Indian, and occasionally Asian); to semi-coercive institutions and practices such as encomiendas, repartimientos, debt peonage, and the *mita;* to salaried work. Mines all across the hemisphere thus propelled the other slavery.[39]

# 5

# The Spanish Campaign

A CENTURY BEFORE THE American and French Revolutions, the Spanish crown set out to free the slaves around the world. The intended beneficiaries were not Africans but Indians living in the far corners of the empire. And the leaders of this crusade were not fiery revolutionaries but a mystical king, his foreign-born queen, and their sickly son.[1]

This movement began with one of the least likely figures to get embroiled in an idealist quest. Philip IV was a worldly man fond of hunting, bullfighting, and the arts. Of all the Spanish monarchs, he stands as the most avid and discerning collector and patron of painters, beginning with his own court painter, the extraordinary Diego Velázquez. But Philip's true passion, like that of many of his contemporaries, was the theater. In his youth, he was a regular at the *corrales*, or theaters, of Madrid, enjoying the latest plays by the prolific Lope de Vega, the cantankerous Francisco de Quevedo, or some other luminary of Spain's Siglo de Oro (Golden Age). Since court etiquette prevented kings from going to the theater, Philip attended incognito, often wearing a mask. Plays were represented in courtyards surrounded by houses overlooking the stage. In one of these second-floor apartments, above the crush and din of the crowd, the Spanish king was able to spend many pleasurable afternoons taking in comedies or dramas without being noticed.[2]

Philip IV was a great patron of the arts. Numerous paintings now in the Museo Nacional del Prado in Madrid were acquired, received as gifts, or commissioned by him. His favorite painter was Diego Velázquez, who made several portraits of the king, including this one in 1623–1624.

These escapades also afforded Philip IV the opportunity to indulge his other great passion: women. At the Corral de la Cruz, he became smitten with a sixteen-year-old actress named María Inés Calderón, who took Madrid by storm with her sweet voice and captivating manner. After one of her performances, the king invited her to join him in his apartment, which caused the king's passion to grow even wilder. Thus began an intense but short-lived relationship. Philip had a son with María Inés and would go on to father more than twenty illegitimate children with as many women.[3]

Philip was not, however, just a pleasure seeker. Almost incongruously, he was also extremely religious. When in his thirties, he suffered a personal crisis that steered him toward mysticism. As a result, he sacked the man he had relied on to rule his enormous empire for more than twenty years, the Count-Duke of Olivares, and announced that he would henceforth govern using no intermediaries. *"Yo tomo el remo"* (I take over the oar), he wrote to one of his governors. Philip summoned mystics from across Christendom so that he might "rule and govern in harmony with their revelations." During this critical time, he met Sor María de Ágreda, an abbess from Old Castile who was regarded as the preeminent mystic of her time. After a brief encounter, the two struck up an extraordinarily candid correspondence that would last for twenty-two years, until the end of their lives in 1665. Through the more than six hundred letters they exchanged, it is possible to peer into Philip's soul.[4]

Philip IV believed that God followed his every move and rewarded or punished the whole of the empire according to his conduct. He confided to Sor María that his sexual appetite was the cause of Spain's misfortunes: "I scarcely have any trust left in myself, because I have sinned a great deal and I deserve the punishments and afflictions that I suffer, and the greatest gift I could receive is for God to punish me rather than these kingdoms, for I am the one to blame and not them who have always been true Catholics." As the contrite Philip sought to rule in a way that would please God, Sor María urged him to dispense "true justice" and stamp out "vices and all manner of sin."[5]

Of the many matters that required Philip's attention, the enslavement of Indians in the New World was decidedly secondary. We do not know what Philip's personal views on the subject may have been, but during the early years of his reign he favored the iron fist. The kingdom of Chile, for instance, had experienced a massive Indian insurrection at the close of the sixteenth century. The situation had been so critical that Philip's father and predecessor, Philip III, had taken the drastic step of stripping the Mapuche Indians of the customary royal protection against enslavement in 1608, thus making Chile one of the few parts of the empire where slave taking was entirely legal. Philip IV inherited this morass when he ascended to the throne and could have done something to improve relations. Instead, in 1625, four years into his reign, the young monarch not only endorsed his father's policies but made them even harsher by ordering "an offensive war in the same way that it used to be waged before the King our lord and my father (may his soul rest in peace) stopped it and made it defensive only. And in particular you will make sure that all Indians captured in the war will be distributed as slaves." Under Philip's pointed directions, the traffic of Indians flourished in Chile for decades.[6]

Yet in the twilight of his life, Philip came to grips with the failure of his policies as he struggled to save his soul. In 1655, after thirty years of insurrection, the Mapuches launched yet another attack, making clear that the conflict was not close to an end. Philip's offensive war had produced not a Spanish victory and a durable peace but a perpetual state of warfare kept going by slave takers and owners of Indian slaves, who were its chief beneficiaries. So the monarch and his ministers changed course. The crown's policies toward the Natives of Chile became markedly softer. In 1656 Philip issued a strongly worded order prohibiting the so-called *esclavitud de la usanza,* or customary slavery, in which Natives willingly sold family members; in 1660 he curtailed textile sweatshops, which were notorious for using Indian slaves; and in 1662 he issued no less than three royal orders forbidding the trafficking of Chilean Indians into Peru. That same year, Philip requested a reassessment of the imperial policies in Chile and expressed his belief that slave taking had become the main obstacle to peace with the Mapuche Indians. Philip's opinion had changed much since the confident years of his youth. Yet the king died before he could set the Indians of Chile free and discharge his royal conscience.[7]

But Philip was not alone in trying to make things right. His wife, Mariana, was thirty years younger than he, every bit as pious, and far more determined. The crusade to free the Indians of Chile, and those in the empire at large, gained momentum during Queen Mariana's regency, from 1665 to 1675, and culminated in the reign of her son Charles II. Alarmed by reports of large slaving grounds on the periphery of the Spanish empire, they used the power of an absolute monarchy to bring about the immediate liberation of all indigenous slaves. Mother and son took on deeply entrenched slaving interests, deprived the empire of much-needed revenue, and risked the very stability of distant provinces to advance their humanitarian agenda. They waged a war against Indian bondage that raged as far as the islands of the Philippines, the forests of Chile, the *llanos* (grasslands) of Colombia and Venezuela, and the deserts of Chihuahua and New Mexico. And yet both were exceedingly unlikely emancipators.

Mariana was an Austrian by birth who had arrived in Spain when she was fifteen years old to be betrothed to the aging Philip. Because she was originally a foreigner and a great deal younger than her late husband, some authors have depicted Queen Mariana as a weak ruler operating in a world of influential men. The facts run contrary to this view, however, as she was notoriously strong willed. As one scholar of the Spanish court put it, "Her commendable fixity of ideas sometimes degenerated into obstinacy and her laudable code of conduct into stubbornness." If anything, she could be faulted for attempting to extend her power beyond her regency and into her son's reign.[8]

King Charles II was an even more improbable champion of Indian rights. Carlos was only three when his father, Philip IV, died, and already showing signs that something was wrong with him. "He seems extremely weak, with pale cheeks and very open mouth, a symptom, according to the unanimous opinion of the doctors, of some gastric upset," wrote a French diplomat, "and though they say he walks on his own feet and that the cords with which the Menina [maid] guides him are simply in case he makes a false step, I doubt it, since I saw him take his nurse's hand to hold himself up when they retired." Carlos grew to be a listless adolescent. He walked slowly alongside walls or tables to steady himself and showed little interest in his surroundings. Few believed that he possessed an independent will. His physical and mental traits led his subjects to refer to him as "el Hechizado" (the Bewitched).[9]

The many orders and decrees that have come down to us illuminate Queen Mariana's and then King Charles's determination to protect the Indians. They speak of the "gravity of the matter of Indian slavery" and "the scruples of conscience that their enslavement causes." Mariana often referred back to Philip's precedents, revealing a widow's desire to bring to fruition a project cut short by death. Something similar is true

La V. M. Maria de Iesus de Agreda. Predicando a los Chichimecos del Nuebo-mexico.

More than a century after Sor María's reported apparitions in northern Mexico, her memory lived on. This 1730 woodcut shows the "lady in blue" spreading the Gospel among nomadic Indians in New Mexico.

of Charles. In his most important decree, freeing all the slaves of the American continent, he devoted admiring words to his mother's efforts. Theirs was a family enterprise passed from one member to the next.

Perhaps the great mystic of Ágreda lurked behind their family's resolve. Philip became deeply impressed by Sor María's earnest injunctions to rule in a Christian spirit by fighting oppression and providing justice, notions that extended so naturally to his indigenous subjects. Moreover, there had been an episode in Sor María's past that connected her directly to the Indians. Back in the early 1620s, when Philip was busy prosecuting the war against the Indians of Chile, Sor María was gaining renown for her trances. During these spells, and without ever leaving her room in Ágreda, she traveled to the Americas. Cloaked in blue, she also appeared to the Indians of New Mexico and Texas, preaching the Gospel and urging them to accept the holy water of baptism. Sor María herself could not tell whether she had actually bilocated — that is, had been in Europe and America at the same time — or, as she would later be more inclined to think, it had been "an angel in my shape that appeared there and preached and taught them, and over here the Lord showed me what was happening." But the fact was that many Natives of New Mexico had witnessed multiple apparitions of a white nun. Friars reported meeting Indians who had never been in contact with the Spanish but already knew the rudiments of the Catholic faith. When asked how they knew, they had simply replied, "The lady in blue." This is how Sor María first came to Philip's attention and how their paths began to converge.[10]

In their correspondence, neither Sor María nor Philip wrote a single word about this episode. It was just too sensitive a subject, and the letters could fall into the wrong hands. At least on two occasions, the Inquisition investigated the nun's claims, and Philip probably used his influence to protect her. Yet Sor María's unique connection to the New World and its peoples must have impressed not only Philip but his successors as well. Queen Mariana corresponded with the mystic of Ágreda, and after María's death in 1665, Mariana supported her canonization. Charles II was no less devoted. In 1677, during the thick of his antislavery campaign, he made a point of visiting Ágreda to honor Sor María's legacy and perhaps to gain some strength and guidance for the difficult road ahead.[11]

## An Empire of Slaves

The Spanish antislavery crusade generated letters, testimonies, and reports about the slaving grounds of the empire: twelve hundred pages of campaign-related documents for northern Mexico, one thousand for the Philippines, three hundred for southern Chile, and decreasing amounts for Argentina, the coasts of Colombia and Venezuela, and other places. The source of these documents reveals a great deal about the geography of Native bondage. In the early days of conquest, European slavers were attracted to some of the most heavily populated areas of the New World, including the large Caribbean islands, Guatemala, and central

Mexico. But by the time the antislavery crusade got under way in the 1660s, nearly two centuries after the discovery of America, the slaving grounds had shifted to remote frontiers where there were much lower population densities but where imperial control remained minimal or nonexistent and the constant wars yielded steady streams of captives.[12]

Five major slaving grounds are evident in the documentation of the antislavery crusade of the seventeenth century. The most daunting and morally fraught was in Chile, where slave taking had remained legal between 1608 and 1674. With the crown's explicit permission, slavery had flourished there. A Spanish chaplain who had lived in Chile for thirty years (fifteen of those among the Mapuche Indians) penned a clear-eyed report for Queen Mariana describing how Spanish captains lured the Indians with false promises of friendship, asking them to come to an appointed place with their families and animals. In some instances, the Indians were in the process of preparing a meal to celebrate and formalize their alliance with the Europeans when they were mercilessly attacked and taken prisoner. These were not vague accusations but precise reports including names and numbers: "The cacique Catilab was killed with spears and they took 17 captives from him"; or "The cacique Ancayeco fell dead there, and he had brought 12 family members with him and they took all of them." By the chaplain's count, one raid in 1672 netted 87 captives and another 274. In previous years, he had reported slaving raids resulting in 300 to 400 captives, "and I could describe many other unjust raids and abusive deaths in the past." Governor Juan Enríquez affirmed categorically in 1676 that "in Chile there are many more Indian slaves than Spaniards," an estimate that even if halfway accurate would put their number in the tens of thousands. Slaves were so plentiful that merchants also shipped them to Peru, where cities and mines were perennially in short supply of laborers. Indians branded on the face arrived "in great numbers" at the port of Callao, the gateway to Lima, "where they were all thrown out onto the plaza and some were sold and others only shown."[13]

Across the Andes, a second major slaving zone extended through the provinces of Paraguay, Tucumán, and adjacent areas. In the 1660s and

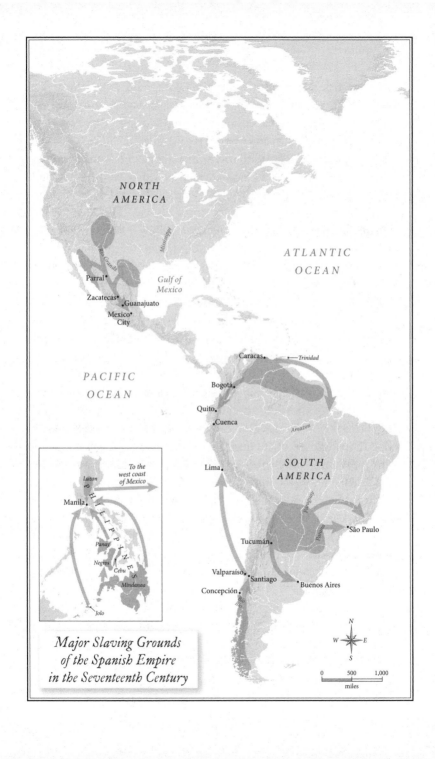

NORTH
AMERICA

ATLANTIC
OCEAN

Gulf of
Mexico

Parral

Zacatecas
Guanajuato

Mexico
City

Caracas — Trinidad

Bogotá

PACIFIC
OCEAN

Quito
Cuenca

Amazon

SOUTH
AMERICA

Lima

To the
west coast
of Mexico

Luzon

Manila

P H I L I P P I N E S

Panay

Negros
Cebu

Mindanao

Jolo

São Paulo

Tucumán

Valparaíso
Santiago

Concepción

Buenos Aires

N
W E
S

0      500    1,000
miles

*Major Slaving Grounds*
*of the Spanish Empire*
*in the Seventeenth Century*

1670s, Spanish slavers staged raids in the Calchaquí Valleys, an area in Tucumán of stunning rock formations and forbidding gorges, where various Indian groups had coexisted since pre-contact times and were now being hunted down and shipped throughout the Río de la Plata basin. The Spaniards were not the only ones raiding in this area. From the coast of Brazil, small parties of *bandeirantes* — a cross between pathfinders, prospectors, and slavers — also mounted devastating expeditions into the interior. Over the centuries, Brazilians have celebrated the *bandeirantes* in poems, novels, and sculptures, hailing them as the founders of the nation. Yet the *bandeirantes* took upwards of sixty thousand captives in the middle decades of the seventeenth century, snatching mostly Indians congregated in the Jesuit missions of Paraguay.[14]

The llanos of Colombia and Venezuela, the vast grasslands crisscrossed by tributaries of the Orinoco River, were a third zone of enslavement. Here Spanish traffickers competed with English, French, and above all Dutch networks of enslavement, all of which operated in the llanos. Interestingly, the Carib Indians — whom the Spaniards had long sought to exterminate — emerged as the preeminent suppliers of slaves to all of these European competitors of the Spanish. The Caribs carried out raids at night, surrounding entire villages and carrying off the children. A Spanish report summed up these activities: "It will not be too much to say that the Caribs sell yearly more than three hundred children, leaving murdered in their houses more than four hundred adults, for the Dutch do not like to buy the latter because they well know that, being grown up, they will escape." The victims of this trade could variously wind up in the Spanish haciendas of Trinidad, the English plantations of Jamaica, the Dutch towns of Guyana, or as far west as Quito, Ecuador, where some of them toiled in the textile sweatshops for which this city was famous.[15]

A fourth major slaving ground lay in northern Mexico. "There is nothing more forbidden since the beginning of conquest than Indian slavery," pithily began a report that Queen Mariana received from a member of the Audiencia of Guadalajara, "yet it is very common to see slaves being sold and held in these provinces, especially the Chichimecs of Sinaloa, New Mexico, and Nuevo León." As we have seen, this large and internally fragmented slaving area supplied laborers to the ranches, silver mines, and towns of northern Mexico and as far south as Mexico City.[16]

The last major area of enslavement, and perhaps the largest, was in the Philippines, where Europeans had stumbled on a dazzling world of slaves. "Some are captured in wars that different villages wage against each other," wrote Guido de Lavezaris seven years after the Spanish had first settled in the Philippines, "some are slaves from birth and their origin is not known because their fathers, grandfathers, and ancestors were also slaves," and others became enslaved "on account of minor transgressions regarding some of their rites and ceremonies or for not coming quickly enough at the summons of a chief or some other such thing." Traffickers also targeted the Muslim-dominated islands in the southern part of the archipelago, such as Mindanao and Jolo, or the dark-skinned Negritos or Negrillos — equivalent to sub-Saharan Africans in the eyes of many slavers — who inhabited the islands of Negros, Panay, and Cebu. A variety of slaves were offered in the markets of Manila, and many were transported across the Pacific on the Spanish galleons bound for Mexico and delivered to their owners there.[17]

Slavery was not new in these five major regions of enslavement. All of them possessed traditions of Indian-on-Indian bondage harking back to pre-contact times. Yet with the arrival of white colonists, these varied traditions of captivity were subsumed under the blanket term *esclavitud,* or slavery. Highly ritualized, idiosyncratic, and regional practices of bondage gradually became adapted to suit the needs of white colonists. Thus the traffic of Natives became commodified and expanded geographically. Apaches from New Mexico were sold as far south as central Mexico and eventually into the Caribbean. Mapuches from southern Chile, accustomed to cold or temperate climates, were marched to the port of Valparaíso and transported by ship to the scorching coastal plains of Peru. And Filipinos crossed the Pacific Ocean to reach their final destination in America. These forced migrations spanning hundreds or even thousands of miles, and the slaving networks that made such long-distance transactions possible, were unthinkable before the arrival of Europeans.[18]

## Freeing the Indians

The start of the Spanish antislavery crusade cannot be dated with precision. It began somewhat nebulously as Philip addressed the insurrection in Chile in 1655 and attempted to clear his royal conscience by issuing a raft of orders curtailing the enslavement of Indians. But the ailing king's approach was gradualist and the pace too slow. His correspondence with viceroys, governors, and bishops stretched over months and years and dragged on until his death in 1665. Queen Mariana brought renewed energy to the abolitionist crusade. If we had to choose an opening salvo, it would be the queen's 1667 order freeing all Chilean Indians who had been taken to Peru. Her order was published in the plazas of Lima and required all Peruvian slave owners to "turn their Indian slaves loose at the first opportunity." When the viceroy of Peru learned of this order, he could not hide his disbelief. He praised "the royal clemency of Her Majesty" but went on to write a long letter explaining "the dire consequences" of an order that would "reignite the war in Chile" and allow the freed Indians to "go back to their heathen rituals and preserve their ferocious character." The viceroy's letter conveyed the unmistakable sense that the queen was a well-meaning lady but completely unaware of the realities of the New World.[19]

As she gained experience and confidence, Mariana became bolder. In 1672 she freed the Indian slaves of Mexico, irrespective of their provenance or the circumstances of their enslavement. Her decree of emancipation fell like a thunderbolt on a clear day, as we shall see later in this chapter. Two years later, Mariana seized on an unexpected message from the outside to strike again. In October 1674, the papal nuncio to Spain wrote that "the groans of the poor Indians of Chile, who have been reduced to miserable slavery with various pretexts by the political and military authorities of that kingdom, have reached the ears of the Holy Father," and he wondered why slavery persisted in Chile "in spite of the many and repeated edicts of the most powerful Kings, predecessors of Your Majesty, and of the orders of the Holy Faith." Mariana and her councilors waited only a few weeks to respond, banning all forms of slavery in Chile. They extended the same prohibition to the Calchaquí

Valleys on the other side of the Andes. The campaign to liberate the Indians had kicked into high gear.[20]

With the accession of Charles II to the throne in 1675, the antislavery crusade neared its culmination. In 1676 Charles set free the Indian slaves of the Audiencia of Santo Domingo (comprising not only the Caribbean islands but some coastal areas as well) and Paraguay. Finally, on June 12, 1679, he issued a decree of continental scope: "No Indians of my Western Indies, Islands, and Mainland of the Ocean Sea, under any circumstance or pretext can be held as slaves; instead they will be treated as my vassals who have contributed so much to the greatness of my dominions, and I will remain very vigilant and careful because this is a very grave matter." In a separate order issued on the same day, el Hechizado freed the slaves of the Philippines, thus completing the project initiated by his father and mother of setting free all Indian slaves within the Spanish empire, a clear — if unacknowledged — milestone in the long and checkered history of our human rights.[21]

The most detailed pronouncement of the Spanish monarchy with respect to the enslavement of Indians appears in the monumental compilation of laws of the Spanish colonies known as the *Recopilación de las leyes de Indias,* an attempt at legal systematization that required decades of painstaking work before its publication in 1680. One section of the *Recopilación* is devoted to the freedom of the Indians, emphatically prohibiting their enslavement under all circumstances, even if taken in just wars or ransomed from other Indians. Unlike the French and American revolutionaries of the late eighteenth century, however, the Spanish monarchs did not arrive at the notion of "self-evident" or "inalienable" rights that applied in all cases and at all times. Instead, considering each case on its own merits, they consented on occasion to the enslavement of some of their most recalcitrant subjects. And thus the *Recopilación* prohibited the enslavement of Indians "except when expressly permitted in this same legal compendium." As it turned out, they excluded two groups from their broad royal protection: the inhabitants of the island of Mindanao in the Philippines, "who have taken up the sect of Muhamad and are against our Church and empire," and the Carib Indians, "who attack our settlements and eat human flesh."[22]

In principle, Philip, Mariana, and Charles were free to rule the colonies of the empire as they saw fit. They issued one decree after another, expecting prompt and dutiful compliance, as if they could change everything with the scratch of a pen. We may doubt the efficacy of their method — the Spanish monarchs themselves were not so naive as to think that this would happen in every case — but their direct orders did carry enormous weight. In Trinidad, for example, Governor Sebastián de Roteta wrote to King Charles, "After several pleas and predictions of the utter destruction of this island, of its poverty, and of the benefits to the Indians themselves who are much better off enslaved than eaten by the Carib Indians, and disregarding the accidents and dangers that I faced on account of such a great novelty, my resolve was to comply entirely with Your Majesty's royal orders."[23]

Governor Roteta requested that all residents of the capital city of San José de Oruña, as well as those of other outlying settlements, bring their Indians to the governor's house. Failure to report each slave would be punished with a fine of 100 pesos (roughly the market value of an Indian). Roteta then compiled a list of all the slaves turned over and recorded each one's name, age, place of origin, and former masters before setting them free. He began the list with the thirteen Indians who had served as domestics in his own household. Other prominent residents followed suit: Vicar Alonso de Lerma presented four Indians, Father Andrés de Noriega gave up another four, Sergeant Major Don Pedro Fernández brought ten, and so on. In all, they surrendered 334 slaves. The brief biographical information contained in the slave list provides an inkling of the ravages of the slave trade in the llanos: "Diego, 20 of age, Indian from the missions of Píritu in the province of Cumaná (coast of Venezuela)"; "Teresa, 25, Carib Indian from the Caura in the Orinoco River"; "Pedro, 22, Indian from the Dutch town of Berbis [Berbice] at the mouth of the Orinoco River." The vast majority said they had come from "the town of Casanare," which was nothing but a crude port at the mouth of the Casanare River on the coast of Colombia from which the slaves from the interior were shipped to Trinidad. Many of them were young children when they were enslaved and no longer remembered the names of the towns and communities of their parents.

All of these Natives found themselves suddenly and unexpectedly free. In addition to prying them loose from their masters, Governor Roteta made sure to wipe out their debts, saying that doing otherwise would have been "an even greater burden than leaving them as slaves." As would happen upon the abolition of African slavery in the United States and Britain, some Indian slaves chose to stay with their former masters, but many decided to live independently. They were happy to receive plots of land at some distance from San José de Oruña where they attempted to remake their lives. This group consisted mostly of women and children "in a miserable state" who could not understand one another, as they spoke different languages. Within a few months, however, they had built thirty or forty shacks clustered in two pueblos. Their fate is unknown.

In other parts of the empire, the campaign generated excitement but also tremendous opposition. In Mexico, Fernando de Haro y Monterroso, a member of the Audiencia of Guadalajara, became the moving spirit of the crusade. He publicized the queen's antislavery decrees, heard complaints from mistreated Indians, and wrestled with "powerful personages over the issue of the personal service of the Indians." Nothing in Haro y Monterroso's history as a sober and conscientious lawyer would predict his antislavery ardor. His persistent letter writing to governors and alcaldes (magistrates) secured the release of close to three hundred Indian slaves, as well as five "Chinese" slaves from the Philippines in Guadalajara. Furthermore, buoyed by these early victories, Haro y Monterroso requested the expansion of the campaign. "My actions are not enough if we do not do the same in the Audiencias of Mexico and Guatemala," he wrote to Queen Mariana, "because these provinces [Sinaloa, New Mexico, and Nuevo León] are so large and the Indians have so little spirit that they are often sold in other jurisdictions." The queen and the members of the Council of the Indies were only too glad to dispatch the necessary orders.[24]

While Haro y Monterroso managed the campaign from above, lower-level officials fought a difficult public relations war in western and northern Mexico. In the province of Sinaloa, for instance, they fanned out into towns and villages to inform the public of the liberation orders. In

San Felipe y Santiago, the provincial capital, the alcalde Miguel Calderón himself read aloud the royal decrees on a Sunday morning, immediately after mass as the throng was filing out of church: "From now on all male and female Indians of this province are free." Over the next three weeks, the determined alcalde and his entourage visited the pueblos of Nío, Guasave, Tamazula, and others, "informing them about Her Majesty's commands" and emphasizing both in Spanish and Nahuatl (through translators) that no soldier or friar had a right to make the Indians work without pay.[25]

Predictably, the campaign bred suspicion and hostility. The Jesuits of Sinaloa, for instance, felt unfairly accused and used their influence to blunt the crusade. "The Indians began to lose all sense of shame and became so restless that they killed some cattle that belonged to the padres," one irate missionary reported, "and the ministers are heartbroken to see that the Indians are losing respect and may not attend [church] as it is their obligation." At the same time, the Jesuit fathers attempted to discredit the principal leader of the antislavery crusade in the province, the *protector de indios* Francisco Luque, by questioning his motives. The Society of Jesus had previously accused him of living in concubinage with an Indian woman. The dominant opinion among the Jesuits was that Luque was no beacon of freedom but an opportunist who, on learning of his impending imprisonment on account of his concubinage, had latched onto the antislavery cause to strike back at the Society of Jesus. Soon enough, a series of accusations and counteraccusations made their way to the Audiencia of Guadalajara. In addition to the Jesuits of Sinaloa, the military commanders and other prominent residents closed ranks against the crusade. Haro y Monterroso struggled to keep the campaign alive, but in the end the opposing coalition proved much too strong in Sinaloa.[26]

The antislavery crusade also affected the notorious traffic of New Mexican Indians to the silver mines. Slavers engaged in this trade were so active and brazen that in the 1650s and 1660s, they had actually used the royal carriages — meant to keep New Mexico supplied with manufactured goods and foodstuffs — to transport their captives, in complete and even mocking disregard of the royal regulations. From time to time, colonial authorities in Parral and elsewhere cracked down on such activities. For instance, in 1662 the governor residing in Parral, on learning of the impending arrival of 120 New Mexican slaves, posted notices forbidding the buying or selling of Indians "according to the royal orders and wishes of His Majesty." Any offender risked losing his slave. When the Indians finally arrived in Parral, the governor had them brought out to the central plaza. In plain view of everyone and with the help of an interpreter, he told them that they were free to go wherever they wished and could not be bought or sold by anyone. It must have been a perplexing moment for both the slaves and the slaveholders.[27]

These early crackdowns failed to stop the Indian slave trade, however. Residents continued to buy Indians clandestinely, and slavers continued to supply them. But the crusade certainly made life more difficult for the traffickers. Shortly after this episode in Parral, Juan Manso, a former governor of New Mexico and a prominent trafficker, found himself on the road leading a caravan with more than seventy Indian captives. Heading to the town of San Juan Bautista, in the province of Sonora, Manso sought to prepare the ground by writing to the alcalde, who happened to be an old acquaintance of his, reportedly asking "as a friend to receive permission to enter the town to sell the Indians and as a reward he would deliver to the *alcalde* two or three pieces." The alcalde refused. Manso and his colleagues found similar problems elsewhere. In the mining town of San Miguel, they had to contend with Fray Alonso de Aguilera, a friar known for preaching that Indian slavery was "a grave sin" and for refusing entrance to the church to anyone connected with the traffic of Indians, particularly "the man from New Mexico who sold the Indians."[28]

Queen Mariana and her ministers were outraged when they discovered that the royal carriages had been used to carry New Mexican Indians to the mining centers. Via the Audiencia of Guadalajara and the tireless Haro y Monterroso, the queen ordered that all slave owners of Nuevo León, Nueva Vizcaya, and New Mexico relinquish their Indians within three days. Slaveholders released 202 Indian slaves in Parral and 72 in Zacatecas, and they promised to release more in the future. The queen's orders also brought down the number of Indian slaves exported from New Mexico.[29]

Although the Spanish campaign garnered some successes in places such as Trinidad and northern Mexico, it also underscored the very real limitations of monarchical authority. It worked in places where determined officials such as Governor Roteta and audiencia member Haro y Monterroso upheld the royal decrees. However, in many areas of the empire, the very officials charged with freeing the Indians were also in collusion with the slavers.

In Chile, where slavery had been legal between 1608 and 1674, the links between crown officials and slavers were extremely close—so close that royal and ecclesiastical authorities had become the very guarantors of the slave markets. In the southern town of Concepción, for example, a Jesuit named Pedro de Soto was the man in charge of examining the captives brought into town to determine whether they could be legally enslaved. On December 30, 1668, a raiding party rode into Concepción and presented its human cargo, including a twenty-year-old woman named Coypue and her baby son. Father de Soto pronounced the captives "lawfully enslaved" and issued "the usual certification." A few weeks later, Governor Bernardo de Monleón Cortés, residing in Valdivia, issued a second certification declaring Coypue "to be a slave in perpetuity" and her son "to be subject to *esclavitud de servidumbre* [temporary enslavement] until turning twenty at which time he would be set free." There was nothing unusual about these certifications. Quite the opposite, their formulaic, businesslike tone makes clear that they circulated widely. Setting aside the possible kickbacks implied in these documents (I could find no evidence that Father de Soto or Governor Monleón Cortés received any fees for their certifications, although it is likely that they were somehow compensated for their time and effort), they reveal the absolute complicity of religious and civil authorities in the traffic of Indians.[30]

Such was the state of affairs when Queen Mariana proscribed all forms of Native enslavement in Chile on December 20, 1674. Understandably, Governor Juan Enríquez remained unmoved. In an unusually frank letter to the king, Enríquez wrote that the royal order posed great inconvenience to the owners, depriving them of their slaves and cheating them out of "the great sums of money" they had spent acquiring them. For instance, the decree directed slave owners to seek compensation for their lost property from the sellers. The governor found this provision entirely counterproductive, as it would give rise to "a seedbed of lawsuits and unrest," all of which would be futile, because in the end "the Indians and soldiers who took the slaves" would be held accountable, and they "do not have property with which to pay."[31]

But the governor's most serious objection was over security. He reasoned that since there were "many more slaves than Spaniards," the entire province would be in grave peril: "Having set them free, they would convene gatherings and conspire with the natural hatred that they profess toward the Spaniard . . . and our enemy would derive such an overwhelming advantage that it would lead to our total ruin." Governor Enríquez added sententiously that "the fields will remain fallow and the colonists will not be able to sustain themselves, nor will the ecclesiastics derive their rents and tithes, and everything will collapse, and together with the horror of the enemy, the extreme need and poverty will compel everyone to leave." The tenor of the governor's letter was defiant, but it was consistent with a medieval legal tradition that can be summed up in the curious dictum *"Obedezco pero no cumplo"* (I obey but do not comply). In a vast empire such as Spain's, royal officials used this response to show both their respect for royal authority and the inapplicability of a decree or order to a particular kingdom.[32]

Governor Enríquez used every means at his disposal to avoid compliance. He delayed making public the abolition decree of 1674. When the Audiencia of Santiago required Enríquez to follow through, he responded that "it was up to him [when] to publish and explain the said decree," adding that as governor and captain general of Chile, he was responsible for the security of the kingdom, which had already been threatened by rumors that had prompted some slaves to flee. In the meantime, the governor put in practice what seemed to him a more promising strategy. He ordered all owners to register their Natives, who would no longer be called "slaves" but would merely be held "in deposit." The members of the Audiencia of Santiago believed that this change would render the abolition decree completely ineffectual, "because the Indians thus deposited would remain with their masters and owners in the same terms as before and even worse because they no longer would have access to the Audiencia."[33]

In his 1679 comprehensive ban of all Indian slaves in the hemisphere, Charles II recounted how much his mother had done on behalf of the Indians of Chile and specifically stated that notwithstanding the arguments advanced by Governor Enríquez, he must set the Indians free. The governor refused even then. He clung to the belief that freeing the slaves was tantamount to losing Chile, a kingdom that had been ravaged by a long war with the Mapuches but that nonetheless was necessary to keep because it was "adjacent to the Strait of Magellan which is the best passage to the South Seas [the Pacific Ocean]." The governor had taken the *Obedezco pero no cumplo* dictum as far as it could go, and the Indian slaves in Chile remained in limbo.[34]

The backlash against the campaign to free the Indians was strongest in the Philippines. The royal order of June 12, 1679, specifying that "no native could be held as a slave under any circumstance" and that "all Indians enslaved up to now are hereby set free as well as their children and descendants" caused a great deal of turmoil in Manila. As in Chile, the first recourse in the Philippines was to stall using the traditional formula: "This *cédula* [royal order] is of the kind that must be obeyed but not complied with," observed the members of the Audiencia of Manila, "and we must write back to the Prince so that better informed he could send us his orders." Their displeasure was patent. "When royal orders are so far apart from the natural law, they cannot be executed," wrote an irate audiencia member to Charles II, "and with all due respect, even less so when that natural law is for the benefit of those who have been vanquished in war, for the victors would have a right to take their lives but only choose to take away their liberty."[35]

Yet even in the distant Philippines, there were some courageous crusaders. While waiting for the king's reply, the audiencia's attorney prodded his reluctant colleagues to make public the emancipation decree. The immediate result was a flood of requests: "So many were the slaves who crowded around this Royal Audiencia to claim their liberty that we could not process the multitude of their papers, even when being extracted in brief and summarily." Many slaves around the capital abandoned their masters, who were left "without service," as the archbishop of Manila, Felipe Pardo, observed.[36]

It was in the provinces that the situation became truly critical. Native Filipinos faced total ruin, as they had most of their wealth invested in their slaves. Moreover, the slaves supplied much of the rice and other basic foodstuffs of the islands, and now "agitated and encouraged by the recent laws setting them free [they] went to the extremity of refusing to plant the fields." The greatest threat of all was that "by setting these slaves free, the provinces remote from Manila may be stirred up and revolt, such as those in the Visayas and Nueva Segovia; and in the island of Mindanao, the malcontent Caragas and Subanos might well join forces with the Muslim insurgents there."[37]

In Chile the governor had taken the lead in opposing the Spanish campaign, but in the Philippines all branches of the imperial administration, including the governor, the members of the audiencia, the city council of Manila, members of the military, and the ecclesiastical establishment beginning with the archbishop, sent letters to Charles II requesting the suspension of the emancipation decree. Among the petitioners were Native Filipinos, for whom slavery had been a way of life since time immemorial. "When a principal native walks around town or visits a temple," observed a Spanish chronicler, "it is with great pomp and accompanied by male and female slaves carrying silk parasols to protect their masters from the sun or rain, and the *señoras* go first followed by their servants and slaves, and then come their husbands or father or brothers with their own servants and slaves." The emancipation decree came as a great annoyance to these Native slave owners. Those of Pampanga, a province on the northern shore of Manila Bay, in central Luzon, resolutely opposed the liberation of their slaves, whom they regarded as "the principal nerve and backbone of our strength." They wrote a long letter to the king of Spain explaining how the Spanish galleons were built in the nearby shipyards of Cavite with teak and mahogany supplied in part by slaves: "And while our women together with our slaves plant the seeds, we men are up in the hills cutting wood for the royal yards." By emancipating the slaves of Pampanga, the empire stood to lose its ships.[38]

In the end, the Audiencia of Manila rescinded the king's emancipation decree on September 7, 1682, and replaced it with a new decree: all previously liberated slaves had to return to their duties within fifteen days upon penalty of one hundred lashes and one year in the galleys (forced service as a rower aboard a galley, or ship). Charles II continued to press his case for liberation, but ending formal slavery in the Philippines proved very difficult.[39]

The Spanish campaign washed over the frontiers of the empire in the closing decades of the seventeenth century. But it followed such different trajectories that assessing its overall impact is as daunting as were the goals of the campaign itself. Most tangibly, it brought freedom to a few thousand Native slaves out of some three to six hundred thousand. In Trinidad, northern Mexico, and even Chile and the Philippines, slave owners felt compelled to free some of their slaves. Yet these freedmen constituted but a fraction of the total number of Native slaves in the empire. The crusade thus brought into sharp relief the limits of monarchical power, especially in distant lands and backwaters.

The crusade also had a chilling effect on European slavers. For all of his reluctance to free the slaves, Governor Enríquez of Chile did issue orders prohibiting soldiers from launching slave raids and taking Indian captives after 1676. In the Philippines, where the proslavery coalition had proved much too strong and had defied royal orders, the Audiencia of Manila nonetheless agreed to suspend for a period of ten years the enslavement of Filipino Natives who were in the habit of hiding from Spanish authorities. The monarchy's newfound determination to prosecute and punish slavers surely made their work much riskier.[40]

The Spanish campaign also pushed the slave trade further into the hands of Native intermediaries and traffickers, whether in northern Mexico, Chile, or the llanos of Colombia and Venezuela. The crown had some power over Spanish slavers and authorities, but its control over indigenous slavers was extremely tenuous or nonexistent. The late seventeenth and early eighteenth centuries witnessed the emergence of powerful indigenous polities that gained control of the trade. The Carib Indians consolidated their position in the llanos as the preeminent suppliers of slaves to French, English, and Dutch colonists, consistently delivering hundreds of slaves every year. In the far north of Mexico, the Comanche Indians came to play a similar role and began a breathtaking period of empire building.

Another unanticipated result of the antislavery crusade was that it raised the expectations of Indians throughout the empire, which in the vast majority of cases remained unmet. Their experience of the campaign was marked by dashed hopes, anxiety, and restlessness. In some instances, uncertainty and turmoil culminated in major insurrections, as in the Pueblo Revolt of 1680 in New Mexico.

Although the Spanish campaign often fell short of its stated goals, it foreshadowed future abolitionist movements. In 1833 Great Britain emancipated nearly eight hundred thousand colonial slaves, but emancipation was gradual and equivocal. The "freed" slaves were first subjected to an unpaid "apprenticeship," which gave owners "slavelike" labor for a period of time. Twenty-five years after the launching of the British experiment, many believed that the former slaves were worse off than before. Similarly, at the conclusion of the American Civil War, Congress passed the Thirteenth Amendment to the U.S. Constitution, granting freedom to all slaves within the nation. The subsequent decades, however, witnessed the rise of draconian codes in some states aimed at restricting the rights of African Americans, as well as the enforcement of labor practices that amounted to involuntary servitude. As with the Spanish campaign, these grand emancipation declarations delivered less than they promised.

Yet the alchemical ingredients of emancipation were in the air during the closing decades of the seventeenth century. Right at the time when the Spanish campaign was gaining momentum in 1671–1672, the lord proprietors of the English Carolina colony ordered that "no Indian upon any occasion or pretense whatsoever is to be made a Slave, or without his own consent be carried out of Carolina." It is unclear whether the proprietors derived some inspiration from the Spanish monarchs, but their pronouncement shows that the idea of Indian emancipation was circulating widely in the Americas. Other precocious abolitionists of the era included Francis Daniel Pastorius, a Quaker from Germantown, Pennsylvania. Based on the biblical admonition "Do unto others as you would have them do unto you," Pastorius protested against African slavery in 1688 and urged his contemporaries to avoid discriminating against others, making "no difference of what generation, descent, or Color they are." In 1700 Samuel Sewall, a Boston judge, published an antislavery tract that offered incisive rebuttals of the main arguments traditionally used to justify the enslavement of Africans. Epifanio de Moirans, a French Capuchin missionary living in Havana, probably came closest than anyone else in the seventeenth century to understanding that Indian slavery and African slavery were two sides of the same coin. Europeans "seize the lands of the natives of the Indies once they have killed them or enslaved them," he wrote in *A Just Defense of the Natural Freedom of Slaves* in 1682, "and they also expel the Blacks from their own lands and reduce them to the perpetual slavery of someone shipped to America or transported to Europe."[41]

# 6

## *The Greatest Insurrection Against the Other Slavery*

IN THE SPRING of 1680, the Pueblo Indians of New Mexico devised an audacious plan of liberation. The Pueblo world consisted of some seventy settled, self-contained communities scattered throughout the upper reaches of the Rio Grande and its tributaries. Each pueblo, the Indians secretly agreed, would rise up on the same day and kill its friars and civil authorities, burn down its churches, destroy its Christian images and rosaries, and unmake all Christian baptisms and marriages. In one decisive coup, these Indian villages would erase most traces of the Spanish presence. The Pueblos had by then coexisted with Europeans for eighty-two years, merely three generations. An Indian named Juan Unsuti, who must have been more than one hundred years of age at the time of the insurrection, still recalled "as though it were yesterday when the Spaniards had entered this kingdom." He remembered life before the white intruders and believed, along with many other Natives, that this earlier way of life could be retrieved.[1]

The rebels' greatest strategic insight was that all or nearly all the pueblos should act simultaneously. If they could marshal their vast numerical superiority, they could dislodge the Spaniards swiftly. In 1680 there were about two thousand Spanish colonists scattered throughout New Mexico, perhaps three thousand if we include their indigenous and mestizo dependents. Unlike other provinces with booming silver mines, New Mexico remained a backwater, unable to attract a significant Spanish presence. Those few settlers lived among seventeen thousand Pueblo Indians — thousands more if we include the Apaches, Utes, Navajos, Mansos, and others. In some outlying pueblos, such as the Hopi villages of what is now northeastern Arizona, the European presence was limited to the bare minimum: two Franciscan friars at Oraibi, one at Shungopovi, and one at Awatovi. Killing these isolated friars and destroying their temples could be accomplished with ease. Other pueblos along the Rio Grande had a sprinkling of Spanish families in addition to the local friar. Subduing these settlers would be only marginally more difficult. The greatest resistance could be expected in Río Abajo, around the southern pueblos of Isleta, Alameda, and Sandia — where the Spanish population density was higher — and above all in the Spanish city of Santa Fe, where a thousand Europeans and their dependents resided. As the seat of government, Santa Fe also boasted the *casas reales,* a sturdy building capable of withstanding a siege. But even here, the Spaniards were outnumbered by the surrounding Indians of the Galisteo Basin.

The plan was brilliant, but it hinged on getting the villages to act together while also maintaining secrecy. Taos, the cradle of the plot, lay at the northeastern edge of the Pueblo world. It was 70 miles from Taos to the city of Santa Fe, almost three times the length of a marathon. Messengers on foot would require an entire day and a grueling effort to cover that distance. And Santa Fe was just the start. To communicate with the southern pueblo of Isleta, the couriers would have to run 140 miles, or the equivalent of five marathons; to get to the mesa-top pueblo of Acoma, they would have to journey 180 miles, or almost seven marathons; and to reach the Hopi pueblos, they would have to cover upwards of 300 miles, or twelve marathons. Distance mattered greatly when success depended on dozens of Indian communities rising up on the same day. If some pueblos could not be notified in time or acted too early or too late, the insurrection could easily turn into a prolonged and debilitating war against the Spanish.

Even more challenging than geography were the cultural differences. Although the Spaniards used the generic term *pueblos* to refer

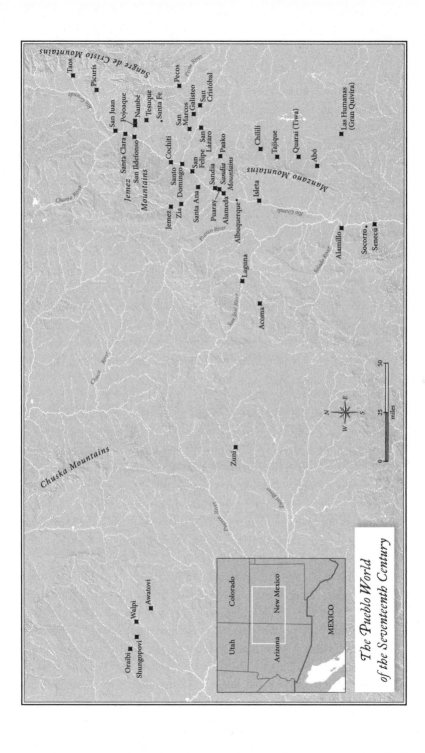

The Pueblo World
of the Seventeenth Century

to all of these compact Native communities, in fact they spoke different languages and possessed different traditions and beliefs. Several of the pueblos spoke related languages of the Tanoan linguistic family, but interspersed among them were villages that spoke Keresan languages such as Cochiti, San Felipe, Zia, and Acoma. Yet other pueblos spoke languages completely unrelated to either the Tanoan or Keresan families, among them Zuni and Hopi. As they plotted the insurrection, the leaders had to bridge ancient linguistic and cultural divisions. Ironically, Spanish already served as a lingua franca and probably facilitated the anti-Spanish conspiracy.

The most formidable obstacle was neither geographic nor cultural but political. The plotters had to secure the participation of each pueblo individually, as there was no political unit larger than the notoriously autonomous village. The Pueblo Indians had wanted to shake off Spanish rule for thirty years, but every time they tried, they either failed to persuade a sufficient number of pueblos or their plans had been revealed. In 1650 the Spaniards had learned about a plan to "destroy the whole kingdom," which had led to nine Native leaders being hanged and to many others being sold as slaves for ten years. A few years later, the ever restless pueblo of Taos had "dispatched two deerskins with some pictures on them signifying conspiracy after their manner," but the plan had been abandoned due to the refusal of some pueblos. In 1665 New Mexico's governor, Fernando de Villanueva, had learned of yet another conspiracy and had some rebels "hanged and burned in the Pueblo of Senecú as traitors and sorcerers." The projected revolt of 1680 was just the latest incarnation of a plan that had been long in the making — and had failed on every previous attempt.[2]

Undaunted, Pueblo leaders gathered during the spring and summer inside underground ceremonial centers, or kivas, where no whites were allowed. Several leaders were involved in the plot, but a fifty-year-old Indian named Po'pay became the most visible head of the movement. He spoke "with a voice that carried above all others," as one witness later recalled. Many Natives believed he was in contact with Poseyemu, a culture hero recognized by all the pueblos and whom the Spaniards believed to be the Devil.[3]

Once the conspiracy got under way, Po'pay would stop at nothing to see the revolt through. He killed his own son-in-law to prevent word of the plot from leaking out. The murder occurred in Po'pay's house — quite likely at his own hands. His unshakable resolve carried a history. Five years earlier, the governor of New Mexico, General Juan Francisco Treviño, had launched a campaign against Native "sorcerers and idolaters." On charges that they had bewitched a friar and some of his relatives at the pueblo of San Ildefonso, forty-seven shamans, including Po'pay, were rounded up and brought to Santa Fe. After an initial investigation, three prisoners were taken to the pueblos where they had allegedly used their supernatural powers — Nambé, San Felipe, and Jemez — and hanged. A fourth committed suicide before his execution. Among the rest, the luckier ones received lashings or were sold into slavery. After a fierce flogging, Po'pay was released. He returned to his native pueblo of San Juan, where he stayed for some time. In the face of more threats, he retired to distant Taos, where he bided his time and planned his revenge.[4]

Po'pay and the other plotters set the date of the uprising for the full moon of August, after the corn had ripened. Since the leaders were medicine men — *hechiceros* (sorcerers) in the damning parlance of Spanish authorities — they used a network of medicine societies to negotiate and forge alliances. Each pueblo possessed a medicine association or society that structured the town's ceremonial life. Only members of this society could take part in its gatherings and rites, although visiting medicine men from other pueblos were welcome. Through the spring and summer of 1680, medicine associations all across the Pueblo world prepared quietly for the insurrection. Young Pueblo Indians captured by the Spaniards during the rebellion claimed that they knew little about the conspiracy but that "among the old men many juntas had been held with the Indians of San Juan, Santa Clara, Nambé, Pojoaque, Jémez, and other nations." In fact, these "old men" were by and large the only ones who knew the details of the plan. Most of the others had only an inkling of the revolutionary changes about to occur.[5]

Sometime in late July or early August, the plotters made their final preparations. Po'pay dispatched runners to dozens of Indian communities. Word traveled on their feet. These runners, keepers of accurate

The tradition of Pueblo running has continued through the centuries. Here two runners compete in the Hopi Basket Dance races in 1919.

information and athletes of astonishing endurance, ran in the summer heat, pushing as far south as Isleta and as far west as Acoma and the distant mesas of the Hopis. In pairs they snaked through canyons and skirted mountains, trying to remain inconspicuous as they covered hundreds of miles with ruthless efficiency. They were sworn to absolute secrecy. And even though they would convey an oral message, they also carried an extraordinary device: a cord of yucca fiber tied with as many knots as there were days before the insurrection. "[Each pueblo] was to untie one knot to symbolize its acceptance," observed one medicine man from San Felipe who was implicated in the plot, "and also to be aware of how many knots were left." The countdown had begun.[6]

In early August, as the knotted cord traveled through the Pueblo lands, the first signs of dissension appeared. Po'pay had failed to notify the Piros, the southernmost pueblos, of the plan, probably anticipating that they would not agree to participate. Worse, as the day of the uprising approached, some pueblos around Santa Fe refused to go through with the plot. They had initially supported the plan even though they would bear the brunt of the fighting against the Spaniards residing in the capital city. But during the waxing moon, they began to reconsider the grave consequences of an all-out war against a foe that possessed firearms and horses. With the moon nearly full and only two knots left in the cord, the Native governors of Tanos, San Marcos, and Ciénega fatefully decided to switch sides. They journeyed to Santa Fe to denounce the conspiracy and, in a more personal and insidious betrayal, alert the Spanish authorities to the whereabouts of two Indian runners, Nicolás Catúa and Pedro Omtuá, who were still making the rounds with the knotted cord.

Uncharacteristically, the Spanish governor and captain general of New Mexico, Antonio de Otermín, sprang into action. Since he had arrived in New Mexico two years earlier, Governor Otermín had permitted a clique of influential locals to run the province in his name. He could not be bothered with the drudgery of government. Instead, he pursued his own economic interests with abandon, granting a free hand to his *maestre de campo* (chief of staff), a wily New Mexican named Francisco Xavier. On August 9, however, upon receiving word of the Pueblo conspiracy, Otermín and his inner circle came alive.[7]

The governor first ordered a detachment to intercept the two runners. Catúa and Omtuá were brought to him and confirmed that all the pueblos would revolt. Otermín and his close advisers sent warnings to the nearby towns, and the governor took steps to protect Santa Fe. He distributed firearms to the residents, posted soldiers in the main church to prevent its desecration, and made preparations in the casas reales to withstand a siege.

After learning that their plan had been discovered, however, the Indian leaders shrewdly moved up the date of the rebellion to the next day, August 10. Runners were probably sent out again to deliver a most urgent message: strike now.

## Extraordinary Days

The revolt swept throughout the kingdom of New Mexico on August 10–11, destroying houses, ranches, and churches and killing some four hundred men, women, and children, or about twenty percent of New Mexico's Spanish population. The rebels did not engage in wanton destruction or indiscriminate killing. Po'pay and the other leaders gave them clear instructions. They were to destroy missions, churches, and all manner of Christian paraphernalia: "break up and burn the images of the holy Christ, the Virgin Mary, and the other saints, the crosses, and everything pertaining to Christianity." To wash away Christian baptisms, they were urged to "plunge into the rivers and wash themselves with amole, which is a root native to the country, washing even their clothing." And to unmake their Christian marriages, the revolting Indians were to "separate from the wives whom God had given them in marriage and take whom they desired." By many accounts, the rebels did as they were told. In the pueblo of Santo Domingo, a group of Indians descended on the church, killed the three missionaries, and dumped their bodies in the nave. In the pueblo of Sandia, farther south, the rebels destroyed the choir stalls, defecated on the main altar, and sacked all the paintings and religious objects in the church and the sacristy. They left a statue of Saint Francis but chopped off his arms with an ax. They also flogged a large statue of Jesus Christ on the cross.[8]

The rebels also targeted priests and friars. Twenty-one out of thirty-three Franciscans, or about two-thirds of all the friars living in New Mexico, were killed. Those living in outlying communities were the most vulnerable. In Jemez, for example, a throng of Indians surprised Fray Juan de Jesús in the middle of the night. They took him out to the cemetery, which had been lit with many candles, stripped him, and forced him to ride a pig while they beat and mocked him. Then Fray Juan himself was made to get down on all fours, and the assailants took turns riding and whipping him. After the friar had been thoroughly humiliated and could no longer move, the Indians killed him by striking him with war clubs.[9]

Similar fates awaited the missionaries living in the Hopi pueblos of present-day Arizona. At Oraibi, the attackers surrounded the friary in the wee hours of the morning. They broke down the door, to find the room's only occupant — and possibly the only Spaniard living at Oraibi at the time — huddled in a corner. The Hopis promptly slashed the friar's throat, extracted his heart, and dumped his body down the mesa. In nearby Shungopovi, Fray Joseph de Trujillo did not give up without a fight. After exchanging angry words with many Natives surrounding his house, he grabbed a sword and cut down the first Indian who broke in. The embattled friar was then surrounded and disarmed. He spent his last moments dangling over a fire, his hands tied behind his back, until his body was burned completely. Fray Trujillo was a veteran missionary who had served in the Philippines and New Mexico, two of the most exposed frontiers in the Spanish empire, and had repeatedly expressed his desire to become a martyr. In the summer of 1680, he finally succeeded.[10]

Religion was clearly a flashpoint of the conflict. Throughout the seventeenth century, missionaries had made every effort to suppress "idolatry" and "superstition" and to subdue the Native medicine men, who had become their main competitors and antagonists. For their part, the medicine men had retained their traditional beliefs and clandestinely practiced their religion inside kivas. When Po'pay descended victorious from his perch in Taos and toured the pueblos, he commanded the Indians to return to their old traditions and beliefs, declaring that Jesus Christ and the Virgin Mary had died.[11]

Yet earthly reasons also impelled the rebels to strike at the Spaniards, as the unfolding of the conflict makes abundantly clear. Even as the Indians attacked churches, missions, and remote ranches, Santa Fe remained unconquered. Slowly rebels began massing on the outskirts of the Spanish city. Within a week, some five hundred warriors from the pueblos of Pecos, Galisteo, San Cristóbal, San Lázaro, San Marcos, and Ciénega gathered less than three miles to the south of the central plaza. Armed with bows and arrows and stones, they began advancing, while burning cornfields and looting the outlying houses. The rebels made it known that "they were coming to kill the governor and all the Spaniards."[12]

Since the start of the rebellion, the Spanish residents of Santa Fe had congregated in the casas reales in the central plaza. In the seventeenth century, the plaza of Santa Fe, an unkempt swampy area shaded by large trees, was roughly twice as large as it is today. Somewhere in this large quadrangle (archaeologists do not know exactly where) stood the Spanish stronghold. It was not a spacious building. Thus the atmosphere must have been infernal as a thousand refugees huddled together in anticipation of the attack, crowding every room while improvising beds, latrines, and cooking areas. Despite the continuous wailing of children and women, the "war whoops" from the outside were audible.[13]

On the morning of August 15, five days into the rebellion, an Indian fully decked out for war rode into the plaza and stopped in front of the casas reales. Indians were barred from riding horses and bearing arms, yet this man had arrived on a horse, wearing a protective leather jacket, and carrying a harquebus, a sword, and a dagger — all Spanish weapons. As a further provocation, he wore a sash of red taffeta that had been looted from the church in Galisteo. Governor Otermín and some of his soldiers recognized the rider as a Pueblo chief who spoke Spanish and was known among the colonists as Juan. The governor came out of the building for a parley. It was only then that Otermín finally heard what the rebels wanted. Juan requested that "all classes of Indians held by the Spanish be given back." He also demanded "that his wife and children be given up to him" and that "all the Apache men and women whom the Spaniards had captured in war be turned over to them, inasmuch as some Apaches who were among them were asking for them."[14]

Governor Otermín, who had been in New Mexico for two and a half years, must have heard Juan's demands with trepidation. Like his predecessors, Otermín had been involved in the traffic of Indians. The antislavery crusade of the early 1670s had temporarily reduced the number of New Mexican Indians exported to the silver mines. But the slave trade had bounced back later in the decade, and Otermín had been a major reason for this resurgence. In 1678 and 1679, the new governor had dispatched slave-bearing caravans from New Mexico and offered safe passage to other traffickers, "inviting everyone to go together in a convoy," as one witness put it. Although it is tempting to portray Otermín as a grasping, covetous governor, in reality he was no worse than other seventeenth-century governors throughout the Spanish colonies, all of whom had to purchase their offices from the crown. Not only did they have to finance their positions up front, but they also had to be content with only half their yearly salary, as the crown kept the other half in the form of a special tax called the *media anata*. To recoup their considerable investments, governors had little choice but to aggressively pursue all economic opportunities within their jurisdictions, including the trafficking of Indians.[15]

Otermín was still an outsider governor with little knowledge of the kingdom that he was supposed to rule. After the parley, he must have gone back inside the casas reales to discuss the rebels' demands with his closest collaborators, including his *maestre de campo*, Francisco Xavier, "to whom the governor had granted all of his authority and power." It was Xavier who may well have introduced Otermín to the slave trade and acted as his partner. Sources describe Xavier as "a man of bad faith, avaricious, and sly," who had driven the Indians of New Mexico "to the ultimate exasperation." When the rebels had surrounded the Spanish stronghold, they had reportedly shouted, "Give us Francisco Xavier, for whom we have revolted, and we will return to peace as before."[16]

Xavier evinced a rare combination of religious intolerance and ruthless ambition. His zealotry was not new. Nearly twenty years earlier, he had started complaining about the kachina dances performed by the Indians of Isleta, San Ildefonso, and other pueblos. Even though colonial authorities had authorized the dances, Xavier remained adamant that they were inspired by the Devil. On that occasion, his misgivings had little effect. But fourteen years later, after Xavier had ascended to secretary of New Mexico, he was able to act on his strict religious sensibilities. He presided over the infamous 1675 campaign against "Indian sorcerers and idolaters" and the roundup of Po'pay and forty-six other medicine men. He personally oversaw their trials and punishments. Unquestionably, Po'pay regarded Xavier as his personal enemy.[17]

As a long-standing and notorious participant in the Indian slave trade, Xavier had made other Indian enemies, particularly among the Apaches. Xavier's signature appears on a 1666 receipt that required him to furnish "two Christian boys of the Apache nation, one of them ten years old and named Baltazar, and the other eight or nine and named Andrés," to Governor Fernando de Villanueva (1665–1668). Shortly before the outbreak of the Pueblo Revolt of 1680, he had welcomed a group of Apaches who had arrived in the pueblo of Pecos to trade. (Pecos had long been a trading post linking the Plains Indians living to the northwest and Spanish New Mexico.) The unsuspecting Apaches entered the pueblo ready to do business, but in spite of numerous assurances, Spanish soldiers promptly imprisoned them on Xavier's orders. He distributed some of the Apaches in Pecos and sent most of them to Parral to be sold as slaves. It is likely that these were the Apaches whom Chief Juan requested from Governor Otermín during their parley.[18]

Otermín, Xavier, and other members of the ruling elite faced a stark decision: comply with the rebels' demand to release "all classes of Indians held by the Spanish" or resist. The first choice would have been the more sensible, as it would have relieved the Spaniards of the difficult conditions in their stronghold and allowed them to evacuate Santa Fe unencumbered by unwilling prisoners. Perhaps it would have paved the way for further peace negotiations. But the governor was not inclined to compromise. He questioned Chief Juan's motives, arguing that it was not true that the Apaches were allied with the Pueblos (in this the governor was misinformed) and that "these parleys were intended solely to obtain his wife and children and to gain time for the arrival of the other rebellious nations to join them and besiege us."[19]

To understand the unwillingness of Otermín, Xavier, and many other colonists to part with their Indian slaves, one has to examine who the people inside the casas reales were. We do not have a full list, but we have an excellent proxy. A few weeks after the siege of Santa Fe, Governor Otermín conducted a muster "of all the soldiers and persons who are here today . . . so that it may be known how many men bearing arms are here at present who can enter the royal service, and how many people may be dead at the hands of the enemy." In addition to the thousand people who took refuge in the casas reales, the muster list includes five hundred survivors from Río Abajo who later joined the contingent from Santa Fe. In other words, the muster list accounts for every surviving "Spaniard" and his or her "dependents," as well as their animals and weapons. It is an extremely rare and valuable snapshot of frontier society.[20]

In round numbers, the muster list includes a total of fifteen hundred persons. If we could have observed them standing in line, the first thing that would have caught our attention would have been the children. Perhaps two-thirds of those mustered were minors. We would also have been immediately struck by the groupings. Instead of an undifferentiated line, the survivors would have arranged themselves into extended families. Seven of these clans included dozens of servants/slaves and herds of twenty, thirty, or up to eighty horses. Thomé Domínguez de Mendoza, for instance, reported that the enemy had robbed his cattle, houses, and crops and killed "thirty-eight Spanish persons, all being his daughters, grandchildren, sons-in-law, sisters, nephews, nieces, and sisters-in-law as is common knowledge." But this New Mexican patriarch still passed muster with fifty-five persons, including his wife, four married sons with eight children in their families, "male and female servants, young and old," and thirty horses. Governor Otermín's circumstances were similar. He traveled with an entourage of thirty "servants, Spaniards, negroes, and Indians" and thus passed muster with "thirty attendants and servants."[21]

Standing next to these clans, we would have noticed some twenty families not quite as rich as the governor but still well-off — mostly the families of ranchers and military officers — each of which possessed half a dozen to a dozen servants and some horses. The rest were poor New Mexicans: Indians from central Mexico, convicts sent to New Mexico to serve out their sentences, widows with large progenies, rank-and-file soldiers, and others. Yet even some of them had servants. Apolinar Martín passed muster "on foot, naked, and without arms." The muster secretary thought it appropriate to add that he was "extremely poor." And yet Martín declared three servants. Similarly, Catalina de Zamora was a widow who passed muster with four grown nieces, "all on foot and extremely poor." But she reported five servants. And a convict named Cristóbal de Velasco listed his wife, a small child, and two female servants.

By the time of the muster, the Spanish colonists had already lost two or three hundred servants to the rebellion. Some of these servants had fled in the early days of the insurrection, while others had been carried off by the attackers or had died in battle. But the colonists retained many more. In rough numbers, one thousand Spaniards owned five hundred servants, collectively worth a fortune of about 50,000 pesos. Indeed, it was the Spaniards' pervasive take in the human loot of New Mexico that had brought them to their bloody stand.[22]

Back in Santa Fe, Governor Otermín, his close circle of advisers, and many other colonists, defying almost all logic, refused to surrender their captives and prepared for a long fight. But with the passing of each day, their situation became more desperate. Following the ineffective parley, and as the Pueblo warriors began advancing from the south toward the Spanish stronghold, Spaniards and Indians fought in alleyways and adobe houses in the barrios to the south of Santa Fe. Having barely stopped this advance, Spanish soldiers learned on August 17 that another contingent of Indians from Taos and Picurís had entered Santa Fe from the north, setting up camp on a strategic elevation not far from the casas reales. The Indian attackers now numbered about two thousand. "They surrounded us from all parts," wrote a chronicler, "and set fire to the main church and to other houses and took up positions in several buildings." The rebellious Indians also managed to cut off the water supply to the casas reales.[23]

The Spaniards' situation was becoming untenable, but they held out for a few more days. At last, on August 21, "reduced to the extremity of dying inside or going out to fight," the Spaniards made their move. A stream of one thousand people flowed out of the casas reales and straggled southward, fleeing for their lives. The adult males bearing arms numbered only about a hundred. They were posted at the front and rear and along the flanks of the crowd of women, children, servants, and animals. The armed men had to not only fend off Indian attacks from the outside but also guard against escape attempts from the inside. The first day, the refugees walked merely one league, or about three miles. They spent the night in a broad field just outside town where they could easily spot any approaching warriors. The rebels were now in complete control of Santa Fe.

Over the next few weeks of their journey, the Spaniards got their first look at the devastation in the wake of the insurrection. They passed through abandoned pueblos and passed burned churches and ranches with strewn corpses as they moved southward, following the banks of the Rio Grande. The victorious rebels followed the retreating Spaniards but left their way unimpeded. Within two months, the Spanish had abandoned the kingdom of New Mexico and would not be back for twelve years. The Pueblo Revolt of 1680 had succeeded.

## Explaining the Insurrection

For more than three centuries, the Pueblo Revolt of 1680 has fascinated churchmen, public officials, booksellers, scholars, and the public at large. This was "the secret rebellion that drove the Spaniards out of the Southwest," as the subtitle of one book proudly proclaims. But what motivated the Indians to risk their lives in an uncertain insurrection in the first place? What compelled them to bloody their hands torturing and killing?[24]

Ever since the seventeenth century, religion has been offered as the primary driver of the Indians' acts. Indeed, Spaniards who lived through the rebellion pointed their fingers at the Devil. We may scoff at such an explanation, but seventeenth-century Christians fervently believed that the Devil roamed in the world and mingled with humans. Satan preyed especially on the weak. In Europe he tempted credulous women and turned them into witches. In fact, witchcraft trials peaked in Europe and North America in the seventeenth century (the famous Salem witch trials took place in 1692). In the New World, the Devil had a field day among unconverted or recently converted Indians. Particularly on remote frontiers, he tricked them into performing human sacrifices, adoring idols, and rejecting Christianity. Throughout the seventeenth century, northern Mexico was rocked by rebellions reportedly inspired by the Devil. In regard to an anti-Spanish movement that broke out in northwestern Mexico in 1601, one Jesuit wrote, "These old Indians were the principal instigators of the uprising, because by means of a diabolical spell they made their people believe the Christian Spaniards were against them." At midcentury a priest in Durango similarly declared that Indians "are subject to the influences of shamans, instruments of the devil, who incite their listeners to rebel and commit atrocities." In such a charged spiritual landscape, Po'pay's machinations in New Mexico could only have been interpreted as the Devil's latest ploy to roll back the kingdom of Jesus Christ on earth.[25]

A much later generation of Anglo-American writers of the Southwest arrived at a different interpretation of the Pueblo Revolt. Historians and authors of the late nineteenth century rejected the preternatural explanations advanced by their colonial predecessors. Yet they continued to place religion at the core of the insurrection. In their view, the fanaticism and zealotry of Spanish church officials drove the Indians of New Mexico to the breaking point. The verdict of L. Bradford Prince, governor of the territory of New Mexico from 1889 to 1893, is quite typical: "Religious feeling was a very strong element among the causes which led to the revolution," Prince wrote in 1883, "and a bitter hatred of the Christianity of the Spaniards was evinced in every act during the struggle."[26]

The most influential articulator of this view was the San Francisco–based collector extraordinaire and entrepreneur Hubert Howe Bancroft. A far cry from a self-effacing historian, Bancroft was the imperious CEO of H. H. Bancroft & Co., the largest bookselling concern in the western United States. This transplanted easterner progressed rapidly from book dealer to collector to author. His approach to history writing was, like much else he did, industrial. He set up a literary workshop that employed more than six hundred individuals. These assistants not only cataloged his vast collection of books and documents but also took notes and assembled data on the known "facts" of a particular area and period, composing preliminary texts of their findings. Bancroft went over these drafts, revised them (sometimes minimally), and published them under his name. Bancroft's operation published thirty-nine hefty volumes offering a grand historical panorama of Central America, Mexico, the

American Southwest, and the Pacific coast as far north as Alaska. One of his tomes dealt with New Mexico and naturally included a section on the Pueblo Revolt of 1680.[27]

Using the most formidable array of seventeenth-century documents from New Mexico assembled up to that time, Bancroft surveyed half a century of New Mexico's history prior to the uprising. He regretted that he could not offer a "continuous and complete narrative" (a mild reproach to his helpers, no doubt). Despite these gaps in his knowledge, Bancroft anchored his narrative firmly on Spanish Christianization efforts and Pueblo resistance. As he summed up the process, the Spanish friars "worked zealously to stamp out every vestige of the native rites; and the authorities had enforced the strictest compliance with Christian regulations, not hesitating to punish the slightest neglect, unbelief, or relapse into paganism." As for the Pueblos, Bancroft ventured the opinion that they "seem to have been more strongly attached than most American tribes to their aboriginal faith, and they had secretly continued so far as possible the practice of the old forms of worship." The stage was set and the conclusion inescapable: the clash of 1680 rested, "largely, on religious grounds."[28]

Scholars of the past thirty years have revised Bancroft's interpretation. Their explanations of the Pueblo Revolt combine multiple causes, including short-term disruptions such as famines and epidemics and long-term or structural factors such as religious antagonism. But while all leading explanations are now multicausal, they continue to emphasize the religious character of the revolt. Historian Ramón Gutiérrez has advanced what remains the most convincing formulation of the religious thesis. According to Gutiérrez, in the early decades of New Mexico's colonization, the Pueblo Indians accepted Christianity peacefully, or at least did not actively oppose it. But starting in the 1640s, they grew disillusioned. As their lives deteriorated markedly due to famine, illness, and intensified raids from Apaches, the Pueblos came to believe that the god of the missionaries was unable to protect them. Gutiérrez writes, "The Franciscans were no longer the supermen they had once seemed. The novelty of their gifts had worn off and their magic had proven ineffectual in producing rain, health, prosperity, and peace." Pueblo confidence was further undermined in the late 1660s when the province suffered a four-year famine, followed by an epidemic in 1671. The Natives increasingly shunned Catholicism and turned to traditional shamans for guidance and relief. In turn the missionaries of New Mexico grew alarmed at these developments. For two generations, they had worked hard to Christianize the Pueblos. They had built more than forty churches and chiseled a community of believers out of the desert. Now, suddenly, the entire spiritual enterprise appeared to be in jeopardy. The missionaries felt betrayed and responded "as any father would have with disobedient children," Gutiérrez tells us. "Punishments began."[29]

What makes this picture of the Indians' disillusionment leading to increased Spanish severity especially convincing is that plenty of evidence of religion-inspired oppression and cruelty exists in the available documentation. Some duress and occasional corporal punishments are to be expected on a remote frontier where a handful of missionaries attempted to enforce religious orthodoxy on recalcitrant communities. The reality, however, was far worse. Near impunity permitted friars to extract unpaid Native labor. Governor Bernardo López de Mendizábal (1659–1661) flatly accused the missionaries of exploiting the Indians under the pretense that it was "for the temples and divine worship" and forcing "all the Indians of the pueblos, men as well as women, to serve them as slaves." Some of the friars also abused their privileged position to procure sex. Oral traditions from the Hopi villages — which are corroborated at least in part by documentary information — detail how some friars at Oraibi and Shungopovi would send the men to fetch water in distant places so that the friars could be with the women during their absence.[30]

Most threatening of all was the missionaries' capacity to torture and kill in the name of God. The worst offender was the aptly named Salvador de Guerra, a friar who terrorized the Hopi pueblos during the 1650s. Like other friars working in near-complete isolation, he lived with a concubine in spite of his vows of celibacy. He also forced the Indians to weave cotton *mantas*, setting minimum quotas they had to meet to avoid punishment. And when it came to fighting the Devil, Friar Guerra had few peers. Not only did he beat suspected idolaters and hechiceros, but he also soaked them with turpentine and set them on fire. In one instance, a witness reported, a luckless Native who survived the turpentine treatment "got up, and desiring to go by a certain road where there is a tank of water to throw himself into it, took another road which leads to Santa Fe, and Fray Salvador de Guerra mounted a horse, thinking that the Indian was going to complain to the government, and followed him, and rode over him with the horse until he killed him."[31]

There is no question that the religious thesis of the Pueblo Revolt explains a great deal. But, like all historical explanations, it hinges on highlighting certain episodes and personalities while de-emphasizing others. The religious character of the movement is so striking and seductive that it overshadows the material motivations of the uprising, which often appear as mere "catalysts" or "triggers" subordinated to the more fundamental religious cleavage.

Especially in the past decade, the research on Indian slavery/servitude has opened new vistas on the turning points of the Pueblo Revolt. New understanding of rising levels of exploitation and enslavement as New Mexico became integrated into the silver economy of northern Mexico — a story told earlier in this book — indicates that it was this pressure, rather than a burst of inquisitorial activity, that led to the growing turmoil in the years leading up to 1680. Surely factors other than "the other slavery" were causes of the rebellion: long-simmering religious animosities, famine, and illness made the mix even more volatile. But rising levels of exploitation, which can be documented in the archival record, belong at the core of this story. In the course of the seventeenth century, the silver economy expanded, and it was New Mexico's misfortune to function as a reservoir of coerced labor and a source of cheap products for the silver mines. It did not take the bad behavior of too many Spanish governors, friars, and colonists — compelling Indians to carry salt, robbing their pelts, locking them up in textile sweatshops, and organizing raiding parties to procure Apache slaves — to bring about widespread animosity, resentment, and ultimately rebellion.[32]

The case of the Pueblo Revolt as a rebellion against the other slavery rests on three types of evidence. The first comprises testimonies of Pueblo rebels. The Spaniards had few opportunities to learn about the causes of the rebellion during their hasty exodus from New Mexico. A year and a half would pass before they were able to gather additional intelligence. At the end of 1681, Governor Otermín led a group of Spanish soldiers and colonists back to New Mexico. During this foray, they were able to capture nine Pueblo Indians, who were brought before the governor for questioning. Their depositions were recorded over a two-week period in late December 1681 and early January 1682. Understandably, Pueblo captives were vague when asked pointedly about the "cause and reasons that led all the Indians of this kingdom to rise up." Still, out of the eight extant testimonies, four contain concrete references to Spanish exploitation. An eighty-year-old Indian from San Felipe named Pedro Naranjo, for example, declared that in the wake of the insurrection, the Indians had remained "free from the work requested by the friars and the other Spaniards which they could no longer bear, and that this was the real reason and legitimate cause that they had to rise up." A twenty-year-old *ladino* (Hispanicized) Indian named Joseph similarly declared that "the causes generally given were the ill treatment and abuses that the Indians received from the current *secretario* Francisco Xavier and the *maestro de campo* Alonsso Garcia and the *sargentos mayores* [sergeant majors] Luis de Quintana and Diego López because they had hit them and taken away what they had and made them work without paying them anything." Two other prisoners, brothers Juan and Francisco Lorenzo, also named Francisco Xavier as a major reason for the rebellion. These few surviving testimonies may be too slender a reed on which to hang an interpretation of the overall rebellion, but they are very suggestive nonetheless.[33]

The timing of the insurrection also lends credence to the theory that Indian slavery was the cause of the rebellion. As already noted, the Pueblo Revolt was long in the making. On at least three different occasions between 1650 and 1680, the Pueblos had attempted to launch a unified movement against their Spanish overlords. Yet this period of Pueblo insurgency is puzzling because it was characterized by relative demographic stability. A few sources mention famines and epidemics, particularly toward the late 1660s. But this famine/pestilence episode does not jibe with the upheaval of 1680. At least to my knowledge, there is not a single testimony claiming that the Pueblos rebelled in 1680 or 1681 because of famine or pestilence. However, this thirty-year period of Pueblo unrest corresponds admirably with the deepening of commercial ties between New Mexico and the silver mines of northern Mexico. Since its founding in 1631, Parral had attracted resources and peoples to its flourishing mines. As we have seen, New Mexican officials and private citizens responded to these new economic opportunities by stepping up the seizure of Indian products, pressing Natives into New Mexican textile sweatshops, or raiding Apache rancherías to procure slaves. The Indian slave trade blossomed during the 1650s, 1660s, and 1670s — precisely when the Pueblo Indians were plotting against the Spaniards.[34]

The last body of evidence that suggests that the Pueblo Revolt was triggered by labor coercion has to do with the ethnic and geographic scope of the insurrection. Though generally known as the Pueblo Revolt of 1680, the movement in fact spread far beyond New Mexico and came to involve not only Pueblos but also the Apaches, Mansos, Conchos, Sumas, Pimas, Janos, Salineros, Tobosos, and many other groups. Some scholars even refer to this multiethnic insurrection as the Great Northern Rebellion. But regardless of labels, the geography of the revolts of the 1680s and early 1690s is quite intriguing. Broadly speaking, the rebellion spread along two corridors, one running due south from New Mexico into the El Paso–Janos area then on through central and southern Chihuahua "to the doors of El Parral and La Vizcaya," and the other extending west into what is today Arizona and Sonora to the mines of San Juan Bautista, Opodepe, and Teuricachi. What these regions and their indigenous inhabitants had in common was that they had all been subjected to the gravitational pull of the silver economy. The geography of the rebellion maps exceedingly well onto the slaving corridors leading to Parral.[35]

Explaining the motives of peoples in times that are remote from our own is a dicey business. And, of course, rebellions are seldom triggered by a single cause. Still, it is remarkable how writers and historians

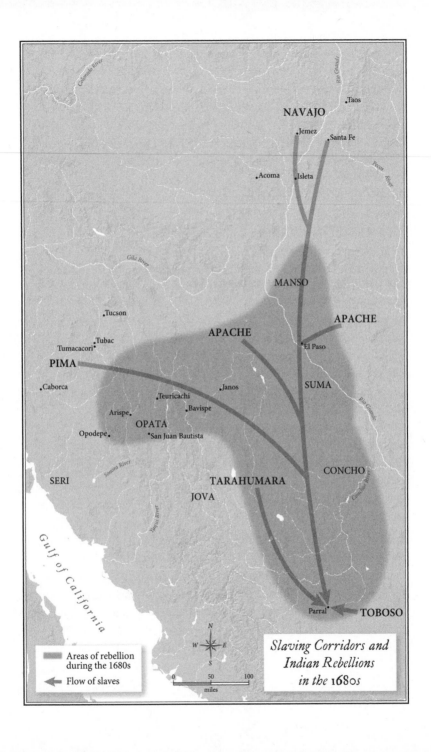

Colorado River

Rio Grande

.Taos

NAVAJO

.Jemez

.Santa Fe

.Acoma    Isleta

Pecos River

Gila River

MANSO

.Tucson

APACHE

APACHE

.El Paso

.Tubac

Tumacacori.

PIMA

.Janos

SUMA

.Caborca

.Teuricachi

Rio Grande

Arispe.    .Bavispe

OPATA

Opodepe.    .San Juan Bautista

SERI

Sonora River

CONCHO

Conchos River

TARAHUMARA

JOVA

Yaqui River

Gulf of California

N
W    E
S

Parral.    TOBOSO

0    50    100
miles

Slaving Corridors and
Indian Rebellions
in the 1680s

Areas of rebellion
during the 1680s
Flow of slaves

have accorded Indian slavery so modest a role in their explanations of the Pueblo Revolt. Without a doubt, however, the rebellions that raged through much of the 1680s and 1690s redefined labor relations in northern Mexico. Indians in New Mexico, Chihuahua, Durango, Sonora, and Coahuila challenged slavery and forced important changes in the ways the traffic of humans was conducted in the following century.[36]

# 7

# Powerful Nomads

NATIVE AMERICANS WERE involved in the slaving enterprise from the beginning of European colonization. At first they offered captives to the newcomers and helped them develop new networks of enslavement, serving as guides, guards, intermediaries, and local providers. But with the passage of time, as Indians acquired European weapons and horses, they increased their power and came to control an ever larger share of the traffic in slaves.

Their rising influence was evident throughout North America. In the Carolinas, for instance, English colonists took tens of thousands of Indian slaves and shipped many of them to the Caribbean. In the period between 1670 and 1720, Carolinians exported more Indians out of Charleston, South Carolina, than they imported Africans into it. As this traffic developed, the colonists increasingly procured their indigenous captives from the Westo Indians, an extraordinarily expansive group that conducted raids all over the region. Anthropologist Robbie Ethridge has coined the term "militaristic slaving societies" to refer to groups like the Westos that became major suppliers of Native captives to Europeans and other Indians. The French in eastern Canada had a similar experience. They procured thousands of Indian slaves during the seventeenth and eighteenth centuries, but as they moved away from Quebec and Montreal and into the Great Lakes region and upper Mis-

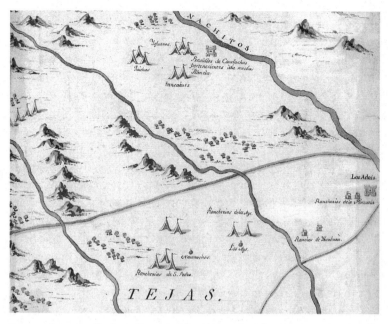

One can learn much about frontier regions through maps. José de Urrutia's 1769 map of northern Mexico, for example, identifies towns, missions, ranches, and presidios — unmistakable evidence of Europe's march into the region — while also making clear that Indian nations (rancherías) held sway over vast swaths of this territory. In the eighteenth century, the frontier was still a patchy grid of European enclaves overlaid on a sea of indigenous peoples.

sissippi basin, they encountered a world of bondage they could scarcely comprehend, let alone control. Indians preyed on one another to get captives whom they offered to the French in exchange for guns and ammunition and to forge alliances. Throughout North America, Natives adapted to the sprawling slave trade and sought ways to profit from it.[1]

The most dramatic instances of Indian reinvention occurred in what is now the American Southwest. Multiple factors propelled Indians of this region to become prominent traffickers. The royal antislavery activism of the Spanish crown and the legal prohibitions against Indian slavery dissuaded some Spanish slavers of northern Mexico, leaving a void that others filled. Moreover, the Indian rebellions of the seventeenth century that culminated in the Great Northern Rebellion restricted the flow of Indian slaves from some regions and led to the opening of new slaving grounds, creating new opportunities. Most important, the diffusion of horses and firearms accelerated at this time, giving some Indians the means to enslave other people. Thus new traffickers, new victims, and new slaving routes emerged in the seventeenth and eighteenth centuries. Some Native communities experienced a process of "deterritorialization," as Cecilia Sheridan has called it, becoming unmoored from their traditional homelands, fusing with other groups, and reinventing themselves as mobile bands capable of operating over vast distances. They made a living by trading the spoils of war, including horses and captives.[2]

The Pueblo Revolt of 1680 succeeded in expelling the Spaniards from New Mexico. When the colonists returned in 1692, the world as they had known it had changed during their twelve-year absence. The returning Spaniards noticed that the Pueblo Indians had forged closer ties with the surrounding nomads. When the Spaniards approached the pueblo of Jemez, for example, they were greeted by a mixed force of Pueblos and Apaches. Once inside the pueblo, the Spanish leader, Diego de Vargas, spotted Apache warriors walking about freely. Other Spaniards observed much the same situation in various parts of the Pueblo world. At the Hopi pueblo of Walpi, in northeastern Arizona, several Indian nations made a show of force. "Some of them were of the Ute nation," Vargas recorded in his diary, "and others were Apaches and Coninas [Havasupais], and all of them were the allies and neighbors of the Hopi pueblos." The colonists thus encountered a tangle of newly forged alliances. Each pueblo had become like the hub of a wheel connected through the spokes to various bands of hunter-gatherers. The easternmost pueblos of Pecos and Taos befriended Apache bands that lived farther to the north and east, while the pueblos of Acoma and Jemez, in western New Mexico, developed alliances with groups of Navajos and Utes.[3]

Before the arrival of Europeans, such interactions had been common. In the period between 1450 and 1600, Pueblo Indians had enjoyed close trading relationships with outlying nomads. In spite of their strikingly different lifestyles, town dwellers and nomads complemented each other well. The Pueblos exchanged corn and ceramics with hunter-gatherers for bison meat and hides: carbohydrates for protein, and pottery for hides. The Spaniards' arrival in 1598 severely reduced this trade. The Pueblos now had to surrender their agricultural surplus to encomenderos and missionaries and therefore retained few, if any, items to exchange. The archaeological record shows fewer bison bones and bison-related objects among the Pueblos during the seventeenth century. Additionally, the Spaniards launched raids against outlying hunter-gatherers, further disrupting Pueblo-Plains trading networks. With the Spanish exodus in 1680, the Pueblos had a chance to reestablish their old ties with the nomads. This trade appears to have been reinvigorated in a very short time.[4]

Not only were Plains Indians more present in the pueblos of New Mexico, but they were also far more assertive. Horses had ushered in a revolution in the region. As historian Pekka Hämäläinen ably puts it, equestrian Indians did everything better than their counterparts who traveled by foot — move, hunt, trade, and wage war. Equestrian Indians could even challenge the Spaniards. The horse revolution unfolded by fits and starts during the 1600s, speeding up considerably with the Pueblo Revolt. When Spanish colonists hastily abandoned New Mexico in the summer of 1680, they left behind the largest herd of horses anywhere in northern Mexico. The Pueblo Indians lost little time in appropriating these animals and trading them away. The Apaches, Navajos, Utes, and others thus gained strength during the tumultuous final decades of the seventeenth century.[5]

Spanish officials were forced to tolerate the Pueblo-Plains ties and to keep vigilant in case of an all-Indian alliance against them. Such a scenario was not far-fetched. In 1704–1705 New Mexican governor Juan Páez Hurtado conducted a full-scale "investigation into the friendship between the Pueblos and the surrounding heathens" after learning that some Indians in the pueblo of San Juan had brokered a peace agreement with the Navajos, Utes, various bands of Apaches (Jicarilla, Trementina, Acho, Faraon, and Gila), and other pueblos. It looked like a formidable cabal that could easily lead to a general insurrection. Governor Páez

Hurtado's vigorous investigation prevented such an outcome, but the episode is significant because it illustrates how Apaches, Navajos, Utes, and other outlying Indians learned to use their newfound ties with the Pueblos to put pressure on the Spaniards—and to extract commercial privileges.[6]

The case of the Comanches reveals how thoroughly the adoption of horses could change a group of peripatetic Indians. The Comanches were newcomers to the region. Only in the final decades of the seventeenth century did they start to move south toward New Mexico or to begin experimenting with horses, which they probably first obtained from the Utes, their linguistic cousins. No Spaniard had ever heard of the Comanches until the early years of the eighteenth century. They and the Utes shared a homeland somewhere north of the Pueblo world, possibly in the eastern Colorado Plateau, and together they muscled their way into the trading fairs held in New Mexico. The Spaniards and Pueblos soon became wary of these two stalwart equestrian peoples. Rumors swirled that the Comanches and Utes were mounted barbarians descending on New Mexico in order to pillage. But these nomads also brought valuable trade items, including tanned bison hides, bison meat, and Indian captives.[7]

Comanche captive taking introduced Apaches from the east, Navajos from the west, and Pawnees from the north into New Mexico. The Comanches' radius of action was astonishing. In 1731 a New Mexican friar asked one of the Comanches' captives to which nation he belonged and how far it was to his country of origin. The slave responded that he was a "Ponna" (quite possibly a Pawnee, whose traditional homeland was along the North Platte and Loup Rivers in present-day Nebraska). The Indian also said that he had traveled with his captors for "one hundred suns," moving at a rate of about ten leagues (thirty miles) for each one. The friar estimated that in the course of a year, Comanches might travel "more than one thousand leagues [three thousand miles] from New Mexico," a distance that may have been entirely possible, considering that Pawnee country was eight hundred miles away from northern New Mexico and that the Comanches traveled to and from these lands, making various detours along the way.[8]

The Comanches sold their first slaves in New Mexico sometime in the first decade of the eighteenth century. By the 1720s, they had become well-established traders. And by the 1760s, they were acknowledged as the preeminent suppliers of captives in the region. Their visits to New Mexico became signal events in the yearly calendar that mobilized the entire province. In 1761 a New Mexican friar wrote to the viceroy of Mexico:

> Here the governor, alcaldes, and lieutenants gather together as many horses as they can; here is collected all the ironware possible, such as axes, hoes, wedges, picks, bridles, machetes, *belduques* [heavy knives used in the hide trade], and knives; here in short is gathered everything possible for trade and barter with these barbarians in exchange for deer and buffalo hides, and what is saddest, in exchange for Indian slaves, men and women, small and large, a great multitude of both sexes, for they are gold and silver and the richest treasure for the governors who gorge themselves first with the largest mouthfuls from this table, while the rest eat the crumbs.[9]

It is easy to miss the full implications of this traffic of captives. In the seventeenth century, Spanish cavalrymen had attacked the nomadic groups in New Mexico practically at will. One after another, the Spanish governors had ordered slaving raids on the Apaches, Navajos, and other hunter-gatherers, peoples who still possessed very few horses. But while the Spaniards initially held the upper hand, the diffusion of horses evened out the playing field.[10]

After the Spanish retreat following the Pueblo Revolt of 1680, nomadic Indian traders with newfound access to horses began to muscle their way into the markets of New Mexico. In 1694, barely two years after the Spaniards had retaken control of the province, a group of Navajos arrived with the intention of selling Pawnee children. The Spanish authorities initially refused to acquire the young captives—after all, as the *Recopilación de las leyes de Indias* had made clear fourteen years earlier, Indian slavery was illegal in all circumstances, even when slaves were being ransomed from other Indians. Their refusal may also have had something to do with the desire of some New Mexican traders to

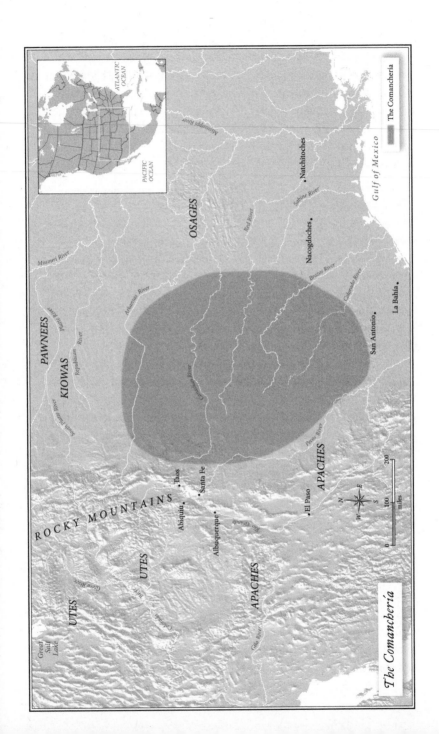

The Comanchería

monopolize the traffic of slaves. But the spurned Navajos did not give up easily. To ratchet up the pressure, the traffickers proceeded to behead the captive children within the Spanish colonists' sight. In the short term, the Utes lost their "merchandise." But in the longer term, the stratagem prompted New Mexican officials to reconsider the ban against "ransoming" Indian captives.[11]

Some years later, in 1704–1705, the Navajos, together with other nomads and Pueblo Indians, increased the pressure even more by threatening an all-out anti-Spanish revolt. Interestingly, it was around this time that New Mexican officials began sanctioning the ransoming of Indian captives sold by these groups. In effect, the Navajos, Utes, Comanches, and Apaches forced New Mexican authorities to break the law and accept their captives. Willingly or not, New Mexicans had become their market.[12]

By the middle of the eighteenth century, these commercial and diplomatic relations had become normalized. In 1752 Governor Tomás Vélez Cachupín reached peace agreements with the Comanches and Utes. Governor Cachupín understood quite well that the best way to achieve a lasting peace with these equestrian powers was by maintaining open trade relations with them and fostering mutual dependence. Thus New Mexico's annual trading fairs became choreographed events in the service of diplomacy. Indeed, Governor Cachupín left to his successor a set of revealing instructions: "It is necessary, when the Comanches come to Taos to trade, that Your Grace present yourself in that pueblo surrounded with a suitable guard and your person adorned with all splendor possible." The governor also urged his successor to show Comanches "every kindness and affection," sitting down with them to smoke tobacco, posting soldiers to relieve them of the responsibility of looking after their horses (something "they appreciate in the highest degree"), leaving them "unmolested in their selling," and making sure that "any appeal for justice is met at once," because "they are always attentive to the governor's actions and decisions from which they draw inferences." According to Governor Cachupín, "The conservation of the friendship of this Ute nation and the rest of its allied tribes is of the greatest consideration because of the favorable results which their trade and good relations bring to this province," and he urged a policy of commercial access that included the selling of Indian captives.[13]

The Comanches flooded the New Mexican market with captives. In the previous century, New Mexicans had kept slaves in their own houses and ranches, and shipped any surplus out to Parral and other mining centers and cities in the south. The New Mexico–Chihuahua trade had functioned as a safety valve, guarding against an oversupply of slaves in New Mexico. Now the Comanches, Apaches, Utes, and others stepped up their selling of captives in New Mexico at the same time the silver mines of Chihuahua were absorbing fewer slaves than before. New Mexico's servile population grew and could no longer be contained in Spanish households and ranches. The clearest symptom was the emergence of new settlements consisting of former slaves. As Friar Miguel de Menchero explained, "Sometimes it happens that the Indians are not well treated in this servitude, no thought being given to the hardships of their captivity . . . and for this reason they desert and become apostates." Many servants escaped, banded together, and mustered the courage to ask for recognition and even request land in outlying areas to start new communities. Such Indians became known as *genízaros,* a term that conjures thoughts of captivity, servitude, and the merging of Plains, Pueblo, and Hispanic cultural traits. In 1733 a group of one hundred Indians who identified themselves as *"los genízaros"* wrote to the governor of New Mexico claiming that they were no longer in servitude to any Spaniard and therefore wished to obtain some land. This first list of genízaros reveals the geography of enslavement at the time, as many of the signatories were Indians from the plains, including Pawnees, Jumanos, Apaches, and Kiowas. Friar Menchero visited a genízaro community south of Albuquerque in 1744. This crude community called Tomé consisted entirely of "nations that had been taken captive by the Comanche Apaches." In the 1750s and 1760s, more genízaro settlements came into existence, an indication of the slaving prowess of the Comanches and other providers.[14]

Indian captivity not only transformed New Mexico but also refashioned the Comanches and their principal victims. The quest for loot caused the Comanches to leave the tablelands and mountains of the

Colorado Plateau and move to the plains. In the 1720s, merely one generation after having acquired horses, these mounted Indians abruptly shifted their base of operations to the east. They descended onto the immense grasslands, with their rolling hills and abundant herds of bison. But more than the bison, what initially attracted the Comanches to the plains were the isolated Apache villages.[15]

In the fifteenth and sixteenth centuries, the Apaches led a nomadic existence on these plains. They did not have horses, so they moved from camp to camp on foot and with the help of dogs pulling travois. In the late seventeenth century, however, the Apaches began to settle down. Once again, the Pueblo Revolt of 1680 was a major catalyst for this change. The rebellion and subsequent reconquest by the Spaniards impelled many Pueblo Indians to flee New Mexico and join these outlying bands. In 1696, fearing reprisals from the returning Spaniards, the Pueblos of Picurís loaded their horses, gathered their goats, and left for the lands of their longtime Apache trading partners. The Apaches already practiced limited forms of agriculture, but the Pueblo refugees introduced new agricultural methods that enabled the Apaches to remain in place all year round. In the fifty-year period between 1675 and 1725 — the blink of an eye in archaeological terms — dozens of Apache settlements sprouted up along the streams, lakes, and ponds of the large region between the Rocky Mountains and the 100th meridian, spanning much of modern-day Kansas and Nebraska. In 1706 a group of Spanish soldiers visited one of these mixed communities of Apaches and Pueblos by the Arkansas River named El Cuartelejo. The residents lived in spacious adobe huts and cultivated small plots of corn, kidney beans, pumpkins, and watermelons, in addition to hunting bison.[16]

What began as a series of Comanche raiding excursions on these exposed settlements rapidly evolved into a full-fledged plan of colonization. Archival records contain only faint traces of the life-and-death battles that raged between Comanches and Apaches during the first half of the eighteenth century. The invaders' greatest strategic advantage was their ability to choose when and where to strike. They operated as unified squadrons pitted against scattered settlements. One Spaniard marveled that even though the Comanches were "the most barbarous nation known, nonetheless they conserve such solidarity both on the marches that they continually undertake, wandering like Israelites, as well as in the camps that they establish where they settle." This was a crucial advantage, but the Plains Apaches, who had also acquired horses by the early eighteenth century, were quite capable of defending themselves. The clashes were sometimes ferocious. Around 1724 they fought a battle at an otherwise unidentified place referred to as "the Great Mountain of Iron," which lasted for nine days. Sixty years later, a Spanish official remembered this encounter as a milestone in the all-out war between the two foes.[17]

In the end, the Comanches prevailed, employing captivity as a primary tool to remake the region. They raided Apache settlements, burning houses and fields, probably deliberately adopting a scorched-earth strategy to permanently dislodge their antagonists. To avoid complications, they generally killed the adult males on the spot, then seized the women and children. In 1719 some Jicarilla Apaches recounted to the governor of New Mexico how "they were very sad and discouraged because of the repeated attacks which their enemies, the Utes and Comanches, make upon them. They had killed many of their nation and carried off their women and children captives until they now no longer knew where to go to live in safety." Five years later, a group of Carlana Apaches could well have been describing the same incident: "The Comanche nation, their enemies, had attacked them with a large number in their rancherías in such a manner that they could not make use of weapons for their defense. They launched themselves with such daring and resolution that they killed many men, carrying off their women and children as captives."[18]

The Comanches took many of their captives to New Mexico, where they exchanged them for horses and knives. In the absence of money or silver, women and children constituted a versatile medium of exchange accepted by Spaniards, Frenchmen, Englishmen, Pueblos, and many other Indian groups of the region. But the Comanches also kept some of the victims. Other North American Indians, including the Iroquois and Cherokees, had long raided neighboring groups to avenge or replace deceased relatives. These so-called "mourning wars" could sometimes escalate into all-out conflicts. It is possible that the Comanches and Apaches understood their conflict at least partly in these terms.[19]

Comanche males competed with one another by expanding their kinship networks. The Comanches practiced polygyny, so raids allowed men to acquire additional wives. Successful males could have three, four, five, or up to ten or more wives. Their "main instinct," commented New Mexican governor Tomás Vélez Cachupín in 1750, "was to have an abundance of women, stealing them from other nations to increase their own." This was not just about prestige, sexual gratification, and reproduction. In an equestrian society, women provided specialized labor. For instance, a skilled male hunter could bring down several bison in just one hour. But once the exhilaration of the chase was over, hunters faced the daunting task of processing dead animals spread over great distances. Each carcass could weigh a ton or more. Flaying open a bison, cutting the choice meat from the back and around the ribs, removing the inner organs, cleaning the hide, and severing the legs and head required not just skill but above all untold amounts of labor. Captive women spent endless hours stooping over these large carcasses, withstanding the heat, stench, and exhaustion involved in preparing the hides for their many uses; looking after the horses; and doing the myriad chores of life in an encampment and on the move. Circumstances could vary, but enslaved women usually began at the bottom of the hierarchy of wives and were given the most taxing and unpleasant tasks. They were subordinate not only to their Comanche husbands but also to the "first wives," who tended to be Comanche by birth and who managed the labor of the lower-ranking women on a daily basis.[20]

Captive children faced different circumstances. Older boys, because they could not readily identify with their captors and had difficulty learning the language, were frequently excluded from the Comanche kinship system. These unlucky captives sometimes remained slaves for life. In contrast, younger captives were often adopted into a family and regarded as full-fledged members of it. Comanches showed a marked preference for boys over girls. Anthropologist Joaquín Rivaya-Martínez has assembled a database of more than fourteen hundred Comanche captives in the eighteenth and nineteenth centuries. More than seventy percent of the children in his sample are boys. They were in high demand primarily because of the relative scarcity of males in Comanche society. Constant battles and raids took a heavy toll on the male population. Reportedly, relatively few Comanche warriors reached old age. The marked preference for boys may also have been a result of the growing number of horses the Comanches came to control. Breaking horses and looking after them became major occupations in Comanche society, and boys were deemed more appropriate for such tasks than girls. At the height of their power in the nineteenth century, the Comanches owned so many horses that each boy was responsible for a herd of as many as 150 animals, according to one witness. Looking after the horses was the first task assigned to these young captives; it was a way of testing their loyalty to the group. The boys also had to recognize their captors as their parents, learn the ways of the society, and earn sufficient trust to receive more difficult assignments. In the fullness of time, they were allowed to take part in bison hunts and eventually were invited to accompany the warriors in raids against other Indians, including their former kinsmen.[21]

Indian captivity was at the heart of the transformation of the plains. The Comanches obliterated Apache settlements across an enormous area, carrying off and selling some Apaches in New Mexico, taking Apache women as their secondary wives, and enslaving and adopting Apache children before unleashing them on their former people. In short, the Apachería became the Comanchería largely through captivity. By the 1760s, the Comanches had forged a stable homeland to the east of the kingdom of New Mexico. Stretching from the Arkansas River in the north to the Balcones Escarpment in the south, and from the eastern flank of New Mexico all the way to Spanish Texas, the Comanchería was a forbidding region that non-Comanches entered at their own peril. Fifteen thousand Comanches or more occupied this territory, easily exceeding the number of Spaniards or Frenchmen living in what is now the Southwest. The Comanches became the second most numerous indigenous people after the Pueblos of New Mexico. They also surpassed New Mexico in the number of horses they possessed. Because the Comanches measured their wealth in terms of horses, each ranchería could have hundreds of them. In a profound sense, the Comanches became "the horse people," breeding them, raiding them, and using them widely as an article of trade.[22]

Above all, the Comanchería was better connected than New Mexico to the surrounding Indian and non-Indian peoples. Using bison hides, horses, and slaves as their preferred items of exchange, the Comanches turned their homeland into a trading center. On their western flank, they retained New Mexico as a convenient entrepôt, continuing their yearly embassies to the trading fairs. At the same time, they developed a brisk trade with French Louisiana to the east and with the English to the northeast. Although the Comanches sometimes dealt directly with French and English merchants, these transactions, which could span all of North America, were more commonly mediated by other Indians. In the 1720s and 1730s, Apache captives flowed to places as far away as Quebec, where they came to comprise as many as one-quarter of all Indian slaves of known origin in New France. In return, the Comanches and their allies procured European weapons. During their assault on the San Sabá mission in 1758, for instance, they reportedly carried more than one thousand French muskets — more firearms than were available in all of Spanish Texas.[23]

Scholars of slavery in the ancient Mediterranean and Africa have sometimes distinguished between "societies with slaves," in which slaves were present but did not constitute a majority of the population and were not central to the production of goods, and "slave societies," which were fundamentally dependent on enslaved peoples. At the height of the African slave trade in the eighteenth century, the proportion of African slaves on some Caribbean islands — including Haiti, Jamaica, and Barbados — reached ninety percent. By this traditional yardstick, the Comanches were merely a "society with slaves." The ratio of slaves among the Comanches in the nineteenth century may have ranged between ten and twenty-five percent, according to one tentative estimate. And yet this percentage fails to convey the multiple ways in which slavery gave the Comanches the means to acquire horses and weapons and to use these as powerful levers to forge alliances, seek compliance, punish enemies, and secure their borders. In tangible ways, the Comanchería became a trading center with commercial networks that included many surrounding Indian nations and stretched into the Spanish, French, and British empires.[24]

Although the Comanches became preeminent suppliers of captives on the northern fringes of the Spanish empire, they were not alone. The Utes followed a somewhat different trajectory, but they too became active participants in the exchange of captives. The Utes were the ones who possibly gave the Comanches their first horses. They also brought the Comanches into New Mexico as their junior partners. As we have seen, in the early decades of the eighteenth century, these two equestrian peoples shared a range somewhere to the north of the Pueblo world, trading and plundering together.[25]

But then their relationship soured. In the 1730s, they began having difficulties, and by midcentury they were engaged in open conflict. As the division deepened, their paths diverged. The Comanches descended onto the plains, dislodged the Apaches, and established a new homeland there. Most Ute bands remained up in the mountains and retained their traditional seasonal migration. In the fall and winter, they remained to the west and north of New Mexico, trading in Taos, Jemez, and other pueblos. New Mexico's most northwesterly settlement, Abiquiu, became a regular trading stop for many Utes. In the eighteenth century, Abiquiu was a remote village of genízaros that served as a jumping-off point for the Great Basin. Many Utes overwintered in protected areas not too far from this and other outlying settlements. In the spring, they rode west and north, venturing into the Great Basin and visiting portions of what are now Utah, Nevada, and Arizona, even traveling as far as Wyoming, Idaho, and eastern California and Oregon.[26]

As they moved away from New Mexico, these Utes encountered an array of indigenous groups, all of whom spoke Numic languages and were more or less related to one another. Immediately to the west of the Colorado Plateau, the Utes entered a transitional region inhabited by smaller bands that possessed fewer horses and practiced small-scale farming. They occasionally intermarried with these Indians—known indistinctly as Utes or Paiutes in the historical record—but did not

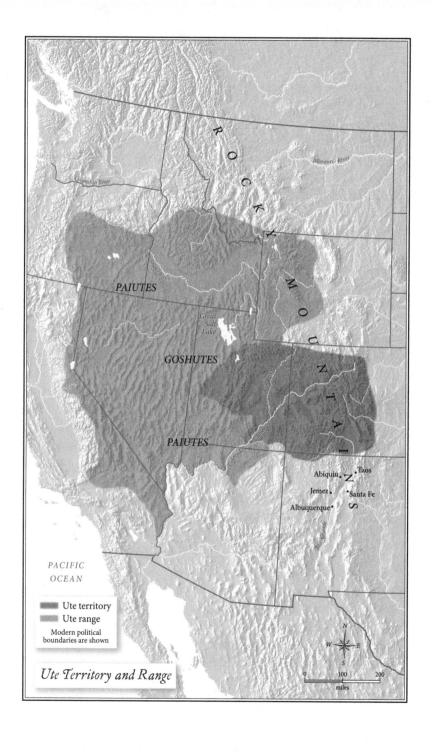

ROCKY MOUNTAINS

*Columbia River*

*Missouri River*

PAIUTES

*Great Salt Lake*

GOSHUTES

PAIUTES

Abiquiu·  ·Taos

Jemez·  ·Santa Fe

Albuquerque·

*Rio Grande*

PACIFIC OCEAN

Ute territory
Ute range
Modern political boundaries are shown

*Ute Territory and Range*

N
W    E
S

0      100      200
miles

treat them quite the same as their own people. As they pushed deeper into the Great Basin, they found peoples to whom they were even more distantly related.[27]

The Great Basin is a low-lying area of around two hundred thousand square miles, an enormous sink wedged between the Wasatch Mountains to the east and the Sierra Nevada to the west. A large depression covered in the last ice age by an inland sea called Lake Lahontan, it is now a stark landscape of dried lakebeds, burnt sienna mountains, bleached deserts, and open spaces. The Paiute Indians occupied much of this area, adapting to its challenging environment. They lived in small groups of closely related family members: husband, wife (occasionally more than one), children, and perhaps a few uncles, aunts, grandparents, and cousins. These camps consisted of as few as ten people and seldom exceeded fifty. Atomization was a necessity, given the scarcity of food. These small bands moved from one campsite to another in carefully planned circuits to procure grasses, pine nuts, and other food resources that were available in different locales at different times of year. Although the Great Basin is generally low, its mountains and hills gave these bands access to various ecological niches at different altitudes. When disaster struck, their atomized social organization enabled them to share their resources with one another. For instance, in cases of drought, frost, insect infestation, or some other environmental calamity, one band could request permission to drink water or eat grasses or roots belonging to a neighboring band without jeopardizing all of the groups' livelihoods. It appears that such requests were usually granted and created bonds of reciprocity.[28]

The sparse conditions of the Great Basin limited the ability of the Paiutes to acquire horses. Horses consumed great amounts of grass, the very food on which the Paiutes depended for survival. Thus the Paiutes *ate* horses instead of keeping them as beasts of burden. As a result, unlike other Numic speakers such as the Utes and Comanches, the Paiutes remained a horseless people, moving on foot in small groups, carrying simple tools, and eking out a living by digging roots and catching animals. Without giving a second thought to the environmental constraints to which the Paiutes were subjected, newcomers to the Great Basin simply assumed that the local Indians were exceedingly backward: "They are an anomaly, apparently the lowest species of humanity, approaching the monkey," opined William Wolfskill, one of the earliest American trappers to behold Paiutes during a visit to the Great Basin in 1830. He also noticed how these Indians fed "like cattle"; communicated mostly through songs, as they knew but few words; and did not possess hatchets or any other instruments to cut even the softest wood. Such views endured for decades. Even Mark Twain later pronounced the Indians of eastern Nevada to be "the wretchedest type of mankind," adding that "from what we could see and all we could learn . . . our Goshoots are manifestly descended from the self-same gorilla, or kangaroo or Norway rat, whichever animal-Adam the Darwinians trace them to."[29]

The Utes and Paiutes may once have had similar ways of life, but by the middle of the eighteenth century, the large equestrian bands of the Colorado Plateau and the small bands of the Great Basin had diverged dramatically. Varied environmental constraints, long-term cultural adaptations, and the dispersal of horses out of New Mexico created two entirely different societies living within striking distance of each other. And that difference brought opportunity. Ute horsemen rode down the Wasatch Mountains and preyed on the Indians of the basin below. To them, procuring Paiute slaves may have seemed like a specialized kind of hunting. They would ride into the Paiute camps and intimidate parents into surrendering their children or husbands into giving up their wives. According to later testimonies, the Utes preferred to conduct these raids in the spring, when the Paiutes were starving and at their most vulnerable. Occasionally the raiders would even offer an old horse as payment — a negligible compensation that nonetheless allowed the Ute traffickers to present the transactions as "voluntary." All over the Americas, slave catchers claimed as much, when in fact such transactions often amounted to outright kidnapping or were involuntary sales conducted under extreme conditions of starvation or duress.[30]

At the sight of approaching intruders, Paiute women and children hid. Only old men, the least likely to be enslaved, ventured out to meet outsiders. The Spaniards who first journeyed into Paiute country in 1776 remarked on their extreme timidity. "It pained us to see them frightened so much that they could not even speak," wrote Fray Silvestre Vélez de Escalante, the diarist of the expedition, as they traversed what is now Beaver County in southwestern Utah. The passing Spaniards had to exert themselves greatly to catch one of these fleeing Indians. The momentary prisoner was "overly vivacious and so intimidated that he appeared to be out of his mind. He stared in every direction, watched everyone closely, and any gesture or motion on our part startled him beyond measure." On another occasion, the friar and his companions spotted five Paiute Indians. When the visitors turned toward them, four of them hid, while one remained in sight but proceeded to climb a very large and difficult rock and would not come down. "At each step we took, as we came closer to him," Fray Vélez de Escalante wrote, "he wanted to take off. We let him know that he did not have to be afraid, that we loved him like a son and wanted to talk with him. And so he waited for us making a thousand gestures to show that he feared us very much." This first party of Spaniards referred to the local inhabitants as "coward Utes." Yet against the background of slaving raids recurring year after year, such behavior was entirely rational.[31]

The Utes made the ferrying of Paiute Indians from the Great Basin into New Mexico a part of their seasonal movements. Mounted Indians procured slaves in the spring, moved about with them in the summer, and sold them at the New Mexican fairs in the fall, only to repeat the cycle the following year. The best evidence for this trade can be found in New Mexico's parish records, especially those of Abiquiu, as historian Ned Blackhawk has observed. It is hard to tell much from these bare-bones entries. Maria Rosa Abeyta, a four-year-old "Ute" girl of unknown parents, was already at her baptism serving one Juan Antonio Abeyta, who appears as her sponsor, or godfather, in the records. María Gertrudis Gutiérrez, also of unknown parents, was introduced as a "genízara yuta," whose godfather was Antonio Gutiérrez. Gertrudis Olguín, another "Ute" girl of unknown parents, was serving Juan Olguín when he took her to be baptized. Although these short entries lack individual detail, some things are obvious. First, in more than ninety percent of cases, the parents of Indian children specifically identified as "Ute" were unknown, which is what one would expect after multiple transactions involving Indian and Spanish traffickers. In Spanish America, a society obsessed with lineages, the fact that the parents of all of these Native children were unknown is a strong indication that they arrived in New Mexico through the slave trade. Second, "godfathers" and "godmothers" were quite evidently the owners or masters of these children. In post-Reformation Catholic practice, godparents were responsible adults who took a special interest in the proper Christian education and upbringing of the children whose baptisms they sponsored. In cases in which parents died or went missing, godparents could even act as surrogate parents. But in New Mexico, the institution was adapted to legitimize the purchase of Indian captives, and with the scratch of a pen, a slaveholder became a respectable godparent.[32]

The term "yuta" in these church records requires some explanation. It almost certainly does not refer to Utes — who after all were at peace with New Mexico after the 1740s — but more broadly to Numic-speaking peoples. Some Utes may well have been enslaved in clashes with Comanches and Navajos. But the majority of those recorded must have been Paiutes, who were identified as "yutas" by New Mexicans for simplicity or perhaps to denote the ethnicity of the captors rather than the captives. These records also reveal the ups and downs of this trade. "Yuta" begins appearing in New Mexican parish records in the 1740s, just when the Utes and Spaniards forged a stable alliance. The Utes signed a formal agreement with New Mexico in 1752. From then on, the number of "yuta" captives climbed steadily through the second half of the eighteenth century and into the early decades of the nineteenth century, reaching a high point only in the 1840s.[33]

The opening of a trail linking New Mexico and California by way of the Great Basin gave additional impetus to the traffic of Paiute Indians. Using Abiquiu as a staging point, caravans of as many as one hundred New Mexican merchants and mule drivers headed west and north into Ute territory. After entering what is now the southeastern corner of Utah, these intrepid travelers had to ford the upper Colorado and Green Rivers, cross the Wasatch Mountains, and descend into the Great Basin via Salina Canyon. The Old Spanish Trail — as this challenging route became known — then veered south, passing through Las Vegas, across

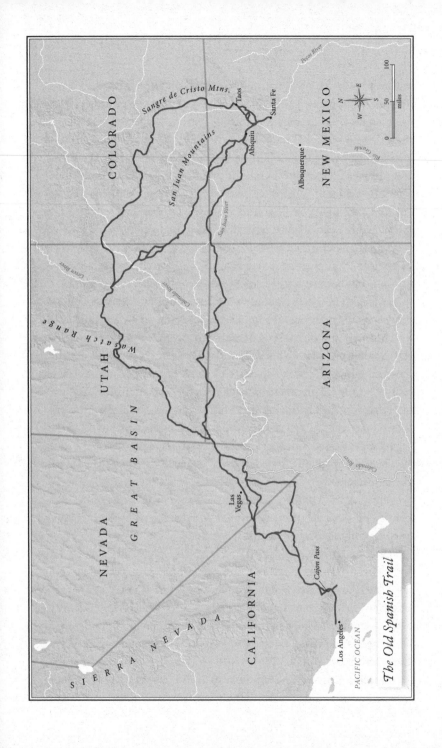

The Old Spanish Trail

the Mojave Desert, and over the San Bernardino Mountains, to end in Los Angeles. Although Spanish explorers had blazed portions of the Old Spanish Trail since the 1760s, it was only during the Mexican period that it became a major thoroughfare used in its entirety.[34]

The Old Spanish Trail forged closer ties between the Spaniards and Utes but also increased the potential for competition and conflict. We have only scattered glimpses of the fraught relationships that developed along the road—alliances that could shift at a moment's notice from peaceful trade to violence. For instance, in the spring of 1813 a group of seven merchants led by Mauricio Arze and Lagos García departed from Abiquiu and journeyed as far north as Utah Lake, in what is now north-central Utah. They called out the surrounding Utes, letting them know that they wished to trade, and waited three days for them to assemble. The Utes were very interested in the Spaniards' horses, but they would pay for them only with Paiute slaves—or so claimed Arze and García in their subsequent judicial depositions. When the New Mexicans requested other goods, many of the Utes became incensed, killing eight of the merchants' mounts and one mule. Thanks to the intervention of one Ute leader, the Spaniards managed to collect the rest of their animals and leave without further losses. On their way home, by way of the Colorado River in southeastern Utah, Arze, García, and the others ran into the ranchería of Chief Wasatch (after whom the mountains running through the middle of Utah are named). Wasatch was waiting there to trade, "as was his custom," and received the New Mexican merchants cordially at first. But when the Spaniards refused to exchange their horses for slaves, the Utes took offense and became hostile. In the end, the New Mexicans accepted 109 pelts and 12 slaves "in order not to receive another injury like the first one." It is hard to know whether the Spaniards were as reluctant to acquire slaves as they said they were, but at the very least their story reveals that the Utes expected the Spaniards to accept slaves as a means of payment all over Utah.[35]

When Americans started trickling into the Great Basin, they found a deeply entrenched and fairly old slave trade conducted by both Utes and New Mexicans. Fur trapper Dick Wootton, a colorful figure widely known as "Uncle Dick," marveled at how common it was during the

1830s to spot parties of Mexicans buying Indian slaves in Utah and admitted to doing business with them: "While we were trapping there I sent a lot of peltries to Taos by a party of these same slave traders, some of whom I happened to know." New England explorer Thomas J. Farnham remarked that many of the slaving victims were Paiute and Shoshone Indians living on the Sevier River of Utah — "poor creatures hunted in the spring of the year, when they are weak and helpless . . . and when taken [they are] fattened, carried to Santa Fé and sold as slaves during their minority." Farnham noted that all ethnicities were already involved in this trade: "New Mexicans capture them for slaves; the neighboring Indians do the same; and even the bold and usually high-minded old [Anglo-American] beaver-hunter sometimes descends from his legitimate labor among the mountain streams, to this mean traffic."[36]

One of the most detailed descriptions of this trade was penned by Daniel W. Jones, a veteran of the U.S.-Mexican War who drifted into New Mexico and in 1850 joined a sheepherding expedition bound for California. On the "down trip," New Mexicans traded with Utes and Navajos along the way, giving them horses in exchange for children procured from "poorer Indians." The sheepherders then took these children all the way to the Golden State, where they sold the captives and used the proceeds to acquire large herds of California stock. On the return trip, the New Mexicans once again engaged their Ute and Navajo suppliers, exchanging their newly acquired horses for more children, now destined for the New Mexican market. According to Jones, boys fetched an average of $100, while girls sold for between $150 and $200 — "the girls having the reputation of making better servants than any others." It would thus appear that by 1850, Indian and Mexican traffickers had found their proper places as two necessary links in the supply chain connecting Great Basin slaves with purchasers in California and New Mexico.[37]

The parallel stories of the Comanches and Utes underscore how the uneven spread of horses enabled them to prey on other Indians. It was not an entirely unprecedented occurrence. In pre-contact North America, the diffusion of agriculture had given rise to an earlier cycle of enslavement. Indian societies that adopted agriculture experienced a sudden population increase and acquired both the means and the motivation to raid other peoples. The Aztecs, Mayas, Zapotecs, Caribs, Iroquois, and many others possessed captives and slaves, as is clear in archaeological, linguistic, and historical records. Nomadic groups also had slaves. But it is possible to find some nomads who were reluctant to accept even individuals who willingly offered themselves as slaves to save themselves from starvation. For some of these groups, taking slaves was simply not economically viable. I do not mean to paint a simplistic portrait of agriculturalist traffickers and nomadic victims. It is clear that different configurations were possible: large urban societies enslaving smaller ones, as in the case of the Aztecs and Tlaxcalans, or agricultural peoples enslaving groups that were still in the process of adopting agriculture. But the fact is that technological differences gave some groups the capacity and incentive to raid others.[38]

In hindsight it is clear that the introduction of horses and firearms precipitated another cycle of enslavement in North America. In the sixteenth and much of the seventeenth centuries, Europeans had maintained their technological superiority, which they had used to enslave tens of thousands of Native Americans. But once the genie was out of the bottle, their initial advantages vanished. By the mid- to late seventeenth century, the Spaniards were able to take fewer and fewer captives as Native Americans rose to the challenge of European colonialism. Some Indian societies negotiated accommodations with the newcomers. Others fled to inaccessible areas. And yet others transformed themselves into powerful forces by taking advantage of the very technologies and markets created by Europeans. All of them became active participants in the other slavery, thus making the system harder to control than ever. In absolute numbers, the other slavery declined during the eighteenth century, but it also evolved and became more deeply entrenched. And it was not just Native Americans who became more adept at taking slaves. In response to this newfound Indian power, Spanish colonists pioneered new practices of enslavement, to which we turn next.

# 8

## *Missions, Presidios, and Slaves*

IN RECENT YEARS, historians have painted a fascinating new picture of Indian power in North America. They have shown that many Indian societies retained a great deal of control in their "native grounds" and at times acted as "militaristic slaving societies," even full-scale "empires." But with so much emphasis on Native control, it is easy to miss the point that Europeans also adapted to the new circumstances. Just as the Comanches and Utes expanded their respective ranges in the eighteenth century, the Spaniards bolstered their religious, military, and demographic presence in northern Mexico. A fantastic silver boom allowed them to dig in their heels. Mexico's production of silver bullion increased by an astounding four hundred percent — from 1,272,680 kilograms (1,403 tons) of fine silver in 1701–1710 to 4,878,510 (5,378 tons) in 1801–1810 — making Mexico the world's leading producer of the white metal. For much of that century, Mexico mined more than half of all the silver extracted in the world. To keep the supply flowing, the crown invested some of the proceeds in military garrisons. In effect, Spain militarized Mexico's northern frontier.[1]

The mission was Spain's first frontier institution. In the early years of colonization, friars boldly ventured into unsettled areas, established contact with Indians, and acted as diplomats, spies, and agents of the crown. In a field-defining essay published almost one hundred years ago, Berkeley historian Herbert E. Bolton argued that just as English backwoods settlers had "driven back the Indian step by step" and French fur traders had "brought the savage tribes into friendly relations with the French government," the missions had played the leading role on the Spanish frontier, teaching millions of Indians the language of Cervantes, introducing them to the mysteries of Christianity, exposing them to every conceivable European plant and animal, and giving them the rudiments of European crafts and agriculture.[2]

Yet for all of these "accomplishments" (now we know that Bolton's approach was decidedly Eurocentric), missions proved inadequate to secure the unsettled frontier. Working alone or in pairs, friars simply lacked the means to control territory or enforce a European-style regime. Missionaries depended on Native leaders to decide whether it was to their peoples' advantage to live within a mission. In many instances, Indians found that life under the mission bell was too regimented for them and ultimately abandoned their missions. As the friars were powerless to retrieve absconding Indians, they had to rely on Spanish soldiers to help them carry out their work of religious instruction. And if the missions' vulnerabilities were noticeable even in cases in which Indians were initially cooperative, they were blatantly obvious when missionaries were dealing with powerful groups such as the Utes, Comanches, and Apaches, who refused to allow missions into their territories. These nations wanted nothing to do with the meddlesome robed men bent on monogamous marriage, a sedentary way of life, and other strictures, and there was nothing the missionaries could do about it.[3]

Spanish officials thus opted for a more forceful means to protect Mexico's silver districts. They ordered the establishment of military garrisons all along the frontier and deployed more soldiers. There certainly had been militias and presidios before, but the shift in emphasis was clear. Although missionaries continued their work throughout the eighteenth century and even expanded into new areas such as Alta California, the military came to play a more prominent role. In 1701 northern Mexico had 15 companies and a total of 562 soldiers. By 1764 the number of units had more than doubled to 23 companies and 13 squads, and the total troop strength was 1,271. To keep southward-moving Indians such as the Apaches and Comanches in check, Spanish policymakers also decided to set up a line of presidios stretching from the Atlantic to the Pacific. This presidial line was very close to today's international border between Mexico and the United States. Of course, the current border took shape only in the middle of the nineteenth century, in the aftermath of the U.S.-Mexican War. But considering that a border is merely the outer rim of an area over which a nation exercises control, this line of presidios overlaid on Indian domains constituted Mexico's northernmost edge of effective control and therefore its border in a more profound way.[4]

For the Indians, the presence of missions and presidios represented both opportunity and danger. Indians preferred to engage these outposts intermittently and on their own terms — perhaps to procure goods or food or even to gain temporary employment, but nothing more. However, their very existence made life risky for Natives living in the vicinity, as they increased the Indians' vulnerability to European labor demands. This was especially true for small nomadic or seminomadic bands that had little else to offer but their labor. The alternatives were stark for them. They could either take to inaccessible areas beyond the pale of Spanish control or strike a bargain with the Devil, so to speak, by joining a mission or presidio while negotiating the best possible arrangement.

Consider the choices available to the Seri Indians. The Seris had been living on the coast of Sonora with little outside interference for centuries, if not millennia. Their language is unrelated to any others in the region — an "isolate" in the parlance of linguists. Seri mitochondrial DNA exhibits a distribution of markers that is extremely rare among the Indians of Mexico or the Southwest (with a high percentage of the haplogroup C founding lineage), and their Y-chromosome DNA reveals low levels of diversity, also suggesting isolation. To be sure, the Seris traded with their neighbors, as the archaeological and historical records make clear. But they could always retreat into their homeland, which was so inhospitable that no other groups wanted to have it. Anyone who has seen this coastal desert would readily appreciate the tremendous difficulty of eking out a living there. Agriculture was

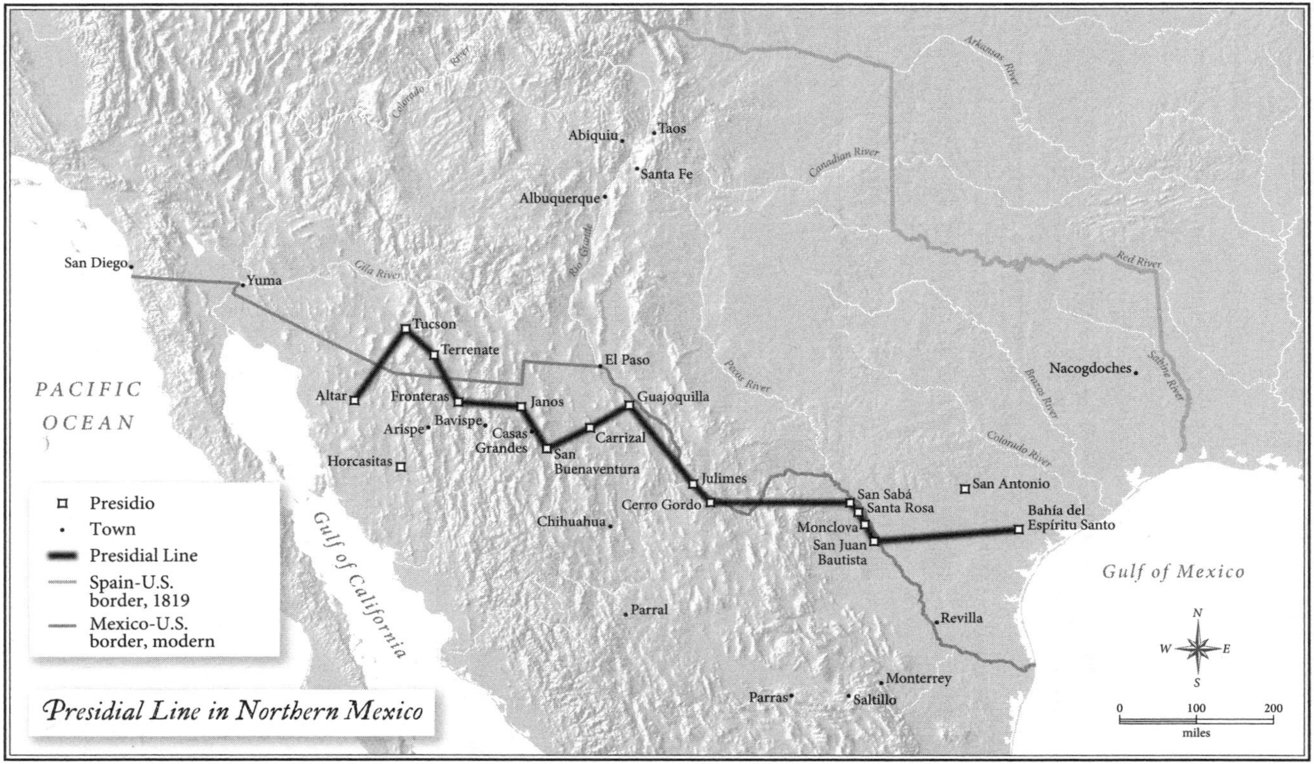
Presidial Line in Northern Mexico
Presidio
Town
Presidial Line
Spain-U.S. border, 1819
Mexico-U.S. border, modern
PACIFIC OCEAN
Gulf of California
Gulf of Mexico
Colorado River
Gila River
Rio Grande
Canadian River
Arkansas River
Red River
Pecos River
Brazos River
Colorado River
Sabine River
San Diego
Yuma
Abiquiu
Taos
Santa Fe
Albuquerque
Tucson
Terrenate
El Paso
Altar
Fronteras
Janos
Guajoquilla
Arispe
Bavispe
Casas Grandes
Carrizal
San Buenaventura
Horcasitas
Julimes
Cerro Gordo
Chihuahua
San Sabá
Santa Rosa
Monclova
San Juan Bautista
San Antonio
Bahía del Espíritu Santo
Nacogdoches
Parral
Revilla
Monterrey
Parras
Saltillo
N
W
E
S
0
100
200
miles

entirely out of the question. The Seris — or Comcáac, as they call them-selves — were true nomads, extremely attuned to a variety of local re-sources. They regularly used as many as 75 different plants and had names for an astounding 350 to 400 of them, as ethnobotanists have been able to determine. The Seris also turned to the bounty of the sea. On flimsy boats made from reeds, they ventured into the Sea of Cortez to hunt turtles — even during the winter months when the animals lay half-buried on the sea floor — and to gather eelgrass when the shoots from the submerged plants broke off and floated to the surface in April. The Seris dried the seeds, ground them, and made a gruel, which they ate with turtle fat or honey. This is the only documented instance of a human population relying on a marine seed plant as a major food source.[5]

Only toward the end of the seventeenth century did the Jesuits be-gin missionizing the Seris. Father Adam Gilg, a native from what is now the Czech Republic, was one of them. In 1688 he journeyed to Sonora to take up his post at the mission of Santa María del Pópulo. The site was nothing but a crude shrine, a few Seri families living in branch huts, and scattered fields irrigated by the San Miguel River. The name Santa María del Pópulo — one shared with an opulent church in Rome — was certainly incongruous. But the most disappointing circumstance for a commit-ted priest like Father Gilg was that the mission lay well outside the Seri homeland. Because the coast would have been too harsh an environment to sustain a community based on agriculture, Pópulo was seventy-five miles inland, merely a beachhead on the edge of the Seri world.

Still, Father Gilg took these drawbacks in stride. This German-speak-ing Jesuit quickly discovered that the Seri language would be a major obstacle to his evangelizing efforts, yet he claimed that their speech re-minded him of German. Gilg was taken aback by the Seris' nakedness, but he found comfort in the fact that their lack of clothes did not seem to cause lewdness or promiscuity. "I have not seen a single unmarried woman sin," he wrote. He even found the Seris' halting attempts at wear-ing clothes amusing: "Some wear only shirts. Others wear only pants. And yet others wear their pants wrapped around the chest . . . and all of these articles pass from hand to hand because the Seris engage in a

Father Adam Gilg drew this sketch of Seri Indians in February 1692. The woman is carrying a basket on her head and a mat under her arm. The men are armed with bows and arrows, as well as knives protruding from their armbands. All the Indians are adorned with necklaces, nose rings, and feathers.

betting game and pay each other with clothes." Father Gilg was generally content with his flock, calling them "my Seris" when he wrote to his brethren in Europe. "This is not the kind of mission where one runs the risk of becoming martyrized," he proclaimed reassuringly, "but not everyone can come here as the work requires missionaries who are able to withstand discomfort and want of everything."[6]

Father Gilg's hopeful letters fit with our image of missions as privileged sites of Indian-European interaction. Like many other idealizations,

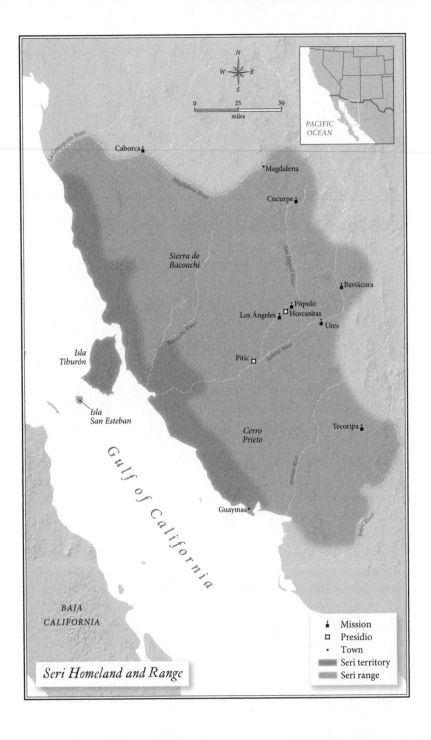

Seri Homeland and Range

this one is based on a modicum of truth. The Seris did receive the Jesuit missionaries peacefully, but one important reason was that the padres gave away food liberally. As one missionary noted, it was necessary to win over the Seris "by their mouths." By all accounts, the robed men delivered. The river valleys of central Sonora were narrow but possessed surprisingly fertile land. By building canals, dams, and wells, using manure as fertilizer, applying European plowing methods, and rotating crops, missionaries were able to get sizeable surpluses.[7]

Just below the surface, however, coercion was also a part of the bargain between missionaries and Indians. The mission of Santa María del Pópulo, for example, had originated as a refugee community in the wake of a series of slaving raids in 1662. A posse of Spaniards had cut a swath through the Seri lands, killing most of the adults of one band and distributing the children in the Spanish towns of Sonora. As Father Gilg himself told the story, "Those who survived, following the advice of my predecessor, Father Juan Fernández, decided to congregate themselves in this place of which I am currently its missionary." Building on this initial nucleus, Father Gilg was able to persuade more Seris to shed their nomadic ways and acquiesce to life under the mission bell. A string of new missions arose, including San Tadeo, San Eustaquio, and Santa María Magdalena de los Tepocas. It is possible that many of the nomads were lured solely by Father Gilg's exhortations — in German laced with a few Seri words, one would imagine — and by his provisions of corn and beef. But at least some of them made their choice under duress. For example, in 1700 Father Gilg accompanied Sergeant Juan Bautista de Escalante and fifteen soldiers on a military incursion into the lands of the Seris. One of their objectives was to bring back ten Seri families that had absconded from Pópulo, taking some cattle in the process. The soldiers caught up with the fleeing Indians, flogged them, and restored them to the mission. For the next six months, Sergeant Escalante and his soldiers crisscrossed the Seri homeland, catching more than two hundred additional Indians and dispatching them to the missions.[8]

The Seris themselves were divided over the question of whether to seek accommodation in a mission or some other Spanish community or to flee to some inaccessible spot. According to anthropologist and historian Thomas E. Sheridan, out of a total population of around three thousand in the early eighteenth century, perhaps ten to twenty percent chose to settle down. The majority pursued the opposite strategy, avoiding contact with Europeans and retreating deep into their environmental refuge. Tiburón, the largest island in Mexico, lies only about a mile and a half from the continent and is clearly visible from much of the central coast of Sonora. But to get to this island, one has to cross the treacherous Strait of Infiernillo. The Spaniards needed good boats to negotiate the strait's strong currents, but the desert coast of Sonora had no trees and therefore no wood for boats. The closest sources of wood would have been the Sierra de Bacoachi or Cerro Prieto. But hauling logs for even a medium-size vessel would have been a formidable task. The Seris were well aware of the Spaniards' difficulties in getting to Tiburón and to the even more remote island of San Esteban, and thus headed there to escape their control.[9]

Negotiating between these two worlds, many Seris chose to straddle them. They would stay in the missions for some time, performing the arduous work of the agriculturalist/stockman, but also frequently flee. Sometimes they would plunder a neighboring mission or nearby ranch, then abscond to the islands. Seri bands also would raid one another's settlements, "hunt" mission cattle as if they were deer, and plunder corn as if it were a wild plant. Ancient animosities, multigenerational vendettas, and rivalries—exacerbated by the emergence of agricultural/ranching oases in the middle of the desert—motivated some of these attacks. They also discovered that they could extend their traditional hunting and gathering activities with the resources recently introduced by Europeans.[10]

The Seri example underscores the weakness of the missionary frontier. After decades of painstaking missionizing, the Jesuits of central Sonora had persuaded only a small share of the Seri nation to settle down and were powerless to prevent them from raiding missions or fleeing from them. A pertinacious pattern of occasional raids and frequent flight became the norm. The padres may have thought that they were "civilizing" the Seris, but the opposite was equally plausible: the Seris had incorporated the missions into their way of life, as they continued to move, hunt, and gather.

The ineffectiveness of the missions eventually prompted Spanish planners to attempt a more forceful approach. As the eighteenth century unfolded, military garrisons and soldiers superseded the missions as the lynchpins of Spain's efforts to stabilize the frontier. With the new approach came new forms of coercion. The word "presidio" captures the dual purpose of garrison and prison. Since Roman times, presidios have been both military establishments deployed in unsettled areas and sites where criminals served out their prison sentences. Today the Spanish word *presidiario* means "inmate or prisoner" rather than garrisoned soldier.[11]

Presidial soldiers were professionals who drew a salary from the crown, but they were underpaid. Thus garrison commanders and soldiers supplemented their earnings by catching Indians and selling them to the Spanish colonists or by turning presidios into supply centers based on coerced labor. These activities were so common that Brigadier General Pedro de Rivera issued a set of military regulations in 1729. Having toured and inspected most of the presidios of northern Mexico (an eight-thousand-mile odyssey through Sonora, Sinaloa, Chihuahua, New Mexico, Texas, and Louisiana), he had plenty of firsthand experience. The very first article of the new regulations forbade governors and presidial commanders "to capture Indians of any sex or age in an expedition of war ... and to claim said prisoners for themselves or divide them under any motive or pretext." The practice was quite common, and in fact these regulations did little to change it. Another grand military inspection, conducted by the Marqués de Rubí almost forty years later, found that soldiers still frequently captured Indians. As Rubí put it, "It is an occasion of abuse against all of their humanity and rights as a people if they are turned over to the citizens, who treat them as slaves, even to the point of selling them."[12]

The Seri nation was among the first to experience this searing transition from a missionary to a presidial frontier. In 1742 the Spanish government established a presidio just to the east of the Seri homeland named

San Pedro de la Conquista del Pitic. The fifty soldiers deployed to Pitic were supposed to bring security to the region, but they had other priorities in mind. A surprise inspection of the garrison conducted only six years after its founding gives an unusual glimpse into its operations. A Mexico City lawyer appeared unannounced on a Sunday morning in the summer of 1748. The licenciado Rafael Rodríguez Gallardo was an imperious man who enjoyed the full backing of the viceroy. He took possession of a dilapidated office inside the presidio, ordered the soldiers to muster, and warned the presidial commander to "stay within his sight at all times." Rodríguez Gallardo then proceeded to the most nettlesome part of his assignment, interviewing the Indians held in the garrison and examining the files detailing their crimes, the length of their imprisonment, and the types of work to which they were assigned. One by one the Indians appeared before a committee of three men: Rodríguez Gallardo, an Indian translator, and an *apoderado* (attorney) of the presidio who had in his possession what few documents regarding the inmates existed. A Native from the Pimería Alta named Nicolás was one of the first to be examined. He appeared "with chains on his legs and said that he had been imprisoned by orders of the Indian governor of the town of Caborca on account of an illicit friendship." When Rodríguez Gallardo asked to see Nicolás's file, the apoderado responded that there was not one. The Indians continued to file into the office: Juan Reyes, a Pima from the town of Buenavista, had been imprisoned for a year for beating up and killing his wife; Ignacio Mendizabal, a Mayo from Navojoa, had been imprisoned for theft; Agustín Tatabutemea had been in the presidio for six years because he had been a principal leader of a revolt against the Spaniards, and so on. The apoderado did not have files for the vast majority of the inmates. Of the eighty-eight Indians who were at the presidio of Pitic at the time of the inspection, only five had been granted proper criminal proceedings. Tellingly, several inmates had been accused of being hechiceros, or sorcerers, and had been sent to the presidio by express orders of the missionaries.[13]

Rodríguez Gallardo's inquest uncovered a microcosm of coercion and enslavement. No matter how serious or light their crimes had been, the Natives, once inside the presidio, were compelled to work from dawn to dusk. Twenty-two Indians labored in shackles, while the remaining sixty-six did not wear chains but were constantly monitored. Since many of the prisoners were married, their wives and children also lived at the garrison. They made tortillas, ground *pinole* (a course flour made of corn and seeds), and fetched water in return for food and clothes. Discipline was extreme. Minor infractions such as being late for work could result in forty or fifty lashes. Some guards were sadistic, beating Indians to unconsciousness, burning their armpits with hot wax, and hanging them from their feet with their heads dangling over a fire. Three Indians accused of being hechiceros at the pueblo of Onavas died after suffering horrifying head burns as presidial soldiers attempted to extract their confessions.[14]

Even "free" Indians at Pitic were compelled to work. A Native named Mateo Osimea declared that for six years, he had been sent to work in a nearby mine. The apoderado immediately noted that Mateo was a free Indian who had been paid for his work. But Mateo countered that instead of wages, he had received a work certificate from the mine and later had been forced to give up the certificate on the grounds that he was a prisoner of the presidio rather than a free worker. Similarly, Salvador Barucia declared that for years he had worked in the presidio as a carpenter. The apoderado affirmed that Salvador was not a prisoner but a *sirviente libre* (free servant), to which the Indian replied that "up to now they do not allow me to leave even though I wish to go back to my pueblo." Salvador received a nominal wage in food and clothes, but he was compelled to stay and work at the presidio. The difference between freedom and slavery at Pitic was deceiving.[15]

The work performed by the inmates should have been for the public good, beginning with building the presidio itself. Yet the garrison remained half-finished after six years. The jail for dangerous criminals consisted of nothing but a grassy area. In fact, the presidio's commanders had used the inmates' labor for private gain. Pitic had been established right next to a large hacienda that belonged to the governor of Sonora and Sinaloa, Agustín de Vildósola. Since the beginning, most of the inmates had been sent to work on his property, building a dam, digging an irrigation ditch, installing fences, and tending the cornfields and wheat fields. Other prisoners had been hard at work carding, spinning, making cloth on looms, and fermenting mescal from the agave plant. Yet others had toiled in the nearby mines. Clearly, the presidio of San Pedro de la Conquista del Pitic had become something of a labor center that serviced the governor's hacienda, made products for sale, and funneled coerced workers to various enterprises in the area.[16]

Rodríguez Gallardo was so repulsed by what he saw that he ordered the immediate closure of the presidio and its relocation to "a more advantageous place." As it turned out, the site selected for the new presidio was in the heart of the Seri mission area, on the San Miguel River, roughly midway between the missions of Pópulo and Los Ángeles. The presidio's relocation proved catastrophic for these communities. Within a year, the soldiers of the new presidio of San Miguel de Horcasitas had taken possession of the best land in the floodplain. In the dry season, the San Miguel River diminished to a trickle, at a time when the fields needed to be irrigated the most. The soldiers simply displaced Indian farmers who had direct access to the river. The presidio's commanders also appropriated the Indians' labor. They seized about seventy Seris from Pópulo and put them to work digging the foundation for the new garrison and making adobe bricks for it. Even the Seri women were made to carry mud, grass, *carrizo* (a type of thick straw), and other building materials. "They are whipped, beaten, and forced to work as though they were evildoers," observed Father Tomás Miranda. The Seris of the mission of Los Ángeles fared no better. Soldiers transported about fifty families to the new presidio and made them work "from sunup to sundown," excepting no one, even pregnant women. There is no reason to assume that these presidios were unusually harsh toward the surrounding Indians. All along the frontier, presidios displaced Natives from well-irrigated lands, appropriated their labor to erect buildings, and seized recalcitrant Indians and turned them into servants, wives, and concubines, occasionally even selling them as slaves.[17]

The final twist to the Seri story shows the tremendous impact of militarization. Initially abused by the Spanish soldiers, the Seris retaliated in 1748–1749 when a party consisting of both mission and non-mission Seris boldly ran off the entire horse herd of the presidio of San Miguel de Horcasitas — thus reducing the soldiers' mobility — and struck half a dozen mining and smelting centers in the area. They unleashed their most serious attack on a mining town called Aguaje, where they killed forty-three residents, burned the houses after looting them, and desecrated the church. According to one priest, they "poured out the holy oils and with infernal fury lanced the painting of Our Great Mother and Lady of Guadalupe nine times, and took the holy vestments, which they burned after having eaten off them." The indigenous rebels even faced off with the soldiers dispatched to apprehend them and succeeded in seizing their muskets.[18]

The Spanish authorities became incensed. In April 1750, they held emergency meetings with colonists and ecclesiastics and formally declared the Seri nation "treacherous, arrogant, incendiary, and apostate" and contemplated a policy of wholesale removal. The principal proponent of "extirpation," as this policy became known, was none other than Rodríguez Gallardo, the licenciado who had been so thorough in his interrogations at Pitic. He made it clear now that what he had in mind was not merely sending away a few *cabecillas* (ringleaders), as had been done in the past. "In times of Governor Manuel Bernal de Huidobro [in 1737], four *cabecillas* from California were driven in shackles by a detachment of five soldiers," Rodríguez Gallardo contended, "and three of these criminals were able to escape while killing Corporal Lucas de Espinosa." Rodríguez Gallardo himself had dispatched a *collera* (chain gang) "of the most famous [Apache and Seri] robbers, arsonists, and killers," with even more disastrous results. Having reached the town of Sinaloa after a journey of two hundred leagues (more than six hundred miles), nine prisoners got away and within days killed all the residents of a nearby ranch.[19]

The worst aspect of this piecemeal policy of punishment from the Spaniards' perspective was that even the Seri captives who had been marched all the way to central Mexico had eventually returned. Their sense of place and direction seemed almost preternatural: "Take a [Seri] Indian into any depths blindfolded, be it mines, dungeons, or intricate labyrinths, and turn him around a thousand times and he will still be able to tell toward what wind or direction he is facing as if he were a living compass." Captives who made their way back to Sonora often became *cabecillas*, who used their newfound geographic and social knowledge to exact revenge: "Two Seris dispatched to the textile factories of Querétaro by Governor Huidobro came back to these coasts, and only these two have put themselves at the head of a group of fugitives causing turmoil and at least 20 homicides."[20]

Rodríguez Gallardo's solution was to deport all Seri Indians to a place from which they would never return. It was not the first time Spanish policymakers had removed Indians in significant numbers. At least since the early 1700s, Spanish soldiers had driven long lines of Tobosos and Apaches, tied together in colleras, from Nuevo León and Chihuahua to central and southern Mexico and the Caribbean islands. The military buildup on the frontier now allowed Spanish officials to envision even more ambitious schemes. By midcentury Rodríguez Gallardo believed that it was possible to remove the entire Seri nation of around three thousand people. All male and female Seris over the age of eight would be sent away, preferably by sea, because "once secured in a boat they will only be able to seek their freedom in their own shipwreck and ruin and without seeing the lay of our continent they would not understand how to return." Given that the textile sweatshops of central Mexico had not been able to keep the Seris from returning home, Spanish officials decided to ship the Indian prisoners to the "ultramarine islands," a vague formulation that probably meant the Caribbean islands and quite possibly the Philippines, where many Mexican vagrants and convicts were already being sent.[21]

The only Seris who would not be shipped away — children younger than eight — would be marched to the Apache frontier to be used as reinforcements. Spanish colonists and their Opata allies had been clinging precariously to their communities in the face of Apache raids in places such as the Valley of Bacanuchi, Terrenate, and San Francisco Xavier de Cuchuta along the headwaters of the San Pedro River. The Seri children would add to their numbers. The governor of Sonora predicted that "the Spaniards or people of reason among whom they intend to place the Seri children will not only agree to it but wish for the children to help them contain the enemy Apaches." In this case, Indian slavery was intended as a demographic strategy to populate a dangerous frontier.[22]

The plan of extirpation unfolded swiftly. In April 1750, Sonoran governor Diego Ortíz Parrilla announced plans to launch an expedition to the island of Tiburón. Over the summer, he gathered men and provisions and had seven large boats outfitted in the Yaqui River to get across the Strait of Infiernillo. When the late-summer rains finally arrived, Spanish soldiers began sweeping the coastal area and arresting Seris in the pueblos of Cucurpe, Opodepe, and Pópulo. In September Spanish soldiers and Pima auxiliaries began crossing over to Tiburón. They faced a determined opponent. At the sight of the approaching boats, the Seris dispersed, poisoning and befouling water holes with herbs and rotting carcasses. In the heat of the summer, they leveraged their superior survival skills while forcing the parched intruders to drink from maggot-infested water sources or import casks of the precious liquid from the mainland.[23]

In spite of the tremendous difficulties, the Spanish-Pima forces prevailed. Adult Seris were led away in ropes and chains, not quite to the Caribbean islands, as originally proposed, but to Guatemala. Even then, some of the men returned. But the women did not come back. An unspecified number of Seri children were also sent to the Apache frontier as planned. The mission records at Tumacácori, in southern Arizona, reveal that some Seris were baptized in the 1750s. The extirpation strategy ultimately failed, however. Many Seris remained in their homeland and had even more reason to rebel. Three years after the expedition to Tiburón, a Seri leader named Chepillo had a frank conversation with a missionary. When the Spanish friar urged the Indian leader to surrender, Chepillo replied, "I know that if we continue fighting we are damning ourselves, but there is no other way. We are accustomed to living with women. We do not know where our wives are, whether they are living or dead. You would not marry us to others, and if we take others, you will order us whipped." Chepillo's reasoning was unassailable. The Seri mission program, which had lasted for more than seventy years, had given way to extirpation and enslavement.[24]

## Colleras and Epidemics

In the course of the eighteenth century, presidios transformed the human landscape of northern Mexico, giving rise to sizeable towns, functioning as reservations, and generally giving Spanish officials and military planners the ability to launch remarkably bold social engineering projects.[25]

The Apaches were notable victims. They drifted southward into the silver-bearing areas of northern Mexico, at first sporadically and then with greater frequency in the 1740s and 1750s. Decades of suspicion and mistrust finally burst into open conflict. To prevent disruptions and to keep the silver flowing, Spanish officials subjected the Apaches to some of the same policies tested earlier on the Seris. According to the estimates of historian Paul Conrad, between 1770 and 1816 some three to five thousand Apaches and other Indians from the north were led away in chains, bound for central and southern Mexico. The most dangerous were shipped to Cuba. The sight of these lines of Indians tied to one another became all too familiar to contemporaries.[26]

At the start of this cycle of deportations, Viceroy Carlos Francisco de Croix felt the need to write a letter of advice to one of his officers on how to conduct these marches. Croix, who was nearly at the end of his tour of duty in the New World, had commanded the Spanish garrison of Ceuta in northwestern Africa earlier in his career and therefore knew a thing or two about transporting prisoners. He was very concerned about potential escapes, as his advice makes clear: "Start the march under the cloak of night . . . keep the Indian men in shackles and the women and children tied with ropes . . . never reveal the route that the collera will follow to minimize the likelihood of an ambush." He recommended that when the caravan set up camp in the middle of the wilderness, far from any settlements, two-thirds of the soldiers form a circle around the prisoners and the last third remain as lookouts. Croix also dispensed some words of wisdom about how to treat the prisoners: "Allow them to have a hot meal at least once a day, do not let the provision of water run out, and do not walk during the hottest hours of the day when the sun is at its most intense but instead have them wash the clothes assigned to them at this time." In spite of Croix's insistence on moderation, these marches were generally dreadful. Soldiers had an incentive to give the prisoners as little food as possible, in order to profit from the budget set aside for food. They also forced the Indians to walk for hours on end in order to wear them down and prevent any escape attempts. Terrible abuse arose from the fact that the majority of the prisoners were women and children, at the mercy of male soldiers. On at least one occasion, some prisoners were able to escape when the Spanish soldiers driving the collera took four female prisoners inside a room while leaving only one guard outside.[27]

Quite apart from the catalog of indignities and abuse during these marches is the incidence of contagious disease. Slavery and epidemics had gone hand in hand since contact. The abundant documentation of the late eighteenth century bears this linkage out. In effect, these drives moved people living in regions of low demographic density to major urban agglomerations such as Mexico City and Veracruz, which were rife with disease. Consider Sergeant José Antonio Uribe's march of 1797. He started in the middle of November from the garrison of Pilar de Conchos, north of Parral, with seventy-one Apaches: thirteen adult males, fifty-seven women, and one girl of about twelve. Sergeant Uribe was somewhat apprehensive, because among the thirteen males there was one individual named Polito, who had already escaped from an earlier collera, and another one called Garlén, "who enjoyed a reputation among his people for his spirit and past deeds of war."[28]

As it turned out, there were no escape attempts. In a little over a month, all but one of the prisoners had reached Mexico City safely; a lone woman had been left at the presidio of San Miguel de Cerro Gordo — now Villa Hidalgo, about sixty miles south of Parral — to receive medical treatment. Other than this medical issue, the drive had been uneventful. The collera reached Mexico City right around Christmastime. The plan was to rest for a few days before resuming the march to Veracruz. On December 26, the thirteen Apache men were escorted into the prison of the Acordada prison, while the fifty-seven females were interned at the Hospice for the Poor.

Disaster struck during this time. Of the fifty-seven Apache females kept at the hospice, fourteen developed skin eruptions characteristic of smallpox. Smallpox is caused by a virus called *Variola major,* which moves from host to host through direct contact. The virus passes from a sick person to a new host through invisible droplets of bodily fluids or secretions, which enter the new host's bloodstream via the mouth, nose, or eyes. Alternatively, dried-out scabs from a recent sufferer also can transmit the virus. A hospice teeming with women from all over Mexico City — easily the largest city in the Western Hemisphere — would have offered nearly ideal conditions for contagion. A face-to-face encounter with an infected person would have sufficed, as would contact with dried-out scabs remaining on floors, beds, or clothes. The Apache women must have become infected almost immediately on arrival.[29]

The incubation period for smallpox is between ten and fourteen days. During this time, only mild discomfort, which could easily be mistaken for a common cold, is apparent. Then the symptoms — high fevers, headaches and backaches, vomiting, and skin eruptions — flare up with frightening rapidity and virulence. Hospice authorities reported the onset of the illness among the Apache women around the middle of January, a little over fourteen days after their initial internment, and on January 17 they wrote that nine of the women had died and five remained gravely ill. Over the next few weeks, the illness continued to spread. Even though the hospice administrators made valiant efforts to contain the outbreak by moving three of the infected Apaches to the Royal Hospital for Indians (where the illness may well have spread even further) and isolating another two who were bedridden and unable to move, other Apaches got sick. By the middle of February, the count had reached thirty-two dead and four infected. The disease had ravaged nearly two-thirds of the Apache women kept at the Hospice for the Poor. They had ended their days with a priest at their bedside offering to baptize them and save their souls from eternal damnation.

The Apache men fared even worse. The Acordada prison, one of the most characteristic buildings of eighteenth-century Mexico City, was still relatively new. But its narrow hallways, dark and damp cells, and extreme crowding offered ideal conditions for the spread of the disease. Not a single Apache inmate was spared. By early February, of fourteen Apache males (thirteen recently arrived in the collera and one more who was already at the Acordada), five had died, seven had become gravely ill, and the remaining two appeared to be recovering as if by a miracle. The conditions of starvation to which these Apaches had been subjected during their march to Mexico City and possibly during their stay at the Acordada must have made their suffering even worse. Studies have revealed a correlation between malnourishment and some of the worst effects of smallpox, especially blindness. For a people like the Apaches, who had lived all their lives free of the disease, the experience must have been terrifying. After the onset of symptoms, the eruptions proliferate, not only on the skin but also along the mucous membranes in the mouth and throat, making basic functions such as eating, drinking, and talking extremely painful. In the worst cases, the pustules "converge." Death is not long in coming after the appearance of these oozing wounds. Even the two Apache males who survived their bout with smallpox remained extremely weak for an extended period. When the order came down from the viceroy to resume the march to Veracruz, only twenty-one women were deemed fit to continue.[30]

We do not know the ultimate fate of these women, but after having tangled with smallpox, they faced a second life-and-death struggle along the Gulf of Mexico coast in the form of two mosquito-borne killers: yellow fever and malaria. Stagnant water, warm temperatures, and a lush tropical environment make the port of Veracruz an ideal habitat for a multitude of insects, including the *Aedes aegypti* (transmitter of yellow fever) and *Anopheles* (transmitter of malaria) mosquitoes. Clouds of mosquitoes cover the swampy coastal areas around the port of Veracruz and are impossible to avoid, least of all in a dungeon holding Indians like San Juan de Ulúa. During the day, one can swat away a few mosquitoes. But at night, while asleep, one is completely at their mercy. Hundreds or even thousands of bites are not uncommon, and all it takes is one bite from an infected female mosquito of either species to get into trouble.

Of these two illnesses, yellow fever was easily the most lethal to a people lacking immunity, like these Indian prisoners from the deserts of northern Mexico and what is now the American Southwest. The yellow fever virus passes through the mosquito's saliva into the bloodstream of the human host and spreads to the liver, where it reproduces, causing chills, muscle pain, and high fevers after three to six days. The skin of the sufferer becomes noticeably yellow as a result of the damage to the liver, hence the illness's name in English. In Spanish it is often referred to as *vómito negro*, or black vomit, because it also causes hemorrhages in the gastrointestinal tract, and the vomited blood is often dark red or black. Yellow fever outbreaks could easily cause mortality rates of more than fifty percent among people who had no prior exposure to *Aedes aegypti*. Although the fragmentary information about the colleras does not permit even a rough estimate of the mortality rates of Indian prisoners held in Veracruz or shipped to Cuba, the constant concern of Spanish officials about "malignant fevers" is a clear sign that yellow fever and malaria lurked in the background.[31]

The colleras of the late eighteenth and early nineteenth centuries show in tangible ways that epidemic disease did not spread evenly across the Americas. Indians living in the interior of North America seemed to have suffered comparatively less from epidemic disease than those inhabiting coastal regions or residing in large urban agglomerations. In the dry and sparsely populated regions of northern Mexico and the American Southwest, pathogens had a harder time spreading than in coastal areas, where tropical diseases reigned supreme, and in urban centers, where the "crowd diseases" — for example, smallpox and cholera — were common. There is little doubt that the colleras of the late eighteenth century were an ideal mechanism for infecting Indians from the north. By forcing them into close and even intimate contact with Spanish soldiers for a month or longer; parading them through towns and cities; compelling them to mingle with criminals and paupers in jails and hospices in the large cities of central Mexico; and finally marching them to the Gulf coast, thus exposing them to another suite of mosquito-borne diseases, the Spaniards made these Indians as vulnerable as possible to smallpox, yellow fever, and other deadly illnesses.[32]

It is also likely that the colleras facilitated the spread of epidemic disease from south to north, as soldiers and drivers moved back and forth and Indian prisoners already exposed to pathogens in central and southern Mexico escaped and found their way back to their home communities in the north. This is one of the most elusive, but tantalizing, aspects of the Indian drives of the late eighteenth and early nineteenth centuries. From 1775 to 1782, North America experienced a smallpox epidemic of continental proportions, from the Atlantic to the Pacific and from the Caribbean and southern Mexico to Canada, as has been documented by historian Elizabeth A. Fenn. The exact origin of this major outbreak is unknown. But sometime in 1779, it reached Mexico City. With its 130,000 inhabitants and its many jails, hospices, churches, schools, and other nodes of infection, the largest city in the Western Hemisphere offered a most auspicious environment for the spread of smallpox. When the first cases were reported in the late summer of 1779, the illness seemed eerily mild, but it gained strength during the fall. By late December, more than 44,000 Mexico City residents had come down with smallpox, and an estimated 18,000 had succumbed to the disease. Indians from northern Mexico must certainly have been affected. In 1778 no less than three different colleras, originating in Tamaulipas, Coahuila, and Chihuahua, had arrived in the city.[33]

From Mexico City, the disease radiated out in all directions. Fenn looked at the burial records in various parishes, tracking the increasing number of deaths as the disease moved like a tidal wave from town to town. Although priests seldom indicated the cause of death, the skyrocketing number of burials leaves no doubt as to the reason. Smallpox's relentless march north is easy to document. During the winter of 1780, *Variola* made dramatic inroads through much of central Mexico. By the late spring and early summer, it had reached the mining areas of Parral and Chihuahua. By the end of the year, it had spread all the way to New Mexico, as well as to the coast of Sinaloa and Sonora and to portions of Tamaulipas and Texas. And by the summer of 1781, it had reached the Comanchería. Of course, it is impossible to correlate specific Indian drives with the spread of this devastating epidemic. But it is remarkable that even in the midst of this outbreak, the colleras continued: one in 1780 and three more in 1781. These Indian drives, moving dozens of susceptible indigenous hosts and requiring soldiers to move back and forth between central and northern Mexico, would have been excellent carriers of the disease.[34]

# 9

## Contractions and Expansions

By the early nineteenth century, Indian slavery had nearly disappeared on the east coast of North America. In colonial times, the Carolinas had been a major Indian slaving ground; New Englanders had impressed rebellious Indians and shipped them to the Caribbean; and French colonists in eastern Canada had impressed thousands of Natives from the interior. During the eighteenth and early nineteenth centuries, however, the traffic of Natives was replaced almost completely by that of African slaves. Only a few vestiges of the old trade networks remained, notably in Florida. There Indian traditions of captivity harking all the way back to pre-Columbian times continued to function. But even these practices became redirected toward blacks. The Seminoles, for instance, took Africans as slaves. Not surprisingly, Americans living along the Eastern Seaboard lost any awareness of earlier forms of indigenous bondage. When they spoke or wrote about slavery in the nineteenth century, they invariably meant African slavery.[1]

Yet Indian slavery continued to thrive in the West and even expanded as traffickers capitalized on some of the momentous changes of the early 1800s. Mexico's struggle for independence from Spain (1810–1821) was probably the most important catalyst of this expansion. Ironically, the leaders of the insurgency called for "the abolition of slavery forever" and the elimination of "all distinctions of caste so we shall all be equal." And they made good on their promises. The newly independent government granted citizenship rights to all Indians living in Mexico and abolished slavery in 1829. However, presaging what would happen later in the century in the United States, with the Civil War and Emancipation Proclamation, these measures, far from ending Indian slavery, paved the way for its transformation and further expansion.[2]

More immediately, Mexico's eleven-year struggle spelled economic disaster. Much of the fighting took place in the mining districts, prompting workers to abandon the silver mines. With no workers there to pump out the water that accumulated as a result of rainstorms and underground seepage, the mines became completely flooded, and these extraordinary engines of growth became mere holes in the ground. It would take half a century for Mexico's mineral exports to return to late-colonial levels. In the meantime, the economic decline led to a breakdown of most frontier controls. The number of soldiers posted in northern Mexico dwindled, presidios were abandoned, and the region became vulnerable to Indian attacks. The Comanches, who had been expanding for a century, and the Apaches, who knew the terrain extremely well, pushed deep into Mexico, descending on haciendas and abandoned mines and capturing women and children.[3]

## The Comanches in Mexico

The Comanche expansion into Mexico started suddenly and coincided with the initial turmoil of independence. Few testimonies are as eloquent as that of landowner and politician Miguel Ramos Arizpe, who had grown up in the state of Coahuila (just south of Texas) during the halcyon days of the Spanish silver boom. A line of presidios running along the Rio Grande had afforded his home state a measure of security that had made it wealthier and better populated than Texas. Though not impassable, these garrisons presented a real obstacle to Indian raiding. As Ramos Arizpe explained, "The various tribes of the Comanchería lived in the enormous plains and sierras between Texas and New Mexico north of the line of presidios . . . and they knew very well that the

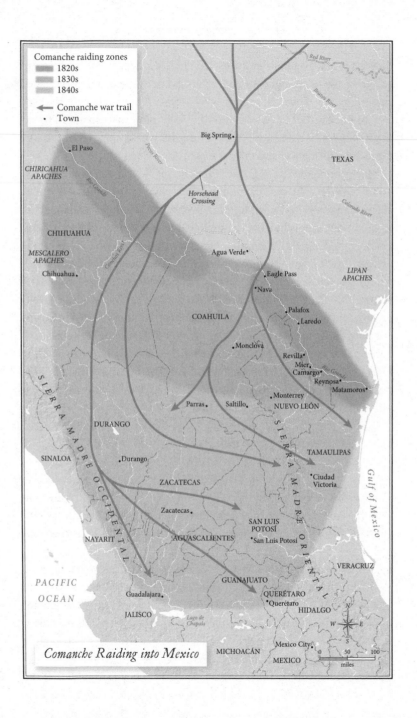

Comanche raiding zones
1820s
1830s
1840s

← Comanche war trail
• Town

*Red River*

Big Spring•

*Pecos River*

TEXAS

El Paso•

CHIRICAHUA
APACHES

*Rio Grande*

*Colorado River*

*Horsehead
Crossing*

CHIHUAHUA

MESCALERO
APACHES

Chihuahua•

Agua Verde•

LIPAN
APACHES

Eagle Pass•
•Nava

COAHUILA

•Palafox
•Laredo

•Monclova

Revilla•
Mier•
Camargo•
Reynosa•
Matamoros•

*Rio Grande*

SIERRA  MADRE  OCCIDENTAL

Parras•

Saltillo•

•Monterrey

NUEVO LEÓN

DURANGO

•Durango

SINALOA

ZACATECAS

Zacatecas•

TAMAULIPAS

•Ciudad
Victoria

SIERRA  MADRE  ORIENTAL

Gulf of Mexico

NAYARIT

AGUASCALIENTES

SAN LUIS
POTOSÍ

•San Luis Potosí

PACIFIC

OCEAN

Guadalajara•

GUANAJUATO

QUERÉTARO
•Querétaro

VERACRUZ

JALISCO

*Lago de
Chapula*

HIDALGO

N
W   E
S

*Comanche Raiding into Mexico*

MICHOACÁN

Mexico City•

MEXICO

0    50    100

miles

principal access into the interior provinces of Coahuila, Nuevo León, and Tamaulipas was closed off to them."[4]

Yet the struggle for independence opened the floodgates. "We observed that the heathen Indians who during entire centuries had taken just a handful of children as captives," Ramos Arizpe recounted, "in the short years between 1816 and 1821 took more than two thousand captives of all kinds, genders, and ages, and killed as many people or more in Coahuila, Nuevo León, and Tamaulipas." He was personally affected by the upsurge in Comanche activity. Ramos Arizpe owned eight hundred square leagues (more than four million acres) of well-irrigated land on the Rio Grande. But he could neither protect nor develop his vast domain because it lay in the path of Comanche expansion. His property included the ruins of the old presidio of Agua Verde, a poignant reminder of Mexico's military retreat.[5]

The Comanches would go on to wage a ruinous war in northern Mexico in the 1830s and 1840s, as historian Brian DeLay has shown. They mounted more than forty raids into Mexico during this period — more than two per year on average. Half of them were actually large-scale military operations involving up to a thousand warriors. Considering that the total Comanche population may have been between ten and twelve thousand, and assuming that there was one warrior for every five Comanches, a "raid" of one thousand men amounted to half the Comanche fighting force, as DeLay notes. Just as impressive was their geographic scope. They came to engulf much of Chihuahua, Durango, Coahuila, and Nuevo León, as well as half of Tamaulipas, reaching as far south as Zacatecas, San Luis Potosí, and Querétaro, not far from Mexico City.[6]

These raiding campaigns were not intended solely or even primarily to take captives. Later interviews with Comanches make clear that the acquisition of horses was the principal objective. Warriors competed with one another over the number of mounts they possessed and sought to procure as many horses as they could by any means. Chief Esakeep expressed great pride in his four sons because they could steal more horses than the other young men in the tribe. In fact, horses were an absolute necessity for any long-distance raid. To conduct these campaigns, Comanches needed to travel hundreds of miles. And once deep in Mexico, they needed to retreat swiftly, carrying captives and loot. Having sufficient animals and the ability to change to fresh mounts was critical.[7]

Procuring goods was another major goal of these incursions. The Comanchería was a trading center that absorbed a variety of commodities that were consumed internally or traded to other groups. Clothes and textiles were excellent forms of plunder — lightweight, easy to transport, and always in high demand. Raiders went through the trouble of removing the clothes of their prisoners before killing them and taking shirts and pants from corpses during a raid. They also paid special attention to metal objects. Knives, lances, and firearms were obviously important. But Comanche raiders also took latches, nails, bolts, and other metal objects that could be transformed into valuable tools with a forge.[8]

Even though taking captives was not the primary purpose of these raids, Comanches took hundreds of them in the 1830s–1850s. Each could fetch anywhere between 50 and as much as 1,000 pesos (or dollars, for in that golden era, there was parity between the two currencies). In other words, by the middle of the nineteenth century, a captive was far more valuable than a horse or a mare. A group of Apaches traveling near the Pecos River in February 1850, for example, exchanged a ten-year-old boy from Saltillo for "one mare, one rifle, one pair of drawers, thirty small packages of powder, some bullets, and one buffalo robe." Around the same time, a twelve-year-old boy from Mexico was traded east of the Rio Grande somewhere in New Mexico for "corn and tobacco, one knife, one shirt, one mule, one small package of powder, and a few balls." The Comanches and Apaches must have developed a good sense of the value and desirability of each type of captive, which varied greatly depending on the circumstances. Anglo-Americans and well-off Hispanics (people of Mexican origin living in what is now the American Southwest) were especially attractive because they could be held for ransom; women were more valuable than men; youngsters (but not babies) were preferred over older folks; boys were preferred over girls; and adult males were generally not worth the trouble except in unusual circumstances.[9]

Any Comanche man could propose a raid, spread the word that a war party was about to leave, and invite all others to join in. Proven leaders had an easier time gaining a following. Less experienced or poorer males typically fielded smaller parties. A council was often held to approve the raid — which necessarily would have political consequences — and to work out the details: where to go; what route to follow; how many warriors, horses, and weapons to take. These parties could target other Indians, American caravans, or particular communities. During the 1830s–1870s, most of the raids were directed against Mexicans. Coahuila, Nuevo León, Chihuahua, Durango, Zacatecas, and some other Mexican states were far enough from the Comanchería and possessed enough animals, textiles, tools, and potential captives to make them attractive targets. According to the recollections of Comanche elders interviewed decades later, the day before departure all members of the raiding party, decked out in their war costumes, paraded on horseback around the tepees so that everyone could see the strength and members of the group. Other men could join the party at this time. A dance, in which only those going on the raid could participate, followed. The members of the raiding party also sang and invited young women to sing with them. This was a propitious time for marriage proposals and elopements.[10]

Once they were on the trail, the first order of the day was to acquire sufficient animals. Ideally, each warrior had to have a riding horse and a pack animal to carry his clothes and other belongings. Additionally, each raiding party included a "cook" who was responsible for the supplies of the entire group. This person was "selected for industry, activity, alertness, and willingness to do what was needed" and was often, interestingly, a Mexican captive. To carry all the water and food the group needed, the cook required sufficient beasts of burden. Consequently, it was not unusual for raiding parties to spend a lot of time getting the necessary animals. The warriors descended on barns or corrals, killing wranglers and stampeding or leading away the animals. When it came time to divide the spoils, the cook frequently got to choose first because horses and mules were so necessary for his work.[11]

Comanche war parties undertook long-distance journeys of reconnaissance and discovery that lasted weeks or even months — comparable to the Spanish expeditions of the sixteenth century, but in the other direction. After all, Chihuahua City was 270 miles away from the Comanchería, Durango 660 miles, and Zacatecas nearly 800 miles. Just getting there was a considerable feat. The raiders sometimes traveled at night and slept during the day to avoid detection. Surviving the desert of northern Mexico was no less challenging for Comanches than it was for other parched travelers. Because the terrain was unfamiliar, party members had to rely on intelligence culled from a variety of sources: Indian allies, trading partners, captives, and an assortment of unwilling informants. When the attackers at last neared their target, they hid in the woods or another protected area. They rested before striking and desisted from lighting a fire. Each man selected his best horse and prepared for the raid. The cook and some sentries usually stayed behind with the supplies and any captives they already had in their possession. Everyone had precise instructions about when and where to rendezvous and made contingency plans.[12]

Witnesses emphasized the stealth of these Indian attacks, which in an instant could turn a placid night into a surreal scene of mayhem, complete with screams of *"Los bárbaros!,"* gunshots, galloping horses, and flying arrows. Outlying ranches, isolated houses, and shepherds plying their trade in remote areas were easy pickings. But Comanche warriors sometimes targeted large Mexican towns as well. In December 1840 and January 1841, a group of Indian attackers spent two weeks raiding ranches in the vicinity of Saltillo, the capital of the state of Coahuila, moving from one ranch to the next, as if in complete defiance of any Mexican retribution. In a feat of "inconceivable audacity," as the Mexican press labeled it, they appeared right on the outskirts of the city before being driven away by a hastily assembled Mexican force. Similarly, in August 1846, during one of the most daring and brazen raids of all, some five hundred Comanches cut a swath through Chihuahua and Durango. George F. Ruxton, an Englishman who was traveling through northern Mexico at the time, left us a bleak portrayal: abandoned ranches, impassable roads, and barricaded towns living in dread of Indian raids. When he reached the city of Durango in September, he was astonished to learn that the talk of this town of some eighteen thousand inhabitants was not about the ongoing U.S.-Mexican War, but about a possible Indian invasion by Comanches who had been ravaging haciendas to the northeast of the city.[13]

Along with horses and trade goods, Comanches made away with captives. The testimony of Abelino Fuentes is fairly typical. He was walking with three brothers and one sister along a path in the vicinity of Monclova sometime in 1838 when a group of thirty warriors descended on them. The attackers immediately killed the oldest brother, Pedro, put the other children on horses, and began retreating. Abelino was seven years old at the time. The following day, a Mexican force caught up with the Comanches, forcing them to shed all their captives except Abelino. The raiders then continued to travel north. Captives like Abelino sometimes tried to escape while they were still close to their home communities and in relative proximity to other Mexican towns. That is why Indians often bound captives with ropes before going to sleep or even while riding. After crossing the Rio Grande and especially after having reached the Comanchería, such precautions became unnecessary. Lacking horses, weapons, and provisions, it was extremely risky for captives to set out on their own in the immense southern plains.[14]

By the nineteenth century, the market for captives along the U.S.-Mexico border was well developed with suppliers, buyers, and widely known intermediaries. Although most Indian groups took captives, not all were involved to the same degree. Because of their geographic location and strength, some bands of Comanches, Apaches, and other Plains Indians did much of the actual enslaving of Mexicans. Captive Fernando González singled out the Yamparicas (a band of Comanches), the Kiowas (a group closely allied with the Comanches), some Apache bands (Lipanes, Mescaleros, and Gileños), and the Sarigtecas (or Saritʉhkas, a generic term for Plains Indians used by the Comanches) as the principal captive takers in northern Mexico. These bands often traded their prisoners away, but they also retained many captives who were incorporated into their respective bands and came to comprise significant proportions of their overall populations. According to the American ethnographer James Mooney, who spent five years doing fieldwork among the Kiowa Indians in the 1890s, "At least one fourth of the whole number have more or less of captive blood . . . chiefly Mexicans and Mexican Indians, with Indians of other tribes, and several whites taken from Texas when children." In a census of Comanche families conducted in

Oklahoma Territory in 1902, fully forty-five percent turned out to be of Mexican descent.[15]

If the principal suppliers of captives are few and easy to identify, the customers are somewhat more scattered: New Mexican families in the market for servants, the Plains Indians themselves, and Anglo-American merchants and fort operators on the frontier. The Bent brothers, William and Charles, are an excellent case in point. They started trading with the Indians of Dakota in the early 1820s before moving their operation to the upper Arkansas River in what is now southeastern Colorado, where they built an imposing square structure out of adobe bricks in 1828–1829. Their sense of geography (and timing) could not have been better: right along the U.S.-Mexico border, on the edge of the Comanchería, and a necessary stopover point for the caravans traveling between Missouri and New Mexico. In its heyday in the 1830s and 1840s, Bent's Fort employed more than a hundred individuals, including merchants, teamsters, hunters, herders, and laborers. Many of these employees were Mexicans whom Colonel William Bent had purchased from Comanche and Kiowa Indians. "I know of several instances of this kind, and there must have been many others," recalled George Bent, William's half-white, half-Cheyenne son. "One peon who was bought by my father from the Kiowas in [the] early days is now living down here at the Kiowa Agency . . . Another captive my father bought was a German who was carried off by the Kiowas from the German colony in Texas when he was a small boy." Comanches and Kiowas regularly headed to Bent's Fort to trade horses and other plunder, including captives. From these visits George Bent was able to ascertain that "among the Kiowas and Comanches nearly every family had one or two Mexican captives. The women captives married into the tribe, . . . the boys and men were employed by the Indians as herders, to guard the horses when out grazing; but after the men had lived with the Indians a number of years they became regular warriors, and the more intelligent and brave ones led war parties of Indians on raids into Mexico and Texas."[16]

From published and unpublished sources, Rivaya-Martínez has identified 470 captives taken by Comanches from the 1820s to the 1860s. It is impossible to know how many cases went unrecorded. From this sample, however, it is clear that most of the victims were Hispanics (seventy-five percent), followed far behind by other Indians (fourteen percent) and Anglo-Americans (ten percent). Traditionally, perceptions of Comanche captivity have been shaped by a handful of sensational accounts given by Americans who fell into their hands, as Rivaya-Martínez has noted. The treatment of Matilda Lockhart, for example, a thirteen-year-old girl abducted from her family's homestead on the Guadalupe River in Texas, became well known through the writings of Mary A. Maverick. When Matilda "returned to civilization," she had bruises and sores all over her body, and her nose had been cut off, her nostrils "wide open and denuded of flesh." Maverick recounted how Matilda's captors would wake her "by sticking a chunk of fire to her flesh, especially to her nose, and how they would shout and laugh like fiends when she cried." Similarly, American readers learned of the ordeal of Rachael Plummer, who wrote *Narrative of Twenty One Months Servitude as a Prisoner Among the Commanchee Indians,* and became acquainted with the misfortunes of the Horn family after the publication of *A Narrative of the Captivity of Mrs. Horn and Her Two Children with That of Mrs. Harris by the Comanche Indians.* Undoubtedly, such experiences did occur among Comanche captives. But proportionally, the Comanches took few Anglo-American captives, and the ones they did take were often ransomed and released as soon as practicable. Far more abundant and typical were the experiences of humble Mexicans, whose lives were changed in an instant when they were captured, and who frequently remained with the Natives for several years, if not forever. Lacking the necessary means and connections, the families of these captives were unable to ransom their children and wives and were otherwise powerless to demand their return. Rash actions by aggrieved parents wishing to pursue Indian abductors could easily result in further injury.[17]

The fate of these captives varied according to ethnicity, social standing, and the vagaries of the slave traffic. Young Mexican captives from poor families who were unlikely to be ransomed were frequently traded back and forth among different clans and different bands. Twelve-year-old Jesús María Guzmán, for example, was abducted in May 1848 from a hacienda near Sabinas Hidalgo, in Nuevo León. The Comanche abductors crossed the Rio Grande near Laredo and traveled through western Texas for a month. Before reaching their ranchería, they spent a few days at an encampment of Lipan Apaches, who attempted to buy Jesús María. On that occasion, the Comanche warrior who had captured the boy refused to sell him at the price that was offered. However, the Lipan Apaches remained interested. Eighteen days later, they paid a visit to the Comanche ranchería. Offering a higher price, they were able to complete the transaction. There are numerous instances of captive exchanges among Comanches and Apaches at this time. In the late 1840s, the Comanches and Lipan Apaches were allied, visited each other regularly, and traded captives as a matter of course. Jesús María actually met most of the captives living in both rancherías, and "during the three years that he lived with the Indians, he noticed how Lipanes and Comanches campaigned together and how Comanches often came to invite his Indians to go raiding together."[18]

Anglo-Americans and well-off Mexicans stood a better chance of being ransomed. Their families often hired agents or worked with government officials to locate their abducted relatives and negotiate their release. Naturally, the Indians themselves must have been aware that some of their captives were eminently "ransomable" and were thus inclined to negotiate with intermediaries in a manner that could not have been too different from modern-day negotiations regarding abductions. Such negotiations were sometimes conducted by agents who remained in regular contact with Indian bands, knew about the captives held by each group, and either acted on behalf of the relatives of the abductees or participated in this human traffic on their own account and for their own benefit. Hispanic merchants who made a living by trading with the Plains Indians were the principal intermediaries. Given the strong ties linking New Mexico with these Indians, it is no wonder that most of these merchants, known as *comancheros,* were based in that territory. The celebrated American merchant Josiah Gregg described them as a class of "indigent and rude" individuals from the frontier villages "who collect together several times a year, and launch upon the plains with a few trinkets and trumperies of all kinds, and perhaps a bag of bread or pinole." Comancheros made the purchase of Indian, Mexican, and

Anglo-American captives a regular part of their overall commercial activities. Sometimes they acted on behalf of the victims' families. In late 1849, for example, a party of Apaches ambushed a wagon train of Americans on the Santa Fe Trail, taking a white woman (Mrs. White) and her small daughter with them. After news of this fateful event reached Santa Fe, James S. Calhoun, the Indian agent for New Mexico, tried to find a solution. He quickly concluded that a military effort would not succeed. Instead, Calhoun hired the services of a comanchero. "This man is well known to respectable people here, as a daring, fearless, and withal a discreet man," he reported to Washington. "I promised to pay him one thousand dollars, and other gratuities, if he succeeds in bringing in to me Mrs. White and her daughter." The Mexican merchant departed within an hour, "manifesting the greatest confidence in his ability to command success." In spite of his speedy dispatch and confidence, the comanchero returned empty-handed. By the time he reached the Apaches, they had killed the woman and absolutely refused to sell the daughter.[19]

More commonly, comancheros ransomed captives to resell them at a higher price. Traditionally, they had acquired captives held by Comanches, Apaches, and other Indians and resold them as chattel in New Mexico. With the rise in the number of Mexicans taken in the nineteenth century, comancheros simply folded this new stream of captives into their business. Americans on the frontier marveled at how these merchants treated their own kith and kin as chattel. Comancheros sometimes justified the acquisition of these captives by citing their compassion for fellow Christians stranded among heathens. In spite of this pious posturing, in reality such "ransomed" individuals had now become the property of their "redeemers" and were certainly not free to return home. Instead, the comanchero was now in a position to negotiate another "ransom" with the captive's family or attempt to resell him or her at a higher price.

Remarkably, some comancheros may actually have specialized in the traffic of Mexican captives, as the Mexican government discovered while investigating the case of the Frescas family. Juan José Frescas and his nine-year-old son, Concepción, had been out cutting wood near

Chihuahua City when a party of Indians attacked them in the summer of 1845, killing the father and taking the boy. He was "a blond, long-faced, chubby boy with a big nose," easy to recognize. For three months, the mother made inquiries, until she learned that her son was being held by a man named Juan Gutiérrez, who lived in the little town of Padillas, near Socorro, in southern New Mexico. Further investigations revealed that Gutiérrez held not only Concepción but also "many others because he takes part in that type of traffic." Gutiérrez "ransomed" most of his Mexican captives from the Apaches. Other merchants, the governor of New Mexico ruefully admitted, conducted a similar traffic with Comanches and Navajos.[20]

These cases emphasize the complicity of all ethnicities in the captive exchange that flourished along the border. The line separating captors from captives was blurry. We tend to think of Indians, Mexicans, and Anglo-Americans as self-contained billiard balls colliding with one another on the frontier. In reality, however, one-fourth of all Kiowa Indians and nearly half of all Comanches were of Mexican descent, and many of them surely participated in raids against fellow Mexicans. Conversely, some Mexican communities, such as San Carlos, in Chihuahua, were notorious for acquiring the spoils offered by Indians — including captives taken elsewhere in Mexico — in much the same way that Bent's Fort on the Arkansas River "ransomed" captives to work there and New Mexico absorbed goods and individuals stolen by Indians in Chihuahua. It is clear that in the harsh frontier environment, ethnic and national loyalties frequently mattered less than the glint of profit and the imperative of survival.[21]

## A Family Story

The Apaches were transformed by the general breakdown in Mexico's control of the border. Although their experience resembled that of the Comanches, it also differed in some crucial respects. In colonial times, the Apaches had been among the worst victims of enslavement. In the seventeenth century, they had been forcibly transported to the silver mines of northern Mexico, and in the eighteenth century they had suffered in colleras bound for Mexico City and the Caribbean. But with the end of the silver boom, their ordeal came to a halt. The colleras ceased after 1816 as the presidios declined or were abandoned altogether.[22]

The celebrated Chiricahua Apache chief Geronimo and his family lived through these searing transitions in western New Mexico and eastern Arizona. Geronimo's grandfather, Mahco, had been chief of the Bedonkohe band at the height of Spanish militarization of the frontier. The presidios in Chihuahua and Sonora had exerted so much pressure on the Chiricahua Apaches that many of them sued for peace in the 1780s. Threatened by the horror of enslavement and deportation, they agreed to settle in fixed communities under the watchful eye of Spanish officials. Thus began a thirty-year social engineering experiment. The Spaniards gave seeds, animals, farming tools, and even firearms to the Apaches, and in return they were expected to become sedentary agriculturalists. The transition was never complete. The settled Apaches continued to move around, hunting, gathering, and even raiding on occasion, doing their best to maintain their traditional way of life. But they did become more reliant on crops and more dependent on Spanish clothes, weapons, and ammunition. Mahco was remembered as "a man of peace and a successful rancher" who enjoyed "good repute among the Mexicans." Much of his life coincided with this extraordinary period of relative calm.[23]

Yet these Indian settlements depended on the continuing flow of money and the presence of the military. Mexico's struggles for independence eroded both of these pillars. The annual expenditures at the presidio of Janos — the closest to the Bedonkohe band — plummeted by more than ninety percent. The number of soldiers and the overall civilian population residing at the garrison also declined significantly in the 1820s. As had happened elsewhere along the frontier, Mexico's prolonged wars and economic ruin fanned the fires of change. Geronimo was born around 1823, barely two years after Mexico's independence. As the country's defenses crumbled, the Bedonkohe people abandoned their settlements and retreated into New Mexico's Mogollon Mountains, a compact, extremely rugged range thirty miles in length. Peaks soaring

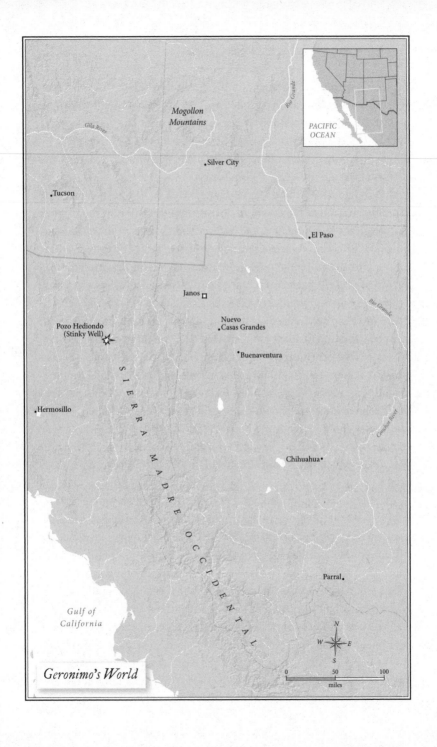

Mogollon
Mountains

Gila River

Rio Grande

.Silver City

.Tucson

El Paso.

Janos ▢

Nuevo
.Casas Grandes

Pozo Hediondo
(Stinky Well) ✧

.Buenaventura

.Hermosillo

Rio Grande

Conchos River

S I E R R A

M A D R E

Chihuahua.

O C C I D E N T A L

Parral.

Gulf of
California

PACIFIC
OCEAN

N
W ✦ E
S

0      50      100

miles

*Geronimo's* World

above ten thousand feet, deep canyons and gorges, and mesas buffeted by strong winds and violent storms offered these Apaches a nearly impregnable refuge, as well as immediate access to various Mexican communities and ranches.[24]

During Geronimo's youth, no single individual led the Chiricahua Apaches, or even the Bedonkohe band, which was further subdivided into local groups and extended families, each with its own chief. But there was one warrior who captured the imagination of many young Apaches. The Mexicans knew him as Fuerte (Strong) or Mangas Coloradas (Red Sleeves). At six feet five inches tall, he towered above other Apaches and Mexicans alike. He was "clothed with muscles," according to the enthusiastic description of an American physician, and had deepset dark eyes and a posture as "straight as a reed from which his arrows were made." This formidable man helped pioneer a new relationship between the Chiricahuas and Mexico. In one of his earliest raids, probably between 1812 and 1815, Mangas Coloradas took a Mexican captive named Carmen and made her one of his wives. (This young woman turned out to be so willful that some Apaches complained she "didn't know her place," a reminder that even captives could improve their situations and assert power.) During the 1820s and 1830s, as Mexico pared down its rationing system and reduced the number of soldiers posted in Sonora and Chihuahua, many Apaches left their communities around the Mexican presidios. After more than a generation of relative peace, many Chiricahuas were still eager to reach an accommodation with the Mexican government. But many others became restless and quite receptive to war leaders such as Mangas Coloradas. By the 1840s, this impressive individual had emerged as the preeminent leader of the war faction among all the Chiricahua bands.[25]

Geronimo came of age hearing stories of Mangas Coloradas and quite possibly training under his supervision. (Adolescents sometimes accompanied raiding parties but were limited to observing the campaign from a distance.) His apprenticeship finally ended in 1846, as Mexico and the United States teetered on the brink of war. As Geronimo later recalled, "Then I was very happy for I could go wherever I wanted and

This is the image most Americans have of Geronimo: a determined-looking man clutching a Winchester rifle, with one knee planted on the ground to steady his aim. In the United States, Geronimo is widely remembered as a tragic hero, fighting to preserve his homeland from westward-moving whites. Yet Americans did not take notice of him until he was in his fifties. By then he had spent a lifetime straddling the U.S.-Mexico border engaged in raids and counterraids, taking Mexican captives while seeing members of his family being killed or impressed by Mexican soldiers.

do whatever I liked. I had not been under the control of any individual, but the custom of our tribe prohibited me from sharing the glories of the warpath until the council admitted me." Geronimo also had another incentive. For some time, he had wished to marry Alope, the daughter of a Bedonkohe man named No-po-so, but No-po-so was not favorably disposed toward him. When the young man asked for Alope's hand, No-po-so demanded many ponies. "I made no reply," Geronimo recalled, "but in a few days appeared before his wigwam with the herd of ponies and took with me Alope." The "days" must have been weeks, during which Geronimo gathered the required animals from Mexican ranches and towns.[26]

The couple's early life coincided with a great increase in the number of Chiricahua raids into Mexico. At the conclusion of the United States' war with Mexico in 1848, the international border was redrawn, and the Chiricahuas ended up on the American side. They could now raid Mexico, then retreat across the border, where Mexican troops could not follow. Officials in both countries recognized the seriousness of this problem. According to article 11 of the Treaty of Guadalupe Hidalgo, which officially ended the war, "Considering that a great part of the territory is now occupied by savage tribes, and whose incursions within the territory of Mexico would be prejudicial in the extreme, it is solemnly agreed that all such incursions shall be forcibly restrained by the Government of the United States whensoever this may be necessary." If policing a two-thousand-mile border today is difficult, it was utterly impossible at a time when there were no fences, passports, or other impediments to the people's movements. The Chiricahuas, headed by an extraordinary cadre of leaders, continued to launch raid after raid into Mexico. Among their leaders were Mangas Coloradas, who even at sixty years of age remained a formidable presence on the battlefield; Cochise, whose reputation for courage was unsurpassed among the Apaches; Miguel Narbona, who as a boy had been kept for a decade in Mexico as a servant and whose seething resentment toward his former captors made him a formidable foe; Juh, a cousin of Geronimo's who had a speech impediment but was able to lead his warriors by using hand signals; and Geronimo himself, who showed great promise from an early age. During this period of active raiding, both Apaches and Mexicans took captives, frequently using them as chips to bring the other side to the bargaining table or to retrieve prisoners.[27]

One of the Chiricahuas' raids changed Geronimo's life forever. At the start of 1851, the Chiricahuas launched two simultaneous campaigns into the Mexican state of Sonora. One was headed by Mangas Coloradas and included Cochise, Miguel Narbona, Juh, Geronimo, and about 150 battle-tested men. This formidable party made its way almost to the outskirts of the capital city of Hermosillo. The other Apache force was similar in size and kept to the west of the first, targeting the mountain communities and ranches of the Sahuaripa district in the Sierra Madre Occidental. The two parties met less resistance than anticipated. The people of Sonora seemed overwhelmed and even paralyzed by the simultaneous raids. The group of Mangas Coloradas and Geronimo succeeded in rounding up around three hundred head of stock and no less than one thousand horses. But on January 20, a Mexican patrol spotted a large cloud of dust produced by the returning Indians just to the south of a place called Pozo Hediondo (Stinky Well). The soldiers dutifully moved into position and set up an ambush. The battle that ensued started with bullets and arrows but soon devolved into hand-to-hand combat. Mangas Coloradas, never given to exaggeration, called it "a war to the knife." In the part of the field where Geronimo fought, he was the only man left alive. The Mexican losses were unprecedented. Out of one hundred men, twenty-six were killed — including most of the officers — and forty-six sustained serious wounds. A mere fifteen were left unscathed. It was the most crushing Apache victory over Mexican troops in history.[28]

For Geronimo, however, this great victory was a prelude to tragedy. One month after the showdown, Mangas Coloradas, Geronimo, and the other leaders caught everyone by surprise by riding into the presidio of Janos in the neighboring state of Chihuahua. The Apaches were there to sound out the local authorities before opening peace negotiations with Sonora. But their visit also had a commercial purpose. The victorious Apaches needed to dispose of their plunder, and the merchants of Janos had long made their living by acquiring and reselling Indian loot.

One of the Apaches, named Tapilá, began shopping around a saddle that had belonged to the Sonoran captain killed at Pozo Hediondo. His successor as military commander of Sonora, Colonel José María Carrasco, exploded with rage on hearing that these Apaches, who had killed so many Mexicans, had been warmly received at the presidio. On impulse, Colonel Carrasco gathered his men and crossed into Chihuahua without informing anyone. His forces descended on Janos and encircled the nearby Apache encampment, where Geronimo's family was still bartering. The Apache men were absent from the camp at the time of the attack. Only when they began to gather at nightfall, in the thicket of a nearby river, did they realize the full extent of their losses. As Geronimo put it, "I found that my aged mother, my young wife, and my three small children were among the slain." He had lost everything that day. "I silently turned away and stood by the river," Geronimo went on. "How long I stood there, I do not know. But when I saw the warriors arranging for a council I took my place."[29]

For the rest of his life, Geronimo harbored a great hatred for Mexicans. As he said, "My feelings toward the Mexicans did not change . . . I never ceased to plan for their punishment." And to a remarkable extent, he was able to exact his revenge. His raids are the stuff of legend. "We never chained prisoners or kept them in confinement, but they seldom got away," he remembered. "Mexican men when captured were compelled to cut wood and herd horses. Mexican women and children were treated as our own people." Reflecting on the arc of his life in 1905–1906, when he was over eighty years of age, he said, "I am old now and shall never go on the warpath again, but if I were young, and followed the warpath, it would lead into Old Mexico."[30]

## The Rising Tide of Servitude

Comanche and Apache raids ravaged northern Mexico in the middle decades of the nineteenth century, resulting in hundreds of captives being taken, but the expansion of the other slavery went far deeper than that. After independence, Mexico extended citizenship rights to all

Indians residing there and abolished slavery. In the absence of slavery, the only way for Mexicans to bind workers to their properties and businesses was by extending credit to them. As a result, debt peonage proliferated throughout Mexico (and in the American Southwest after slavery was abolished there in the 1860s) and emerged as the principal mechanism of the other slavery (see appendix 6).

The trappings of debt peonage were in place in Mexico as early as 1587, when an Indian from Michoacán recounted how some Spaniards had advanced him money "at a far higher price than it was worth and then seized my possessions and took me and my wife and children, and they have kept us locked up for twelve years, moving us from one textile factory to another." The Indian did not know the amount he still owed or how much money he and his family had earned during their twelve years of forced servitude. But he was certain that peonage was worse than slavery because unlike the Africans with whom he toiled, he was not allowed to wander the streets freely even on Sundays. Over the centuries, debt peonage spread. As the Spanish crown abolished Indian slavery in 1542, prohibited the granting of new encomiendas in 1673, and phased out repartimientos after 1777, debt peonage gained ground.[31]

After Mexico declared its independence from Spain, the process gained momentum. States throughout the country enacted servitude and vagrancy laws. The state of Yucatán, for example, regulated the movement of servants through a certificate system. No servant could abandon his master without having fulfilled the terms of his contract and could not be hired by another employer without first presenting a certificate showing that he owed "absolutely nothing" to his previous employer. In Chiapas the state legislature introduced a servitude code in 1827 allowing owners to retain their workers by force if necessary until they had fulfilled the terms of their contracts. Lashes, lockdowns, and shackles were commonly used. The same was true in Coahuila. In 1851 the state legislature there allowed owners to flog their peons. Interestingly, the governor opposed the measure because it would affect more than one-third of all the people of Coahuila, according to his calculations. Peonage in neighboring Nuevo León may have been just as common and was especially galling because it was customary to transfer debts from fathers to sons, thus perpetuating a system of inherited bondage. In these ways, servitude for the liquidation of debts spread all over Mexico. Although Mexico's faltering economy kept the demand for workers in check in the early decades after independence, once economic growth resumed later in the century, employers went to great lengths to procure and retain coerced laborers.[32]

A muckraking American journalist named John Kenneth Turner had unique access to this expanding world of servitude and provided the most detailed portrait of its workings. Posing as a millionaire investor, Turner traveled to Yucatán in 1908. He made his way to Mérida, a town that boasted extravagant mansions and was surrounded by about 150 henequen haciendas. The planters there received the American warmly. These "little Rockefellers," as Turner called them, had grown rich by selling rope and twine made from the henequen plant. In the early years of the century, Yucatán's total exports of henequen had reached nearly 250 million pounds a year. But a panic in 1907 had cut severely into their profits, "so they needed ready cash, and they were willing to take it from anyone who came," Turner explained. "Hence my imaginary money was the open sesame to their club, and to their farms."[33]

Turner's disguise as a prospective investor also allowed him to ask freely about how workers were hired. "Slavery is against the law; we do not call it slavery," the planters told him again and again. They generally referred to the Mayas, Yaquis, and even Koreans working at their haciendas as "people" or "laborers," never as slaves. The "henequen kings" were quite forthcoming about how debt served as a tool of coercion. "We do not consider that we own our laborers; we consider they are in debt to us," the president of the Agricultural Chamber of Yucatán told Turner. "And we do not consider that we buy and sell them; we consider that we transfer the debt, and the man goes with the debt." In spite of this verbal obfuscation, the fact was that an Indian worker could be acquired for $400 (400 pesos) in Yucatán. "If you buy now, you buy at a very good time," Turner was told. "The panic has put the price down. One year ago the price of each man was $1,000." Obviously, the reason the going rate was uniform was not that all peons were equally in debt, but that there was a market for them irrespective of their debt. "We don't keep much account of the debt," clarified one planter, "because it doesn't matter after you've got possession of the man." After paying the price, Turner was told, he would get the worker along with a photograph and identification papers. "And if your man runs away," another planter added reassuringly, "the papers are all the authorities require for you to get him back again."[34]

Turner asked candidly about how to treat his workers. "It is necessary to whip them — oh, yes, very necessary," opined Felipe G. Canton, secretary of the Agricultural Chamber, "for there is no other way to make them do what you wish. What other means is there of enforcing the discipline of the farm? If we did not whip them they would do nothing." The American journalist witnessed a formal beating, with all the workers assembled, during one of his hacienda visits. The young man received fifteen lashes across his back with a heavy, wet rope. All henequen plantations had *capataces,* or foremen, who carried canes to prod and whack the Indians. Turner wrote, "I do not remember visiting a single field in which I did not see some of this punching and prodding and whacking going on."[35]

Slavery in Mexico in the twentieth century? "Yes, I found it," wrote Turner in his extraordinary exposé, published on the eve of the Mexican Revolution. "I found it first in Yucatan." According to him, the slave population of Yucatán consisted of 8,000 Yaqui Indians forcibly transported from Sonora; 3,000 Koreans, who had departed from the port of Inchon and were on four- or five-year labor contracts; and between 100,000 and 125,000 Mayas, "who formerly owned the lands that the henequen kings now own." Turner estimated that in all of Mexico, there may have been 750,000 slaves, a figure that is almost certainly exaggerated but that underscores the expansion of the other slavery during the last few decades of the nineteenth century.[36]

# 10

---

## *Americans and the Other Slavery*

AMERICANS POURED INTO the West during the first half of the nineteenth century. In 1800 they occupied a band of settlements along the Atlantic coast that reached from western New York and upper Ohio south along the Ohio River, then through central Tennessee and the Cherokee lands into southern and coastal Georgia. Fifty years later, they were spilling across the plains of Michigan, the hills of Wisconsin, and into eastern Iowa, Missouri, and Arkansas. They were also washing over the Gulf coast from Florida west to Texas and, after the discovery of gold in the late 1840s, all the way to California and Oregon. Larger than any country in western Europe, this area recently opened to settlement became home to about ten million Americans who represented an astounding forty-four percent of the total U.S. population in 1850.[1]

Not only were these pioneers experiencing the novelty of the region, but they were also embarking on a journey of self-discovery and reexamination of their beliefs about human relations. Accustomed to African slavery, they were now confronted by the existence of Indian slavery. Variations of the same story unfolded in many quarters of the West: easterners went from surprise to curiosity and, depending on their temperament and persuasion, either acceptance or outrage.

## Into New Mexico

The best evidence of these reactions comes from letters and diaries of westbound settlers. James S. Calhoun had never set foot in New Mexico when he was appointed Indian agent for that territory in April 1849. He had grown up in the South, where he had divided his time between managing a shipping firm based in Columbus, Georgia, and pursuing a successful career in state politics. Sensibly, before taking up his post, he traveled to Washington, D.C., to gather information. But as the commissioner of Indian affairs warned him, "So little is known here of the condition and situation of the Indians in that region, that the Department relies on you to furnish it with such statistical and other information." All the agent could find was a memorandum listing New Mexico's principal Indian nations: Apaches, "an indolent and cowardly people"; Utes, "a hardy, warlike people subsisting by the chase"; Navajos, "an industrious, intelligent, and warlike tribe"; Comanches, "a numerous and warlike people," and so on. The document estimated that there were thirty-seven thousand Indians (excluding Pueblos) in New Mexico, a figure that already gave Calhoun a sense of the enormity of the task at hand.[2]

Yet nothing could have prepared this Georgian for what he found on the ground. Along the way to Santa Fe, Calhoun heard rumors about Native hostilities against Americans that made him apprehensive. He even offered to raise a regiment of volunteers on behalf of the federal government to provide protection. Once he was in Santa Fe, his concerns only increased. He reported that Indian relations in New Mexico were "of a much more formidable character than had been anticipated" and feared that the number of U.S. troops — six hundred infantrymen in total — was utterly insufficient to control the Indians. This was still speculation.[3]

Calhoun's first tangible experience occurred one month after his arrival, when he joined an expedition to "the seat of the supreme power of the Navajo tribe of Indians," the famous Canyon de Chelly of Arizona. It was a daring undertaking. For three years, the Navajos had been stepping up their raids on New Mexico's settlements. To put an end to these attacks and force the Navajos into signing a peace treaty, the territorial

The Canyon de Chelly, "the seat of the supreme power of the Navajo tribe of Indians," as Indian agent James Calhoun described it, was both an extraordinarily fertile homeland and a formidable refuge. Timothy H. O'Sullivan took this photograph of "Camp Beauty" in 1873.

governor decided to visit the Navajo stronghold, accompanied by a detachment of soldiers and the recently arrived Calhoun. From Santa Fe, the party traveled due west through the wide-open, parti-colored plains. After a week of slow progress and difficult conditions, which included camping in places with no water, wood, or grass, they finally reached the gigantic fan-shaped gash in the earth that is the Canyon de Chelly.

The travelers entered the canyon in silence. Streams of water laced the sides and bottom of this enormous oasis that supported extensive fields of corn, wheat, melons, squash, and beans, as well as peach orchards, which would have been especially green and lush in early September. Groves of pine, juniper, and cedar were visible all around, and water "in any desirable quantity" could be procured simply by digging a few feet into the stark reddish soil. Hundreds of Navajo warriors, taking up positions on the surrounding heights and "dashing with great speed from point to point, evidently in great perturbation," closely monitored the progress of the American delegation.[4]

Early the next morning, the head chief of the Navajo nation, Mariano Martínez, presented himself with some warriors and requested to see the New Mexican governor. The two leaders had a long conversation and agreed to sign a treaty the very next day. In the past, whenever the Navajos had faced punitive expeditions sent out by the Spaniards, Mexicans, or Americans, they had been quick to negotiate. And in every case, the treaty-making ritual had involved giving up some captives. Chief Martínez returned the day after the initial conversation accompanied by four captives: Antonio José, a ten-year-old from Jemez; Teodosio, another boy taken from "a corral near the Rio Grande"; Marceito, a young man from Socorro who had been held in captivity for many years and was no longer able to speak Spanish; and José Ignacio, an adult originally from Santa Fe who had refashioned himself as a Navajo and had two wives and three children, even though he still belonged to an Indian named Wato. Exactly how Chief Martínez persuaded the owners to part with these four individuals is not known.[5]

At that time, the Navajos held hundreds of slaves seized in raids on the Pueblos, Utes, Apaches, Hispanics, and Americans. These multiethnic captives rendered valuable services tending orchards and cornfields and looking after the large flocks of sheep accumulated by the people of the canyon. Indeed, a slaveholding class seems to have emerged among the Navajos. A dozen or so "rich" headmen each held up to forty or fifty slaves and peons, along with many other Navajo dependents. A key provision of the treaty between Martínez and the New Mexican governor required the Navajo nation to surrender "all American and Mexican captives . . . on or before the ninth day of October next," exactly one month after the day of the signing. As for the four captives about to be released, although the two boys were excited to return to their families, the adults were not as enthusiastic. The novelty of a home in a New Mexican town "seemed to excite [Marceito] somewhat," while José Ignacio much preferred to remain with his Navajo family, "notwithstanding his peonage."

Agent Calhoun met these captives and followed their fates until they were returned, except for the one "so fortunately married," who was allowed to stay with the Navajos. This was his first recorded experience with the other slavery. The Georgian had lived all his life surrounded by black slaves and was not particularly interested in Indians in general.

His letters are entirely lacking in references to the ancient ruins or theories of past civilizations that impressed so many other travelers. But his familiarity with chattel slavery in the South made him an ideal observer of Indian bondage in the West, apt to elaborate on its details and draw comparisons.

By the time Calhoun had spent six months as an Indian agent, he had formed a clear image of New Mexico as a land with a core population of Pueblo Indians, Mexican villagers, and Americans surrounded by what he called "the four wild tribes" — the Apaches, Navajos, Utes, and Comanches. "Those within the circle and those who form the circle look upon each other as natural enemies," Calhoun explained to his superiors in Washington, "and they are eternally at war, robbing and enslaving each other." Out of the four "wild tribes," the Navajos alone possessed all the necessities of life, according to Calhoun. They cultivated the soil very successfully, owned enormous herds of goats and sheep, and wove some of the finest blankets in the region. They could live on their own without preying on others. The agent was convinced, however, that the other three groups survived "chiefly" by their depredations. Getting the Apaches, Utes, and Comanches to stop their raiding campaigns would require enormous outlays of money by the U.S. government and a strong military presence. Nothing less would accomplish a lasting peace.[6]

In the meantime, a market for captives thrived in New Mexico. Calhoun described this market in some detail. The first thing he observed was that Indian captives in New Mexico were not referred to as "slaves" but as "peons." Clearly, the shift to debt peonage was well under way there, and the system was highly coercive. According to Calhoun, peons could escape their servitude only by paying a certain amount to their owners. Indeed, the Indian agent likened peonage to chattel slavery: "*Peons*, you are aware, is but another name for *slaves* as that term is understood in our Southern States," he explained in a letter to the commissioner of Indian affairs, adding that the main difference was that the peonage system was not confined to a particular "race of the human family," but applied to "all colors and tongues." Indians purchased other Indians, and Mexicans bought other Mexicans, and yet no one seemed to have the slightest objection to being purchasers of their own "kith and kin." Quite to the contrary, they believed that "the right to buy and sell captives is perfect and that no human power can disturb that right."[7]

After broaching the terminology and describing the enthusiasm with which New Mexicans engaged in this other form of enslavement, Calhoun provided some details about the market for captives and relationships with peons. Unlike Georgia or Louisiana, where slave auctions were held in public and centralized places, in New Mexico the traffic of humans was a great deal more fragmented, as owners bought captives from comancheros and acquired "the labor" of convicts at public auctions. They also haggled privately with their peons over debts and terms of service. Despite the nature of these scattered transactions, New Mexicans tacitly agreed on approximate price ranges for different types of captives, criminals, and peons. Their value depended on "age, sex, beauty, and usefulness," reported Calhoun. "Good looking females, not having passed the 'sear and yellow leaf,' are valued from $50 to $150 each; males, as they may be useful, one-half less, never more." This remarkable price premium for females harked all the way back to the sixteenth century.[8]

Like many other Americans, Calhoun accepted the bondage system that existed in the West. He reported the practice to his superiors and learned many details about it, but he did nothing to prevent Hispanics and Anglo-Americans from holding men, women, and children in peonage. Only in cases covered by article 11 of the Treaty of Guadalupe Hidalgo, which required the return of all Mexican captives, did the Indian agent make efforts to secure the release of those in bondage. Even in those cases, Calhoun purchased the captives from their owners, thus validating the system, even as he returned them to their families across the border.[9]

## American Ranchers

Calhoun merely tolerated the other slavery of the West, but other Americans went several steps beyond that by actively practicing it and enshrining it in law. In the 1840s, colonists were attracted to California because of its broad valleys and booming ranching economy. There they found a baronial society that impressed them deeply. About one hundred Mexican families owned princely domains scattered from San Diego to San Francisco Bay. It is easy to imagine the rolling hills, the properties that in some cases extended all the way to the spectacular California coastline, and the large houses made of thick adobe walls. These houses were a curious combination of grandeur and lack of material comforts, however, as there were few possessions inside. These enormous ranches had originated in a well-meaning but ultimately disastrous order from Mexico City. In 1833 the Mexican government had mandated the dismantling of the Spanish missions that had long served as California's social and economic backbone. Mission Indians were to receive plots of land, seeds, cattle, and tools. The predictable result, however, was a landgrab, as wealthy and well-connected individuals took the lion's share of the land.[10]

In northern California, the personification of the ranching baron was a rotund man with bushy sideburns named Mariano Guadalupe Vallejo, or Don Guadalupe for short. As military commander, Don Guadalupe personally welcomed foreigners. He spoke French well and English tolerably (according to one discerning witness) and was quite gregarious. Indeed, Don Guadalupe invited recent arrivals into his home and displayed a hospitality that became legendary. The Vallejos killed cows and turkeys to feed guests and offered tamales and enchiladas liberally. After these meals, guitars were tuned, and singing and dancing could be expected. Englishmen, Americans, Frenchmen, Swedes, Swiss, and Russians all passed through the Vallejos' *casa grande* in Sonoma.[11]

One of the first things visitors noticed at the Vallejos' home was the ubiquitous crews of servants. In a custom reminiscent of the antebellum South, each of Don Guadalupe's children, boys and girls, had a dedicated Indian servant. Don Guadalupe's wife, Doña Francisca Benicia Carrillo, had two servants catering to her personal needs. Besides these personal valets, the Vallejos kept a sizeable staff around the house: five or six women grinding corn and making tortillas, six or seven laboring in the kitchen, "and though not learned in the culinary art as taught by Italian and French books, they made very palatable and savory dishes,"

Ranch scene in Monterey, California, around 1849. A wealthy Mexican couple ride by a sturdy house as an Indian servant butchers a cow on the right, and Indian girls make bread in the background.

recalled Don Guadalupe's younger brother, Salvador Vallejo. There were five or six women washing clothes and up to a dozen sewing and spinning. According to the younger Vallejo, it was not uncommon for wealthy Californians to keep retinues of twenty to sixty Indians.[12]

Foreign visitors who ventured out of Don Guadalupe's home and onto his nearby Rancho Petaluma were able to gain a great deal more insight. At its peak in the early 1840s, this 66,000-acre ranch was tended by seven hundred workers. An entire encampment of Indians, "badly clothed" and "pretty nearly in a state of nature," lived in and around the property and did all the work. As Salvador Vallejo recalled, "They tilled our soil, pastured our cattle, sheared our sheep, cut our lumber, built our houses, paddled our boats, made tiles for our houses, ground our grain, killed our cattle, dressed their hides for the market, and made our unburned bricks; while the women made excellent servants, took good care of our children and made every one of our meals." The Vallejos were quick to paint a picture of benevolent patriarchy. "Those people we considered as members of our families," Salvador Vallejo remembered. "We loved them and they loved us. Our intercourse was always pleasant: the Indians knew that our superior education gave us a right to command and rule over them."[13]

But what seemed pleasant and natural to the Vallejos was decidedly less so to the Indians. Some workers at Rancho Petaluma were former mission Indians. As administrator of the mission of San Francisco de Solano, Don Guadalupe had ample opportunity not only to dispose of mission lands and resources (in fact, his Sonoma home, the military barracks, and the entire plaza lay on former mission lands) but also to bind ex-neophytes to his properties through indebtedness. Faced with dwindling resources and loss of land, former mission Indians had little choice but to put themselves under the protection of overlords like the Vallejos. Other Indian laborers had been captured in military campaigns north of Sonoma. As *comandante* (commander) of the northern California frontier, Don Guadalupe had a guard of about fifty men to keep order in the region and prevent Indians from stealing cattle. He also used his guardsmen to procure servants. He was not alone in doing so. Especially after the secularization of the missions in 1833, Mexican ranchers sent out armed expeditions to seize Indians practically every year — and as many as six times in 1837, four in 1838, and four in 1839.[14]

Mexican ranchers pioneered the other slavery in California, but American colonists readily adapted to it. They acquired properties of their own and faced the age-old problem of finding laborers. Their options were limited. No black slaves existed in California, at least not in the open, as Mexico's national government had abolished African slavery in 1829. Asian workers were still rare. In the early 1840s, Don Guadalupe kept four Native Hawaiians at Rancho Petaluma, as did a neighboring American rancher named John Sinclair and some others. The "coolie" (Asian) trade began after the gold discoveries of 1848 and would reach significant numbers only years later. Indian labor was the only viable option. Although the indigenous population of Alta California had been cut by half during the Spanish and Mexican periods — roughly from 300,000 to 150,000 — Indians still comprised the most abundant pool of laborers. Short of working the land themselves, white owners had to rely on them.[15]

Traces of the earliest Euro-American settlers are still visible in northern California. John Sutter was the proprietor of a large fort by the junction of the Sacramento and American Rivers that is now a major tourist attraction in midtown Sacramento. George C. Yount was the first Euro-American to settle permanently in the Napa Valley; the wine-sipping town of Yountville is named after him. Pierson B. Reading was the recipient of a huge land grant that would give rise to the city of Redding. And Andrew Kelsey, a ruthless entrepreneur, built a ranching operation just south of Clear Lake that is now the town of Kelseyville. These foreigners were acquisitive, possessed good business sense, and were quick to appreciate the advantages of coerced Indian labor.

Josiah Belden, a member of the first wagon train of Americans traveling from Missouri to California, characterized the local Indians as "primitive and inoffensive" and observed that their apprenticeship in the Spanish missions had made them "very useful servants and laboring men for the rancheros and citizens." John Bidwell of the same group pointed out that it was possible to employ "any number of Indians by giving them a lump of Beef every week, and paying them about one dollar for same time." A Massachusetts doctor named John Marsh offered clearer guidance on how to treat Indian workers: "Nothing more is necessary for their complete subjugation but kindness in the beginning, and a little well timed severity when manifestly deserved." And even when the latter method became a necessity, Dr. Marsh reassured his readers, the California Indians "submit to flagellation with more humility than the negroes."[16]

Perhaps no one expressed the views and opinions of that first generation of American settlers better than Lansford W. Hastings, author of *The Emigrants' Guide to Oregon and California*, published in 1845. In a heady mix of boosterism and insight, Hastings first waxed lyrical about California's valleys "of unequalled fertility and exuberance," its "unheard of uniformity and salubrity of climate," and its "inexhaustible resources," so that no country is "so eminently calculated by nature itself, in all respects, to promote the unbounded happiness and prosperity of civilized and enlightened man." According to Hastings, the only disquieting aspect of California was that the local Indians were "in a state of absolute vassalage, even more degrading and more oppressive than that of our slaves in the south." Luckily, even this problem could be turned into an advantage: "Whether slavery will eventually be tolerated in this country in any form, I do not pretend to say, but it is quite certain that the labor of Indians will for many years be as little expensive to the farmers of that country, as slave labor, being procured for a mere nominal consideration."[17]

There is no question that Americans benefited from the peonage system, but there were significant differences in how they put it into practice. On one end of the spectrum were the decidedly paternalistic *patrones* (landowners), such as John Bidwell. In several expeditions through northern California, he became acquainted with Natives living on ranches and at large. The fact that he was fluent in Spanish and learned several Indian words greatly facilitated communication. Like many other owners, Bidwell regarded Indians as children of nature — credulous, superstitious, and gullible — and sometimes resorted to manipulation. To intimidate them, he carried the paw of a very large grizzly bear and showed it to them, knowing that they viewed grizzlies as especially powerful, and even evil, spirits. He also told them that he would become very angry if they came near his camp when he slept and would command the lightning to fall on them.[18]

Bidwell's need for Indian workers became critical during the gold rush years. He was among the lucky few who struck gold and was able to establish a productive gold-mining camp on the Feather River. During the frantic mining seasons of 1848 and 1849, he and his partners managed to recruit between twenty and fifty Natives from the Butte County area, including some Mechoopda Indians with whom he retained a lifelong association. Through his good fortune and their efforts, Bidwell amassed a fortune in a short time. He was a pragmatist who used his personal rapport with the Indians and his provisions to his advantage. Bidwell paid his workers with food and clothing rather than cash, but to his credit, he did not use debt or coercion to get his way. In fact, when he served as alcalde at the mission of San Luis Rey a few years earlier, he specifically refused to return fugitive workers to their Mexican masters because of unpaid debts.[19]

Bidwell's peculiar blend of pragmatism and paternalism was perhaps best expressed at Rancho del Arroyo Chico, a 22,000-acre property east of the Sacramento River and north of Chico Creek (encompassing what is now the town of Chico) that he had acquired with his mining wealth. When he first moved onto the ranch in 1849, there were no Indians on the premises. Therefore his first goal was to convince the Mechoopda Indians living immediately to the south to come to his ranch. Bidwell gave them work and asked them to stay. He offered the ranch as a refuge where they could hunt, fish, gather acorns, conduct communal grasshopper drives, and generally maintain their way of life and culture at a time of rapid change throughout California. A couple of hundred Mechoopdas resettled in a new ranchería barely one hundred yards from Bidwell's residence. One visitor commented that Bidwell had found these Indians "as wild as a deer and wholly unclad," but through his protection and employment, they had built "happy homes with their own gardens, fruit trees, and flowers." With the passage of time, they erected bark huts and even some adobe structures arranged in the shape of a cross.[20]

It is difficult to gauge the exact nature of the ties between this American *patrón* and the resident workers. An article that appeared in the *Yreka Semi-Weekly Union* in 1864 accused Bidwell of keeping "a slave pen" at Rancho Chico and alluded to an incident in which an Indian man had been beaten with a club while his hands and feet were tied together over a barrel. The article urged Bidwell to stop the hypocrisy of supporting the abolition of black slavery while at the same time enslaving Indians. For his part, Bidwell contended that the Natives at Rancho Chico had never been profitable to him and that his only objective had been to protect them. The record makes clear that this was disingenuous: Bidwell derived tangible advantages by having a stable workforce on-site. At the same time, he protected "his Indians" on more than one occasion. In one dramatic instance in July 1863, he defended the ranch Indians when they were accused of the brutal killing of two white children nearby. He even faced an armed mob led by the outraged father, Samuel Lewis, and went so far as to call out the army rather than allow his resident Indians to be murdered or driven away.[21]

The last phase in the evolving relations between Bidwell and the Mechoopdas began in 1868, when the aging owner married Annie Kennedy, a young, socially active woman who was also a devout Presbyterian. For the past twenty years, Bidwell and the Mechoopdas had forged a mutually convenient arrangement, with the Indians providing some services for him around Rancho Chico while still being able to retain much of their culture. The close ties between protector and protected are best illustrated by Nopanny, an Indian woman in her late twenties or early thirties who worked for Bidwell as a cook and housekeeper. Bidwell enjoyed Nopanny's cooking, including her grasshopper cakes, which he proudly offered to his guests. Nopanny also served as a key intermediary between the American rancher and the Mechoopdas. When Annie Bidwell began to take control of the household after 1868, Nopanny reportedly confronted her and tried to put her in her place: "No, me Mrs. Bidwell number one, you Mrs. Bidwell number two." Although it is not possible to confirm the accuracy of this exchange and one can only speculate about the true nature of the relationship between John Bidwell and Nopanny, we do know that Annie Bidwell did not let things stand. She replaced all the Indian house servants with Chinese cooks and Irish maids.

The changes did not stop there. When the Mechoopdas disturbed Annie's sleep with their mourning ceremonies, which lasted late into the night, she had the entire ranchería moved to another site about a mile away from the house. Annie also set out to instruct a group of Natives whom she regarded as much too wild. Her civilizing and religious campaigns especially targeted the children but also were aimed at a few adults. One of Annie's pupils, Elmer La Fonso, gained some fame in the community for singing gospel songs "with a fine baritone voice." A blind Indian named Austin McLain became a violin player, and a group of Natives formed a brass band that played in the Fourth of July parade and at other celebrations. In the end, upon her death in 1918, Annie Bidwell

A blind Indian named Austin McLain plays the violin in front of a home in the Chico Ranchería.

deeded twenty-eight acres of land to the ranchería. This final act of generosity, however, failed to provide a stable home for the Mechoopdas. Eventually the federal government took over the land Annie had left to them.[22]

If Bidwell was a relatively benevolent *patrón,* Captain John Sutter was the personification of the hard-driving frontier entrepreneur. From the time of his arrival in California in 1839, this Swiss-born officer was bent on carving out an empire for himself. As he put it, "I preferred a country where I should be absolute master." Carrying an armful of letters of introduction and surrounded by his European and Hawaiian employees, Sutter took pains to project an aura of confidence, wealth, and far-reaching vision. His theatrics must have worked on some level. In short order, he obtained a grant from the California government, selected a propitious embankment by the Sacramento River, and began building an establishment that looked more like a fort than a farm. He was soon able to parlay his meager resources into an impressive enterprise.[23]

A Swedish doctor named Sandels visited Sutter's fort in 1843, four years after it was built. Dr. Sandels was taken by the beauty of the land-scape as he ascended the Sacramento River, with its many turns and lush canopies on both sides. He also was impressed by the scale of Sutter's building, a two-story quadrangular adobe structure enclosing a very large area. Dr. Sandels arrived very early in the morning and found Captain Sutter already issuing orders for the day. It was time for the wheat harvest, and the place was bustling, as several hundred Indians "flocked in" for their morning meal. They rushed toward several troughs made of hollowed-out tree trunks in the middle of the patio. Crouching on their haunches, they reached into the troughs with their bare hands to scoop up a thin porridge, which they quickly stuffed into their mouths. "I must confess I could not reconcile my feelings to see these fellows," Dr. Sandels would later write in his memoir, "as they fed more like beasts than human beings." After having "half satisfied their physical wants," they were given sickles and hooks and driven off to the fields.[24]

To fellow Euro-Americans, Captain Sutter came across as an affable frontiersman, frank and generous. But his outsize ambitions also made him imperious and demanding toward his dependents. To sustain his fort, Sutter bought cattle and foodstuffs on credit from his neighbors. Indeed, throughout his life the Swiss officer had shown a propensity to take on more debt than was prudent. "He would perhaps have bought anything at any price if it could be obtained on credit," opined the nine-teenth-century historian Hubert Howe Bancroft. And in 1841, the al-ready overextended Sutter was presented with the buying opportunity of a lifetime.[25]

Since the dawn of the nineteenth century, the Russian empire had explored the west coast of North America from Alaska to California. In 1812 the Russians bolstered their presence by establishing Fort Ross by Bodega Bay. For some years, this outpost near the rugged coast of northern California thrived. But when the population of sea otters be-gan to decline due to overhunting, the Russians decided to sell their fort, which consisted of twenty-four main buildings (complete with wooden floors and glass windows), ten kitchens, eight sheds, and eight bathhouses. They identified Captain Sutter as a possible buyer. In early September 1841, the governor of Fort Ross, Alexander Rotchev, made his way to Sutter's home with the surprising offer to sell him the entire fort and its outlying ranches, including furnishings, tools, and cattle, for $30,000. Sutter already owed nearly $4,000 to the Russian-American Company. The price of the fort would simply be added to his existing account. Sutter was elated by the opportunity and flattered by the confidence the Russians placed in him. The contracting parties drew up a payment plan. Sutter would pay the company only $2,000 in 1841, but his payments would increase to $5,000 in 1842 and 1843, then balloon to $10,000 in 1844 and 1845. In the cash-starved economy of Mexican California, however, these enormous sums could only be paid in kind. For Captain Sutter this meant thousands of bushels of wheat and hundreds of quintals of soap, peas, beans, suet, and tallow. (One quintal in colonial Mexico equaled 46 kilograms, or about 100 pounds.) Ever the optimist and without thinking too much, Sutter accepted the terms. After all, he had lived on credit all his life.[26]

To meet his enormous obligations, Sutter resorted to every tool in the labor kit. Sutter's fort lay on the border between the Miwoks and Nisenans, so he began luring workers from these groups by giving out presents of beads, blankets, and shirts. He also assiduously cultivated Miwok and Nisenan headmen. Once these Indians had moved close to Sutter's fort, its proprietor offered them porridge every morning — as Dr. Sandels witnessed — and paid them with clothes. In fact, Sutter established something of a "company store" system. In lieu of cash, Indian laborers received metal disks that they donned as necklaces. Star-shaped holes were punched in the disks to keep track of the amount of work they did. They could then redeem the disks in Sutter's store: two weeks of work would earn a cotton shirt or a pair of pantaloons. Using this method, Captain Sutter was able to attract and maintain hundreds of Miwoks and Nisenans for each working season. But in addition to dangling carrots, Captain Sutter also resorted to the proverbial stick. The famous trailblazer John C. Frémont visited Sutter's fort in 1843–1844. He noted that at first the proprietor had faced some difficulties with the Indian laborers, "but by the occasional exercise of well-timed

authority, he had succeeded in converting them into peaceable and industrious people."[27]

After settling down in California, Sutter's first objective had been to
raise a private army. At first it consisted of a small group of white men,
but it soon grew to about 150 infantrymen and 50 cavalrymen, the majority of them Indian soldiers. They wore uniforms acquired from the
Russians — green and blue with red trim — and responded to commands
issued in German. It was an unusual martial display in the wilds of California. One of the occupations of this army was to persuade reluctant or
uncooperative Indians to work. A Nisenan man named William Joseph
recalled that although Sutter paid his workers, if they failed to work, his
henchmen "whipped them with a big whip made of cowhide." Working
for Sutter was evidently not a choice but an obligation, especially in the
critical years when the large payments to the Russian-American Company were due.[28]

Sutter's private army also allowed him to participate in the Indian
slave trade. Over the years, Sutter learned much about this traffic. As he
wrote in his personal reminiscences, "It was common in those days to
seize Indian women and children and sell them; this the Californians
did as well as Indians." Early on, Captain Sutter had to deal with slavers operating in his domain. In the fall 1840, a group of Indians from
the mission of San José arrived at Sutter's fort. They were bearing passports from the Vallejos and asked for permission to visit some of their
friends and relatives in the area. Instead, however, they struck a nearby
ranchería of Yalisumni Nisenans while the men were away working for
Sutter, killing the elderly and carrying off the women. The attackers intended to sell their prisoners to the ranches by the coast, "as was common in those days." But this was not to be. Sutter personally led a detachment of soldiers in pursuit of the marauding Indians, caught the
perpetrators, and brought them to his fort for execution.[29]

Such experiences paved Sutter's way into the slaving business. But
what really pushed him into that traffic was the need to punish hostile
Indians and the realization that this could be done in an economically
advantageous manner. Sutter's presence by the Sacramento River had
polarized the indigenous inhabitants. Some Miwoks and Nisenans were

his allies and laborers—however reluctantly—but many others refused to submit and attempted to steal from Sutter and even murder him. In 1844–1845, when Sutter's political influence was on the wane and huge payments to the Russians were due, he opted to use an iron fist on the Natives. "I see now how it is," Sutter wrote to his most trusted agent, who was in the process of developing a new farm; "if they are not Keept strickly under fear, it will be no good."[30]

Sutter's personal army came alive in those years, persuading unreliable laborers, breaking up bands of hostile Indians, and punishing cattle rustlers. All of these activities became potential sources of slaves. Unguarded private letters reveal the deliberate way in which Sutter approached this line of business. "I shall send you some young Indians," Sutter wrote to his neighbor and creditor Antonio Suñol in May 1845, "after our campaign against horse-thieves, which will take place after the wheat harvest." A few weeks later, true to his word, Sutter dispatched thirty-one Indians, "as usual, dying of hunger." Some other such transactions have come to light.[31]

It is difficult to gauge the full scope of Sutter's slaving activities. In Hubert Howe Bancroft's monumental history of California, based on many firsthand accounts, including Sutter's, the historian concluded that from the start, the Swiss captain had seized Indian children, "who were retained as servants, or slaves, at his own establishment or sent to his friends in different parts of the country." Similarly, Albert Hurtado, the scholar who is most familiar with Sutter's correspondence, has observed that the Indian wars undoubtedly helped Sutter improve his balance sheet vis-à-vis his creditors. One of Sutter's employees, Heinrich Lienhard, even claimed that his boss kept a harem of Indian women and young girls in a room right next to this office. These accusations, while plausible, remain uncorroborated.[32]

Although Captain Sutter combined some features of the peonage system with occasional slave raiding, other Euro-American settlers became more specialized in the traffic of Indians. Andrew Kelsey and his brothers arrived in California in the first overland wagon train from Missouri in 1841. By 1844 Andrew, Benjamin, and Samuel had settled in the Napa Valley, where they raised cattle for the tallow trade. During these years, the Kelseys interacted closely with the Vallejos, who lived in the adjacent valley. The Kelseys, as well as other ranchers in the area, relied on Indian workers brought from the Clear Lake region directly to the north.[33]

Today, State Route 29 runs north through the wineries of the Napa Valley before meandering through Mount Saint Helena and descending to Clear Lake. Visitors are astounded by the size of the lake — the largest freshwater lake entirely within California. (Lake Tahoe straddles the California-Nevada border.) Though far less famous than the Napa Valley today, Clear Lake has its own share of visitors, who enjoy the houses and condos along the shore. The lake itself is alive with water-skiers, kayakers, and motorboaters. Fortunately, Clear Lake is large enough to accommodate these human activities and still sustain remarkable wildlife. Egrets, herons, bald eagles, hawks, ospreys, and many other birds can be spotted in the area. Anglers are especially keen on the lake's bass. Clear Lake ranks as one of the top bass-fishing spots in the United States and is sometimes called "the Bass Capital of the West."

It is precisely this natural abundance that has made Clear Lake a magnet for human populations since time immemorial. In the early nineteenth century, the lake was even bigger than it is today. It supported eighteen different rancherías, each consisting of about 100 to 150 individuals occupying different islands or portions of the shore. They were mostly Pomo Indians, with Miwok and Wappo linguistic groups represented at either end of the lake. Each band claimed some lands and hunting grounds and enjoyed a diverse diet. In the spring, the Indians caught the plentiful fish swimming upstream in basket traps or even with their bare hands. In the summer, they dived for clams and dug up roots to eat. In the fall, they gathered acorns and hunted the thousands of water fowl descending on the lake. Even though they possessed an extraordinarily varied and abundant supply of food, the Indians of the lake also traded actively among themselves and with more distant tribes. The lake rancherías exchanged everyday necessities such as fish, baskets, animal skins, and clams. From the coast they imported salt and seashells, while exporting in return obsidian from nearby Mount Saint Helena (an extinct volcano), fish, and acorns. Despite being threatened by smallpox in the 1830s, the total indigenous population living around Clear Lake in the early 1840s was probably about three thousand.[34]

The first outsider to establish a beachhead in Clear Lake was none other than Salvador Vallejo. Around 1839 or 1840, he built a log house and a corral on the southern shore of the lake just north of present-day Kelseyville. It was little more than a rude wooden shelter and a few poles driven into the ground forming a kind of stockade. The younger Vallejo kept a *mayordomo* (caretaker) there to manage the place and direct the dozen or so Pomo Indians who constructed buildings, maintained the property, and tended the horses and cattle brought from Sonoma. Subsequently, on the basis of these improvements, Vallejo applied for a land grant encompassing much of the southern shore.[35]

From time to time, Salvador Vallejo also visited Clear Lake to recruit Indian workers for the ranches in Sonoma and Napa, thus setting an important precedent. In one notorious expedition in 1843, he led a group of eighty Mexican ranchers and as many Indian allies into the region. The riders first attempted, unsuccessfully, to recruit the Koi Indians by giving them beads and other presents, while asking them to relocate to the Mexican ranches. Next they approached the Elem Indians, on Rattlesnake Island, who also refused. Finally they reached the Kamdot Indians, who organized a great council in a *temescal*, or sweathouse, to which Vallejo was invited. The Indians began gathering in the conical structure, about the size of a circus ring, by the lake. The building was completely enclosed except for a small hole at the top to let out the smoke. The only way in or out was through a narrow tunnel that could be used by only one person at a time. The participants set a fire in the middle of the structure, and once they were sweating profusely, they would escape through the tunnel to plunge into the lake. According to Vallejo's own version of events, he believed that the sweathouse invitation was a ruse. So with half the Indian men inside, naked and unarmed, he and his men set the building on fire while blocking the tunnel. Then the rest of the men and "the squaws and children were made prisoners and driven down into Napa Valley and there compelled to go to work" — a prize of three hundred Indians, young and old, male and female.[36]

The American takeover of California forced the Vallejos to consolidate their holdings. In 1847 Salvador Vallejo sold his Clear Lake cattle operation to Andrew Kelsey and a younger American named Charles Stone. The two partners promptly relocated to the southern shore of the lake and treated the Indians like slaves. They forced four or five hundred Pomo Indians to build a sturdy adobe house measuring about forty feet long and fifteen feet wide, complete with a fireplace, in only two months. The Americans meted out cruel punishments for minor infractions. Perhaps the very isolation of these two white men living in a remote outpost, completely surrounded by Natives, as well as the need to keep firm control, prompted them to terrorize the local inhabitants. Whatever the cause, the accounts of both whites and Indians are consistent. Americans who stayed with Kelsey and Stone reported that their hosts flogged Indians for entertainment and even shot random Natives just for the fun of seeing them jump. Thomas Knight, an American who settled in the Napa Valley in 1845, said that one of the preferred methods of punishment was to hang Indians by their thumbs in the adobe house for two or three days, allowing their toes to just touch the floor. Kelsey and Stone also raped young Indian women. Indeed, according to another white Napa Valley resident, one of their motivations for relocating to remote Clear Lake was to gain the freedom to satisfy "their unbridled lusts among the youthful females."[37]

In the meantime, the conscription of Indians continued. In 1848 Kelsey and Stone rounded up 172 Indians and had them driven to the ranches of Napa and Sonoma for compulsory work. The discovery of gold brought even more misery to the Indians of the lake. In the fall of 1849, the two partners sent around 50 Pomo Indians to the headwaters of the Sacramento River to pan for gold. The timing of this venture could not have been worse. At the absolute peak of gold fever, throngs of prospectors from Oregon and southern California were converging on the region. Benjamin Kelsey drove the Pomos to the goldfields without incident, but once there he realized that the hordes of prospectors had created an acute shortage of provisions. Basic foodstuffs were fetching extremely high prices. Thus Kelsey was persuaded that he and the other investors would be better off if they simply sold all their provisions rather than look for gold. And so he liquidated his supplies, leaving the Indians to fend for themselves. Hunger was not the only peril. The gold-fields were in an area surrounded by the traditional enemies of the Pomos. An outbreak of malaria made their situation even more difficult. Of the 50 or so Indians who went to the goldfields, only three made it back to Clear Lake. As one contemporary chronicler wrote, "Sons and brothers who had gone away in the full prime of their manhood, had fallen victims to hunger, disease, and the enemy's bow and arrow."[38]

When the survivors returned and news of their ordeal spread, the Pomos became infuriated. Still, Kelsey and Stone remained undaunted. In fact, they added insult to injury by planning to relocate all the Indians of the lake to the Sacramento River by Sutter's fort. According to Augustine, a Pomo chief working as overseer for the two partners, the idea was to drive everyone away except the Indian vaqueros working directly in the cattle operation. To that effect, they commanded the Indians to make rope "to bind the young men and the refractory ones, so as to be able to make the move into the Sacramento Valley." But having endured two years of unrelenting and vicious exploitation, having mourned the deaths of dozens of their brothers sent to the goldfields, and facing the prospects of massive relocation, "finally the Indians made up their minds to kill Stone and Kelsey, for, from day to day they got worse and worse in their treatment of them," declared Chief Augustine a few years later, "and the Indians thought that they might as well die one way as another, so they decided to take the final and fatal step." One morning in December 1849, the Indians charged the adobe house, killing Kelsey and Stone with arrows and striking their heads with rocks. The specific details of these killings vary from one version to another, but they all agree that the end of the two partners was grisly.[39]

The scant literature on the early history of Clear Lake focuses on the cruelty of Andrew Kelsey and Charles Stone and the episodic massacres. But it tends to overlook a larger point: although the two American partners may have been unusually (even pathologically) cruel, they were able to enslave these Indians because such activities were common throughout the region and there was a thriving market for Indian slaves. Indeed, their deaths did not stop the trafficking of Clear Lake Indians.

The trade resumed in 1850 and became especially active from 1854 to 1857, when traffickers, revolvers in hand, regularly descended on small Indian bands, shot the men and sometimes the women, and caught the boys and girls between the ages of eight and fourteen. "Not many of the present generation of Californians know," wrote Henry Clay Bailey, a Kentuckian who arrived in California at midcentury, "that in the early '50s a regular slave trade was carried on in the mountains bordering the upper Sacramento valley from Clear Lake to Strong Creek." The bounty of resources at the lake sustained a significant Indian population there that slavers continued to tap for years.[40]

The prevalence of the other slavery in the mid-nineteenth century was reflected in legal statutes. Even as California hung in the balance between Mexico and the United States, on September 15, 1846, Captain John B. Montgomery, commander of the Northern Department of California, issued a proclamation warning people who "have been and still are holding to service Indians against their will" to desist and urging the general public not to regard Indians "in the light of slaves." Yet the proclamation went on to state that all Indians living in the settled portions of California could not "wander about in an idle and dissolute manner," but were required to obtain employment. Once their contracts had been fulfilled and their debts paid off, they were free to leave their employers. But they had to find another employer or master immediately, or they were liable to be arrested and drafted into public works.[41]

The next step in the process of formalizing the peonage system was to give teeth to Montgomery's proclamation, which is exactly what Henry W. Halleck, secretary of state of California, did by introducing a certificate and pass system in 1847. All employers were required to issue certificates of employment to their indigenous workers. If these workers had to travel for any reason, such as to visit friends or relatives or to trade, they also had to secure a pass from the local authorities. These certificates and passes allowed employers and local officials to monitor and control the movements of Indians. "Any Indian found beyond the limits of the town or rancho in which he may be employed without such certificate or pass," Halleck ordered, "will be liable to arrest as a horse thief, and if, on being brought before a civil Magistrate, he fail to give a satisfactory account of himself, he will be subjected to trial and punishment." This system accomplished a number of goals. It allowed ranchers to hold Indians in place, as the certificates typically listed the "advanced wages" that had to be repaid before the certificate bearer would be free to go. This was the very cornerstone of the peonage system. The certificate and pass system also sought to minimize conflict among employers. Understandably, Indians often fled from ranches and mines and took up work with other employers. With these documents, prospective employers could determine at a glance if an Indian seeking employment had any outstanding debts. And finally, the pass system went beyond previous ordinances in distinguishing between Natives gainfully employed and all others — regardless of where they lived — who were automatically considered vagrants or horse thieves and therefore subject to the labor draft.[42]

Captain Montgomery's 1846 proclamation and Secretary Halleck's 1847 pass system were important steps in the process of enshrining the peonage system into law. But by far the most sweeping piece of California labor legislation during the pre–Civil War era was the Act for the Government and Protection of Indians of 1850. As usual, this benign-sounding law was not what it purported to be. The committee that crafted it included the baronial Mariano Guadalupe Vallejo; David F. Douglas, a southerner from Tennessee with plenty of experience with the peculiar institution; and John Bidwell, the only moderate in the group. Bidwell was ill at the time, however, so it was up to the Mexican rancher and the former Tennessean to hammer out the final details. Their proposal quickly passed both houses on April 19, 1850, and was signed into law three days later.[43]

It was an unwieldy piece of legislation containing twenty sections. Some of them were largely declarative; section 15, for example, prohibited the sale of alcohol to Indians. Otherwise the Indian Act of 1850 was like a piñata with something for everyone who wished to exploit the Natives of California. For instance, section 20 stipulated that any Indian who was able to work and support himself in some honest calling but was found "loitering and strolling about, or frequenting public places where liquors are sold, begging, or leading an immoral or profligate course of life" could be arrested on the complaint of "any resident citizen" of the county and brought before any justice of the peace. If the accused Indian was deemed a vagrant, the justice of the peace was required "to hire out such vagrant within twenty-four hours to the best bidder . . . for any term not exceeding four months." In short, any citizen could obtain Indian servants through convict leasing.[44]

Another section established the "apprenticeship" of Indian minors. Any white person who wished to employ an Indian child could present himself before a justice of the peace accompanied by the "parents or friends" of the minor in question, and after showing that this was a voluntary transaction, the petitioner would get custody of the child and control "the earnings of such minor until he or she obtained the age of majority" (fifteen for girls and eighteen for boys).[45]

The apprenticeship provision worked in tandem with yet another section of the Indian Act of 1850 that gave justices of the peace jurisdiction in all cases of complaints related to Indians, "without the ability of Indians to appeal at all." And "in no case [could] a white man be convicted of any offense upon the testimony of an Indian, or Indians." Understandably, these provisions gave considerable latitude to traffickers of Indian children. In northern California, this trade flourished, especially in the mid-1850s, and became so important that some newspapers began writing about the inhumanity of it. In 1857 the newspapers launched what one witness described as "an agitation against the California slave trade" and "a general crusade." Very few traffickers were ever caught, however, and even those who were apprehended simply continued about their business after receiving just a slap on the wrist. Such was the protection afforded by the law.[46]

These labor laws, and the debates surrounding them, harked back to the early colonial days. California declared that Indians were free, but they were not free to be idle, in much the same way that the Spanish crown in the middle of the sixteenth century abolished Indian slavery but still compelled Natives to work for their own good.

# 11

# *A New Era of Indian Bondage*

THE AMERICAN OCCUPATION of the West did not reduce the enslavement of Indians. In fact, the arrival of American settlers rekindled the traffic in humans. Conditions varied from place to place, of course. As the gold rush played out, California experienced the greatest demand for coerced Indian labor, but other territories had similar experiences. Easterners who had never participated in the market for Indians became immersed in it just by virtue of relocating to the West.

The Mormons began arriving in Utah in 1847 and attained a resident population of forty thousand by 1860 and eighty-six thousand by 1870. Scattered in settlements all around the Great Salt Lake and south of it, they eked out a living in the desert with considerable difficulty.

With respect to slavery, the Church of Jesus Christ of Latter-day Saints had no set doctrine. However, Brigham Young, the undisputed Mormon leader, believed that slavery had always been a part of the human condition. "Eve partook of the forbidden fruit and this made a slave of her," he affirmed in a major speech. "Adam hated very much to have her taken out of the Garden of Eden, and now our old daddy says I believe I will eat of the fruit and become a slave too. This was the first introduction of slavery upon this earth." Young went on to explain how Cain murdered his brother Abel, and for this crime God put a special mark on all of Cain's descendants: "You will see it on the countenance of every African

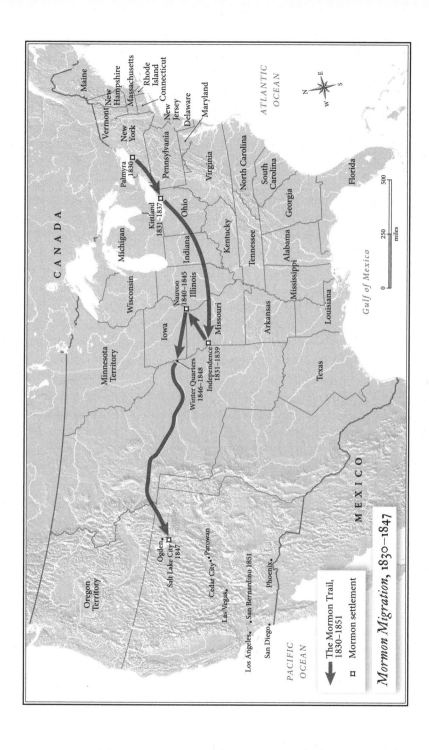

Mormon Migration, 1830–1847

you ever did see upon the face of the earth, or ever will see." Some of the earliest Mormon pioneers possessed black slaves, and the Compromise of 1850—a set of congressional bills designed to defuse a confrontation between slave and free states—permitted Utah to decide whether to legalize chattel slavery by popular sovereignty.[1]

Interestingly, Mormons had an explanation for the perceived characteristics of the Indian slaves they encountered in the West. According to the Book of Mormon, in ancient times different tribes of Israelites crossed to the New World. These tribes warred with one another until the only survivors were the descendants of Laman. For this reason, Mormons often referred to Indians as Lamanites. Like the Africans, the Lamanites were cursed by God, assumed a "dark and loathsome countenance," and over the centuries grew fierce and warlike. Cut off from the teachings of God, the Lamanites became a degraded people. But since they were originally from the blood of Israel and therefore God's chosen people, there was a glimmer of hope. One day the Lamanites could "blossom as the rose on the mountains," as Wilford Woodruff, the fourth president of the Church of Jesus Christ of Latter-day Saints, put it so arrestingly, "Their chiefs will be filled with the power of God and receive the Gospel, and they will go forth and build the New Jerusalem." This would be a magnificent redemption in which the Mormons could play a part.[2]

The path toward redemption began with enslavement. As the Mormons reached Utah in the summer of 1847, they began building a fort. That fall a band of Utes made camp in the vicinity. These Indians were just returning from a raiding campaign and had two girls whom they intended to exchange for firearms. The Mormons were initially reluctant to trade. They were not accustomed to acquiring Indians, rifles were scarce in Utah, and it was not wise to arm the surrounding Natives. As the Mormons could not agree on a deal among themselves, the Utes killed one of the prisoners and began torturing the other, a girl of about seven years of age. The traffickers made clear that they would kill her unless a rifle was forthcoming. Charles Decker, Brigham Young's son-in-law, was the first to break down. He gave up his gun and took the girl. "She was the saddest looking piece of humanity I have ever seen," recalled one witness. "They had shingled her head with butcher knives and fire brands . . . She was gaunt with hunger and smeared from head to foot with blood and ashes."[3]

News of this transaction spread quickly. Over the next few years, Indians living in Utah made their way to the Mormon settlements, offering captives. These traffickers expected willing customers, but they were prepared to use the hard sell, displaying starving captives to arouse the pity of potential buyers. A Ute chief named Walkara became the most well-known supplier. "He has never been here with his band without having a quantity of Indian children as slaves," recalled Brigham Young, "and I have seen his slaves so emaciated that they were not able to stand upon their feet. He is in the habit of tying them out from his camp at night, naked and destitute of food, unless it is so cold he apprehends they will freeze to death." Other colonists had similar experiences: "[Walkara's] children captives were like living skeletons," wrote Solomon Nunes Carvalho, a Sephardic Jew who accompanied the famous frontiersman and explorer John C. Frémont on a visit to the Ute chief's camp, "and were usually treated in this way, that is, literally starved to death by their captors."[4]

Initially, Brigham Young had been cautious in his dealings with the Indians. He had counseled his brethren not to sell guns to them. He had also sought to restrict their presence inside the fort that he and his followers had built near the Great Salt Lake. "When the Lamanites are about, you will keep your gates closed and not admit them within the walls," Young had said as he prepared for an extended absence. "So far as you come in contact with them, treat them kindly but do not feed them or trade with them or hold familiar intercourse with them within the city. But if you wish to trade with them, go to their camp and deal with them honorably."[5]

However, once Young gained more confidence and understood that the Indian slave trade had existed in the region for centuries and was deeply rooted, he changed his mind. By 1850 or 1851, he had become persuaded that the way to move forward was by buying Indians. "The Lord could not have devised a better plan than to have put the saints where they were to help bring about the redemption of the Lamanites and also make them a white and delightsome people," Young said to the members of the Iron County Missions in May 1851. Other church leaders were no less enthusiastic. "The Lord has caused us to come here for this very purpose," said Orson Pratt, one of the original Mormon "apostles," in 1855, "that we might accomplish the redemption of these suffering degraded Israelites."[6]

Yet there was one major drawback. By buying Indian children, the Mormons would be giving impetus to a terrible traffic that caused bloodshed, mayhem, and war. Therefore Brigham Young's solution was to steer a middle and contradictory course: he cracked down on some traffickers but also advocated the passage of the Act for the Relief of Indian Slaves and Prisoners of 1852, which enabled Utah residents to become guardians of Indian minors for up to twenty years. In this way, Young intended to curb the most brutal aspects of the Indian slave trade and at the same time pursue the Mormon goal of Indian redemption.[7]

New Mexican traffickers were the first to feel the effects of Young's policies. For seventy years, Hispanic merchants had been involved in the overland trail to California and had grown accustomed to bartering horses and slaves along the Old Spanish Trail, which cut a swath through Utah. This was still the case in the fall of 1851 when a New Mexican from Abiquiu named Pedro León Luján found himself leading a party of merchants through central Utah. Luján was bearing a trading license from the governor of New Mexico, and his intention was to barter for captives. But Luján was a prudent man. He knew that his license was about to expire, so he sought out Brigham Young to extend it. Luján and his companions spent days tracking down the Utah governor, but when he found Young, the meeting did not go well. Through an interpreter, Governor Young explained that since the signing of the Treaty of Guadalupe Hidalgo, the laws of the United States applied in Utah. Such laws, he said, prohibited the enslavement of Indians—an argument that must have amused the hardened New Mexicans, whose predecessors had operated in contravention of Spanish and Mexican law since the sixteenth century. "The Mexicans listened with respect," observed the interpreter, "and all seemed satisfied and pledged their words that they would return to their homes without trading for children." However, on the way back to New Mexico, Luján did acquire some Indian children and one woman — perhaps forced by the circumstances, as he would later testify, but more likely in defiance of the governor's prohibition. In any case, he was subsequently apprehended, tried, and found guilty. Luján's property was confiscated, including the captives, who were promptly placed in Mormon homes.[8]

The trial and conviction of Don Pedro León Luján sent a clear message to New Mexicans wishing to do business in Utah. It was an important precedent, but it did not spell the end of the traffic of Indians. In 1851 Utah was vast — far larger than it is today, as it included portions of Nevada, Colorado, and Wyoming — and therefore utterly impossible to police. During the 1850s and 1860s, New Mexicans continued to rendezvous with Utes and Navajos at lonely outposts, exchanging horses for humans. Luján himself continued to own Paiute Indians, as the 1870 census reveals. Governor Young's unenforceable interdiction merely drove the traffic underground and made it more difficult to detect, as had occurred in centuries past.[9]

Brigham Young's next target was Chief Walkara, or "the Hawk of the Mountains," as the Ute leader called himself. Walkara was the most important supplier of Indian children in Utah, but Young had to tread lightly, as Walkara's band was powerful and could inflict serious damage on exposed white settlements. By the 1840s, Walkara had a lock on the middle section of the Old Spanish Trail between New Mexico and California. John Frémont met Walkara in 1844 and reported that the Ute chief was "journeying slowly towards the Spanish Trail to levy the usual tribute upon the great California caravans." The Ute chief also sold Paiute Indians to the passing merchants, thus turning the Old Spanish Trail into a great source of power and wealth. Walkara was well known among New Mexican traffickers, but he also conducted business at the trail's southern end. In California he sold bison robes as well as Indian children. According to one witness, one time Walkara was mistreated by California ranchers who confiscated his property. So the Hawk of the Mountains retaliated by stealing horses. A single horse-stealing campaign in 1839–1840 through Cajon Pass, near Los Angeles, reportedly netted three thousand animals, making it one of the biggest hauls in the annals of horse thievery. Walkara's band is an example of an equestrian power operating across different Euro-American groups, exploiting weaker indigenous groups, and thriving on the basis of superior mobility and the chief's keen business sense.[10]

When the Mormons first arrived in Utah in 1847, Chief Walkara welcomed them as potential trading partners and customers. It also helped that the Mormons initially settled by the Great Salt Lake, well to the north of Walkara's domain in southern and central Utah. But as the Mormons continued to migrate into Utah in the 1850s, their settlements spilled southward into Ute lands. Adding insult to injury, the Mormons' conviction of Pedro Luján delivered a major blow to Chief Walkara's livelihood. Walkara and his family greatly resented these trading restrictions. A few months after Luján's Indian trafficking trial, Walkara's brother Arapeen arrived in the town of Provo to sell children. When the Mormons refused to buy, Arapeen went into a rage, saying that they had no right to prevent Mexicans such as Luján from buying children unless they themselves acquired them. What Arapeen did next became etched in Daniel W. Jones's memory: "Several of us were present when he took one of the children by the heels and dashed his brains out on the hard ground, after which he threw the body toward us telling us that we had no hearts or we would have saved its life."[11]

It is tempting to think that the Mormons opposed Indian slavery and that the trial and conviction of Luján and the difficulties with Chief Walkara were steps toward the total elimination of it in Utah. But such an interpretation is impossible to reconcile with the passage of the Act for the Relief of Indian Slaves and Prisoners in 1852. The discussions that took place prior to this act reveal that Young and other Mormon leaders did not so much want to do away with Indian slavery as to use it for their own ends. They objected to Indian children and women being left in the hands of Ute captors to be tortured and killed and to allowing them to fall into the "low, servile drudgery of Mexican slavery." But they were fully in favor of placing Native children and women in Mormon homes to associate them "with the more favored portions of the human race." Mormons used euphemisms such as "buying the slaves into freedom" to refer to this equivocal process. In fact, the Act for the Relief of Indian

Slaves and Prisoners allowed any white resident of Utah to hold Indians through a system of indenture for a period of up to twenty years — longer than in California or New Mexico. Masters in Utah were required to clothe their indentured Indians appropriately and send youngsters between seven and sixteen years of age to school for three months each year. Other than that, they were free to put them to work.[12]

Determining the total number of Indians acquired through slavery and indenture in Utah requires painstaking research in census records, diaries, genealogies, and assorted documents. Richard D. Kitchen has identified more than four hundred Indians taken into Mormon homes between 1847 and 1900. The actual number must have been much higher considering that many indentured Indians died immediately after contact or survived only a few months or years, thus leaving little or no paper trail. We know, for example, that T. D. Brown acquired five Indian children but only two were still alive by the end of the year; Zadok and Minerva Judd adopted at least three children but only one reached adulthood; and the Cox family adopted a seven-year-old Indian girl, Sylvia, who promptly died during a measles epidemic. There were many other such cases. Without question, Indians of the Great Basin were especially susceptible to new illnesses introduced by white colonists. When the Mormons first reached Utah in 1847, there were an estimated 20,000 Native Americans within the territory. By 1900 the number had plummeted to 2,623. In other words, eighty-six percent of the Indians in Utah vanished in half a century. It would not be until the 1980s that the Indian population there regained its pre-Mormon levels. As usual, it is impossible to disentangle the extent to which biological and man-made factors contributed to this catastrophic decline. But Indian slavery was certainly a major factor.[13]

More questions revolve around the living and working conditions of the indentured Indians. All along Mormons claimed that they acquired Indian children with the intention of civilizing rather than enslaving them. Between the 1830s and 1860s, some of them actually wrote sketches of their indigenous dependents. Often these were edifying stories of obedience and contentment, such as those of Ammon, a young boy who refused to play with the other children but nonetheless became "a good student, also religious, honest, and industrious"; Rose, who was raised by the Daniels family and was "apt and willing to learn and became a very good cook and housekeeper and did the work about the home as any girl or daughter would do in the home of a large family"; and Mary Thomson, who was employed in many of the homes of the town of Ephraim "and became a faithful, devoted friend to the members of those families." And yet additional evidence reveals less uplifting stories of Indians who ran away from their adopted homes or had difficulty integrating into Mormon society. The *Deseret News* of September 18, 1852, for example, includes an ad from one Christopher Merkley offering a reward for the return of a twelve-year-old boy who had fled from his possession and spoke very little English. Similarly, Thomas Forsythe traded a horse and saddle in exchange for a boy named Moroni. He grew up to be very useful around the farm. But one day when he failed to bring in the cows, Forsythe, who was an ill-tempered man, reprimanded Moroni severely, prompting him to flee.[14]

Some Mormons viewed Indians as outright slaves, or at least treated them as an underclass that could be readily exploited. Over the winter of 1849–1850, a posse of about one hundred Mormon men from Parowan, in southern Utah, gave chase to some Indians who had been raiding their cattle. They succeeded in killing about twenty-five or thirty warriors and taking their women and children. In effect, their retaliatory expedition had turned into a slaving raid. One member of the posse, Joel H. Johnson, recorded in his diary how he had kept two women and three children "who were all sick, occasioned by exposure after having the measles." Of the five, only a ten-year-old boy survived. Yet this did not deter Johnson from acquiring more Indians. In a letter to the editor of the *Deseret News* on January 25, 1853, Johnson observed that he employed several Paiutes to assist him in tending a herd and doing chores. "When employed and fed by the whites they are a great help to the farmers," Johnson affirmed, "and will do as much work as most any white man in a day and can be hired for their board and some small present, by way of old clothing." Many colonists believed that agricultural work was the best way to redeem the Indians of Utah. Brigham Young himself

Early in 1850, a force of about one hundred Mormons killed several Indian males and took about forty prisoners, mostly women and children. According to Captain Howard Stansbury in his book *Exploration and Survey of the Valley of the Great Salt Lake of Utah* (1852), "They were carried to the city and distributed among the inhabitants, for the purpose of weaning them from their savage pursuits, and bringing them up in the habits of civilized and Christian life."

repeatedly wrote about the beneficial effects of the "peaceful avocation of herding or cultivating the soil" as a way to curb the Indians' "wilder and more dangerous exploits of predatory war" and to counter their natural tendencies toward idleness.[15]

The original goal had been to turn the Indians into "a white and delightsome people." But the reality was frequently one of persistent separation. Brigham Young specifically urged his followers "never to condescend to their level, but always seek to elevate them to a higher, purer, and, consequently, a more useful and intelligent existence." Mormons who adopted Indians had to strive to erase their Native cultures and curb their wild instincts. Some testimonies are quite explicit about this: "I have a little Indian boy and girl," said Elder E. T. Benson to a group that congregated in Provo in 1855, "and it is certainly repugnant to my feelings to have to put up with their dirty practices." Benson rejoiced that the little boy was becoming quite bright and perceptive but acknowledged that "he yet has some of his Indian traits, and I presume it will be some time before they are all erased from his memory." These comments and others reflect a pervasive attitude that prevented Indians from fully integrating into Mormon society.[16]

Historians Juanita Brooks and Michael K. Bennion have established that Native Americans who grew up in Mormon households married at significantly lower rates than the population at large. One would think that in a polygamous society, Indian women would have been readily incorporated as secondary wives, but this occurred rarely. Contemporaries such as John Lee Jones could not hide his astonishment at finding a Mormon man with an Indian wife, calling it "quite a novel circumstance to me." Church leaders had divergent views about the wisdom of taking Lamanite wives: some supported this practice as the most expedient means to "amalgamate with the natives," while others emphasized their cursed condition, so that it was "better to let them alone." Anecdotal evidence illustrates the difficulties Indian women brought up in Mormon households faced in finding marriage partners. Susie Leavitt, for example, had two children out of wedlock. When she was called before the local church authorities to answer for her sins, she famously replied, "I have a right to children. No white man will marry me. I cannot live with the Indians. But I can have children, and I will support the children that I have . . . God meant that a woman should have children." For Indian males, the situation was dire. Few Native American men are known to have married white women. One of them was David Lemmon, who was exceptional in many ways: strikingly tall and athletic, and an extraordinary violin player who traveled frequently to play at dances and thus had many opportunities to socialize. He married a Swedish woman named Josephine Neilson. Far more common, however, are stories like that of Tony Tillohash. He proposed to a white girl from the Heaton household, where he had worked for years. The parents quickly discouraged him and advised him to marry among his own people. Eventually he went to live on the reservation of a Paiute band called the Shivwits.[17]

Before the Mormons moved to Utah, they never anticipated acquiring Indians and keeping them in their homes as "indentures." Their curious ideas about the origins of Indians and their impulse to help in their redemption eased their transformation into owners and masters. But even without these notions, they would have become immersed in an extraordinarily adaptable and durable system that had long flourished in the region. In colonial times, Spanish missionaries had acquired Indians to save their souls. In the nineteenth century, the Mormons' quest to redeem Natives by purchasing them was not too different. Yet both ended up creating an underclass, in spite of their best wishes. Such was the staying power of the other slavery.

In New Mexico, the Civil War led to the greatest Indian slavery boom in the territory's recorded history. Although the conflict began in the East, it quickly spilled into the West. Texas was a conduit for the westward expansion of the conflict. As a cotton state, it had opposed the election of Abraham Lincoln and favored secession from the United States. The Lone Star State formally joined the Confederacy in March 1862. As the sectional conflict intensified, Confederate leaders in Texas and elsewhere looked to New Mexico as the gateway to the mineral wealth of Colorado and the coast of California. Thus, barely three months into the conflict, Texas troops entered New Mexico. By early March 1862, the Texans had taken control of Albuquerque and Santa Fe. It was a rapid and impressive advance that nonetheless soon came to a grinding halt. Moving south from Colorado, Union troops engaged the Texans just east of Santa Fe in the famous Battle of Glorieta Pass, sometimes grandly referred to as "the Gettysburg of the West." The Union forces could not defeat the Texans, but they did destroy the wagon train containing most of the Confederates' supplies, thus making their continued presence in New Mexico difficult. The final blow came from California, where Colonel James H. Carleton had raised a volunteer force of about two thousand men known as the California Column. Under Carleton's vigorous leadership, these volunteers braved the Mojave Desert and marched eight hundred miles via Tucson to arrive in southern New Mexico in the summer of 1862, just in time to drive out the last Confederate remnants.[18]

This is how Carleton found himself in New Mexico, at the head of a sizeable force and with no visible enemy. He had to remain vigilant in case the Texans returned. Otherwise he merely awaited the unfolding of the Civil War in other parts of the country. Still, there were some things he could do with his men and resources. Like many other officers of the day, Carleton had fought in the U.S.-Mexican War and subsequently taken part in various Indian campaigns in the western territories. In the early 1850s, he had spent nearly five years in New Mexico fighting the Apaches. During this formative period, Carleton had witnessed the never-ending cycle of war and peace with the Indians of the West. U.S. officials signed treaty after treaty with the Apaches, Utes, and Navajos, compacts that were sometimes not ratified by Congress and were routinely violated by one or both parties. It was an ineffectual and confusing situation, all the more so because policy concerning the Indians was mired in a petty rivalry between the Department of War and the Department of the Interior. Carleton learned one important lesson from these experiences: the only lasting solution to the "Indian problem," as he called it, was to move the tribes onto reservations by means of forceful military action. When he took military command of New Mexico in the fall of 1862, he had a unique opportunity to do just that. With New Mexico under martial law, now General Carleton enjoyed practically unlimited authority.[19]

Of the various Indian groups surrounding New Mexico, the Navajos, or Diné, had been the most menacing in recent years. In the spring of 1860, they had assembled the largest war party ever recorded in Navajo history, and their intention had been nothing less than to overrun the only American military outpost established within Navajo territory, appropriately called Fort Defiance. In the predawn darkness of April 30, 1860, more than one thousand Navajo warriors (perhaps as many as two thousand according to some sources) arranged themselves in three groups and took up their positions. It was an unprecedented maneuver in terms of daring, planning, and scope. The Navajos possessed few firearms and were at a tremendous disadvantage against a fully manned fort designed to resist such attacks. But their frustration had reached the boiling point. They began their attack in the early daylight, mostly with bows and arrows, seizing some of the outlying buildings, killing one soldier, and wounding several others. The assailants kept pounding Fort Defiance for several hours, finally reaching a stalemate. The Navajos carried on their fight through the spring and summer of 1860, as Navajo riders struck communities throughout western New Mexico as far south as Acoma. A Santa Fe newspaper estimated that the Navajo offensive claimed the lives of some three hundred individuals and resulted in a loss of property amounting to $1.5 million. These figures are almost certainly too high, but they reflect the very real concern among New Mexicans.[20]

Multiple reasons impelled the Navajos to fight. One of the most important was the dynamics of the captive exchange. Thanks to the painstaking work of anthropologist David M. Brugge, it is possible to plot the ebb and flow of the traffic of Navajo children and women into New Mexico as revealed by baptismal records. These documents run continuously for nearly two centuries, from the 1690s to the 1870s (see appendix 7). The peaks correspond with known military campaigns, Indian wars, and sometimes adverse environmental conditions. For example, the initial baptisms in the 1700s can be explained by Governor Francisco Cuervo y Valdés's "vigorous war" against the Navajos in 1705; the upswing in the number of baptisms in the 1740s was almost certainly a result of a major war between the Navajos and Utes, exacerbated by a drought in 1748; and the captive boom of the 1770s coincided neatly with the breakdown of a half century of peace between the Spaniards and Navajos. After the 1770s, there was a forty-year lull (with minor exceptions), which nonetheless ended with an unprecedented upsurge in Navajo captives during the 1820s. Starting in the 1820s, Navajo baptisms continued decade after decade until the 1870s. During this sixty-year period, the Navajos replaced the Apaches and Utes/Paiutes as the most heavily enslaved Indian nation in New Mexico.[21]

A closer look reveals that the initial captive taking led to raids and reprisals that yielded yet more captives and gave rise to a vicious circle of mutual predation that was very difficult to break. In the late 1700s, the New Mexicans and Navajos had developed protocols and practices that made open warfare infrequent and brief. These protocols, however, broke down as slave taking proliferated. In particular, as Hispanics and Anglos became more numerous and dominant in New Mexico, they insisted on unequal captive exchanges that caused resentment among the

Natives. A Navajo headman named Armijo explained this phenomenon better than anyone during a visit to Santa Fe in January 1852. "More than 200 of our children have been carried off and we know not where they are," Armijo told Indian agent John Greiner. "The Mexicans have lost but few children in comparison with what they have stolen from us." The Navajo man went on to explain how for five years, his people had tried to get their children back, to no avail. "Eleven times have we given up our captives — only once have they given us ours," Armijo said. "My people are yet crying for the children they have lost. Is it American justice that we must give up everything and receive nothing?" Indian parents had seen their children grow up in bondage in New Mexican homes. In many instances, they knew where their sons and daughters were being held but were not permitted to get close to them after three decades of unrelenting slave taking. The Diné had had enough. This was the tinder for the 1860 Navajo attack on Fort Defiance and the campaign against the New Mexicans.[22]

But a counterattack was beginning to gather strength, and it would rage against the Navajos with extraordinary force. Years later the Navajo chief Manuelito spoke of the fateful time "when this world was dark with dirt and sand flying, and the stones were raised by the wind . . . [and] when all the Nations came against us, then we lost our children."[23]

Manuelito's assertion that "all the Nations" turned against the Navajos was not an exaggeration or rhetorical flourish, but a verifiable reality. The first to mobilize were the Hispanics in New Mexico. In the wake of the Navajo attacks of 1860, the residents of frontier communities such as Cubero, Cebolleta, and Abiquiu banded together to form local militias. Historically these exposed towns had served as military outposts and staging areas for raids into Navajo and Ute lands. They had skilled commanders, impoverished soldiers motivated by the prospect of acquiring loot, and vast campaign experience stretching back to Spanish presidial times. According to New Mexico's Militia Law of 1851, "Any man of experience & good character" could raise a volunteer force as long as his campaigns were conducted in good faith and according to the rules and customs of war of the United States. Indeed, the New Mexican territorial government was required by law to provide arms to such volunteer units, and Governor Abraham Rencher was ready to comply. Whereas in the 1850s militia units had been required to give up their Indian captives "to be disposed of as the governor shall direct," an amendment introduced in January 1860 by the territorial legislature omitted any reference to the disposal of Indian captives. Though seemingly minor, this omission allowed frontiersmen to raise forces for the explicit purpose of capturing Indians. In effect, the amendment legalized the enslavement of hostile Indians.[24]

Hispanic militia units fanned out through the Navajos' lands during 1860. They varied in size and success. Ramón A. Baca of Cebolleta commanded as many as three hundred men and was extraordinarily effective. During an expedition in June, his forces took six women, eight children, fifty horses, and two thousand sheep. Adhering to frontier tradition, they drove the prisoners to Cebolleta, where they promptly sold them off. Other Hispanic militias were smaller and less successful. In July Jesús Gallegos of Abiquiu led one hundred twenty-five men into Navajo territory, but they were able to kill only four Navajos, wound a few others, and take four ponies. Yet other militias experienced disaster. Joaquín Candelario, also of Cebolleta, had a fierce encounter with Navajos at Laguna Grande, leaving thirty of his men dead. Candelario and thirteen survivors, seven of them badly wounded, straggled back into Fort Defiance on June 27, 1860.[25]

Encouraged by the example of the frontier towns, other New Mexicans clamored for stern retribution. In August a crowd gathered in Santa Fe and issued an immediate call for one thousand volunteers. Men began signing up in Santa Fe, Bernalillo, Rio Arriba, San Miguel, and Valencia Counties. Together these companies formed a citizen battalion of nearly five hundred men under the command of Manuel A. Chaves and took to the field against the Navajos in September.[26]

The Navajos had to worry not only about these New Mexican volunteer forces but also about other Indians. The Pueblo Indians dispatched their own warriors. Forty Indians from the pueblo of Jemez, led by the pueblo's governor, Francisco Hosta, heeded the call. Pueblos and Apaches also acted as scouts and auxiliaries for both the militias and the U.S. military. These Natives were glad to make common cause with

Euro-Americans against their mutual enemy and regarded this service as a way to secure horses, sheep, and captives. Even more dangerous than the Pueblos and Apaches were the Utes. The rivalry between the Navajos and Utes stretched back for centuries, but their different historical trajectories had given the Utes some advantages. Over the years, the Navajos had settled down in a multiplicity of clans in northwestern New Mexico, eastern Arizona, and parts of Colorado and Utah, accumulating large herds of sheep and developing fruit orchards and other crops that tied them to the land. Some twelve thousand Navajos lived in this homeland they called Dinétah. Their pastoral and fragmented existence made them vulnerable to attack, however, especially from the Utes, who lived just to the north and had adopted an equestrian and mobile existence.

Up to 1856, the Utes and Navajos had raided each other from time to time, but that year the U.S. military began receiving news of a state of generalized warfare between the two nations. Although it was hard to determine the true extent of this conflict at any given time, there were obvious flashpoints. In September 1860, the Utes assembled a war party of five to six hundred individuals — larger than New Mexico's entire volunteer force. Two colorful figures led this party: Chief Kaniache of the Muache Utes and a German-born Indian subagent for the Capote Utes named Albert H. Pfeiffer. (Both would go on to play crucial roles in the ultimate removal of the Navajo nation to the Bosque Redondo reservation.) Little is known about the daily operations of this extraordinary war party, but one thing is clear: it became the most successful military unit operating against the Navajos. In short order, the Utes killed six Navajos and took nineteen captives, five hundred horses, and no less than five thousand sheep.[27]

Last to enter the fray against the Navajos was the U.S. military. Regular soldiers gathered at Fort Defiance in September and October 1860 and mounted a three-pronged advance into Navajo country. The army's participation was brief but significant. Together with New Mexican militias and Indian war parties, the three American columns pursued the Navajos through the winter. In February 1861, thirty-two Navajo headmen, their resistance broken, sued for peace and signed a treaty. This state of affairs would not last for long. The Navajo nation was divided

Albert H. Pfeiffer grew up in Germany but immigrated to the United States when he was a young man. In 1858 he was appointed the Indian subagent operating out of Abiquiu. The cape he is wearing here, made of buckskin and red flannel, was presented to him by the Ute Indians. He wore it in public with marked dignity. According to the 1860 census, Pfeiffer and his wife kept at least eight Indian servants.

between wealthy families owning orchards, herds, and captives and other families with few possessions. Rich Navajos favored peace to preserve their wealth, but poorer Navajos, who had suffered disproportionately, had strong incentives to continue fighting. Hispanic New Mexicans distinguished between these two groups, unabashedly classifying them as either *ricos* (rich) or *ladrones* (thieves). The military campaigns of 1860–1861 had only exacerbated the plight of the poor Navajos, who saw their children and women taken away and their few animals stolen. Seeking to recover what they had lost, they launched another cycle of raids. By the end of 1861, the U.S. officer who had been in charge of the army's earlier campaign, Colonel Edward Canby, recognized that at least some of the Navajos had resumed their attacks.[28]

This was the situation when General James Carleton arrived from California, oversaw the final withdrawal of Confederates from New Mexico, and considered ways to put his military might to good use. He made preparations for an all-out offensive, with the intention of removing the entire Navajo nation four hundred miles away to a reservation on the windswept plains of eastern New Mexico called Bosque Redondo. This time there would be no compromises or temporary arrangements, only a scorched-earth campaign designed to bring about the Diné's unconditional surrender. The choice would be simple: total extermination or wholesale removal.

The Navajo campaign of 1863–1864 would not involve large armies clashing in epic battles like those elsewhere during the Civil War. Instead, General Carleton likened the Navajo campaign to a chase for wild game. As he put it, "An Indian is a more watchful and a more wary animal than a deer." He therefore encouraged his soldiers to follow the enemy's tracks "day after day with a fixedness of purpose that never gives up," using "all sorts of wiles to get within gunshot of it." Carleton's basic strategy consisted of fielding small units working in different areas of Dinétah to keep the Navajos continually on the run. His forces would ravage the land—burning crops, orchards, and food stores; setting fire to hogans and tepees; and tracking Navajos over long distances—all the while denying them food and shelter until they became utterly exhausted. It would be a relentless chase through Navajo country.[29]

General Carleton chose the legendary scout Christopher "Kit" Carson to lead the offensive. It was an inspired choice, first because the two men knew each other well and shared the same ideas concerning the importance of stealth, mobility, and endurance in the campaign. In 1854 a group of Indian scouts under Carson had guided Carleton and his soldiers as they followed a group of Apaches. The chase lasted "more than a fortnight" but was successful in the end, thus demonstrating how a few resolute men with a little bacon, flour, and coffee could effectively track down an elusive enemy. Apart from shared experience and ideas, Carson was an excellent choice because he had access to the best possible scouts to fight the Navajos. From 1854 to 1861, he had worked as an Indian agent, representing the U.S. government to the Indian nations of northern New Mexico. At his home in Taos, he had given out presents and received Indian visitors almost daily. Over the years, he had become especially close to the head chief of the Muache Utes, a remarkable leader named Kaniache, who had saved Carson's life on one occasion. When Carson took charge of the campaign against the Navajos, he knew exactly where to get his scouts.[30]

In the summer of 1863, General Carleton dispatched eleven hundred American soldiers to Dinétah. Divided into seven companies, they fanned out to give chase. Even though Carson was in the field and nominally in charge, General Carleton remained a hands-on commander. From his perch in Santa Fe, he insisted on being informed of every company's moves and in return constantly wrote letters containing instructions. Like a stern father, Carleton directed, praised, and scolded. When he had gone too long without news from Carson, he would fire off a short missive: "Make a note of this: You will send me a weekly report, *in detail,* of the operations of your command, a certified copy of which I desire to send to Washington." When a company stayed too long in one place or spent weeks without encountering any Indians, Carleton ordered the men to move and get into the action. When Carson expressed some misgivings about entering the Canyon de Chelly, the Navajos' stronghold, and requested permission to return home for the winter, Carleton tersely replied, "It is desirable that you go through the Cañon de Chelly before you come." In all cases, the commanding general gave clear orders about how to dispose of the Navajos: "You will promptly attack and destroy any and all grown male Indians whom you may meet. Women and children will not be harmed, but will be taken prisoners and will be securely guarded until further orders."[31]

In theory Carleton's soldiers were supported by Indian scouts. But the reality could be quite different, as the day-to-day workings of Carson's command readily attest. Routinely, Carson and his Ute scouts would leave camp early in the morning, riding ahead and moving quickly while the rest of the regiment made preparations to start the march. This advance party was the first to make contact with enemy Indians and frequently did much of the fighting. By the time the rest of the troops arrived, it was usually all over. The American soldiers spent much of their time burning crops and hogans. Ironically, the Ute scouts were often referred to as "auxiliaries," but in truth they did all the tracking and much of the fighting, while the U.S. troops were the ones performing auxiliary functions.[32]

Carson naturally relied on Kaniache for this campaign, and because the Ute head chief and his men anticipated doing much of the hard work, they also assumed they would keep the spoils of war. Accordingly, Carson forwarded an extraordinary request to Carleton:

> It is expected by the Utes, and has, I believe, been customary to allow them to keep the women and children and the property captured by them for their own use and benefit, and as there is no way to sufficiently recompense these Indians for their invaluable services, and as a means of insuring their continued zeal and activity; I ask it as a favor that they be permitted to retain all that they may capture.

Carson made this request as a concerned commander who wished to retain his Indian scouts. But his letter went further, expressing an opinion that must have been shared quite widely throughout New Mexico's frontier society:

> I am satisfied that the future of the captives disposed of in this manner would be much better than if sent even to the Bosque Redondo. As a general thing the Utes dispose of their captives to Mexican families, where they are fed and taken care of and thus cease to require any further attention on the part of the government. Besides this, their being distributed as Servants thro' the territory cause[s] them to loosen that collectiveness of interest as a tribe, which they will retain if kept together at any one place.

Carson, who was married to a Hispanic woman from Taos, knew these things from personal experience. He had Navajo captives in his household, as did Subagent Pfeiffer and other soldiers, officers, and civilians all the way up to Governor Henry Connelly.[33]

Even so, General Carleton refused to grant Carson's request. "All prisoners which are captured by the troops or employees of your command will be sent to Santa Fe by the first practicable opportunity," Carleton replied in his characteristically brash style. *"There must be no exception to this rule."* In the heat of the battle, however, Carson overlooked this pointed order. Kaniache continued to complain about doing all the hard work but not receiving sufficient compensation until he and his Utes finally left Carson's service. Revealingly, Carson noted that the real reason for the Utes' departure was that they had already gathered sufficient stock and captives. As for Kaniache and his men, they continued to operate against the Navajos, but "on their own account" and free from the strictures of the U.S. military.[34]

The fight against the Navajos continued unabated through the fall. But even with more than a thousand U.S. soldiers and an undetermined number of Indian scouts on the prowl, New Mexico remained unsafe. "There are parties of fives and tens and twenties of Navajoes and Apaches, most always well mounted, stealing throughout the country and committing depredations," Carleton reported in August to his superiors in Washington. To assist the troops, Carleton proposed a plan to raise volunteer forces in each county. As was the case two years earlier, frontier towns such as Cubero, Cebolleta, and Abiquiu were the first to respond. And also as before, they immediately launched what amounted to full-scale slaving raids into Dinétah.[35]

None of these raids was more successful than Ramón Baca's in November 1863. Baca led a group of 116 Hispanic volunteers on a six-day foray in a northwesterly direction from Cebolleta: "We encountered about 200 Indians, very poor, without stock of any consequence," Baca reported. "The Indians ran at once. We killed five men and one woman and took three children prisoners." Since its founding in the early nineteenth century in western New Mexico, Cebolleta had developed as a rough frontier outpost and a buffer community consisting of convicts, soldiers, and their families. An Indian subagent named Nathan Bibo lived in Cebolleta and years later wrote about the Indian fighters, with their "shirt and trousers made of unbleached cotton (manta), the very large brim Old Mexico straw hat (poblano), sandals of home-made fabric, leather belt . . . and their long hair braid hanging way down the back of the body." These men, by means of their superior knowledge of Indian hiding places, took "hundreds of prisoners who, as was the custom of those early days, were sold as domestics all over the territory, sometimes at very high prices," according to Bibo. If the number is accurate, Baca and his men were by far the most successful slavers of the Navajo campaign.[36]

The campaign culminated in the dead of winter with the occupation of the Canyon de Chelly. Carson's argument against entering this forbidding landscape rested on the belief that it would be better to wait "until the weather opens sufficiently to permit more extended operations." The old scout also hoped to spend the winter with his family in Taos. General Carleton would have none of that. He prodded Carson in multiple missives, impressing on him the fact that the winter was precisely the time to ratchet up the pressure. There was little else Carson and about four hundred men could do but move into position in early January 1864. Their plan was to skirt around the canyon in order to enter it through the more distant western end. Meanwhile, veteran campaigner and former Indian subagent Albert H. Pfeiffer would enter through the east entrance with one hundred men. The two groups intended to meet at the bottom in order to cut off all the escape routes, but the plan quickly unraveled.

Rounding the Canyon de Chelly turned out to be extremely difficult. Carson's oxen were dying every day from pulling the supply wagon through enormous heaps of snow. Although Pfeiffer entered the canyon, his mules kept breaking through the thin crust, stumbling, and falling. As Pfeiffer and his men zigzagged to the bottom, Indians appeared at every turn, jumping onto the rock ledges "like mountain cats." In one fatal exchange, the Americans killed two Navajo males and "one squaw who obstinately persisted in hurling rocks and pieces of wood at the soldiers." Pfeiffer covered the entire length of the canyon, about thirty miles, in four days, and saw that thousands of Navajos had taken refuge in caves and rocks all along the canyon's walls. The two sides for the most part kept their distance. "At the place where I encamped," Pfeiffer wrote, "the curl of the smoke from my fires ascended to where a large body of the Indians were resting over my head, but the height was so great that the Indians did not look larger than crows, and as we were too far apart to injure each other no damage was done, except with the tongue, the articulation of which was scarcely audible."[37]

On January 14, Carson's command finally made its way to the bottom of the canyon and caught up with Pfeiffer's company. As the old scout put it, "We have shown the Indians that in no place, however formidable or inaccessible, are they safe from the pursuit of the troops of this command." General Carleton was even more bombastic: "This is the first time any troops, whether when the country belonged to Mexico or since we acquired it, have been able to pass through the Cañon de Chelly which, for its great depth, its length, its perpendicular walls, and its labyrinthine character, has been regarded by eminent geologists as the most remarkable of any 'fissure' (for such it is held to be) upon the face of the globe."[38]

During Pfeiffer's march across the canyon, nineteen Indians on the brink of starvation had turned themselves in. Carson's orders were to send them to the Bosque Redondo reservation. Instead, he gave them food and turned them loose to spread the message that the Americans were not waging a "war of extermination" and that the Diné would be well treated if they accepted relocation to eastern New Mexico. Indeed, during his brief stay in the Canyon de Chelly, Carson did everything possible to persuade the Navajos that the government's intentions were "eminently humane and dictated by an earnest desire to promote their welfare." It was a shrewd decision. After having spent months on the run and suffered starvation throughout the winter, many Navajos received this proposal with newfound interest. And there was one additional consideration: following in the Americans' footsteps, Utes began appearing in the canyon. They were reportedly "on the loose, riding horseback, and were dangerously aggressive."[39]

Carson's tactic worked. By the end of January, five hundred Navajos had surrendered. This trickle became a tidal wave within weeks, reaching five thousand by the end of March, thus surpassing even the most wildly optimistic projections and overwhelming the army's capacity to feed and transport so many Indians. The U.S. troops turned their attention to addressing this monumental logistical challenge. But while U.S. soldiers ceased all hostilities, Hispanic and Indian bands, sensing an unprecedented opportunity to finish off their enemies, pressed their attack.[40]

As the snow began to melt and Navajo families tried to surrender, bands of Hispanic and Indian volunteers took to the field. Several attacks occurred over a one-week period in late April and early May. On April 29, a distraught Navajo man arrived at Fort Canby (as Fort Defiance was now called) to report that he and his family had been intercepted by a party of Mexicans while en route to the fort to surrender. He stated that "all of his family had been either killed or captured and his herds taken by the Mexicans." Other survivors confirmed the incident. A U.S. officer heard these testimonies and filed a report, offering one final and extremely insightful observation: "The Mexicans, Utes, Zuni, & Moqui Indians are aware that the wealthy Navajos are about to come in for the purpose of emigration to the Bosque Redondo, and take advantage of the fact and prosecute a war against them knowing that the Navajos are unprepared and are relying on the protection of the Gov't."[41]

Another attack occurred three days later, this one against Navajos who were under the nominal protection of U.S. troops. This group had already surrendered and was on its way to Bosque Redondo, passing through the vicinity of Albuquerque, when some of its members became ill and fell behind. As the leader of the Americans, Captain Francis McCabe, did not wish to delay the rest of the column, he decided to leave the ill Navajos in charge of a petty chief with sufficient provisions. They were resting when "6 Mexicans came from the town and took 13 of them prisoners, 8 women and 5 children, and took them back into the town; they also robbed them of their provisions." The overstretched Americans seemed unable to protect the thousands of Indians on the move. One small distraction was all the slave takers needed to strike.[42]

Bad as this was, three days after that the commanding officer at Fort

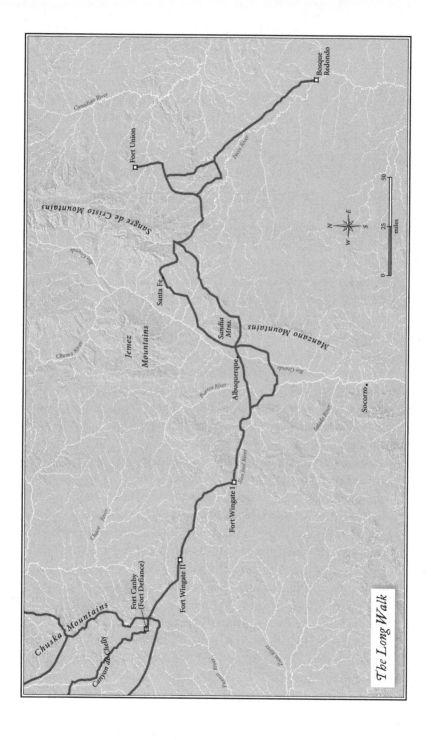

The Long Walk

Canby received an urgent letter informing him that "a man who lives in Cebolleta, N.M. named Romaldo [Ramón] Baca has organized here & at other points, a party of 200 men, to go out with him, and steal the stock of the rich Navajos, now coming in to your Post." Writing from Albuquerque, Major J. C. McFerron made one additional point: "Those belonging to his party are to leave for the general rendezvous in small parties so as not to excite attention to their movements." Evidently Baca was well aware of the impending surrender of the rich Navajos and wished to make the most of the situation. He enjoyed great success, if we are to judge from other sources. For instance, one of his victims was the niece of a prominent Navajo chief named Herrero. She was eventually rescued and described in front of a military court how an armed party of "Mexicans from Cebolleta" attacked her camp at Casa Blanca, near Moqui, killing seven men and taking twelve prisoners, all women and children. Her two sisters were sold at Ranchos de Atrisco, close to Albuquerque, while some of the other prisoners were taken to southern New Mexico near Isleta, where they were finally disposed of. The geographic scope of these sales is noteworthy. Baca's hometown of Cebolleta was already saturated with Navajos. A survey conducted in February 1864 yielded ninety-five Navajo peons, a remarkable number for such a minuscule settlement.[43]

Ute war parties also were active. The historical record contains only sporadic references to their activities and is mostly lacking in detail. But we have indirect proof of their tremendous effectiveness. In July 1865, officials in Costilla County, in southwestern Colorado, conducted a detailed census of all Indians held in bondage. Sixty individuals were identified and listed by name, age, ethnicity, and date of capture. Fifty of them, or eighty-three percent, were Navajos, mostly children and women taken during the 1863–1864 campaign, as one would expect. In addition, the census provided rare information about the sellers. Of the sixty Indians listed, forty-eight had been sold by Mexican traffickers, ten by Utes, one by Apaches, and one by an unidentified individual. Clearly, Mexican dealers had the upper hand in Costilla County. However, an identical survey conducted in neighboring Conejos County told a very different story. Eighty-eight Indian peons were listed there, of whom sixty-three, or seventy-one percent, were Navajos. In this case, fully forty-five had been sold by Utes, forty by Mexicans, two by Apaches, and one by an unspecified trafficker. Essentially, Ute and Mexican traffickers had split the slaving business in half in Costilla and Conejos Counties.[44]

We can thus infer that both Mexican and Ute bands worked tirelessly that fateful spring of 1864. The situation was so dire that Kit Carson requested additional troops to pursue and capture "whatever bands of citizen marauders may come here for the purpose of thwarting the laudable actions of the government." Similarly, Governor Henry Connelly issued a proclamation declaring all citizen forays into Navajo country "positively prohibited under the severest penalties" and warning against "further traffic in captive Indians." It is doubtful, however, that Connelly's proclamation made much of a difference.[45]

The wholesale removal of the Navajo nation was tremendously disruptive not only for those who made it to Bosque Redondo but also for the scores of Navajos who were captured en route and sold off throughout New Mexico, Colorado, and northern Mexico. With good reason, the Navajos refer to this period as "the Fearing Time." By the end of 1864, 8,354 Navajos were living at the Bosque Redondo reservation, according to reliable military censuses. That still left three to four thousand Navajos unaccounted for. Considering that a few hundred remained at large in remote areas and that hundreds more had perished during the campaign, it seems reasonable to assume that the number of enslaved Navajos was between one and three thousand. (Nearly seven hundred Navajos appear in baptismal records as dependents.) Wealthy New Mexicans each possessed four, five, or more Navajo slaves.[46]

Americans had them too, from the governor down. The chief justice of New Mexico, Kirby Benedict, stated quite clearly that he had seen Indian slaves at the house of Governor Connelly, "but whether claimed by his wife, himself, or both, I know not." The chief justice was also aware that superintendent of Indian affairs for New Mexico Michael Steck—the very federal official charged with enforcing U.S. policies toward Indians—possessed one female servant, "but I cannot state by what claim she is retained." As far as the Indian agents working under Superintendent Steck, the chief justice assumed that "*all of them, ex-*

*cept one,* have the presence and assistance of the kind of persons mentioned." Their ranks included Kit Carson and Albert Pfeiffer, as we have seen. The situation was much the same among the American judges of New Mexico. Chief Justice Benedict recalled how in the spring of 1862, he had traveled with Associate Justice Sydney A. Hubbell with the intention of taking their families to the East, "and he informed me at Las Vegas that he sold one Indian woman to a resident of that place preparatory to crossing the Plains."[47]

The chief justice's candid deposition makes clear that by the summer of 1865, nearly all propertied New Mexicans, whether Hispanic or Anglo, held Indian slaves, primarily women and children of the Navajo nation, who were "bought and sold by and between the inhabitants at a price as much as is a horse or an ox." He estimated that the total number of Indian slaves in New Mexico ranged from fifteen hundred to three thousand, "and the most prevalent opinion seems to be that they considerably exceed two thousand." In absolute terms, such figures may not sound like much, but the percentage was extremely high for the Navajo nation. For the present-day United States as a whole, it would be as if the population of California, Texas, or New York and New England combined were suddenly sold off into slavery.[48]

The enslavement of Navajos in the 1860s was a direct result of the American conquest of the West. The federal government's policies of removal gave Indian slavers extraordinary opportunities to ply their trade. The total number of Indians baptized in New Mexico in the 1860s was 846, almost seven times more than in the previous decade and far more than in any other decade going all the way back to the 1690s. Fully ninety-three percent of these baptized Indians were Navajos (see appendix 7). But at least there was some small consolation. Word of this sordid affair reached the ears of Washington politicians and abolitionist societies in the East. Something had to be done. After all, the United States was fighting a civil war ostensibly over slavery.

# 12

## The Other Slavery and the Other Emancipation

AMERICANS TODAY ARE well aware of some of the milestones in the antislavery movement, such as the Underground Railroad, the publication of Harriet Beecher Stowe's *Uncle Tom's Cabin* in 1852, and the Thirteenth Amendment to the U.S. Constitution, which abolished slavery throughout the United States in 1865. Very few, however, would be able to say specifically when or how the enslavement of Indians ended. This blind spot harks back to the Civil War era. American leaders of the 1850s and 1860s became aware of the phenomenon of Indian slavery only slowly, and Washington's crackdown on the other slavery occurred by fits and starts.

To be sure, federal agents in the West kept sending reports to Washington about Indians held in bondage. But the West was still a world away prior to the completion of the first transcontinental railroad in 1869: months of travel by wagon across the plains or by ship around South America. Easterners readily identified the South's system of chattel slavery as a major national problem, but they had tremendous difficulty rallying against the West's kaleidoscopic, shadowy, and ever-changing labor practices concerning Chinese coolies, Mexican peons, and American Indian slaves. And yet the solution had to come from the East, as local, territorial, and state authorities in the West were either implicated in the traffic and exploitation of Indians or unable to act against local and regional elites that were too entrenched and dependent on coerced Native labor.

Abolitionist societies in the East did concern themselves with the plight of Native Americans from time to time. Events such as the Seminole Wars in Florida during the 1810s and 1830s, the Cherokee removal in the 1830s, and the Indian wars of the 1860s sparked discussions and calls for action. Abolitionists' awareness of the condition of the original inhabitants of North America is at times remarkable. In 1838 the editor of the *Pennsylvania Freeman*, John Greenleaf Whittier, understood that "the same despotic, cruel, and diabolical spirit that oppresses the African race acts in all its unearthly force and virulence against the poor Indians." One year later, the man who served as lawyer for the Cherokee nation, James G. Birney, spelled out in an open letter how white settlers had "traversed the seas, invaded another continent, set on fire the humble dwellings of the unoffending heathen and enslaved their young men and maidens." Yet these early insights did not translate into concrete action. The main problem was conceptual. Abolitionists (and nineteenth-century Americans more broadly) believed that the nation consisted of a collection of races afflicted by different problems. Blacks were thus defined by the American system of chattel slavery. This gave abolitionists a clear target. In contrast, the condition of Indians arose from multiple factors, including land dispossession, removal to reservations, wanton murder at the hands of white colonists, disappearance due to illnesses to which they had no immunity, and, only in passing, enslavement. This layering of different forms of abuse prevented abolitionists from seeing the common threads of labor oppression that affected Africans and Native Americans alike.[1]

The impetus to eradicate Indian slavery did not originate in abolitionist groups. Instead, it came from that much-maligned institution, the United States Congress. Congressmen were called on to review legislation emanating from the western territories, and sometimes they did not approve what they received. In 1851 New Mexico's territorial assembly passed the Law Regulating Contracts Between Masters and Servants, which contained the usual provisions about debt obligations that had to be repaid through labor. Congress went along with that legislation. But in 1859 New Mexico's legislature made the servitude code more draconian by allowing masters to "correct their servants" without the intervention of any court. Adding insult to injury, that same year the legislature reissued an act declaring all black slaves the legal property of their masters. These two territorial laws proved much too controversial in Washington. Some legislators began referring to them as the "white slave code," which allowed "all white laboring men and women to be whipped by their employers," and the "black slave code," which allowed "any person to arrest anyone whom he calls an absconding slave by force and without any legal process from any court or magistrate." The ensuing sectional spat prompted Ohio representative John A. Bingham to introduce a bill "to disapprove and declare null and void all Territorial acts and parts of acts heretofore passed by the Legislative Assembly of New Mexico which establish, protect, or legalize involuntary servitude or slavery within said Territory, except as punishment for crime, upon due conviction." The bill narrowly passed in 1860.[2]

Congress thus intervened to nullify New Mexico's servitude laws. Yet as the nation plunged into war, the matter of Indian servitude took a backseat to the burning question of black slavery. In 1862 the U.S. House of Representatives enacted a broader law prohibiting "slavery and involuntary servitude in any of the Territories of the United States." In theory Congress had proscribed all forms of bondage in the territories, but in practice the overriding concern was to prevent the spread of black slavery into the West. Even within New Mexico, Congress's nullification of the indenture laws in 1860 and the prohibition of slavery and involuntary servitude in 1862 made little difference in the ongoing traffic of Indians. As we have seen, Indians held in bondage reached record numbers in New Mexico during the Navajo campaign of 1863–1864.[3]

Indian slaves had to wait until the end of the Civil War to get additional attention from the federal government. As the North gained the upper hand in the war, a group of congressmen began to think about the nation that would emerge after the conflict. One of the most ebullient was Senator James R. Doolittle of Wisconsin. In a Senate speech in January 1864, he asserted that "we shall come out of this struggle with slavery utterly done away with; that we shall be redeemed and regenerated as a people; that we shall stand hereafter, as we have stood heretofore, in the vanguard of the civilized nations." Senator Doolittle was a deeply religious man who believed that the Declaration of Independence was "the new gospel of man's redemption" and the Fourth of July "the Birthday of God's Republic, second only in history to the birth of Christ." Doolittle's opportunity to play a part in perfecting the Union after the Civil War was not long in coming. On March 3, 1865, Congress passed a resolution creating the Joint Special Committee on the Condition of the Indian Tribes, a bicameral committee charged with investigating their treatment by the civil and military authorities of the United States. Doolittle had been serving as chairman of the Committee on Indian Affairs in the Senate, so it was only natural that he would also chair this joint committee, which received considerable backing from Congress.[4]

The task before the Doolittle Committee was gargantuan. Three senators and four representatives could not possibly collect all the necessary information about a continent-size nation, let alone process it and craft a report based on a comprehensive examination of the evidence. Nonetheless, the committee used the powers vested in it to call witnesses and request reports from military officers, Indian agents, superintendents, and "other persons of great knowledge in Indian affairs." Through circular letters and questionnaires, the committee soon amassed hundreds of pages of information. During the summer recess of 1865, the committee members also toured the West. Two of them journeyed to California, Oregon, Nevada, and the territories of Washington, Idaho, and Montana. Another two were assigned to Minnesota, Nebraska, Dakota, and upper Montana. Senator Doolittle and the last two members went to Kansas, Indian Territory, Colorado, New Mexico, and Utah. After these travels, the committee faced the daunting task of making sense of it all and writing a report. Remarkably, the final draft consisted of only ten pages—followed by testimonies and documentation running for more than five hundred pages. The short expository portion of the report lacked any concrete proposals. It merely rehashed familiar tropes about the disappearance of the Indians as a result of wars with whites, disease, and Indian intemperance—and even as a Darwinian outcome of an inferior race coming into contact with a superior one. Still, the Doolittle

Report accomplished much. Among other things, the report substantiated the traffic of Indian slaves and the prevalence of peonage. It was the first time many easterners and Washington politicians had heard about these other forms of bondage.[5]

One of the high-ranking officials who kept abreast of the findings of the Doolittle Committee was Secretary of the Interior James Harlan. He was an ardent opponent of slavery with boundless energy who had just assumed his duties as secretary in the cabinet reshuffle following President Lincoln's assassination. Harlan found the information about the slaving practices in New Mexico troubling and decided to take up the matter with President Andrew Johnson. After a few preliminary meetings, the president must have come around to Harlan's point of view. On June 9, 1865, President Johnson issued a statement from the executive mansion affirming that the Indians of New Mexico had been "seized and reduced to slavery." It is significant that he used the "s" word — with its great emotional charge in the immediate aftermath of the Civil War — to describe the condition of the Natives of New Mexico. Johnson also ordered "that the authority of the Executive branch of the Government should be exercised for the effectual suppression of a practice which is alike in violation of the rights of the Indians and the provisions of the organic law of said Territory."[6]

The president's directive was all Secretary Harlan needed to take additional action. He ordered the commissioner of Indian affairs to launch a parallel investigation into the condition of the Indians of New Mexico. And thus the wheels of government began turning. The commissioner appointed a bank clerk from Dubuque, Iowa, named Julius K. Graves as "special agent" in charge of this second investigation. Graves was a methodical and persistent man who did much to explain the depth of the Indian slavery problem to the eastern establishment. In September Graves received his final instructions and, after a harrowing trip that left some of his limbs frozen, reached Santa Fe on December 30, 1865. On New Year's Day, Special Agent Graves began his investigation by attending the opening session of the territorial legislature. "The Indian question was the all absorbing topic of conversation among the entire community," Graves reported to his superiors in Washington. "Each individual seemed to have peculiar ideas upon the subject, and freely announced and advocated them." He correctly surmised that New Mexico's peonage system had been in existence for more than a century. In Graves's words, it remained "the universally recognized mode of securing labor and assistance; and the results of that system were identical to that of Negro slavery as formerly practiced in the southern states." Graves distinguished between the ordinary Mexican form of peonage, which he described as "a state of continual imprisonment or service for debt," and a second system derived from the practical enslavement of captive Indians taken in raids. About the first system, Graves merely reported that the New Mexican peons received salaries of between $2 and $15 per month. After deducting food, clothing, and other expenses, they were left with little to pay down their debt. The result in most cases was compulsory service for life.[7]

Graves was more interested in documenting the second system. The special agent pointed out that New Mexicans continued to send expeditions that all too often were nothing but slave raids. He believed that these actions were "calculated to keep alive the Indian troubles, and indeed, provoke the savage beings to continued acts of vengeance." Although in theory expedition leaders were supposed to turn over all their Indian captives to the territorial authorities, "in most cases the captives are either sold, at an average of $75 to $400, or held in possession in practical slavery." According to Graves, this system persisted all over New Mexico, "to an alarming extent" and in spite of the various acts of Congress and President Johnson's more recent executive order. From what the special agent had been able to observe, Santa Fe alone may have had four hundred Indian slaves. He also mentioned that "nearly every federal officer holds peons in service," including New Mexico's superintendent of Indian affairs, who had half a dozen. No wonder the orders from Washington had gained little traction in New Mexico. Graves concluded with an impassioned plea, urging the federal government to take vigorous action in New Mexico, because failing that, the enslavement of Indians would continue for years. His assessment would prove entirely correct.[8]

While Doolittle and Graves conducted their inquiries, congress-men in Washington struggled to ratify and implement the Thirteenth Amendment — the first constitutional amendment in sixty years. Its wording was succinct and full of possibilities:

Section 1. Neither slavery nor involuntary servitude, except as a pun-ishment for crime whereof the party shall have been duly convicted, shall exist within the United States, or any place subject to their ju-risdiction.

Section 2. Congress shall have the power to enforce this article by ap-propriate legislation.

American leaders had proposed the Thirteenth Amendment as a way to guarantee the Union's victory over the Confederacy and ensure the abolition of African slavery. Lincoln's Emancipation Proclamation of 1863 had been a necessary first step, but an executive order could al-ways be ruled unconstitutional by the courts or reversed by Congress or future presidents. The idea of a constitutional amendment thus emerged as an expedient and almost accidental solution to the imper-manence of Lincoln's proclamation. Rather than leaving this great act of emancipation to the executive branch alone, Supreme Court justice Samuel Miller would later explain, Congress "determined this [amend-ment] to place this main and most valuable result in the Constitution of the restored Union as one of its fundamental articles." The intended beneficiaries of the Thirteenth Amendment were unquestionably Afri-can slaves. But the adoption of the term "involuntary servitude," a for-mulation borrowed from the Northwest Ordinance of 1787, opened the possibility of applying it to Indian captives, Mexican peons, Chinese coolies, or even whites caught in coercive labor arrangements. Dur-ing Reconstruction, legislators and justices were thus forced to come to grips with the precise meaning and extent of the Thirteenth Amend-ment and its related legislation.[9]

To understand the intentions and values of the framers of this legisla-tion, one has to begin with the free labor ideology that developed in the

1850s and emerged triumphant at the end of the Civil War. The elections of November 1864 not only gave Lincoln a landslide victory for a second term but also produced a Congress solidly dominated by Republicans and former Free-Soil Party members deeply committed to the ideal of a nation of free workers. Republicans had almost unanimous control of the Senate and a three-fourths majority in the House of Representatives. These men did not agree on a single definition of free labor, but they believed in the superiority of free over slave labor. Perhaps the closest they came to a common understanding of free labor was their insistence that every man should be "entitled to the fruits of his labor." They repeated this phrase over and over like a mantra, beginning with President Abraham Lincoln, who had become the greatest ideologue and most conspicuous advocate of free labor. In speeches and writings, Lincoln emphasized how northerners were "neither hirers nor hired," but instead worked "for themselves, on their farms, in their houses, and in their shops, taking the whole product to themselves, and asking no favors of capital on the one hand, nor hirelings or slaves on the other." The ideal of a nation of self-reliant men who owned their own plots of land, tools, and animals resonated powerfully with a president who had grown up working on small farms in Kentucky, Indiana, and Illinois. After winning the war, Lincoln and the Republican majority in Congress intended to extend this bountiful system to the entire nation. As Republican leader and textile entrepreneur Edward Atkinson of Massachusetts affirmed, it had been "a war for the establishment of free labor, call it by whatever name you will."[10]

These advocates of free labor first had to secure passage of the Thirteenth Amendment. They had little trouble in the Republican-controlled Senate, but in the House of Representatives, the Democratic minority was able to block the bill because of the two-thirds majority required to pass a constitutional amendment. On January 31, 1865, the Thirteenth Amendment came up for a second vote after frantic negotiations. When the final tally was announced, it had passed with only two votes to spare, 119–56. The spectators in the gallery broke into cheers. "Members joined in the shouting and kept it up for some minutes," wrote a congressman in his journal. "Some embraced one another, others wept like children.

I have felt, ever since the vote, as if I were in a new country." To many Americans, the passage of the Thirteenth Amendment represented the dawn of a new era.[11]

Yet the struggle over free labor proved far more protracted than anticipated. In 1865–1866 southern states enacted the infamous Black Codes aimed at restricting the freedom of former slaves. Adopting tried-and-true tactics such as vagrancy laws, convict leasing, and debts, white southerners sought to nullify the provisions of the Thirteenth Amendment. The Mississippi legislature was the first to introduce these measures, which were quickly copied, sometimes word for word, in South Carolina, Georgia, Florida, Alabama, Louisiana, and Texas. Mississippi's Vagrancy Act of 1865, for instance, required that "all free negroes and mulattoes over the age of eighteen carry written proof of employment." Without such a document, a free black would be immediately deemed a vagrant and hired out to any white man willing to pay the $50 fine incurred by a convicted vagrant. "Free negroes" could also be convicted for "mischief," "insulting gestures," and the "vending of spirituous or intoxicating liquors." These forms of labor coercion harked back to the eighteenth century or were copied from labor arrangements that existed in other parts of the country. In either case, the similarities between the new labor regime that emerged in the South and the other slavery that prevailed in the West are remarkable. Indian captives, servants, and peons in Utah, California, New Mexico, or Yucatán would have instantly recognized the purpose and spirit of the Black Codes. African slavery may have been abolished, but the methods of the other slavery were spreading to the South.[12]

Partly to counter the Black Codes, Congress passed the Civil Rights Act of 1866, which extended to all males in the United States, "without distinction of race or color, or previous condition of slavery or involuntary servitude," the same rights enjoyed by white citizens. The idea was to give former slaves the tools to fight against the labor practices that came to replace formal slavery. They would be able to sue in court and generally enjoy the same legal protections of their persons and property as whites. Several legislators believed that the Thirteenth Amendment and Civil Rights Act of 1866 were sufficient to free blacks. After all, the Thirteenth Amendment was categorical in prohibiting "involuntary servitude." As Justice Samuel Miller explained in 1873, "The word 'servitude' is of larger meaning than slavery . . . and the obvious purpose was to forbid all shades and conditions of African slavery."[13]

Free labor advocates and congressmen could see that coercive labor practices also existed in the West, and some of them intended to take their crusade into that region. Yet as they turned westward, they faced both internal disagreement and external opposition, particularly from the Supreme Court. The first question was whether the Thirteenth Amendment could be extended to peoples other than African Americans. The Supreme Court took up this issue in the landmark Slaughter-House Cases (1873). Justice Stephen Field argued for an expansive interpretation of the term "involuntary servitude" to include such varied practices as "serfage, vassalage, villenage, peonage, and all other forms of compulsory service for the mere benefit or pleasure of others." Justice Field boldly stated that the Thirteenth Amendment was intended "to make everyone born in this country a freeman . . . and [able to] enjoy the fruits of his labor." However, the man who wrote the majority opinion, Justice Samuel Miller, held for a more restrictive understanding. He affirmed that even though "only the fifteenth amendment mentions the negro by speaking of his color and his slavery, it is true that each of the other articles [Thirteenth and Fourteenth Amendments] was addressed to the grievances of that race, and designed to remedy them, as the fifteenth." Only hypothetically did Miller contemplate the possibility that "if Mexican peonage or the Chinese coolie labor system shall develop slavery of the Mexican or Chinese race within our territory, this amendment [Thirteenth] may safely be trusted to make it void." Miller's view was that the Thirteenth Amendment was intended chiefly to end slavery in the South, and a majority of the justices concurred with him.[14]

As various legal scholars have noted, in the Slaughter-House Cases and others, such as the Civil Rights Cases of 1883, the Supreme Court moved steadily to restrict the scope of the Thirteenth Amendment. Wary of the expansion of national power at the expense of the states, the highest court in the land interpreted the Thirteenth Amendment increasingly as a narrow rule that applied to a dwindling number of situations. By the turn of the century, that "grand yet simple declaration of the personal freedom of all of the human race within the jurisdiction of this government" had become largely a historical relic.[15]

The Civil Rights Act of 1866 and the Fourteenth Amendment in 1868 also failed to bring relief to Native Americans held in bondage. These statutes protected and conferred citizenship rights on "all persons born or naturalized in the United States, and subject to the jurisdiction thereof," but quite crucially excluded "Indians not taxed." As early as the U.S. Constitution of 1787, "Indians not taxed" had been excluded from population counts to determine the apportionment of the House of Representatives and comprised all Indians residing on reservations or living on their own, in bands or individually, in unsettled regions of the United States. Only those who had left their Native communities and joined the majority society were counted as "taxed." It boiled down to a distinction between "wild" and "civilized" that deprived the vast majority of Native Americans of basic citizenship rights and protections. According to the census of 1870, only eight percent of American Indians were classified as "taxed," and even that small minority were eventually stripped of their citizenship rights.[16]

In 1880 John Elk, a Winnebago Indian who had left his reservation to live in Omaha, Nebraska, tried to register to vote. The case brought on his behalf eventually reached the U.S. Supreme Court, which ruled against him. The majority opinion in *Elk v. Wilkins* (1884) held that the question of whether "any Indian tribes, or any members thereof, have become so far advanced in civilization that they should be let out of the state of pupilage, and admitted to the privileges and responsibilities of citizenship" had to be decided by the nation as a whole "and not by each Indian for himself." In other words, the existing legislation did not grant citizenship to any Indian. In a strongly worded dissent, Justice John Marshall Harlan accused the majority of creating "a despised and rejected class of persons with no nationality whatever, who, born in our territory, owing no allegiance to any foreign power . . . are yet not members of any political community, nor entitled to any of the rights, privileges, or immunities of citizens of the United States." It would not be until the Indian Citizenship Act of 1924 that Congress unequivocally offered federal citizenship to all Indians living in the United States.[17]

Congress thus failed to eradicate the other slavery of the West through constitutional amendments. It was a major defeat for the free labor advocates and radical Republicans who held power immediately after the Civil War. Resorting to federal appointments and piecemeal legislation to address the plight of the Indians, they were able to achieve only mixed results.

California, for instance, was a major bastion of the other slavery in the 1850s and early 1860s. Indians had to demonstrate that they were legally employed or face charges of "vagrancy," which would result in compulsory work awarded to the highest bidder for a period of four months. Natives convicted of crimes were regularly leased to whites who paid their bail. Most jarringly, thousands of Indian children were awarded to white families as "apprentices." According to the Act for the Government and Protection of Indians of 1850, any white person could go before a justice of the peace and secure the "custody, control, and earnings" of an Indian minor as long as the "parents or friends" gave their consent. What is more, an amendment to the act introduced in 1860 eliminated the need to secure this consent and required only the assent of the "person or persons having the care or charge" of the Indian child in question. This resulted in more kidnapping parties roaming the Golden State to obtain suitable children and murder their parents, as well as the intensification of the Indian wars in the early 1860s.[18]

To counter this Indian slave trade, President Lincoln appointed a fierce abolitionist named George M. Hanson as superintendent of Indian affairs for northern California. Hanson did not mince words, calling the apprenticeship system "virtual slavery," denouncing the "unholy traffic in human blood and souls," and recognizing that the market for Indians was at the root of the ceaseless conflict with the Natives of California. Superintendent Hanson appointed citizens to monitor the activities of kidnappers in the countryside and worked with local and state courts to bring slavers to justice. He also waged his campaign in the court of public opinion. In 1862 Hanson secured the apprehension and conviction of George H. Woodman, who was caught transporting sixteen Yuki and

Pomo children as he crossed into Napa County. Woodman's captives were confiscated, but he was let go with only a slap on the wrist. The kidnapper remained unrepentant. A few weeks later, he tried to explain himself. "I have a lot of Indians living with me from Nearly evry tribe In those mountains," Woodman wrote to Hanson in an unusually candid letter. "There has bin a Regular skeam of Warfare Carried on against the Indians By the authority of the State for the last 3 years — leaving unprotected thousands of Indian children and the Cheafs of those tribes are anxious that thare ofen Children Shall Liv with the whites . . . and wish me to take charge of the children & Provide them with homs." Superintendent Hanson released the letter to the press along with his own reply, questioning Woodman's "philanthropy" and "disinterested benevolence" and challenging him to surrender all his Indian children, whom the superintendent promised to place in good homes at no charge.[19]

Hanson also worked with the legislature to repeal California's apprenticeship laws and strike down the provisions that allowed the leasing and whipping of Indian convicts. Achieving these legislative goals proved difficult, however, especially in the state senate, which was controlled by Democrats. At last, the state elections of 1863 brought into power a new coalition of Republicans and free-soil Democrats. Four months after President Lincoln issued the Emancipation Proclamation, the California legislature followed suit by repealing some aspects of the apprenticeship laws. It is tempting to interpret these events as part of an inexorable move toward freedom, but the reality in California was sobering. White households continued to hold Indians by the thousands. Historian Brendan C. Lindsay has compiled the most detailed information about the extent of the apprenticeship system through school district reports. The numbers are astounding. In 1863 no less than 4,500 Indian children under the age of seventeen were still living in white households. Far from decreasing after the legislative changes, the number of apprenticed children actually *increased* to nearly 6,000 in 1864 and remained at that level in 1865. There was a decline in subsequent years, but the practice did not disappear. In the 1870s, the number of Native children living in white households hovered between 1,300 and 1,500 — very large numbers considering that California Indians were

Senator Charles Sumner, circa 1865.

vanishing by then. The Golden State was simply unable to eliminate the other slavery.[20]

The same pattern of piecemeal federal involvement and local resistance to ending the other slavery characterized New Mexico. It was only because the Doolittle Commission had turned up such damning information about the condition of Indians living in the West that Secretary of the Interior James Harlan had launched a parallel investigation into New Mexico, which in turn had led Special Agent Julius K. Graves to file a report that circulated in Congress. Things could have ended there had it not been for Senator Charles Sumner of Massachusetts, who picked up the report.

Senator Sumner was one of the staunchest free labor advocates in the entire U.S. Congress and a power to be reckoned with. His efforts to emancipate African Americans, as well as his bold ideas about forcibly reconstructing the South, are familiar to those interested in the Civil War. Far less well known are Senator Sumner's activities on behalf of Indians. He had learned about the peonage system by corresponding with New Mexicans, and on January 3, 1867—after having read Graves's report and pleas for vigorous action—he raised the issue on the floor of the Senate. "I think you will be astonished when you learn that the evidence is complete, showing in a Territory of the United States the existence of slavery," Sumner informed his colleagues. "During the life of President Lincoln, I more than once appealed to him, as head of the Executive, to expel this evil from New Mexico. The result was a proclamation, and also definite orders from the War Department; but, in the face of [the] proclamation and definite orders, the abuse has continued, and, according to official evidence, it seems to have increased." Senator Sumner then introduced a resolution to consider further legislation to stop the enslavement of Indians in New Mexico. Two months later, Congress passed "An Act to abolish and forever prohibit the System of Peonage in the Territory of New Mexico and other Parts of the United States." The Peonage Act of 1867, as it became known, was a further elaboration of the Thirteenth Amendment. While the Thirteenth Amendment banned only "involuntary servitude," the Peonage Act defined peonage as "the voluntary or involuntary service or labor of any persons as peons, in liquidation of any debt or obligation." Masters often justified peonage on the grounds that it originated in a contract signed voluntarily by both parties. But the definition of peonage adopted by Congress overrode such a justification. Those who insisted on holding peons now became subject to fines of up to $5,000 and prison sentences of up to five years. In New Mexico, Governor Robert B. Mitchell publicized the Peonage Act and declared all peons free on April 14, 1867. Yet the written word was not enough to do away with the nexus of practices and customs that had lasted for centuries. Few peons invoked the protection of this act, and fewer masters still were prosecuted.[21]

More than a year passed before legislators addressed the problem of Indian bondage again. This time the trigger was money. Congress had appropriated $100,000 for the upkeep of the Bosque Redondo reservation where the Navajo nation had been confined. By early 1868, however, the appropriation had been exhausted, and the reservation was headed for catastrophe. Scurvy ran rampant; Comanches had begun attacking and carrying off herds of animals; and the interned Navajos had been unable to raise crops due to insect infestations, floods, and droughts. Faced with the specter of maintaining seven thousand Navajos in desperate circumstances, Congress set up a peace commission and dispatched it to eastern New Mexico to find a solution. Its most prominent member was Lieutenant General William T. Sherman, the second-highest-ranking officer in the United States, behind Ulysses Grant. Sherman was not known as a champion of Indian rights. In fact, over the years he had disagreed with eastern humanitarians over the army's conduct toward Indians. But at least he made direct contact with Native Americans. As a member of the peace commission, he traveled to Bosque Redondo and in late May conferred with various Navajo chiefs. Sherman was shocked by what he saw: "I found the Bosque a mere spot of green grass in the midst of a wild desert," the general wrote to Grant, "and the Navajos had sunk into a condition of absolute poverty and despair." The only viable options were either to move the Navajos to Indian Territory or to return them to their homeland in northwestern New Mexico and northeastern Arizona.[22]

During the negotiations, Sherman learned about the hundreds or possibly thousands of Navajos held in captivity. On May 29, the Navajo chief Barboncito got straight to the point: "I want to drop this conversation now and talk about Navajo children held as prisoners by Mexicans. Some of those present have lost a brother or a sister and I know that they are in the hands of the Mexicans. I have seen some myself." Sherman replied that Congress, "our great council," had passed a law that prohibited peonage, "so that if any Mexican holds a Navajo in peonage, he is liable to be put in the penitentiary." Another commissioner from Washington,

Barboncito was a member of the Coyote Pass (or Ma'iideeshgiizhnii) clan in the Canyon de Chelly. In the 1840s and 1850s, he tried to mediate between the Navajos and whites, but their conflict persisted. He participated in the Navajo attack on Fort Defiance in 1860 and subsequently tried to reach a settlement with New Mexico's military authorities, again to no avail. He was among the last Navajo leaders to be captured and sent to the Bosque Redondo reservation.

Colonel Samuel F. Tappan, then asked, "How many Navajoes are among the Mexicans now?" The Navajo man replied, "Over half of the tribe." Tappan proceeded with the same line of inquiry: "How many have returned within the five years?" Barboncito could not tell. Sherman assured

Barboncito that he and the other commissioners would do everything possible to return the Navajo children: "All are free now in this country to go and come as they please."[23]

One month later, Congress issued Joint Resolution No. 65 authorizing Lieutenant General Sherman to use any reasonable means at his disposal to "reclaim from bondage the women and children of the Navajo, as well as other tribes now held in slavery in the Territory adjoining their homes and the reservation on which the Navajo Indians have been confined." Sherman then ordered the military commander of New Mexico, Major General George W. Getty, to convey to the Navajos "the substance of the law" and to permit individual Navajos to search for their relatives and offer them financial support for that purpose.[24]

Yet another aspect of this piecemeal process of liberating Indian slaves involved the First Judicial District Court of New Mexico. In 1868 William W. Griffin, a radical Republican and free labor advocate from Virginia bent on change, in his capacity as special commissioner of Indian affairs charged 150 individuals from the Taos area with holding Indian slaves and peons in violation of the law. His work pace was frantic. Not only did he question the masters—who readily admitted to having Indian slaves and peons—but he also requested that the victims be brought to him so that he could personally inform them that under the laws of the United States, they were "absolutely free to live where and work for whom they desired, and were at perfect liberty to go where and when they pleased, and if necessary the power of the Government would be exercised to protect them in that liberty and freedom." Griffin was a man on a mission: "I will be able to reach and liberate every Indian held as a slave, or peon, within my district," he wrote two months later, "and instruct them perfectly as to their rights under the laws and succeed speedily and effectively in breaking up this system of servitude so long a curse to this territory."[25]

Prompted by these proceedings, the U.S. district attorney in New Mexico began a grand jury investigation later in the year. In all, 363 individuals from Santa Fe, Taos, and Rio Arriba Counties who were suspected of holding peons or Indian slaves were subpoenaed. Griffin presented the voluminous evidence that he had gathered. However, the crusading commissioner soon discovered that being on the right side of the law is not always enough. The jurors had peons of their own or had family members and friends who had them. Indeed, many New Mexicans were opposed to the grand jury investigation. Their point of view was best captured by an editorial in a Santa Fe newspaper: "The Navajos are a savage and barbarous people," affirmed the *New Mexican*. "The captives from this tribe have now for years lived among civilized people; have learned the language of the country, have become Christianized . . . Most if not all of those who come under the classification of 'Navajo captives,' prefer to remain in homes where they have so long been domesticated, and where they possess the advantages not only of religion, but of civilized life."[26]

In the end, Commissioner Griffin succeeded in liberating 291 Indian slaves and 60 peons. Although this was a major accomplishment, the majority of owners accused of holding Indians illegally faced no consequences. In subsequent years, however, New Mexicans took fewer slaves, even if reluctantly. In 1868 the number of Navajos appearing in baptismal records was still twenty-eight, but that number dropped to seventeen in 1869 and 1870, nine in 1871, and six in 1872. Even though this evidence shows that Indian slavery diminished in New Mexico, it did not disappear.[27]

One of the most striking observations one can make is that in contrast to the enormous dynamism and adaptability of the other slavery, the legal framework introduced to combat this form of bondage remained narrowly conceived and frozen in time. When legal scholar Jacobus tenBroek assessed the historical significance of the Thirteenth Amendment in 1951, right before the start of the civil rights movement, he concluded that it had played a very minor, even "insignificant" role in ending involuntary servitude among Indians in the West and others in the South. "Designed for the sweeping and basic purpose of sanctifying and nationalizing the right of freedom," tenBroek asserted, "few indeed, have successfully invoked it." This amendment, along with the Peonage Act of 1867, had some impact in New Mexico in the late 1860s; was used to strike down a Black Code in Alabama (1879) that facilitated the leasing of convicts; and was invoked to nullify some statutes in Alabama (1911), Georgia (1941), and Florida (1943) that had the effect of peonizing some residents in those states. This was the sum total of the Thirteenth Amendment's accomplishments up to 1951 — a very modest harvest considering the scope of the problem.[28]

In New Mexico and other parts of the West, the other slavery endured well into the twentieth century. On April 26, 1967, almost as a cruel one-hundredth anniversary commemoration of the Peonage Act, the *Albuquerque Journal* printed a picture of a smiling field worker on its front page. At the height of the civil rights movement, the photo's caption seemed incongruous: "ALLEGED SLAVE: Abernicio Gonzales, a ranch hand in western Sandoval County is suing his employer Joe Montoya for $40,000, which he alleges is due him for wages he earned at a rate of 50 cents a day for the last 33 years. Gonzales claims he was held in peonage at the ranch." Additional details emerged in the lawsuit. Gonzales had started working at the Cabezón Ranch in 1933 when he was thirteen years of age to repay $50 that his mother had borrowed for the wedding of an older brother. In less than three months, Gonzales worked off the debt. However, he agreed to continue working for 50 cents a day plus food, clothing, and shelter. In theory the ranch owner would deposit Gonzales's wages in an account for his old age. But according to the plaintiff's version, he never saw any bank statements or any other accounting of the wages. Moreover, Gonzales was not allowed to leave the ranch to seek other employment. The plaintiff also claimed that he had been punished and threatened, charges the ranch owner denied. By way of context, Gonzales's lawyer added that in some counties of northern New Mexico, as many as forty to fifty percent of rural workers lived in what he characterized as "a state of semi-peonage." Not everyone agreed with such a high amount. The War on Poverty administrator in New Mexico, Alex Mercure, estimated the number of agricultural workers living in "economic peonage" to about 120,000 in the entire state.[29]

EPILOGUE

ACKNOWLEDGMENTS

APPENDIXES

NOTES

INDEX

# Epilogue

IN THE LATE nineteenth century, as the United States emerged as an economic superpower and a magnet for workers from around the world, new forms of the other slavery arose all across the nation. Labor intermediaries, or brokers, known as "padrones" — an Italian term meaning "boss" or "lord" — proliferated at this time. The image of the Italian padrone employing children to sell newspapers in New York City or Chicago became the most familiar. But many other immigrant communities, including Greeks, Croatians, Bulgarians, Japanese, and Mexicans, had padrones too. All of these labor intermediaries made possible the transportation of their compatriots to the United States; brokered their employment in mines, railroads, and other industries; and looked after their basic needs for food, clothing, and shelter. Yet padrones charged handsomely for their services, pocketed much of their employees' salaries, and sometimes held them in virtual or actual bondage. Historian Gunther Peck has examined the activities of padrones among Italians, Greeks, and Mexicans and has underscored the fact that far from being throwbacks to the slave owners of the past, padrones were a product of the new industrial pressures of American capitalism and made use of new means of transportation to mobilize workers from distant corners of the world to create immediate and disposable workforces. And what

Italian American families, including many children who were kept out of school, are shown picking cranberries under the supervision of a padrone in Burlington County, New Jersey, in 1938. As the area surrounding the cranberry bogs was sparsely populated, the padrones had to bring in work gangs when the fruit ripened.

is more, these enterprising individuals justified their activities by casting themselves as champions of progress and even of free labor.[1]

More recently, author Kevin Bales has brought attention to the plight of contemporary slaves. His discussion is anchored in a fundamental distinction between what he calls "the old slavery," based on legal ownership of certain racial groups, and "the new slavery," in which formal ownership has been replaced by a variety of mechanisms of control, such as indebtedness or threats of violence, directed not at a particular race, but at poor and vulnerable populations regardless of color or ethnicity. Following the lead of Bales and others, scholars, activists, and the media are paying considerable attention to the victims of this "new slavery" and are trying to address fundamental questions about numbers and geographic distribution. Currently, the Walk Free Foundation provides yearly estimates of the number of slaves around the world and ranks more than 160 countries according to the prevalence of slavery there.[2]

With this resurgent focus on present-day slavery, what lessons can we derive from the four-hundred-year experience of Native Americans with the other slavery? Three considerations seem especially relevant.

First, the emphasis on the newness of contemporary forms of bondage is myopic. Many social scientists trace the beginnings of the new slavery to the end of World War II or even later, to the economic liberalization of the 1980s and 1990s. Some place the blame on "globalization," that ill-defined catchall term with its popular connotation of newness. They point to the dissolution of the Soviet Union and its related economic dislocations as the origin of the sex trade involving Eastern European women, or to the opening up of the economies of the developing world over the past thirty years, which has led to the proliferation of sweatshops to make products for the developed world. One cannot deny that such situations have indeed promoted and accelerated the traffic and exploitation of humans. But in this book, I have tried to show that the mechanisms of coercion that underpin such practices today are much older than many analysts realize. Historically speaking, "the new slavery" did not replace "the old slavery" (African slavery) but was there all along. This is not just a minor quibble over labels — "other" instead of "new" slavery. By placing the emphasis on the newness of this phenomenon, we underestimate the staying power and extraordinary adaptability of slavery itself. In spite of formal legal prohibitions against Indian slavery in 1542 and African slavery in 1865 — as well as antislavery campaigns conducted by the Spanish crown in the seventeenth century, the Mexican government in the early nineteenth century, and the U.S. government in the Civil War era — extralegal slavery, in various forms, has endured. The long-running experience of Native Americans with the other slavery helps us see its true causes. Modern incarnations of involuntary servitude and human trafficking are hardly by-products of economic dislocations or the growing inequality of the contemporary world. Such nefarious endeavors have existed for centuries as a substitute for formal slavery and have expanded in times of war, revolution, lack of state control, and globalization defined in a broader sense — starting with Portugal's exploration of western Africa and the Admiral's discovery of the New World, as opposed to just the latest twist on this process over the past thirty years. Only by contemplating this longer trajectory can we gain a measure of the breathtaking dynamism and staying power of the other slavery and related forms of involuntary servitude.

Second, the other slavery that affected Indians throughout the Western Hemisphere was never a single institution, but instead a set of kaleidoscopic practices suited to different markets and regions. The Spanish crown's formal prohibition of Indian slavery in 1542 gave rise to a number of related institutions, such as encomiendas, repartimientos, the selling of convict labor, and ultimately debt peonage, which expanded especially in the eighteenth and nineteenth centuries. In other words, formal slavery was replaced by multiple forms of informal labor coercion and enslavement that were extremely difficult to track, let alone eradicate. This remains true today: formal slavery is prohibited practically everywhere in the world, yet there are multiple practices of human bondage and trafficking that have some features in common, as well as others that are unique to each market and region of the world. As Louise Shelley has noted while studying the sex trafficking of Russian-speaking women, the smuggling of children for adoption, and other forms of bondage, there is no one business model for the trafficking of humans. The long experience of Native Americans shows that this variability of practices, supremely adapted to each social and legal context and region, is one of the defining characteristics of the other slavery — and of its related forms of involuntary servitude today.[3]

The third and final lesson of this book has to do with the enormous difficulties of combating the other slavery. It was not enough simply to prohibit Indian slavery. The New Laws of 1542, the Spanish campaign of the late seventeenth century, the Thirteenth Amendment of 1865, and the Peonage Act of 1867 did not end the other slavery. Since those who benefit from forced labor will always find ways to get around the law, it is necessary to deploy a very flexible and dynamic regulatory system that matches the adaptability of involuntary servitude and enforces the law effectively. The Native American experience shows, for instance, that the other slavery was capable of shifting geographically and targeting new groups. Attempts to liberate one group often resulted in the enslaving of a neighboring group. In the long history of Indian slavery, we have seen how Chichimecs, Utes, Apaches, Navajos, Yaquis, Mayas, and others took turns as the most heavily enslaved peoples at different times. When one group became more difficult to enslave, another one took its place. Similarly, in combating human trafficking and slavery today, we should be mindful that the successful reduction of slavery in one group or one region may result in a comparable expansion in another. Attacking the multiple guises of bondage requires real commitment. Spanish monarchs, Mexican independence leaders, and U.S. congressmen historically attempted to end an entrenched web of coercive practices that kept many Indians in bondage throughout North America. However, these actions — well-intentioned as they may have been — were handed down from afar and were ultimately uneven and had mixed results. Dynamic, adaptive, often invisible, stretching the limits of accepted institutions or posing as legitimate work, the other slavery and its related forms of involuntary servitude continue to endure today.

# *Acknowledgments*

THIS IS A hybrid work of synthesis and original research. That means I have relied on the works of many scholars whose insights and documentation have informed this book, as is evident in the chapter notes. Even though historians tend to write single-authored books and articles, history itself remains a collective enterprise. The intellectual debts I have incurred while writing this book are, therefore, too long to list here. Ultimately, the most detailed acknowledgments can be found in the citations.

A more manageable group of individuals had a more personal influence on my writing of *The Other Slavery*. My literary agent, Susan Rabiner, helped me turn a sprawling subject into a reasonable book proposal. All along Susan's suggestions were absolutely essential. In the early stages of the project, Amanda Cook served as my editor, offering excellent advice before accepting a position at another publisher. Deanne Urmy brought the project to fruition with great enthusiasm and the hand of a seasoned editor, for which I am very grateful.

In the history department at UC Davis, my greatest intellectual debts are to Arnold Bauer, Joan Cadden, Ari Kelman, Lorena Oropeza, Alan S. Taylor, Charles F. Walker, and Louis Warren. Arnie, Joan, Ari, and Chuck generously went over chapter drafts and indulged my half-baked ideas. Also at UC Davis, Evan Fletcher read several chapters and made time to talk about them over coffee, for which I thank him profusely. In addition, a cabal of Latin Americanists from various universities in northern California (Latin American Historians of Northern California, or LAHNOCA) occasionally meet to discuss works in progress, and I was fortunate to be the beneficiary of one of these sessions.

Over the years, I have presented various chapters and material pertaining to this book at conferences, symposia, and invited talks; during archival visits and casual hallway encounters; over coffee, beer, or a meal; or just out of the blue in person or email. The scholars who shaped this project in one way or another include (but are not be limited to) Ida Altman, Carolyn Arena, Roberto Baca, Juliana Barr, Arne Bialuschewski, James Brooks, Vera Candiani, Paul Conrad, Susan Deeds, Brian DeLay, Alberto Díaz Cayeros, Maria Manuel Ferraz Torrão, Ross Frank, Alan Gallay, Sarah Barringer Gordon, Steven Hahn, Pekka Hämäläinen, Rick Hendricks, William Kiser, Cármen Mena García, José Moya, Nara Milanich, Brian Owensby, Brett Rushforth, Cecilia Sheridan, Erin Woodruff Stone, David Sweet, Samuel Truett, Jaime Valenzuela Márquez, Eric van Young, and the late David J. Weber. Juliana, Arne, Paul, Susan, Brian, Alan, Pekka, Rick, David, and Sam read chapters or the entire manuscript, for which I am greatly in their debt.

My dear friend Samuel R. Martin has supported this project in multiple ways. Nothing would have been possible without my mother, María Teresa Fuentes Magaña; my wife, Jaana Remes; and our children, Samuel and Vera Reséndez. I do not have words to express my gratitude to them.

# Appendix 1

## Indian Slaves in the Americas, 1492–1900 (in thousands)[1]

| | North America (excluding Mexico) | Mexico and Central America | Circum-Caribbean[2] | South America (excluding Brazil) | Brazil | Totals |
|---|---|---|---|---|---|---|
| 1492–1550 | 2–10[3] | 250–700[4] | 130–200[5] | 40–80[6] | 40–60[7] | 462–1,050 |
| 1551–1600 | 5–15[8] | 110–190[9] | 30–75[10] | 165–270[11] | 120–200[12] | 430–750 |
| 1601–1650 | 15–45[13] | 35–90[14] | 30–55[15] | 190–350[16] | 80–150[17] | 350–690 |
| 1651–1700 | 40–90[18] | 45–90[19] | 20–35[20] | 185–355[21] | 60–100[22] | 350–670 |
| 1701–1750 | 20–40[23] | 20–50[24] | 15–25[25] | 145–260[26] | 50–130[27] | 250–505 |
| 1751–1800 | 15–30[28] | 30–60[29] | 10–20[30] | 100–145[31] | 40–100[32] | 195–355 |
| 1801–1850 | 10–20[33] | 30–80[34] | 15–45[35] | 40–90[36] | 30–90[37] | 125–325 |
| 1851–1900 | 40–90[38] | 70–150[39] | 20–70[40] | 100–180[41] | 70–150[42] | 300–640 |
| Total | 147–340 | 590–1,410 | 270–525 | 965–1,730 | 490–980 | 2,462–4,985 |

# Appendix 2

Slaving Licenses in the Caribbean, 1509–1522[43]

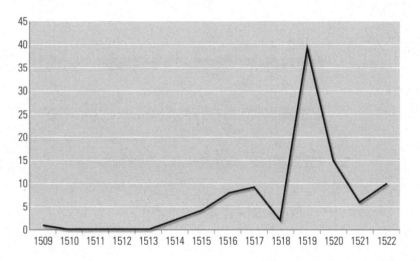

# Appendix 3

Average Price of Indian Slaves by Gender and Age in the Caribbean, 1521–1535[44]

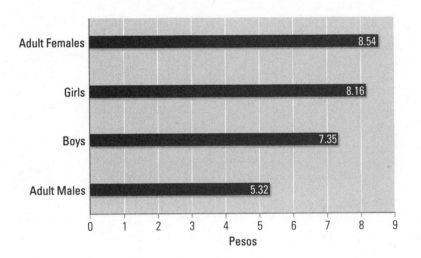

# Appendix 4

Production of Mexican Silver and U.S. Gold, 1520–1900[45]

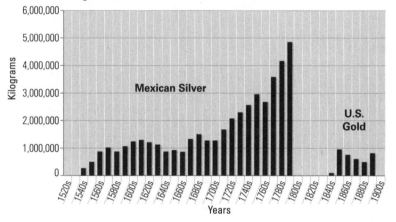

# Appendix 5

Indians from New Mexico Listed in Baptismal Records from Parral, 1634–1700[46]

| | Apaches | Apaches from New Mexico | Indians from New Mexico | Quiviras | Total |
|---|---|---|---|---|---|
| 1634–1639 | 0 | 0 | 11 | 0 | 11 |
| 1640–1644 | 0 | 0 | 0 | 0 | 0 |
| 1645–1648 | 2 | 0 | 5 | 0 | 7 |
| 1649–1655 | 9 | 4 | 8 | 0 | 21 |
| 1656–1660 | 14 | 1 | 34 | 0 | 49 |
| 1661–1665 | 20 | 0 | 8 | 1 | 29 |
| 1665–1670 | 4 | 2 | 95 | 1 | 102 |
| 1671–1675 | 45 | 0 | 22 | 2 | 69 |
| 1676–1680 | 100 | 1 | 15 | 5 | 121 |
| 1681–1685 | 54 | 0 | 10 | 2 | 66 |
| 1686–1691 | 18 | 0 | 2 | 0 | 20 |
| 1695–1700 | 21 | 0 | 1 | 0 | 22 |

# Appendix 6

Indian Slaves in Mexico and North America, 1492–1900 (in thousands)[47]

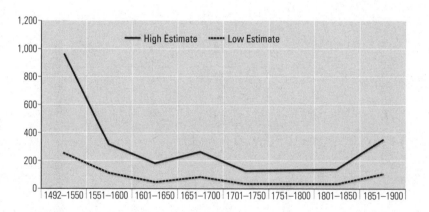

# Appendix 7

Navajo Baptisms in New Mexico, 1690–1880[48]

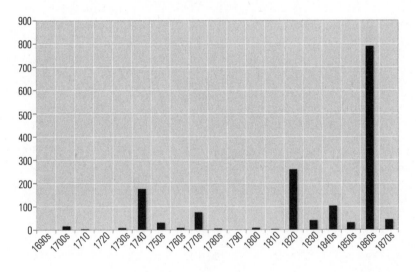

# Notes

## INTRODUCTION

1. For country-by-country estimates of people in bondage today, see the Global Slavery Index, Walk Free Foundation, http://www.globalslaveryindex.org/findings/#rankings.

2. Colonial Americans in places such as New England, Virginia, and the Carolinas had Indian slaves in the seventeenth and eighteenth centuries. But the institution was subsequently eclipsed by African slavery. By the middle of the nineteenth century, the memory of these earlier Indian slaves had been sufficiently erased that many easterners experienced the phenomenon of Indian slavery in the West as a novelty. (See chapter 10.) For a sampling of the new scholarship that is excavating the old Indian slavery in the East, see Alan Gallay, *The Indian Slave Trade: The Rise of the English Empire in the American South, 1670–1717* (New Haven, CT: Yale University Press, 2002); Alan Gallay, ed., *Indian Slavery in Colonial America* (Lincoln: University of Nebraska Press, 2009); Christina Snyder, *Slavery in Indian Country: The Changing Face of Captivity in Early America* (Cambridge: Harvard University Press, 2010); Barbara Krauthamer, *Black Slaves, Indian Masters: Slavery, Emancipation, and Citizenship in the Native American South* (Chapel Hill: University of North Carolina Press, 2013); Brett Rushforth, *Bonds of Alliance: Indigenous and Atlantic Slaveries in New France* (Chapel Hill: University of North Carolina Press, 2012); and Robbie Ethridge and Sheri M. Shuck-Hall, eds., *Mapping the Mississippian Shatter Zone: The Colonial Indian Slave Trade and Regional Instability in the American South* (Lincoln: University of Nebraska Press, 2009).

3. The quotes from the commander are from John B. Montgomery, "A Proclamation to the Inhabitants of the Northern District of California," *California Star,* March 6, 1847, available online in the California Digital Newspaper Collection, http://cdnc.ucr.edu/cgi-bin/cdnc. The proclamation was issued on September 15, 1846. On the impact of the Indian Act of 1850, see Michael F. Magliari, "Free Soil, Unfree Labor: Cave Johnson Couts and the Binding of Indian Workers in California, 1850–1867," *Pacific Historical Review* 73:3 (2004), 349–389; Sherburne F. Cook, *The Conflict Between the California Indian and White Civilization* (Berkeley: University of California Press, 1976), 314–315; Robert F. Heizer, "Indian Servitude in California," in Wilcomb E. Washburn, ed., *Handbook of North American Indians: History of Indian-White Relations,* vol. 4 (Washington, DC: Smithsonian Institution Press, 1988), 414–417;

Stacey L. Smith, *Freedom's Frontier: California and the Struggle over Unfree Labor, Emancipation, and Reconstruction* (Chapel Hill: University of North Carolina Press, 2013), passim; and Benjamin Madley, "'Unholy Traffic in Human Blood and Souls': System of California Indian Servitude Under U.S. Rule," *Pacific Historical Review* 83:4 (November 2014), 626–667.

4. The quotes are from James S. Calhoun, Indian agent, to Orlando Brown, Commissioner of Indian Affairs, Santa Fe, March 15, 1850, in *The Official Correspondence of James S. Calhoun While Indian Agent at Santa Fe and Superintendent of Indian Affairs in New Mexico,* ed. Annie Heloise Abel (Washington, DC: Government Printing Office, 1915), 162; and report of James S. Calhoun, Santa Fe, March 31, 1850, in *Annual Report of the Commissioner of Indian Affairs to the Department of the Interior* (Washington, DC: Office of the Commissioner of Indian Affairs, 1850), 105. "Sear and yellow leaf," a quote from *Macbeth,* refers to the autumn of one's life.

5. Martha C. Knack, *Boundaries Between: The Southern Paiutes, 1775–1995* (Lincoln: University of Nebraska Press, 2001), 56; John G. Turner, *Brigham Young: Pioneer Prophet* (Cambridge: Harvard University Press, 2012), 215–218.

6. Archaeological, linguistic, and historical information leaves absolutely no doubt that captivity and enslavement were practiced in various regions of the Americas prior to contact. See, for example, Elsa M. Redmond and Charles S. Spencer, "From Raiding to Conquest: Warfare Strategies and Early State Development in Oaxaca, Mexico," in Elizabeth N. Arkush and Mark W. Allen, eds., *The Archaeology of Warfare: Prehistories of Raiding and Conquest* (Gainesville: University Press of Florida, 2006); Inga Clendinnen, *Aztecs: An Interpretation* (New York: Cambridge University Press, 1995); Daniel K. Richter, "War and Culture: The Iroquois Experience," *William and Mary Quarterly* 40:4 (October 1983), 528–559; John Parmenter, *The Edge of the Woods: Iroquoia, 1534–1701* (East Lansing: Michigan State University Press, 2010), xliii–xliv, 45–51; William A. Fox, "Events as Seen from the North: The Iroquois and Colonial Slavery," in Robbie Ethridge and Sheri M. Shuck-Hall, eds., *Mapping the Mississippian Shatter Zone: The Colonial Indian Slave Trade and Regional Instability in the American South* (Lincoln: University of Nebraska Press, 2009); Leland Donald, *Aboriginal Slavery on the Northwest Coast of North America* (Berkeley: University of California Press, 1997); and Fernando Santos-Granero, *Vital Enemies: Slavery, Predation, and the Amerindian Political Economy of Life* (Austin: University of Texas Press, 2009). I want to thank Heather F. Roller for bringing the last source to my attention.

7. Many local and regional studies document the trafficking of Indian slaves. For references to all the cardinal points mentioned in this paragraph, see Esteban Mira Caballos, *El indio antillano: Repartimiento, encomienda y esclavitud, 1492–1542* (Seville: Muñoz Moya Editor, 1997); Álvaro Jara, *Guerra y sociedad en Chile* (Santiago: Editorial Universitaria, 1971); Antonio Rumeu de Armas, *La política indigenista de Isabel la Católica* (Valladolid: Instituto Isabel la Católica de Historia Eclesiástica, 1969); and William Henry Scott, *Slavery in the Spanish Philippines* (Manila: De La Salle University Press, 1991).

8. I use the estimate of the number of African slaves from the Trans-Atlantic Slave Trade Database, http://www.slavevoyages.org/tast/index.faces.

9. To my knowledge, Brett Rushforth provided the first comprehensive estimates of Indian slaves in the Americas of between two million and four million. Rushforth, *Bonds of Alliance*, 9–10. My own estimates are somewhat higher, and in appendix 1 I provide a breakdown by region and time.

10. Numerous scholars have discussed the demographic impact of slavery on West Africa. For brief overviews, see John Thornton, *Africa and Africans in the Making of the Atlantic World, 1400–1800* (New York: Cambridge University Press, 1998), 304–334; John Iliffe, *Africans: The History of a Continent* (New York: Cambridge University Press, 1995), 137; and Alan Taylor, *American Colonies* (New York: Viking, 2001), 323–324. On the synergistic relationship between slavery and epidemics, see Paul Kelton, *Epidemics and Enslavement: Biological Catastrophe in the Native Southeast, 1492–1715* (Lincoln: University of Nebraska Press, 2007), passim. David S. Jones makes the additional point that the epidemiological vulnerability of Native Americans was also dependent on environmental factors such as malnutrition or the chaos generated by European colonization. Jones, "Virgin Soils Revisited," *William and Mary Quarterly* 60:4 (October 2003), 703–742.

11. This is an aspect of Indian slavery that has received a great deal of scholarly attention. Some of the key works in this regard include Carl Coke Rister, *Border Captives: The Traffic in Prisoners by Southern Plains Indians, 1835–1875* (Norman: University of Oklahoma Press, 1940); L. R. Bailey, *Indian Slave Trade in the Southwest* (New York: Tower Publications, 1966); David M. Brugge, *Navajos in the Catholic Church Records of New Mexico, 1694–1875* (Tsaile, AZ: Navajo Community College Press, 1985); Knack, *Boundaries Between;* James F. Brooks, *Captives and Cousins: Slavery, Kinship, and Community in the Southwest Borderlands* (Chapel Hill: University of North Carolina Press, 2002); Ned Blackhawk, *Violence over the Land: Indians and Empires in the Early American West* (Cambridge: Harvard University Press, 2006); Pekka Hämäläinen, *The Comanche Empire* (New Haven, CT: Yale University Press, 2008); Brian DeLay, *War of a Thousand Deserts: Indian Raids and the U.S.-Mexican War* (New Haven, CT: Yale University Press, 2008); Lance R. Blyth, *Chiricahua and Janos: Communities of Violence in the Southwestern Borderlands, 1680–1880* (Lincoln: University of Nebraska Press, 2012); Joaquín Rivaya-Martínez, "Captivity and Adoption Among the Comanche Indians, 1700–1875" (Ph.D. diss., UCLA, 2006); Matthew M. Babcock, "Turning Apaches into Spaniards: North America's Forgotten Indian Reservations" (Ph.D. diss., Southern Methodist University, 2008); and Paul Conrad, "Captive Fates: Displaced American Indians in the Southwest Borderlands, Mexico, and Cuba, 1500–1800" (Ph.D. diss., University of Texas at Austin, 2011).

12. For the variability of contemporary forms of bondage, see Louise Shelley, *Human Trafficking: A Global Perspective* (New York: Cambridge University Press, 2010), passim. Several authors have alluded to the multiple forms of bondage that characterized European-Indian relations in North America. For instance, see Juliana Barr, "From Captives to Slaves: Commodifying Indian Women in the Borderlands," *Journal of American History* 92:1 (June 2005), 19–44. Joseph C. Miller has similarly argued that attempting to pigeonhole African slavery as "an institution" has been counterproductive and that historians would be better served by viewing slavery as a process.

Miller, *The Problem of Slavery as History: A Global Approach* (New Haven, CT: Yale University Press, 2012), passim.

## 1. CARIBBEAN DEBACLE

1. The quotes are from Bartolomé de Las Casas, *The Devastation of the Indies: A Brief Account* (Baltimore: Johns Hopkins University Press, 1992), 27; and Christopher Columbus, *The Four Voyages* (New York: Penguin, 1969), 56, 92. The population debates have generated a large literature. For a comprehensive, if dated, introduction, see William M. Denevan, ed., *The Native Population of the Americas in 1492* (Madison: University of Wisconsin Press, 1976). For the best recent treatments with a focus on the Caribbean, see Massimo Livi Bacci, "Return to Hispaniola: Reassessing a Demographic Catastrophe," *Hispanic American Historical Review* 83:1 (2003), 3–51; and Noble David Cook, "Sickness, Starvation, and Death in Early Hispaniola," *Journal of Interdisciplinary History* 32:3 (Winter 2002), 349–386.

2. Alfred W. Crosby, "Virgin Soil Epidemics as a Factor in the Aboriginal Depopulation in America," *William and Mary Quarterly* 33 (April 1976), 289.

3. Las Casas, *The Devastation of the Indies*, 12–13; King Ferdinand to Diego Colón, Seville, July 21, 1511, Archivo General de Indias (hereafter cited as AGI), Indiferente, 418, L. 3, F. 92v–93. Friar Toribio de Benavente considered Las Casas "tempestuous, argumentative, short-tempered, offensive, and harmful." Yet his own analysis of the demographic debacle of Mexico, offered in the guise of ten plagues, is remarkably consistent with the analysis offered by Las Casas. See Massimo Livi Bacci, *Conquest: The Destruction of the American Indios* (Cambridge, UK: Polity Press, 2008), 25–30.

4. On the delayed arrival of smallpox, see Alfred W. Crosby Jr., *The Columbian Exchange: Biological and Cultural Consequences of 1492* (Westport, CT: Greenwood Press, 1972), 46; and Livi Bacci, "Return to Hispaniola," 42. Carl O. Sauer noted as much in the mid-1960s in *The Early Spanish Main* (Berkeley: University of California Press, 1966), 204. Writing in 2002, Noble David Cook made the best case for an early introduction of smallpox to Española but conceded that no one had yet found any mention of the illness among the Taíno population in 1493 or 1494. Cook, "Sickness, Starvation, and Death in Early Hispaniola," 371. On the spread of syphilis, see Gonzalo Fernández de Oviedo, *Historia general y natural de las Indias,* book 2, chap. 13. See also Livi Bacci, *Conquest,* 56–63. For the influenza thesis, see Francisco Guerra, "La epidemia Americana de influenza en 1493," *Revista de Indias* 14:176 (1985), 325–347; and Francisco Guerra, "The Earliest American Epidemic: The Influenza of 1493," *Social Science History* 12:3 (Autumn 1988), 305–325. For a broader consideration of the role of epidemics in the early Caribbean, see Noble David Cook, *Born to Die: Disease and New World Conquest, 1492–1650* (New York: Cambridge University Press, 1998), 15–59.

5. See the sources in the previous note, as well as Cook, "Sickness, Starvation, and Death in Early Hispaniola," 369. Variola can survive outside the human body for weeks according to Frank Fenner, Donald A. Henderson, Isao Arita, Zdenek Jezek, and Ivan D. Ladnyi, *Smallpox and Its Eradication,* cited in Elizabeth A. Fenn, *Pox Americana:*

*The Great Smallpox Epidemic of 1775–82* (New York: Hill and Wang, 2001), 15. The large treatise by Fenner and coauthors is generally considered the definitive work on smallpox.

6. Mira Caballos, *El indio antillano*, 34; Luis Arranz Márquez, *Repartimientos y encomiendas en la Isla Española* (Madrid: Ediciones Fundación García Arévalo, 1991), passim; Livi Bacci, "Return to Hispaniola," 3–51.

7. For a very candid discussion of the methods used by one of the leading High Counters, see Woodrow Borah, "The Historical Demography of Latin America: Sources, Techniques, Controversies, Yields," in Paul Deprez, ed., *Population and Economics: Proceedings of Section V of the Fourth Congress of the International Economic History Association, 1968* (Winnipeg: University of Manitoba Press, 1970), 187–188. See also the more recent discussion by David Henige, "Recent Work and Prospects in American Indian Contact Population," *History Compass* 6:1 (2008), 183–206.

8. Works that revise down the High Counters' estimates for the Caribbean include Arranz Márquez, *Repartimientos y encomiendas*; Mira Caballos, *El indio antillano*, 33–70; and Livi Bacci, "Return to Hispaniola," 3–51. For an interesting study of the synergies between epidemics and the Indian slave trade in a different geographic area, see Kelton, *Epidemics and Enslavement*, passim. Indian vulnerability to disease was greatly affected by malnutrition, overwork, and other environmental factors, as David S. Jones has noted. Jones, "Virgin Soils Revisited," 703–742.

9. Of the many biographies of Columbus, Samuel Eliot Morison's continues to exert enormous influence. Morison, *Admiral of the Ocean Sea: A Life of Christopher Columbus* (Boston: Little, Brown, 1970). For an in-depth, more recent treatment of some of Columbus's geographic assumptions, see Nicolás Wey Gómez, *The Tropics of Empire: Why Columbus Sailed South to the Indies* (Cambridge, MA: MIT Press, 2008). On the negotiations with the Spanish monarchs, see Juan Pérez de Tudela Bueso, "La negociación Colombina de las Indias," *Revista de Indias* 14 (1954), 289–357. In his earlier negotiations with the Portuguese crown, Columbus had insisted on the very same terms he got from Spain.

10. Morison, *Admiral of the Ocean Sea*, 358–359. The first quote is from Ferdinand and Isabella to Columbus, Barcelona, March 30, 1493, cited ibid., 354–355. Note that at this point, Ferdinand and Isabella did not know anything about the lands just discovered by Columbus. By "Indies" they meant distant lands to the west of Spain. On Columbus's triumphal entrance into Barcelona and the other quotes, see Bartolomé de Las Casas, *Historia de las Indias*, 3 vols. (Mexico City: Fondo de Cultura Económica, 1986), 1:332–333. For details of the tropical birds, see Pietro Martire d'Anghiera, *De Orbe Novo*, 2 vols. (New York: Burt Franklin, 1970), 1:65.

11. Sauer, *The Early Spanish Main*, 28.

12. For the meanings, uses, and value of spices in Europe, see Paul Freedman, *Out of the East: Spices and the Medieval Imagination* (New Haven, CT: Yale University Press, 2008).

13. The quotes are from D'Ailly's *Imago mundi*, cited in Wey Gómez, *The Tropics of Empire*, 79–84. Wey Gómez's analysis of how these ideas informed Columbus's expectations is very persuasive.

14. On the connections between heat and gold, see Sauer, *The Early Spanish Main*, 24; and above all Wey Gómez, *The Tropics of Empire*, 40–42, where both Columbus and Ferrer de Blanes are quoted.

15. On Columbus's observations of the color of Indians, see his journal entries for October 11 and 13, 1492, and the quotations in Wey Gómez, *The Tropics of Empire*, 18, 22, 40.

16. The quotes are from Columbus's diary, in Cristóbal Colón, *Textos y documentos completos*, ed. Consuelo Varela (Madrid: Alianza Editorial, 1984), 56. During his first voyage, Columbus took Indians from various places, including San Salvador and Cuba. For the captives from Cuba, see Las Casas, *Historia de las Indias*, 1:232–234; and Carlos Esteban Deive, *La Española y la esclavitud del indio* (Santo Domingo: Fundación García Arévalo, 1995), 45–46. In assessing the reliability of Las Casas's writings, it is important to make a clear distinction between his incendiary *Devastation of the Indies* and his far more meticulous (and seldom read) *Historia de las Indias*.

17. The quote is from the very famous letter of Columbus to Luis de Santángel, Canary Islands, February 15, 1493, in Juan Pérez de Tudela y Bueso, ed., *Colección Documental del Descubrimiento*, 3 vols. (Madrid: Editorial MAPFRE, 1994), 1:256. See also Wey Gómez, *The Tropics of Empire*, 316–317. The distinction made by Columbus seems curious because from the standpoint of most Europeans, all Indians were idolaters. Yet the Admiral initially believed that many Indians possessed no religion.

18. Rui de Pina, "Chronica Del Rei Dom João II," in Antonio Brásio, ed., *Monumenta Missionária Africana*, vol. 1 (Lisbon: Agência Geral Do Ultramar, 1952), 8–14; Morison, *Admiral of the Ocean Sea*, 42; Paolo Emilio Taviani, *Christopher Columbus: The Grand Design* (London: Orbis, 1985), 110–126; P.E.H. Hair, *The Founding of the Castelo de São Jorge da Mina: An Analysis of Sources* (Madison: African Studies Program, University of Wisconsin, 1994), 1–41; Christopher R. DeCorse, *An Archaeology of Elmina: Africans and Europeans on the Gold Coast, 1400–1900* (Washington, DC: Smithsonian Institution Press, 2001), 26–28, 138–144.

19. The quotes are from Columbus to the Catholic monarchs, La Isabela, January 20, 1494, and January 30, 1494, in Pérez de Tudela y Bueso, *Colección Documental del Descubrimiento*, 1:535–536 and 545, respectively. For a general treatment of Indian slavery during these years, including what different Spanish chroniclers have said about this institution, see Deive, *La Española y la esclavitud del indio*, and the more expansive José Antonio Saco, *Historia de la esclavitud de los indios en el Nuevo Mundo*, 2 vols. (Havana: Talleres de Cultural, 1932).

20. The most complete account of the slaves dispatched on February 17, 1495, can be found in Michele da Cuneo to Gerolamo Annari, Savona, October 15, 1495, in *L'isola regalata* (Milan: Viennepierre edizioni, 2002), 30–31. The same episode appears in other sources, including Las Casas, *Historia de las Indias*, 1:405.

21. Columbus's grand proposal is quoted in Las Casas, *Historia de las Indias*, 2:71. See also Rumeu de Armas, *La política indigenista de Isabel la Católica*, 133; and Deive, *La Española y la esclavitud del indio*, 62–63.

22. The quotes from Ferdinand and Isabella are from Rumeu de Armas, *La política indigenista de Isabel la Católica*, 134–138.

23. For an excellent discussion of the practices of enslavement in Spain during the century before the discovery of America, see Debra Blumenthal, *Enemies and Familiars: Slavery and Mastery in Fifteenth-Century Valencia* (Ithaca, NY: Cornell University Press, 2009).

24. Rumeu de Armas, *La política indigenista de Isabel la Católica,* 134–138. Brief accounts of the same events appear in Lesley Byrd Simpson, *The Encomienda in New Spain* (Berkeley: University of California Press, 1966), chap. 1; and Deive, *La Española y la esclavitud del indio,* 68–70.

25. Rumeu de Armas, *La política indigenista de Isabel la Católica,* 134–138. The queen's outburst is reported in Antonio de Herrera y Tordesillas, *Historia general de los hechos de los castellanos en las islas y tierra firme del mar oceano,* book 4, chap. 6.

26. Columbus's memorial is quoted in Las Casas, *Historia de las Indias,* 2:237. The italics are mine. Some of the key texts about Indian slavery in the early Caribbean appear in English translation in Eric Williams, *Documents of West Indian History* (New York: A & B, 1994). For an early work on Indian slavery in the Caribbean, see Edwin A. Levine, "The Seed of Slavery in the New World: An Examination of the Factors Leading to the Impressment of Indian Labor in Hispaniola," *Revista de Historia de América* 60 (1965), 1–68.

27. Las Casas, Oviedo, and Pietro Martire d'Anghiera provide brief accounts of the discovery of gold in Española. Especially detailed is Pietro Martire, *De Orbe Novo,* 1:81–82.

28. Pietro Martire, *De Orbe Novo,* 1:88, 109.

29. The first and third quotes are from Las Casas, cited in Samuel M. Wilson, *Hispaniola: Caribbean Chiefdoms in the Age of Columbus* (Tuscaloosa: University of Alabama Press, 1990), 79, 76. The second quote is from Pietro Martire, *De Orbe Novo,* 1:88.

30. For gold production figures and estimates of Indians working in the mines, see Oviedo, *Historia general y natural de las Indias,* book 4, chap. 8; and Las Casas, *The Devastation of the Indies,* 24–25. For the effects of the pearl rush, see Aldemaro Romero, Susanna Chilbert, and M. G. Eisenhart, "Cubagua's Pearl-Oyster Beds: The First Depletion of a Natural Resource Caused by Europeans in the American Continent," *Journal of Political Ecology* 6 (1999), 57–78. See also Enrique Otte, *Las perlas del Caribe: Nueva Cádiz de Cubagua* (Caracas: Fundación John Boulton, 1977); and Molly A. Warsh, "Enslaved Pearl Divers in the Sixteenth Century Caribbean," *Slavery and Abolition* 31:3 (September 2010), 345–362. As Carl Sauer notes, the meaning and location of Cibao has changed over the centuries. The lowlands that today are known as Cibao were called the Vega Real at the time of Columbus. Cibao proper encompassed the mountains that today constitute the Cordillera Central. Sauer, *The Early Spanish Main,* 80. For the Indian slave trade more broadly, see Erin Woodruff Stone, "Indian Harvest: The Rise of the Indigenous Slave Trade and Diaspora from Española to the Circum-Caribbean, 1492–1542" (Ph.D. diss., Vanderbilt University, 2014).

31. Las Casas, *Historia de las Indias,* 1:417; Livi Bacci, "Return to Hispaniola," 14; Arranz Márquez, *Repartimientos y encomiendas,* 60–64.

32. Oviedo, *Historia general y natural de las Indias,* book 6, chap. 8; Las Casas, *The Devastation of the Indies,* 24–25. The weight calculation assumes a volume of sixty-four cubic feet and a weight of one hundred pounds for each cubic foot of sand.

33. Oviedo, *Historia general y natural de las Indias,* book 6, chap. 8.

34. The quote is from ibid. The host of those parties was a royal accountant named Santa Clara. Las Casas, *Historia de las Indias,* 2:344. Contemporaries offered different figures for gold production in addition to the gold bullion imports recorded in the House of Trade (Casa de Contratación) in Seville. Livi Bacci provides tables with various figures for gold production in Española in the early sixteenth century and gold productivity culled from different gold mines around the world. For the gold mines of Española, he arrived at an upper limit of ten thousand workers, assuming a maximum yearly production of 1,000 kilograms (about 2,000 pounds) of gold and a productivity of about 100 grams (3.5 ounces) per worker. Livi Bacci, "Return to Hispaniola," 11–20.

35. The phrase is often attributed to Francisco de Bobadilla, cited in Arranz Márquez, *Repartimientos y encomiendas,* 82.

36. Ursula Lamb, *Frey Nicolás de Ovando: Governador de las Indias* (Santo Domingo: Sociedad Dominicana de Bibliófilos, 1977), passim.

37. The first quote is from Pietro Martire d'Anghiera, and the second is from King Ferdinand to Diego Columbus, Burgos, February 23, 1512, both cited in Mira Caballos, *El indio antillano,* 96 and 100, respectively.

38. On Ovando's background, see Lamb, *Frey Nicolás de Ovando,* chaps. 1 and 2. See also Rumeu de Armas, *La política indigenista de Isabel la Católica,* 143–145. Ovando had very clear instructions about how to deal with the Indians. See "Instrucción al comendador Frey Nicolás de Ovando," Granada, September 16, 1501, in Richard Konetzke, *Colección de documentos para la historia de la formación social de Hispanoamérica, 1493–1810,* 3 vols. (Madrid: Consejo Superior de Investigaciones Científicas, 1953), 1:4–6.

39. The early encomiendas have been the subject of numerous studies, the best of which are Arranz Márquez, *Repartimientos y encomiendas,* and Mira Caballos, *El indio antillano.* For the European roots of the institution, see Robert S. Chamberlain, *Castilian Backgrounds of the Repartimiento-Encomienda* (Washington, DC: Carnegie Institute, 1939). For the survival of pre-contact labor arrangements, see Francisco Moscoso, *Tribu y clases en el Caribe antiguo* (San Pedro de Macoris: Universidad Central del Este, 1986).

40. The information about the free caciques and villages is from Mira Caballos, *El indio antillano,* 109–111.

41. The quotes are from the Dominican Friars of La Española to Señor de Chiebvres, Santo Domingo, June 4, 1516, cited in Mira Caballos, *El indio antillano,* 37; Oviedo, *Historia general y natural de las Indias,* book 1, chap. 3; Las Casas, *The Devastation of the Indies,* 24–25; and King Ferdinand to Diego Colón, July 21, 1511.

42. The witness is quoted in Mira Caballos, *El indio antillano,* 111.

43. The quotes appear in Las Casas, *Historia de las Indias,* 2:346; and Pietro Martire, *De Orbe Novo,* 4th decade, book 10. Governor Ovando proposed the idea of bringing additional slaves to the island as early as 1507. He dispatched two representatives to Spain, who secured the necessary support from the Spanish crown, as is clear in the instructions to Ovando, Burgos, April 30, 1508, quoted in Mira Caballos, *El indio antillano,* 267.

44. For an excellent archaeological report of the town of Isabela, see Kathleen Deagan and José María Cruxent, *Columbus's Outpost Among the Taínos: Spain and America at La Isabela, 1493–1498* (New Haven, CT: Yale University Press, 2002). For glimpses of the two ports on the northern shore, see Las Casas, *Historia de las Indias*, 1:429; 2:241, 269, 338, 340, 348, 435.

45. The quote is from Oviedo, *Historia general y natural de las Indias*, book 1, chap. 5. Carlos Esteban Deive has gathered the most relevant passages concerning the first contacts with the Carib Indians and the opinions of Europeans about cannibalism. Deive, *La Española y la esclavitud del indio*, 27–34. On the conflation of "Caribe," "Caniba," "cannibal," and other words and the early reports of cannibals, see William F. Keegan, "Columbus Was a Cannibal: Myth and the First Encounters," and Louis Allaire, "Visions of Cannibals: Distant Islands and Distant Lands in Taino World Image," both in Robert L. Paquette and Stanley L. Engerman, eds., *The Lesser Antilles in the Age of European Expansion* (Gainesville: University Press of Florida, 1996), 17–32 and 18–49, respectively. See also Irving Rouse, *The Tainos: Rise and Decline of the People Who Greeted Columbus* (New Haven, CT: Yale University Press, 1992); and Neil L. Whitehead, "The Crises and Transformations of Invaded Societies: The Caribbean, 1492–1580," in Frank Salomon and Stuart B. Schwartz, eds., *The Cambridge History of the Native Peoples of the Americas*, vol. 3, part 1 (New York: Cambridge University Press, 1999), 864–903. Scholarly debates still rage about the ethnic and cultural affiliations of certain islanders. See, for example, Jalil Sued Badillo, "Guadalupe: ¿Caribe o taína? La isla de Guadalupe y su cuestionable identidad caribe en la época pre-colombina; Una revisión etnohistórica y arqueológica," *Caribbean Studies* 35:1 (January–June 2007), 37–85.

46. Following scholarly convention, I use the name Lucayos for the inhabitants of the Bahamas. See Sauer, *The Early Spanish Main*, 159; and William F. Keegan, *The People Who Discovered Columbus: The Prehistory of the Bahamas* (Gainesville: University Press of Florida, 1992), 11. On pearl-related slavery, see Otte, *Las perlas del Caribe*; Julian Granberry, "Spanish Slave Trade in the Bahamas, 1509–1530: An Aspect of the Caribbean Pearl Industry," *Journal of the Bahamas Historical Society* 1 (1979), 14–15; and, more recently, Warsh, "Enslaved Pearl Divers in the Sixteenth Century Caribbean." The term *islas inútiles* often also encompassed the Lesser Antilles.

47. On the early slaving raids in Central America, see the excellent essay by Carmen Mena García and Carmen María Panera Rico, "Los inicios de la esclavitud indígena en el Darién y la desaparición de los 'Cuevas'" (paper presented at the Congreso de la Asociación Española de Americanistas, Barcelona, September 2011); and, more generally, Carmen Mena García, *El oro del Darién: Entradas y cabalgadas en la conquista de Tierra Firme, 1509–1526* (Seville: Centro de Estudios Andaluces, 2011). See also William L. Sherman, *Forced Native Labor in Sixteenth-Century Central America* (Lincoln: University of Nebraska Press, 1979); Linda A. Newson, *Indian Survival in Colonial Nicaragua* (Norman: University of Oklahoma Press, 1987); and Mario Góngora, *Los grupos de conquistadores en Tierra Firme, 1509–1530* (Santiago: Universidad de Chile Centro de Historia Colonial, 1962). For early Indian enslavement on the coast of Venezuela, see Morella A. Jiménez G., *La esclavitud indígena en Venezuela, siglo XVI* (Caracas: Academia Nacional de la Historia, 1986).

48. The royal prohibition against taking Indian slaves and the subsequent exceptions to the prohibition are discussed in numerous works, including Rumeu de Armas, *La política indigenista de Isabel la Católica*, 140–141; Mira Caballos, *El indio antillano*, 266–267; Deive, *La Española y la esclavitud del indio*, 72–83; and, most recently, Nancy E. van Deusen, *Global Indios: The Indigenous Struggle for Justice in Sixteenth-Century Spain* (Durham, NC: Duke University Press, 2015), 3–5. The quote is from Judge Rodrigo de Figueroa, cited in Sauer, *The Early Spanish Main*, 195. The literature discussing Indian cannibalism is vast. For a brief and convincing review, see Neil L. Whitehead, *Lords of the Tiger Spirit: A History of the Caribs in Colonial Venezuela and Guyana, 1498–1820* (Dordrecht: Foris, 1988), 172–180.

49. On Juan Ponce de León's dealings with the Indians of Florida and his royal patent of conquest, see William R. Swagerty, "Beyond Bimini: Indian Responses to European Incursions in the Spanish Borderlands, 1513–1600" (manuscript based on Ph.D. diss., University of California, Santa Barbara, 1981), 38–74; Mira Caballos, *El indio antillano*, 295, 297; and Sued Badillo, "Guadalupe," 46, 49. On Lucas Vázquez de Ayllón's activities, see Paul E. Hoffman, *A New Andalucia and a Way to the Orient: The American Southeast During the Sixteenth Century* (Baton Rouge: Louisiana State University Press, 1990), 41–47; Paul E. Hoffman, "A New Voyage of North American Discovery: Pedro de Salazar's Visit to the 'Island of Giants,'" *Florida Historical Quarterly* 58 (1980), 415–426; and Paul E. Hoffman, "Lucas Vázquez de Ayllón's Discovery and Colony," in Charles Hudson and Carmen Chaves Tesser, eds., *The Forgotten Centuries: Indians and Europeans in the American South, 1521–1704* (Athens: University of Georgia Press, 1994), 36–49.

50. Bartolomé de Las Casas, *En defensa de los indios* (Barcelona: Biblioteca de Cultura Andaluza, 1985), 127. On the use of attack dogs, see John Grier Varner and Jeannette Johnson Varner, *Dogs of the Conquest* (Norman: University of Oklahoma Press, 1982), 3–34. On the holding pens, see the *juicio de residencia a los jueces de Apelación* (a type of judicial proceeding), 1516, quoted in Mira Caballos, *El indio antillano*, 265.

51. Both quotes are from Mira Caballos, *El indio antillano*, 285. For Vázquez de Ayllón's expeditions, see Hoffman, *A New Andalucia*, 44. For transatlantic mortality rates, see Philip D. Curtin, *The Atlantic Slave Trade: A Census* (Madison: University of Wisconsin Press, 1969), 275–290; and David Eltis and David Richardson, *Atlas of the Transatlantic Slave Trade* (New Haven, CT: Yale University Press, 2010), 167–187.

52. On the determined resistance of the Carib Indians, see Mira Caballos, *El indio antillano*, 294–302, and Whitehead, "The Crises and Transformations of Invaded Societies," 875–888.

53. For the number of Lucayos enslaved, see Mira Caballos, *El indio antillano*, 289, 391–399; and Keegan, *The People Who Discovered Columbus*, 218–223. Only a handful of islands became extraordinary refuges where displaced populations of both Taínos and Caribs refashioned themselves and found new homes. The large island of Trinidad, for example, remained populated. In 1511 Spanish authorities had pronounced the people of Trinidad man-eating Caribs, and over the next few years Europeans conducted raids there. But in 1520 the crown reclassified them as "a people of good will and friends of Christians." Although the raids never ceased entirely, the people of

Trinidad survived partly through this flimsy legal protection and primarily by removing themselves from the exposed coastal areas to the inaccessible mountains of the interior. The most remarkable case of a refuge island is perhaps Dominica, in the Lesser Antilles. As late as 1534, Spaniards found twenty villages, dozens of canoes, and thousands of residents there. That so many Carib and Taíno Indians remained on an island so close to Puerto Rico after decades of the most intense slaving bespeaks their resourcefulness and indomitable will to survive. Their survival also shows that in the long run, opposing, fighting, and hiding from the colonists were better strategies than seeking accommodation. Linda A. Newson, *Aboriginal and Spanish Colonial Trinidad: A Study in Culture Contact* (London: Academic Press, 1976), 32, 72. In 1516 the infamous slaver Juan Bono—whom Las Casas called "Juan Bono, Malo" ("John Good, Bad")—built a house on Trinidad, where he intended to enslave the residents of a nearby village. He shipped 180 to 200 of them to Puerto Rico. Las Casas, *Historia de las Indias*, 3:186. In the Lesser Antilles, Santa Cruz became depopulated by the middle of the 1510s, and Guadalupe followed suit by the decade's end. It is quite likely that many of these Indians migrated to Dominica. Sued Badillo, "Guadalupe," 60–85. From the very beginning, a synergistic relationship developed between epidemics and enslavement. As the Caribbean experience shows, death caused by disease spurred slaving raids to replace dead or dying workers, and conversely slaving campaigns spread disease, thus closing an extremely insidious loop. This synergistic relationship has been documented in other regions and times. Historian Paul Kelton, for instance, has shown that it was not the arrival of Europeans in the southeastern United States that devastated the Indians there. Instead, it was the rise of the deerskin trade in the 1650s and the burgeoning Indian slave trade under English auspices that accelerated and magnified the spread of epidemic disease, culminating in what he calls the "Great Southeastern Smallpox Epidemic of 1696." The synergistic relationship between epidemics and enslavement was real and occurred throughout the New World, with terrifying results. Kelton, *Epidemics and Enslavement.*

54. For a sound discussion of population dynamics in Europe during and after the Black Death, see Wally Seccombe, *A Millennium of Family Change: Feudalism to Capitalism in Northwestern Europe* (New York: Verso, 1992), 144–159. For the larger context, see Suzanne Austin Alchon, *A Pest in the Land: New World Epidemics in a Global Perspective* (Albuquerque: University of New Mexico Press, 2003).

55. Livi Bacci, *Conquest*, 6, 231.

## 2. GOOD INTENTIONS

1. A Web-based text of the New Laws can be found at "Leyes y ordenanzas: Nuevamente hechas por S. M. para la gobernación de las Indias, y buen tratamiento y conservación de los indios," *Colección de documentos para la historia de México: Versión actualizada*, Biblioteca Virtual Miguel de Cervantes, http://bib.cervantesvirtual .com/servlet/SirveObras/06922752100647273089079/p0000026.htm. The italics in the quote are mine. The Spanish archives contain very little information about the meetings leading up to the promulgation of the New Laws. For the most detailed

treatment of the laws, see Ernesto Schäfer, *El Consejo Real y Supremo de las Indias*, 2 vols. (Madrid: Marcial Pons Historia, 2003), 2:77–88.

2. I was inspired in this section by recent works such as Brian P. Owensby, *Empire of Law and Indian Justice in Colonial Mexico* (Stanford, CA: Stanford University Press, 2008); van Deusen, *Global Indios*, passim; and Ariela J. Gross and Alejandro de la Fuente, "Slaves, Free Blacks, and Race in the Legal Regimes of Cuba, Louisiana, and Virginia: A Comparison," *North Carolina Law Review* 91 (2013), 1699–1756.

3. The quote is from Harriet A. Jacobs, *Incidents in the Life of a Slave Girl Written by Herself* (Cambridge: Harvard University Press, 1987), 34. For a general study of the workings of the court system in the South, see Ariela J. Gross, *Double Character: Slavery and Mastery in the Antebellum Southern Court* (Princeton, NJ: Princeton University Press, 2000), passim.

4. Van Deusen, *Global Indios*, 21. A thirteenth-century legal compendium known as *Las siete partidas* (The seven books) already regarded slavery as "the most wretched condition into which anyone could fall" and allowed slaves to act in court to lessen their sufferings. For example, in cases of cruel or abusive masters, "a slave may complain to the judge who will need to find the truth, and if so, the slave will be sold to a different master." The fourth book dealt with domestic matters involving marriage, children, and — as an extension — "servants and slaves." *Las siete partidas del sabio rey, don Alfonso el nono, nuevamente glosadas por el licenciado Gregorio López, del Consejo Real de Indias de Su Majestad* (1555) (Valladolid: Diego Fernández de Córdoba, 1587), book 4, law 6. See also Owensby, *Empire of Law*, chap. 5; Robin Blackburn, *The Making of New World Slavery: From the Baroque to the Modern, 1492–1800* (New York: Verso, 1997), 50–52; and Charles R. Cutter, *The Protector de Indios in Colonial New Mexico, 1659–1821* (Albuquerque: University of New Mexico Press, 1986), chap. 1. Studies that show how Indians used Spanish legal mechanisms to advance their interests abound. In addition to the works already cited, see Steve J. Stern, *Peru's Indian Peoples and the Challenge of Spanish Conquest: Huamanga to 1640* (Madison: University of Wisconsin Press, 1993); and William B. Taylor, *Landlord and Peasant in Colonial Oaxaca* (Stanford, CA: Stanford University Press, 1972).

5. For a broad comparative discussion, see Gross and de la Fuente, "Slaves, Free Blacks, and Race." Frank Tannenbaum's classic study *Slave and Citizen* was among the first to draw attention to the significant differences between the legal regimes that emerged in the Spanish and Portuguese colonies — which he believed were relatively benign and conducive to freedom — and the harsher regimes prevalent in British America. Tannenbaum, *Slave and Citizen* (Boston: Beacon Press, 1946). Later social and legal scholars have tended to de-emphasize Tannenbaum's sharp distinction by highlighting the harshness of the plantation slavery that emerged in Latin America. And yet recent scholars such as Gross and de la Fuente have documented the significant impact of the law on slaves' lives. Indians made rapid use of the Spanish legal system to the point of litigiousness. For an excellent case study, see Susan Kellogg, *Law and the Transformation of Aztec Culture, 1500–1700* (Norman: University of Oklahoma Press, 1995). In the early 1570s, a group of indigenous leaders from central Mexico acknowledged as much in a letter to the Spanish king: "In the time of our gentility we did not

often have lawsuits," they wrote. "Now that we are Christians we have many lawsuits with other natives as well as with the Spanish people of your Majesty." *Códice Mendieta,* quoted in Owensby, *Empire of Law,* 2.

6. The exact estimate of the number of Indians sent to Spain is 2,442 according to Mira Caballos, *El indio antillano,* 305–306; and Esteban Mira Caballos, *Indios y mestizos americanos en la España del siglo XVI* (Madrid: Iberoamericana, 2000), 111. See also the introduction to van Deusen, *Global Indios.* When we consider that this estimate is based on fragmentary export licenses and that several Natives were introduced without licenses, it is obvious that the real number was higher, perhaps considerably so. See Alfonso Franco Silva, "El indígena en el mercado de esclavos de Sevilla, 1500–1525," *Gades* 1 (1978), 25–35; and Juana Gil-Bermejo, "Indígenas americanos en Andalucía," in Bibiano Torres Ramírez and José J. Hernández Palomo, eds., *Andalucía y América en el siglo XVI* (Seville: Escuela de Estudios Hispanoamericanos, 1983), 535–555.

7. Gregorio López understood the institution of slavery through the prism of *Las siete partidas.* Ever the legal scholar, he believed that this elaborate set of laws and practical advice was so important to the daily lives of all Spaniards that he went through the trouble of preparing a new annotated edition. For his efforts on behalf of Indians, see "Gregorio López contra propietarios de indios," Seville, 1543–1545, AGI, Justicia, 741, N. 3. More than eight hundred pages of documents survive for these trials alone. They are available online at Portal de Archivos Españoles (hereafter cited as PARES), the digital portal of the Spanish archives, http://pares.mcu.es/.

8. During my own archival work, I counted seventy-nine such trials. The number of lawsuits peaked in 1543, and although they decreased rapidly thereafter (with smaller spikes in 1548, 1553, and 1560), Indians continued to take their masters to court as late as the 1580s. After I wrote this chapter, I read Nancy E. van Deusen's excellent *Global Indios,* which is a far more comprehensive study of these cases. See also Nancy E. van Deusen, "Seeing *Indios* in Sixteenth-Century Castile," *William and Mary Quarterly* 69:2 (April 2012), 205–234; and Nancy van Deusen, "The Intimacies of Bondage: Female Indigenous Servants and Slaves and Their Spanish Masters, 1492–1555," *Journal of Women's History* 24:1 (Spring 2012), 13–43. The closest we can get to an Indian narrative in this early period is a complaint written by a Chichimec cacique named Don Francisco Tenamaztle during his imprisonment in Valladolid, Spain, in 1555. Don Francisco recounted the myriad abuses perpetrated by the Spaniards on his people in northwestern Mexico. But strictly speaking, his voice is that of an aggrieved Indian leader, not that of a slave, and his account is too brief and general to be of much use. "Informaciones hechas en Valladolid este año a pedimento del cacique don Francisco Tenamaztle, remitido preso desde la provincia de Xalisco, de donde era señor," Valladolid, 1555, in Alberto Carrillo Cázares, ed., *El Debate sobre la Guerra Chichimeca, 1531–1585,* 2 vols. (Zamora: El Colegio de Michoacán, 2000), 2:513–535.

9. On sex and age ratios for African slaves, see Eltis and David, *Atlas of the Transatlantic Slave Trade,* 162–166. It is true that sex ratios were somewhat more balanced during the sixteenth and seventeenth centuries than at the height of the transatlantic trade in the eighteenth century. But even in this earlier period, males constituted a

majority of those transported to the New World. African sellers of slaves typically offered more women and children than the buyers wanted. For an excellent discussion of this phenomenon, see David Eltis, *The Rise of African Slavery in the Americas* (New York: Cambridge University Press, 2000), chap. 4. Less than one in every ten slaves was a minor during the sixteenth and seventeenth centuries, a ratio that increased in the eighteenth century, but only to one in five.

10. For excellent discussions of slavery and gender in the Mediterranean, see Sally McKee, "Slavery," in Judith M. Bennett and Ruth Mazo Karras, eds., *The Oxford Handbook of Women and Gender in Medieval Europe* (New York: Oxford University Press, 2013), 281–294; Sally McKee, "Domestic Slavery in Renaissance Italy," *Slavery and Abolition* 29:3 (September 2008), 305–326; Aurelia Martín Casares, *La esclavitud en la Granada del siglo XVI: Género, raza y religión* (Granada: Universidad de Granada y Diputación Provincial de Granada, 2000); and António de Almeida Mendes, "Child Slaves in the Early North Atlantic Trade in the Fifteenth and Sixteenth Centuries," in Gwyn Campbell, Suzanne Miers, and Joseph C. Miller, eds., *Children in Slavery Through the Ages* (Athens: Ohio University Press, 2009), 19–34.

11. Price information for the Caribbean comes from Mira Caballos, *El indio antillano*, 288–289. For Central America, see Sherman, *Forced Native Labor*, 70; for Chile, see Jara, *Guerra y sociedad en Chile*, 143, 147; and for New Mexico, see *The Official Correspondence of James S. Calhoun*, 162.

12. See, for example, "Pleito fiscal: Catalina de Olvera," Santa Olalla, December 9, 1551, to May 4, 1552, AGI, Justicia, 1179, N. 1, R. 2. An Indian from Pánuco named Luis was taken when he was only eleven and transported to Spain, where he remained for about twenty-five years before he mustered enough courage to sue his master, Nuño de Guzmán, the notorious slaver and former governor of Pánuco. See *real cédula* (royal order or decree), Valladolid, June 30, 1549, "Ejecutoria del pleito de Nuño de Guzmán," AGI, Patronato, 281, N. 1, R. 3.

13. See Gaspar's testimony in the trial against his master, Bartolomé Vallejo, Seville, December 12, 1561, "Pleito fiscal: Bartolomé Vallejo," AGI, Justicia, 856, N. 2.

14. Aurelia Martín Casares's excellent discussion about the scholarly stereotypes of enslavement being passed from one generation to the next applies no less to Indians than to Africans. Martín Casares, *La esclavitud en la Granada del siglo XVI*, 26–32.

15. Several documents survive about this story. The most important are those from the trial resulting from Pedro's later lawsuit to regain his own freedom and that of María's children, Ciudad Rodrigo, 1544, "Autos Fiscales, Mexico," AGI, Justicia, 199; and real cédula, n.p., August 7, 1544, "Libertad de ciertos indios residentes en España," AGI, Patronato, 231, N. 1, R. 6. See also real cédula, Valladolid, July 18, 1544, "Hijos y testamento de Juan Marques," AGI, Indiferente, 423, L. 20, F. 775v–776r; and real cédula, Valladolid, April 7, 1544, "Averiguación sobre los descendientes de Juan Márquez," AGI, Indiferente, 423, L. 20, F. 747v–748v.

16. On masters and concubines/slaves in the wider Mediterranean world, see McKee, "Slavery"; Sally McKee, "Inherited Status and Slavery in Late Medieval Italy and Venetian Crete," *Past and Present* 182:1 (February 2004), 31–53; and Yaron Ben-Naeh,

"Blond, Tall, with Honey-Colored Eyes: Jewish Ownership of Slaves in the Ottoman Empire," *Jewish History* 20:3/4 (2006), 315–332.

17. The lengthy trial lasted for the better part of 1544 and required the intervention of two *fiscales*, one member of the Council of the Indies, and four royal decrees bearing the king's signature to establish beyond a shadow of a doubt that Pedro and the children were "free and not subject to any servitude." See "Real cédula a las justicias de estos reinos y de Indias declarando libre a un indio, Juan, hijo de Juan Marques y de María, india de Nueva España," Valladolid, August 29, 1544, AGI, Indiferente, 423, L. 20, F. 789r–789v; "Real cédula a las justicias de estos reinos y de Indias declarando libre a una india, Luisa, hija de Juan Marques y de María, india de Nueva España," Valladolid, August 29, 1544, AGI, Indiferente, 423, L. 20, F. 787r–788r; "Real cédula a las justicias de estos reinos y de Indias declarando libre a una india, Catalina, hija de Juan Marques y de María, india de Nueva España," Valladolid, August 29, 1544, AGI, Indiferente, 423, L. 20, F. 788r–788v; and "Real cédula a los alcaldes mayores y ordinarios de la villa de Dueñas para que quiten a Isabel de Herrera, viuda de Juan Marques, un indio, Juan hijo de este, a quien después de dado por libre, quiere vender como esclavo," Valladolid, October 13, 1544, AGI, Indiferente, 423, L. 20, F. 802r–802v.

18. Francisco Sarmiento on behalf of Catalina Hernández and her sisters, all children of Beatriz Hernández Seville, 1573–1574, "Pleito fiscal: Juan Cansino," AGI, Justicia, 908, N. 1; available online at PARES, http://pares.mcu.es/. Nancy van Deusen addresses this case in *Global Indios*, chap. 1.

19. Nancy van Deusen has shown very well how sixteenth-century litigants developed strategies to create identities, and this case was no exception. See van Deusen, "Seeing *Indios* in Sixteenth-Century Castile," 205–234.

20. Real cédula, Valladolid, August 8, 1544, AGI, Indiferente, 423, L. 20, F. 781r–781v; real cédula, Madrid, February 23, 1552, AGI, Justicia, 831, N. 6, and Patronato, 281, N. 2, R. 95; and real cédula, Madrid, December 9, 1551, AGI, Justicia, 1179, N. 1, R. 2, respectively. Nancy van Deusen notes that an astounding ninety-five percent of indigenous litigants whose cases reached completion were freed. She also notes that such a high percentage may be deceiving, as there were hundreds of Indians who did not pursue their freedom through court proceedings. Van Deusen, *Global Indios*, 23.

21. See Guzmán's request, Valladolid, March 23, 1550, "Receptoría pedida por Nuño de Guzmán," AGI, Patronato, 280, N. 2, R. 137; royal order, Valladolid, January 21, 1551, AGI, Indiferente, 424, L. 22, F. 261v; and royal order, Valladolid, January 21, 1551, "Ejecutoria del pleito de Nuño de Guzmán," AGI, Patronato, 281, N. 1, R. 3. Guzmán was not the only owner to argue that slaves deserved no wages. In a very similar case, Catalina de Olvera, owner of an Indian slave named Ynés, claimed that she did not profit from Ynés, but rather Ynés profited from her. Olvera's attorney noted that she had to spend a great deal of money on Ynés "because after Ynés gave birth many illnesses afflicted her, and her legs became swollen each year, and Olvera had to seek medical help [for her]." "Pleito fiscal: Catalina de Olvera."

22. Esteban Mira Caballos, "De esclavos a siervos: Amerindios en España tras las Leyes Nuevas de 1542," *Revista de Historia de América* 140 (January–June 2009), 95–110.

23. Silvio Zavala has more than enough sources to document the scope of Indian slavery in central Mexico during the first half of the sixteenth century. See Zavala, *Los esclavos indios en Nueva España* (Mexico City: El Colegio Nacional, 1968). Virtually all early chronicles also contain relevant passages. The quotes are from ibid., 1.

24. The quote is from Fray Diego Durán, *History of the Indies of New Spain* (Norman: University of Oklahoma Press, 1994), 561. The earliest encomienda in Mexico often involved "personal services" furnished to the encomendero in addition to products. The crown had some success in limiting this practice in central Mexico but not in other parts, as we will see in chapter 3. Two classic works on the functioning of encomiendas in early Mexico are Lesley Simpson, *The Encomienda in New Spain: The Beginning of Spanish Mexico* (Berkeley: University of California Press, 1966); and Charles Gibson, *The Aztecs Under the Spanish: A History of the Indians of the Valley of Mexico* (Stanford, CA: Stanford University Press, 1976).

25. The quote is from Bernal Díaz, *Historia verdadera,* cited in Zavala, *Los esclavos indios en Nueva España,* 78.

26. Toribio de Benavente, *Historia de los indios de la Nueva España* (Mexico City: Porrúa, 1973), 92. For Indian slave estimates based on royal accounts, see the excellent work by Jean-Pierre Berthe, "Aspectos de la esclavitud de los indios en la Nueva España durante la primera mitad del siglo XVI," in *Estudios de Historia de la Nueva España de Sevilla a Manila* (Guadalajara: Universidad de Guadalajara, 1994), 67.

27. On pre-contact slavery, see Toribio de Motolinía, *Memoriales de Fray Toribio de Motolinía* (Mexico City: Casa del Editor, 1903), especially part 2, chap. 20, "Que trata el modo y manera que estos naturales tenían de hacer esclavos, y de la servidumbre a que los esclavos eran obligados," and chap. 21, "En el cual acaba la materia de los esclavos y se declara las condiciones de su servidumbre y cúales se podían vender y cuáles no"; Bernardino de Sahagún, *Historia general de las cosas de Nueva España* (Mexico City: Porrúa, 1956), passim; and Rushforth, *Bonds of Alliance,* passim. For an excellent discussion of why captivity practices among early Native American societies were tantamount to slavery, see Santos-Granero, *Vital Enemies,* conclusion. On the practice of Indian slavery and slave prices after contact, see Zavala, *Los esclavos indios en Nueva España,* chaps. 1 and 2.

28. These two diverging estimates are well known to scholars, including Berthe, "Aspectos de la esclavitud de los indios," 66–67, and Livi Bacci, *Conquest,* chap. 2. One can get a sense of the number of Indian slaves by the fact that the town of Tlaxcala alone manumitted some twenty thousand Indian slaves just in 1537. See Charles Gibson, *Tlaxcala in the Sixteenth Century* (Stanford, CA: Stanford University Press, 1952), 144.

29. Agreement to form a company between Fernando Alonso and Nicolás López de Palacios Rubio, Mexico City, February 27, 1528, Acervo Histórico del Archivo General de Notarias del Distrito Federal (hereafter cited as AHAGNDF), Notary No. 1, escribano público Juan Fernández del Castillo, vol. 54, file 372, fols. 297–298; sale by Pedro González Nájera in favor of Antón de Carmona, Mexico City, June 3, 1528, AHAGNDF, Notary No. 1, escribano público Juan Fernández del Castillo, vol. 54, file 494, fols. 383v–384; contract between Pedro de Villalobos and Álvaro Maldonado, Mexico City, August 27, 1525, AHAGNDF, Notary No. 1, escribano público Juan

Fernández del Castillo, vol. 52, file 17, fols. 33v–35; special power of attorney given by Juan Domínguez to Alonso Martín de Jerez to sell sixty Indian slaves sent to the mines of Zacatula, Mexico City, February 19, 1528, AHAGNDF, Notary No. 1, escribano público Juan Fernández del Castillo, vol. 54, file 212, fols. 346–347; sale by Martín Vázquez in favor of Alonso García, Mexico City, September 30, 1528, AHAGNDF, Notary No. 1, escribano público Juan Fernández del Castillo, vol. 54, file 715, fols. 554v–555.

30. Contract to create a company between Pedro de Sepúlveda and Martín Sánchez, Mexico City, October 19, 1528, AHAGNDF, Notary No. 1, escribano público Juan Fernández del Castillo, vol. 54, file 816, fols. 633r–633v; other notarial records cited in previous note.

31. Sale by Melchor Vázquez to Hernán Cortés, Mexico City, November 20, 1536, AHAGNDF, Notary No. 1, escribano real Martín de Castro, vol. 33, file 212, fols. 420–423; Hernán Cortés recognizes a debt owed to Juan de Cuevas, Mexico City, November 20, 1536, AHAGNDF, Notary No. 1, escribano real Martín de Castro, vol. 33, file 214, fols. 426–428. Four days later, Cortés formed a partnership with the royal treasurer Alonso de Sosa to work yet another mine in the area, and each partner agreed to provide "all Indian and black slaves that were needed." Contract between Hernán Cortés and Alonso de Sosa, Mexico City, November 24, 1536, AHAGNDF, Notary No. 1, escribano real Martín de Castro, vol. 33, file 225, fols. 449–451. Cortés was also the principal mine owner in Taxco. See Robert S. Haskett, "'Our Suffering with the Taxco Tribute': Involuntary Mine Labor and Indigenous Society in Central New Spain," *Hispanic American Historical Review* 71:3 (August 1991), 447–475; Jean-Pierre Berthe, "Las minas de oro del Marqués del Valle en Tehuantepec, 1540–1547," in *Estudios de Historia de la Nueva España de Sevilla a Manila* (Guadalajara: Universidad de Guadalajara, 1994), 15–24; and Zavala, *Los esclavos indios en Nueva España*, passim. For a fascinating look at how encomienda Indians were forced to support the mining enterprise from the Indian point of view, see Thomas Calvo, Eustaquio Celestino, Magdalena Gómez, Jean Meyer, and Ricardo Xochitemol, *Xalisco: La voz de un pueblo en el siglo XVI* (Mexico City: CIESAS, 1993), 49–108; and Ida Altman, *The War for Mexico's West: Indians and Spaniards in New Galicia, 1524–1550* (Albuquerque: University of New Mexico Press, 2010), chap. 3.

32. "Información hecha en la ciudad de México sobre la libertad de los indios," Mexico City, September 6, 1539, AGI, Justicia, 1029. This struggle over Indian slavery took shape in the 1530s as two diffuse and loosely organized groups for and against it coalesced around the Spanish court. Their intense lobbying efforts and conflicting agendas resulted in contradictory royal decrees first forbidding Indian slavery (1528 and 1530), then reinstituting it with some qualifications (1531), and finally allowing it more broadly (1534). "We cannot comprehend what may have moved your royal Council [of the Indies] into such a cruel decision," complained a group of Mexican Franciscans to the Spanish emperor, "nor do we understand what reasons may have confounded the sage men who make up your illustrious Council." Franciscan friars of Mexico to the emperor, Mexico City, July 31, 1533, in Mariano Cuevas, ed., *Documentos inéditos del siglo XVI para la historia de México* (Mexico City: Porrúa, 1975), 14–15.

33. For the Peruvian case, see James Lockhart, *Spanish Peru, 1532–1560* (Madison: University of Wisconsin Press, 1994), 17, 23, 187; and Lewis Hanke, *The Struggle for Justice in the Conquest of America* (Dallas: Southern Methodist University Press, 2002), 96. For Mexico, see Zavala, *Los esclavos indios en Nueva España,* chap. 2; A. S. Aiton, *Antonio de Mendoza: First Viceroy of New Spain* (Durham, NC: Duke University Press, 1927), 96–98; and Simpson, *The Encomienda in New Spain,* 130–135.

34. The quote is from José Antonio Saco, *Historia de la esclavitud de los indios en el Nuevo Mundo,* 2 vols. (Havana: Talleres de Cultura, 1932), 2:133. The italics are mine. Historian Silvio Zavala described the two camps as one that advocated "absolute abolition as defended by Las Casas" and the other one "characterized by judicial casuistry that was compatible with slavery under certain circumstances." Zavala, *Los esclavos indios en Nueva España,* 115.

35. Altman, *The War for Mexico's West,* chap. 5; Carlos Sempat Assadourian, *Zacatecas: Conquista y transformación de la frontera en el siglo XVI: Minas de plata, guerra, y evangelización* (Mexico City: El Colegio de México, 2008), passim.

36. Sempat Assadourian, *Zacatecas,* 39–49; Zavala, *Los esclavos indios en Nueva España,* 110.

37. The classic study of Zacatecas is Peter J. Bakewell, *Silver Mining and Society in Colonial Mexico: Zacatecas, 1546–1700* (New York: Cambridge University Press, 1971), chap. 1. See also Sempat Assadourian, *Zacatecas,* chap. 2.

38. "Borrador de la instrucción del Príncipe don Felipe a don Luis de Velasco, virrey de Nueva España, acerca de la libertad y buen tratamiento de los naturales que trabajaban en las minas, estancias, e ingenios, 1552," in Mariano Cuevas, ed., *Documentos inéditos del siglo XVI para la historia de México* (Mexico City: Porrúa, 1975), 170–175. For a discussion of Prince Philip's proposal and the emergence of the new labor regime, see Zavala, *Los esclavos indios en Nueva España,* 135–137.

39. The first viceroy of Mexico, Don Antonio de Mendoza (1535–1550), observed that "with respect to the freedom of the Indians, we have followed the law to the last letter." He stated that he had freed some Indians, but it is unclear how exactly he did it and how many. Mendoza, "Relación, apuntamientos, y avisos . . . ," in *Instrucciones y Memorias de los Virreyes Novohispanos,* 2 vols. (Mexico City: Porrúa, 1991), 1:113. See also "Instrucción a Luis de Velasco," Valladolid, April 16, 1550, in *Instrucciones y Memorias,* 125–138; and María Justina Sarabia Viejo, *Don Luís de Velasco virrey de Nueva España, 1550–1564* (Seville: Consejo Superior de Investigaciones Científicas, 1978), 303–309.

40. Melgarejo to the king, Mexico City, May 14, 1551, in Francisco del Paso y Troncoso, ed., *Epistolario de Nueva España,* 15 vols. (Mexico City: Antigua Liberaría Robredo, 1940), 6:47–49. See also Zavala, *Los esclavos indios en Nueva España,* 133–134; Sarabia Viejo, *Don Luís de Velasco,* 305–309; and Berthe, "Aspectos de la esclavitud de los indios," 81.

41. For the total number of freed Indians, see Melgarejo to the emperor, Mexico City, February 10, 1561, in Paso y Troncoso, *Epistolario de Nueva España,* 9:102–106. The procurador himself explained the need for lengthy proceedings in Melgarejo to the emperor, Mexico City, January 3, 1552, in Paso y Troncoso, *Epistolario de Nueva Es-*

*paña,* 6:120–123. Examples of delayed or ongoing proceedings appear in Melgarejo to the emperor, Mexico City, November 17, 1552, in Paso y Troncoso, *Epistolario de Nueva España,* 6:208–209. The procurador of Española mentioned was Alonso López de Cerrato, a strong supporter of the abolitionist faction. He would go on to implement the New Laws in Central America. See Sherman, *Forced Native Labor,* passim.

42. For the slaves made during the Mixtón War and considered justly made, see Melgarejo to the emperor, Mexico City, October 20, 1554, in Paso y Troncoso, *Epistolario de Nueva España,* 7:270–272; Melgarejo to the emperor, Mexico City, April 11, 1557, in ibid., 8:128–130; and Melgarejo to the emperor, Mexico City, June 15, 1558, in ibid., 8:182–184. See also Zavala, *Los esclavos indios en Nueva España,* 132–134.

43. Doctor Quesada, *oidor* (member) of the Audiencia of Mexico, Mexico City, October 30, 1550, cited in Zavala, *Los esclavos indios en Nueva España,* 123. See also Sarabia Viejo, *Don Luís de Velasco,* 308–309.

44. *Visitador* Hernando Martínez de la Marcha to the emperor, Compostela, February 18, 1550, in Sempat Assadourian, *Zacatecas,* 247–260. On the activities of Martínez de la Marcha, see J. H. Parry, *The Audiencia of Nueva Galicia* (New York: Cambridge University Press, 1948), 48–49; Zavala, *Los esclavos indios en Nueva España,* 145–147; and Sarabia Viejo, *Don Luís de Velasco,* 308–309.

45. Jiménez G., *La esclavitud indígena en Venezuela,* chap. 8.

46. Sherman, *Forced Native Labor,* chaps. 9 and 10.

47. Indians in Mexico continued to take their Spanish masters to court through the sixteenth and seventeenth centuries. Indigenous plaintiffs regularly described their condition as "slave-like" or "worse than slavery" and attempted to use whatever protections the law offered. As historian Brian P. Owensby has insightfully argued, these lawsuits served at least to allow Indians to engage their employers and negotiate less coercive terms. Owensby, *Empire of Law,* 151–166.

## 3. THE TRAFFICKER AND HIS NETWORK

1. For a discussion of the number of expelled Jews and the routes they followed, see Haim Beinart, *The Expulsion of the Jews from Spain* (Oxford, UK: Littman Library of Jewish Civilization, 2005), 284–290. Soon after the expulsion decree of 1492, Luis de Carvajal's grandparents formally converted to Christianity. In private, however, various family members continued to practice Judaism. Indeed, the Spanish Inquisition investigated and sentenced Carvajal's great-aunt for just such a transgression. In spite of these brushes with the Holy Office, the Carvajals remained in their ancestral hometown of Sayago, in the old Spanish kingdom of León, until around 1515, when they finally joined the exodus. They did not go far, traveling only about forty miles to the west, crossing the Portuguese border probably by way of Fermoselle, and finally settling in Mogadouro. On Luis de Carvajal's genealogy and family background, see Luis de Carvajal, *The Enlightened: The Writings of Luis de Carvajal, El Mozo,* ed. and trans. Seymour R. Liebman (Coral Gables, FL: University of Miami Press, 1967), 21–26; Stanley M. Hordes, *To the End of the Earth: A History of the Crypto-Jews of New Mexico* (New York: Columbia University Press, 2005), 72–73; and especially

Samuel Temkin, *Luis de Carvajal: A Biography* (Santa Fe, NM: Sunstone Press, 2011), 17–19. Temkin has gone beyond previous scholars in unearthing relevant information about this fascinating figure. As will become clear in this chapter, while I embrace the new information presented in his biography, I fundamentally disagree with Temkin's broad acquittal of Carvajal regarding any involvement in the slave trade.

2. On Carvajal's early life, see Temkin, *Luis de Carvajal*, 18–21.

3. See George E. Brooks, *Landlords and Strangers: Ecology, Society, and Trade in Western Africa, 1000–1630* (Boulder, CO: Westview Press, 1993), 178; John W. Blake, *European Beginnings in West Africa, 1454–1578* (Westport, CT: Greenwood Press, 1937), 73–75; M. Mitchell Serels, *Jews of Cape Verde: A Brief History* (Brooklyn, NY: Sepher-Hermon Press, 1997), 8–9; and, above all, Maria Emília Madeira Santos, coord., *História Geral de Cabo Verde*, vol. 2 (Lisbon: Imprensa de Coimbra, 1995), 21–29. I want to thank Maria Manuel Ferraz Torrão for graciously sharing her knowledge with a complete stranger.

4. Temkin, *Luis de Carvajal*, 22–25. The census data are for 1582, a slightly later date, but are very representative of Santiago's demography. Brooks, *Landlords and Strangers*, 162. For descriptions of Cape Verde at that time, see Anonymous Portuguese pilot, "Description of a Voyage from Lisbon to the Island of São Thomé," n.p., n.d. (circa 1540), in John William Blake, *Europeans in West Africa, 1450–1560*, 2 vols. (London: Hakluyt Society, 1942), 1:147–149; Friar Baltasar Barreira, "Description of the Islands of Cape Verde and Guinea," Cape Verde, August 1, 1606, in Avelino Teixeira da Mota and P.E.H. Hair, eds., *Jesuit Documents on the Guinea of Cape Verde and the Cape Verde Islands, 1585–1617* (Liverpool: Department of History, University of Liverpool, 1989), parts 5 and 13; and, more generally, Brooks, *Landlords and Strangers*, 143–163.

5. On Cape Verde's commercial activities, see especially Madeira Santos, *História Geral de Cabo Verde*, 18–112; Brooks, *Landlords and Strangers*, 143–163; and Blake, *European Beginnings in West Africa*, 73–75.

6. Unfortunately, Carvajal did not leave a paper trail regarding his work as treasurer. Given the obvious economic orientation of the Cape Verde Islands, however, it is clear that he dealt primarily with slaves. Later in life, Carvajal would describe his position as "treasurer and accountant for the king of Portugal." See Carvajal's testimony during his inquisitorial process in Alfonso Toro, ed., *Los judíos en la Nueva España* (Mexico City: Fondo de Cultura Económica, 1982), 281; Madeira Santos, *História Geral de Cabo Verde*, 522; and "Oficio para Luis de Carvalhal tesoreiro das fazendas dos difuntos no islas de Santiago e Fogo no Cabo Verde," Lisbon, December 3, 1559, in Temkin, *Luis de Carvajal*, 23.

7. It is known for sure that Duarte de León and Antonio González owned the contract for Cape Verde and Guinea between 1566 and 1574. Other commercial transactions suggest that they already had this contract in 1562 and quite likely years before that. Madeira Santos, *História Geral de Cabo Verde*, 21 n. 5. On São Domingos, see André Álvares de Almada, "Tratado Breve dos Rios de Guiné . . . ," in Antonio Brásio, ed., *Monumenta Missionária Africana*, vol. 3 (Lisbon: Agência Geral do Ultramar, 1958), 307. Plenty of evidence confirms that Duarte de León dealt in African slaves. For instance, in 1566 the Council of the Indies initiated proceedings against him and his

partners for sending the slave ship *Nuestra Señora de la Victoria* from Lisbon to the Spanish province of Cartagena without a license or authorization. See Jerónimo de Ulloa, *fiscal* of the Council of the Indies, against Blas de Herrera, Duarte de León, and Antonio Gómez González de Guzmán residing in the city of Lisbon, Madrid, May 5, 1566, "Receptoría pedida por Jerónimo de Ulloa," AGI, Patronato, 291, R. 145. See also the legal proceedings initiated by Duarte de León's heirs over three hundred African slaves from Cape Verde and Guinea sold in Española and Puerto Rico, 1588, "Sentencias del Consejo," and 1589, "Pleitos de la gobernación de Puerto Rico," both in AGI, Escribanía, 953 and 119A, respectively; and the proceedings of Duarte de León and his partner Antonio González, both of whom are identified as "contratadores de los Ríos de Guinea," n.p., December 17, 1571, "Pleito Fiscal: Herederos de Hernando del Cardoso," AGI, Justicia, 889, N. 6. Duarte de León and his partner may have had other resident agents in Upper Guinea, including Marcus Fernandes, who was "chief of the contract in the Rio Grande," and Simon de León, who resided in the port called Begundo on the Rio Farim. Blake, *Europeans in West Africa*, 38.

8. On the negotiations between the two monarchies, see Madeira Santos, *História Geral de Cabo Verde*, 23. For an excellent study of how Portuguese families involved in the slave trade were able to increase their economic influence in the port of Seville in the middle decades of the sixteenth century, see Manuel F. Fernández Chaves and Rafael M. Pérez García, "La penetración económica portuguesa en la Sevilla del siglo XVI," *Espacio, Tiempo y Forma*, 4th ser., vol. 25 (2012), 199–222.

9. Fray Nicolás de Vitte to a very illustrious lord of Meztitlán, August 21, 1554, in Mariano Cuevas, ed., *Documentos inéditos del siglo XVI para la historia de México* (Mexico City: Porrúa, 1975), 221–223.

10. Bishop Zumárraga was not a man prone to exaggeration. He named specific shipmasters and listed close to twenty vessels calling at ports in Pánuco — a province that had nothing but humans to export. Modern scholars have confirmed the bishop's estimates. Zumárraga to King Charles V, Mexico City, August 27, 1529, in Joaquín García Icazbalceta, *Don Fray Juan de Zumárraga, primer obispo de México,* 4 vols. (Mexico City: Porrúa, 1988), 2:210–213. On Indian slavery in Pánuco under Guzmán, see Silvio Zavala, "Nuño de Guzmán y la esclavitud de los indios," *Historia Mexicana* 1:3 (1951), 411–428; Donald E. Chipman, "The Traffic in Indian Slaves in the Province of Pánuco, New Spain, 1523–1533," *The Americas* 23:2 (October 1966), 142–155; and Donald E. Chipman, *Nuño de Guzmán and the Province of Panuco in New Spain* (Glendale, CA: Arthur H. Clark, 1967), 206–229. On the cattle boom in Pánuco, see William E. Doolittle, "Las Marismas to Pánuco to Texas: The Transfer of Open Range Cattle Ranching from Iberia Through Northeastern Mexico," in *Yearbook* (N.p.: Conference of Latin Americanist Geographers, 1987). From Guzmán's *residencia* (judicial proceeding) it is possible to extract more precise information about slave shipments to the Caribbean. Future scholars could also derive a wealth of information from sources such as "Información que Su Magestad mandó hacer y enviar a su Real Consejo de las Indias sobre los esclavos que se han sacado de Pánuco . . . ," Mexico City, August 9, 1529, AGI, Patronato, 231 N. 4, R. 1; and the proceedings of two Indian slaves from Pánuco, Pedro and Luisa, against Nuño de Guzmán to gain their

freedom, Valladolid, March 23, 1550, "Receptoría pedida por Nuño de Guzmán," AGI, Patronato, 280, N. 2, R. 137.

11. At least three Englishmen left accounts of their experiences: Miles Phillips, "A discourse written by one Miles Phillips, Englishman, one of the company put on shore northward of Pánuco by M. John Hawkins 1568" (hereafter cited as Phillips's account), and Job Hortop, "The travails of Job Hortop which Sir John Hawkins set on land within the Bay of Mexico on the 8 of October 1568," both in Richard Hakluyt, *The Principal Navigations, Voyages, Traffiques and Discoveries of the English Nation*, 12 vols. (Glasgow: James MacLehose and Sons, 1904), 9:398–465; and "Testimonio de Antonio Godard," Seville, November 2, 1569, AGI, Indiferente, 902, N. 1, R. 3, 5–10. The quotes are from Phillips's account, 410.

12. Phillips's account, 398–405. Hawkins's exploits, including this third slaving voyage, are well documented in Antonio Rumeu de Armas, *Viajes de John Hawkins* (Seville: Escuela de Estudios Hispano-Americanos de Sevilla, 1947); Raynor Unwin, *The Defeat of John Hawkins: A Biography of His Third Slaving Voyage* (London: Readers Union, 1921); Harry Kelsey, *Sir John Hawkins: Queen Elizabeth's Slave Trader* (New Haven, CT: Yale University Press, 2003); and Robert S. Weddle, *Spanish Sea: The Gulf of Mexico in North American Discovery, 1500–1685* (College Station: Texas A&M University Press, 1985), 297–307.

13. Phillips's account, 410–411.

14. Ibid., 414–415. The eyewitness accounts differ in a few details but not in substance. See the discussion in Temkin, *Luis de Carvajal*, 42–52.

15. Phillips's account, 416; Temkin, *Luis de Carvajal*, 50–52.

16. Phillips's account, 417. Although different types of leagues were used at the time and it is not always easy to determine which one is referred to, my general assumption is that 1 Spanish league equals a little over 3 miles or 4.8 kilometers.

17. Phillips's account, 417–420. For an excellent analysis of African coffles, see Joseph C. Miller, *Way of Death: Merchant Capitalism and the Angolan Slave Trade, 1730–1830* (Madison: University of Wisconsin Press, 1988), 190–199. Some Indians transformed themselves into what some scholars have termed "militaristic slaving societies." The term was coined by Robbie Ethridge, "Creating the Shatter Zone: The Indian Slave Traders and the Collapse of the Southwestern Chiefdoms," in Thomas J. Pluckhahn and Robbie Ethridge, eds., *Light on the Path: The Anthropology and History of the Southeastern Indians* (Tuscaloosa: University of Alabama Press, 2006), 207–218. See also, more generally, Ethridge and Shuck-Hall, *Mapping the Mississippian Shatter Zone*; and Brian Ferguson and Neil L. Whitehead, *War in the Tribal Zone: Expanding States and Indigenous Warfare* (Santa Fe, NM: School of American Research Press, 1992).

18. Phillips's account, 420–421.

19. Ibid., 421.

20. Ibid., 421–422.

21. Ibid., 423. As the Englishmen's accounts make clear, they received favorable treatment when compared with Indian slaves. Yet as suspected Lutherans, they were also investigated and sentenced by the Spanish Inquisition, which was formally established in New Spain in 1571. A number of the men, including John Gray, John

Browne, John Rider, James Collier, Thomas Browne, John Keyes, and several others, received lashes or served in monasteries while wearing the *sanbenito,* the garment worn by those convicted by the Inquisition. Miles Phillips was sentenced to serve in a monastery for five years but did not get lashes. The inquisitorial proceedings of some of these men provide some information about Hawkins's expedition and reveal that several of the Englishmen worked in the mines of Guanajuato and Taxco. See the proceedings of David Alejandro and Guillermo Calens, in Julio Jiménez Rueda, ed., *Corsarios Franceses e Ingleses en la Inquisición de la Nueva España* (Mexico City: Imprenta Universitaria, 1945), 231–304 and 307–506, respectively.

22. For an interesting survey of the frequency and location of colonial rebellions, see Friedrich Katz, "Rural Uprisings in Preconquest and Colonial Mexico," in Friedrich Katz, ed., *Riot, Rebellion, and Revolution: Rural Social Conflict in Mexico* (Princeton, NJ: Princeton University Press, 1988), 65–94. On the patterns of rebellion in central Mexico, see William B. Taylor, *Drinking, Homicide, and Rebellion in Colonial Mexican Villages* (Stanford, CA: Stanford University Press, 1979). The classic work on the Chichimec Wars is Philip Wayne Powell's *Soldiers, Indians and Silver: North America's First Frontier War* (Berkeley: University of California Press, 1952). Powell argues that the war lasted from the 1550s to the 1590s. More recently, José Francisco Román Gutiérrez has revised this chronology, showing that the wars started in the 1530s with the arrival of Nuño de Guzmán in northwestern Mexico. Gutiérrez, *Sociedad y Evangelización en la Nueva Galicia durante el siglo XVI* (Guadalajara: El Colegio de Jalisco, 1993), 360–366. See also Carrillo Cázares, *El Debate sobre la Guerra Chichimeca,* 1:40. For Carvajal's journey to New Spain, see Temkin, *Luis de Carvajal,* 26–30. The Englishman John Chilton visited Tampico in 1572. Although some aspects of his account are vague or erroneous, this part jibes with other evidence about the unsettled conditions in town. See Luis Velasco y Mendoza, *Repoblación de Tampico* (Mexico City: Imprenta Manuel León Sánchez, 1942), 13; and Temkin, *Luis de Carvajal,* 212–213 n. 8. For glimpses of Tampico in the sixteenth century, see Velasco y Mendoza, *Repoblación de Tampico,* 10–18. The *Suma de Visitas,* based on an inspection tour of 1548; the *relaciones geográficas,* or questionnaires and maps elaborated in 1579–1585; and the Ortelius atlas, containing a map of the Huasteca region, all help clarify the human geography of this area. See Guilhem Olivier, *Viaje a la Huasteca con Guy Stresser-Péan* (Mexico City: Fondo de Cultura Económica, 2008), 247–256; and the *Suma de Visitas de Pueblos por Orden Alfabético,* in Francisco del Paso y Troncoso, *Papeles de Nueva España* (Madrid: Impresores de la Real Casa, 1905), 230.

23. The quote about the Chichimecs is from Fray Guillermo de Santa María, quoted in Alberto Carrillo Cázares, ed., *Guerra de los Chichimecas* (Zamora: El Colegio de Michoacán, 2003), 117. See also Powell, *Soldiers, Indians and Silver,* 50–51.

24. Kelsey, *Sir John Hawkins,* 71–93; Philip Wayne Powell, *Mexico's Miguel Caldera: The Taming of America's First Frontier, 1548–1597* (Tucson: University of Arizona Press, 1977), 40–45.

25. On the council of 1569 and at least three others that followed, see Carrillo Cázares, *El Debate sobre la Guerra Chichimeca,* 56–57, 223–245; Powell, *Soldiers, Indians and Silver,* 106–107; and Powell, *Mexico's Miguel Caldera,* 68–69.

26. On Archbishop Pedro Moya de Contreras's position, see his letter to chief councilor of the Indies Juan de Ovando, Mexico City, August 31, 1574, in Paso y Troncoso, *Epistolario de Nueva España*, 11, 179.

27. The quotes are from "Comisión título de capitán para Luis de Carvajal," Mexico, April 11, 1572; Viceroy Enríquez to Carvajal, Mexico, April 17, 1572; and testimony by Juan de Urribarri, Mexico City, February 15, 1578, all cited in Temkin, *Luis de Carvajal*, 54, 54, and 61, respectively.

28. Fiscal Arteaga Mendiola to King Philip II, Mexico City, March 30, 1576, and November 2, 1576, both in Temkin, *Luis de Carvajal*, 69.

29. Francisco de Belver, quoted in Primo Feliciano Velázquez, *Historia de San Luis Potosí*, 4 vols. (Mexico City: Sociedad Mexicana de Geografía y Estadística, 1946), 1:330. Carvajal's pronouncement reportedly occurred at the church of Xilitla (or Xelitla), not far from Jalpan. Soldiers Cristóbal Rangel and Martín Robles, who were not present at Xilitla at the time, heard the same version and provided testimony to that effect. Velázquez, *Historia de San Luis Potosí*, 329. Temkin discounts Belver's testimony, claiming that he was one of the soldiers disrupting the peace that Carvajal had achieved in the region in 1576. In fact, to clear Carvajal of all wrongdoing, Temkin goes on to question the motivations not only of Belver but also of the *fiscal* of the Audiencia of Mexico, Eugenio de Salazar, and of the viceroy, Álvaro Manrique de Zúñiga, Marquis of Villamanrique. Temkin, *Luis de Carvajal*, 70–72, 129–171.

30. Philip Wayne Powell, *War and Peace on the North Mexican Frontier: A Documentary Record*, vol. 1 (Madrid: Ediciones José Porrúa Turanzas, 1971), 163–182; Powell, *Mexico's Miguel Caldera*, 54–55, 60.

31. Provinces or regions in the Spanish empire were often referred to as "kingdoms," such as the "kingdom of New Mexico" or the "kingdom of Guatemala." "New Spain" and "Mexico" are used interchangeably in this book to refer to the region that now includes the country of Mexico and the American Southwest.

32. Eugenio del Hoyo, *Esclavitud y encomiendas de indios en el Nuevo Reino de León, siglos XVI y XVII* (Monterrey: Archivo General del Estado de Nuevo León, 1985), passim. In northern Mexico, encomiendas had traditionally amounted to spoils of conquest. In theory Spanish governors gave these grants of Indians to "worthy" or "meritorious" colonists. But in practice the system often operated the other way around: Spanish colonists subdued Indian bands that they subsequently requested be granted to them as encomiendas. In places such as Nuevo León, Durango, and Chihuahua, these roundups of Indians were indistinguishable from slave raids. Over the years, however, the Spanish crown whittled away at the encomenderos' stranglehold on such Indians by reducing the time they could hold their encomiendas — initially from perpetuity to "three lives" (i.e., three generations) and then, by the middle of the seventeenth century, to "two lives." Finally, in the heat of the Spanish campaign of 1673, the crown forbade the granting of new encomiendas altogether. For the constraining role played by colonial officials, see Chantal Cramaussel, "Encomiendas, repartimientos y conquista en Nueva Vizcaya," *Historias* 25 (October–March 1991), 1–18. Bans on encomiendas did not always succeed. In Nuevo León, for example, the abolition of encomiendas led to the rise of *congregas*, forced resettlements of Indians

close to mines and other Spanish businesses, which in many ways retained the same coercive elements. Thus the early eighteenth century witnessed a struggle in Nuevo León between a reformist visitor named Francisco Barbadillo and the local landed elite over how to incorporate the nomadic Indians into the Spanish enterprises and body politic. Sean F. McEnroe, *From Colony to Nationhood in Mexico: Laying the Foundations, 1560–1840* (New York: Cambridge University Press, 2012), chap. 2. See also Susan Deeds, *Defiance and Deference in Mexico's Colonial North: Indians Under Spanish Rule in Nueva Vizcaya* (Austin: University of Texas Press, 2003), 74–75.

33. Governor Carvajal's affidavit appears in a lawsuit by a miner from Zacualpan named Alonso de Nava against Luis de Carvajal the younger over a thirteen-year-old Chichimec Indian named Francisco. Affidavit by Governor Luis de Carvajal, León, March 21, 1586, Archivo General de la Nación (hereafter cited as AGN), Real Fisco de la Inquisición, 1593, vol. 8, exp. 3, fols. 49–68.

34. Viceroy to the king, Mexico City, August 10, 1586, "Cartas del virrey Marqués de Villamanrique," AGI, Mexico, 20, N. 135. The quote is from Affidavit by Governor Luis de Carvajal, León, March 21, 1586.

35. On el Mozo's involvement in the slave trade, see the lawsuit by the Zacualpan miner Alonso de Nava against Luis de Carvajal el Mozo over the thirteen-year-old Chichimec Indian Francisco. AGN, Real Fisco de la Inquisición, 1593, vol. 8, exp. 3, fols. 49–68. In his inquisitorial deposition, el Mozo describes his occupation as "merchant of the mines and other parts." In another part of his deposition, he clearly states that he "went to the town of Pánuco, and from there took provisions to the war of Tamapache, and then in the company of his father came to Mexico City with some slaves that his father was taking to sell." Deposition of el Mozo in the proceedings against Governor Carvajal, in Toro, *Los judíos en la Nueva España*, 237, 242. For the Indians sold by el Mozo, see Affidavit by Governor Luis de Carvajal, León, March 21, 1586. The quote is from Carvajal, *The Enlightened*, 58–60.

36. Currently, the most detailed biography of Carvajal is Samuel Temkin's *Luis de Carvajal*. Temkin has gone beyond previous scholars in unearthing relevant information about this fascinating figure. As stated in his introduction, Temkin believes that a number of present-day scholars who have written critically about Carvajal—highlighting in particular his slaving activities—are biased. As a result, his biography leans heavily on Carvajal's own self-defense. Temkin found corroborating evidence for "every one of the claims Carvajal made" and regards some of the accusations against him as mere "fabrications" and part of a "scheme" by his enemies to bring about his downfall. In his drive to clear Carvajal of *all* charges, Temkin intentionally avoids in his book what he calls "hearsay testimony" and "sworn affidavits by witnesses who stood to benefit from their testimony." As is clear from this chapter, while I embrace the new information presented in Temkin's biography, I fundamentally disagree with his broad acquittal of Carvajal of any involvement in the slave trade. I offer additional information about Carvajal's slaving activities and discuss his life in the context of a frontier environment in which not only he but many other Spanish conquerors, settlers, and officials, as well as many Natives, profited from the sale of Indians. For more critical appraisals of Carvajal's life, see, for example, Vito Alessio

Robles, *Coahuila y Texas en la época colonial* (Mexico City: Porrúa, 1978); Eugenio del Hoyo, *Historia del Nuevo Reino de León, 1577–1723* (Mexico City: Libros de México, 1979); and Velázquez, *Historia de San Luis Potosí.* For Carvajal's activities, see his inquisitorial testimony in Toro, *Los judíos en la Nueva España,* 339; and Temkin, *Luis de Carvajal,* 63–72. The quotes are from viceroy to the king, Mexico City, August 10, 1586; king of Spain to his viceroy and audiencia members, San Lorenzo, August 8, 1587, in Konetzke, *Colección de documentos para la historia de la formación social de Hispanoamérica,* 1:583–584; and Velázquez, *Historia de San Luis Potosí,* 330–337.

37. There is significant controversy about this aspect of Carvajal's story. See Eugenio del Hoyo, "Notas y comentarios a la 'relación' de las personas nombradas por Luis de Carvajal y de la Cueva para llevar al descubrimiento, pacificación y población del Nuevo Reino de León, 1580," *Humanitas* 19 (1978), 251–281; Samuel Temkin, "Luis de Carvajal and His People," *AJS Review* 32:1 (2008), 79–100; and Temkin, *Luis de Carvajal,* 88–100. I agree with Temkin that early scholars have tended to exaggerate by proposing a "Jewish conspiracy." Although Carvajal obtained his capitulation, or contract, through the usual mechanism, the waiving of House of Trade supervision over Carvajal's colonists was extraordinary. I do not find Temkin's two main explanations for this — i.e., that Carvajal was a trustworthy hidalgo and that time was short — convincing, as these would also apply to all the other grantees. The exception remains a mystery.

38. For a chilling transcription of these confessions, see Vito Alessio Robles, *Acapulco, Saltillo y Monterrey en la historia y en la leyenda* (Mexico City: Porrúa, 1978), 297–298. See also Temkin, *Luis de Carvajal,* 167–170. For a full biographical treatment of el Mozo, see Martin A. Cohen, *The Martyr: Luis de Carvajal, a Secret Jew in Sixteenth-Century Mexico* (Albuquerque: University of New Mexico Press, 1973).

39. Deposition of el Mozo in the proceedings against Governor Carvajal, in Toro, *Los judíos en la Nueva España,* 237, 242.

40. Ibid.

41. For a brief treatment of the frontier captains, see the works of Philip Wayne Powell, especially *Mexico's Miguel Caldera,* chap. 5.

42. Alonso de León, "Relación y discursos del descubrimiento, población . . . ," in Genaro García, ed., *Documentos inéditos o muy raros por la historia de México* (Mexico City: Porrúa, 1975), 41, 58.


## 4. THE PULL OF SILVER

1. For two excellent general treatments of the California gold rush, see Malcolm J. Rohrbough, *Days of Gold: The California Gold Rush and the American Nation* (Berkeley: University of California Press, 1997); and Susan Lee Johnson, *Roaring Camp: The Social World of the California Gold Rush* (New York: Norton, 2000).

2. On the silver peso, see Carlos Marichal, "The Spanish-American Silver Peso: Export Commodity and Global Money of the Ancien Regime, 1550–1800," in Steven Topik, Carlos Marichal, and Zephyr Frank, eds., *From Silver to Cocaine: Latin American*

*Commodity Chains and the Building of the World Economy, 1500–2000* (Durham, NC: Duke University Press, 2006), 25–42.

3. I found the best historical information about gold strikes in the United States, along with excellent production data, in James R. Craig and J. Donald Rimstidt, "Gold Production History of the United States," *Ore Geology Reviews* 13 (1998), 407–464. For the founding of silver mines in Mexico, see Brígida von Mentz, "Las políticas de poblamiento y la minería en la llamada provincial de la plata, 1540–1610"; Chantal Cramaussel, "Ritmos de poblamiento y demografía en la Nueva Vizcaya"; and Salvador Álvarez, "Latifundio y poblamiento en el norte de la Nueva Vizcaya, siglos XVI–XVIII," all in Chantal Cramaussel, ed., *Demografía y poblamiento del territorio la Nueva España y México, siglos XVI–XIX* (Zamora: El Colegio de Michoacán, 2009), 95–110, 123–144, and 140–170, respectively. See also Salvador Álvarez, "Minería y poblamiento en el norte de la Nueva España en los siglos XVI y XVII: Los casos de Zacatecas y Parral," in *Actas del primero congreso de historia regional comparada 1989* (Ciudad Juárez: Universidad Autónoma de Ciudad Juárez, 1989), 105–137; Robert C. West, "Early Silver Mining in New Spain, 1531–1555," in Peter Bakewell, ed., *Mines of Silver and Gold in the Americas* (Brookfield, VT: Variorium, 1997), 57–73; Álvaro Sánchez-Crispín, "The Territorial Organization of Metallic Mining in New Spain," in Alan K. Craig and Robert C. West, eds., *In Quest of Mineral Wealth: Aboriginal and Colonial Mining and Metallurgy in Spanish America* (Baton Rouge, LA: Geoscience Publications, 1994), 155–170; and Salvador Álvarez, "La historiografía minera novohispana: Logros y asignaturas pendientes," in Margarita Guerra, ed., *Historias paralelas: Actas del primer encuentro de historia Perú-México* (Zamora: El Colegio de Michoacán, 2005), 99–133.

4. Estimating Mexico's silver production is far from simple. See John J. TePaske, *La Real Hacienda de Nueva España: La Real Caja de México, 1576–1816* (Mexico City: Instituto Nacional de Antropología, 1976); and Michel Morineau, *Incroyable gazettes et fabuleux métaux: Les retours des trésors américains d'après les gazettes hollandaises, XVI–XVIII siècles* (London: Cambridge University Press, 1985), 563, 578–579. The data on silver and gold production used here come from John J. TePaske, *A New World of Gold and Silver* (Leiden: Brill, 2010), 113; and Craig and Rimstidt, "Gold Production History of the United States," 407–464. My conversions assume that 1 troy ounce equals 31.1035 grams. (Troy ounces are used to measure precious metals.) On the shafts, see Haskett, "'Our Suffering with the Taxco Tribute,'" 451; Woodrow Borah, "Un gobierno provincial de frontera en San Luis Potosí, 1612–1620," *Historia Mexicana* 13:4 (April–June 1964), 538–539; and D. A. Brading, *Mineros y comerciantes en el México borbónico, 1763–1810* (Mexico City: Fondo de Cultural Económica, 1975), 183–184. For the larger context, see Kendall W. Brown, *A History of Mining in Latin America: From the Colonial Era to the Present* (Albuquerque: University of New Mexico Press, 2012), passim.

5. The classic work on Parral and its hinterland is Robert C. West, *The Mining Community in Northern New Spain: The Parral Mining District* (Berkeley: University of California Press, 1949). West's pioneering work has been extended by Álvarez, "Minería

y poblamiento en el norte de la Nueva España," 105–137; Cramaussel, "Encomiendas, repartimientos y conquista en Nueva Vizcaya"; Raúl Pedro Santana Paucar, "Acumulación y especialización productiva en la minería colonial (el caso del Distrito Minero de Parral, Chihuahua, 1630–1730)," *Humanidades* 6 (1980), 117–139; Chantal Cramaussel, *Poblar la frontera: La provincia de Santa Bárbara en Nueva Vizcaya durante los siglos XVI y XVII* (Zamora: El Colegio de Michoacán, 2006); and Guillermo Porras Muñoz, *El nuevo descubrimiento de San José del Parral* (Mexico City: UNAM, 1988), among others. Susan Deeds has studied why some Indian groups endured in the region and others disappeared. See Deeds, *Defiance and Deference in Mexico's Colonial North,* passim. On the connection between Parral and Pancho Villa, see Friedrich Katz, *The Life and Times of Pancho Villa* (Stanford, CA: Stanford University Press, 1998), 765–766.

6. Chantal Cramaussel, "Juan Rangel de Biesma: Un descubridor en problemas," *Meridiano 107* (Ciudad Juárez: Universidad Autónoma de Ciudad Juárez and Gobierno del Estado de Chihuahua, 1992), 21–32.

7. Cramaussel, "Juan Rangel de Biesma," 33.

8. West, *The Mining Community in Northern New Spain,* 13; Porras Muñoz, *El nuevo descubrimiento de San José del Parral,* 51–59; Cramaussel, *Poblar la frontera,* 100–110. The quote is from Esquerra de Rosas, cited in Porras Muñoz, *El nuevo descubrimiento de San José del Parral,* 51.

9. Demographic information is from Porras Muñoz, *El nuevo descubrimiento de San José del Parral,* 51–51; and Cramaussel, *Poblar la frontera,* 145. On Francisco de Lima's life, see Rick Hendricks and Gerald Mandell, "Francisco de Lima, Portuguese Merchants of Parral, and the New Mexico Trade, 1638–1675," *New Mexico Historical Review* 77:3 (Summer 2002), 266–287; and Cramaussel, *Poblar la frontera,* 112 n. 125. My description of Parral is based largely on Cramaussel's painstaking research and abundant information in *Poblar la frontera.*

10. On the shafts of Parral and digging techniques, see West, *The Mining Community in Northern New Spain,* 19–23. For the dangers of mining, see Brown, *A History of Mining in Latin America,* 58–70. On the introduction of explosives, see Brading, *Mineros y comerciantes,* 184.

11. West, *The Mining Community in Northern New Spain,* 23.

12. Porras Muñoz, *El nuevo descubrimiento de San José del Parral,* 59–60; Cramaussel, *Poblar la frontera,* 130–131, 196–199, 234–240; West, *The Mining Community in Northern New Spain,* chap. 3. Many judicial proceedings in Parral, especially those involving rebellious Indians, thieves, debtors, murderers, and escaped slaves, resulted in a sentence to the *morteros.* See, for example, the case of Juan Bernabé, 1647–1649, Archivo Histórico Municipal de Parral (hereafter cited as AHMP), Parral, microfilm reel 1649C, frames 1481–1486; the case of an Indian from Sonora named Marcos Cristobal, 1652, AHMP, Parral, microfilm reel 1652D, frames 1939–1983; the cases of a Tarahumara Indian named Sebastián and a Salinero Indian named Pablo, 1654, AHMP, Parral, microfilm reel 1654C, frames 1578–1592; and the cases of three Apache Indians from New Mexico, María, Angelina, and Juan, 1669, AHMP, Parral, microfilm reel 1669B, frames 0874–0888.

13. See the sources in the previous note.

14. Viceroy Martín Enríquez to the king of Spain, Mexico City, May 1, 1572, "Cartas del Virrey Martín Enríquez," AGI, Mexico, 19, N. 83.

15. The quote is from Alonso de la Mota y Escobar, *Descripción geográfica de los reinos de Nueva Galicia, Nueva Vizcaya y Nuevo León* (Mexico City: Editorial Pedro Robredo, 1940), 151. For the black and mulatto slaves of Parral, see Vincent Meyer, "The Black Slave on New Spain's Northern Frontier: San José del Parral, 1632–1676" (Ph.D. diss., University of Utah, 1975); and Cramaussel, *Poblar la frontera*, 201–205.

16. Nicolás de Tolentino requesting his freedom from the heirs of Felipe Catalán, Parral, March 22, 1673, in AHMP.FC.D43.001.008, Justicia, "Peticiones de libertad." The bills of sale documenting Tolentino's life and travels is remarkably complete. Other cases of "Chinese" slaves have come to light, including that of Pedro Marmolejo, the son of María "china," who was from the Philippines and lived in Parral for more than forty years. Freedom request by Pedro Marmolejo, Parral, August 22, 1672, AHMP. FC.A08.001.021, "Gobierno y administración, Informaciones." For the larger context, see Tatiana Seijas, *Asian Slaves in Colonial Mexico: From Chinos to Indians* (New York: Cambridge University Press, 2014), chap. 1. For instance, Nicolás de Tolentino's experience is similar to that of Catarina de San Juan.

17. For this entire section, I rely on the demographic estimates provided in Cramaussel, *Poblar la frontera*, 145.

18. The quote is from Mota y Escobar, *Descripción geográfica*, 151–152. Interestingly, *pepenas* are not mentioned specifically in regard to Parral, although there certainly was a flourishing black market in ore there.

19. As an example of historians' enthusiasm for the mines as engines of free labor, see Alan Knight, *Mexico: The Colonial Era* (New York: Cambridge University Press, 2002), 65. Somewhat more cautiously, D. A. Brading and Harry E. Cross write that "in Mexico forced labor ceased to be an important element among mine workers as early as the middle seventeenth century." Brading and Cross, "Colonial Silver Mining: Mexico and Peru," *Hispanic American Historical Review* 52:4 (November 1972), 557. See also Bakewell, *Silver Mining and Society in Colonial Mexico*, 122. For the persistence of coerced labor, see José Cuello, "The Persistence of Indian Slavery and Encomienda in the Northeast of Colonial Mexico, 1577–1723," *Journal of Social History* 21:4 (Summer 1988), 683–700; Susan Deeds, "Rural Work in Nueva Vizcaya: Forms of Labor Coercion on the Periphery," *Hispanic American Historical Review* 69:3 (August 1989), 425–449; and Chantal Cramaussel, "Haciendas y mano de obra en la Nueva Vizcaya del siglo XVII: El curato de Parral," *Trace* 15 (June 1989), 22–30.

20. For indebtedness in Parral, see West, *The Mining Community in Northern New Spain*, 51.

21. Cramaussel, "Encomiendas, repartimientos y conquista en Nueva Vizcaya," 105–137; Susan M. Deeds, "Trabajo rural en Nueva Vizcaya: Formas de coerción laboral en la periferia," in *Actas del primer congreso de historia regional comparada* (Ciudad Juárez: Universidad Autónoma de Ciudad Juárez, 1989), 161–170; Cramaussel, *Poblar la frontera*, 145, 219–234; Deeds, *Defiance and Deference in Mexico's Colonial North*, chap. 3; and Deeds, "Rural Work in Nueva Vizcaya," 425–449.

22. The full scope of these Indian rebellions can be gleaned from AHMP, section "Milicias y guerra," series "Sediciones." The director of the Parral archives, Roberto Baca, first drew my attention to this rich source, for which I am grateful. See also Roberto Baca, "La esclavitud y otras formas de servidumbre en Chihuahua: Una visión desde los archivos coloniales," in Jesús Vargas Valdés, ed., *Chihuahua: Horizontes de su historia y su cultura*, 2 vols. (Chihuahua: Milenio, 2010), 1:118–145. For additional clues about Indian slavery around Parral, see "Relación of Diego de Medrano," in Thomas H. Naylor and Charles W. Polzer, eds., *The Presidio and Militia on the Northern Frontier of New Spain: A Documentary History*, vol. 1, *1570–1700* (Tucson: University of Arizona Press, 1986), 409–479. In chapter 3 of her illuminating book *Defiance and Deference in Mexico's Colonial North*, Susan Deeds calls the period from the 1620s to the 1690s a "counterfeit peace" because of the labor coercion used against Natives, which prompted them to revolt. Revealingly, Spaniards called Natives who rebelled *indios de media paz*, half-pacified Indians, because of their intractability. Deeds also makes the important point that Jesuit missionaries agreed to participate in the system of Indian exploitation through repartimientos as a lesser evil, in order to protect the Indians somewhat, and as a safeguard against outright slave raiding, which would have depleted the mission Indians. See Deeds, *Defiance and Deference in Mexico's Colonial North*, chap. 3; Deeds, "Rural Work in Nueva Vizcaya," 425–449; and Deeds, personal communication. See also Cramaussel, *Poblar la frontera*, passim; and Christophe Giudicelli, "Un cierre de fronteras taxonómico . . . tepehuanes y tarahumara después de la guerra de los tepehuanes, 1616–1631," *Nouveau Monde Mondes Nouveaux*, March 18, 2008, https://nuevomundo.revues.org/25913?lang=fr.

23. West, *The Mining Community in Northern New Spain*, chap. 3; Cramaussel, *Poblar la frontera*, chap. 4. Governor Lope de Sierra Osorio, based in Parral, wrote that the Tobosos consisted of twelve different Indian nations. Interestingly, he noted that they were "so desperate and valiant that they take or give no quarter, and they make slaves of all the women and children whom they capture." Extract of a report by Governor Lope de Sierra Osorio, undated but subsequent to 1683, in Charles W. Hackett, *Historical Documents Relating to New Mexico, Nueva Vizcaya, and Approaches Thereto, to 1773*, 3 vols. (Washington, DC: Carnegie Institution, 1937), 2:219. On Tobosos, see also Conrad, "Captive Fates," chap. 3; and J. Gabriel Martinez-Serna, "Mobility and Ethnic Spaces in the Texas Borderlands: The Toboso Indians from the Seventeenth Century to Mexican Independence" (unpublished paper, n.d.).

24. In 1573 the Spanish crown issued legislation regulating how the new expeditions of discovery were to proceed in the New World. The changes were far more than cosmetic. Oñate was held to a higher standard than his predecessors in settling New Mexico, although he was still granted considerable freedom. For the legal constraints on Oñate, see Jerry R. Craddock, "La Guerra Justa en Nuevo México en 1598–1599," *Initium* 7 (2002), 331–359; and Marta Milagros del Vas Mingo, "Las Ordenanzas de 1573, sus antecedents y consecuencias," *Quinto Centenario* 8 (1985), 83–101. On the trial of the Indians of Acoma, see George P. Hammond and Agapito Rey, eds., *Don Juan de Oñate: Colonizer of New Mexico, 1595–1628*, 2 vols. (Albuquerque: Univer-

sity of New Mexico Press, 1953), 1:477. John L. Kessell notes that no mention of one-footed Acoma Indians has come to light. Spaniards "may indeed have performed the maimings," he writes, "but a close reading of the documents raises reasonable doubts." Kessell, *Pueblos, Spaniards, and the Kingdom of New Mexico* (Norman: University of Oklahoma Press, 2008), 42. For a full biography of Oñate, see Marc Simmons, *The Last Conquistador: Juan de Oñate and the Settling of the Far Southwest* (Norman: University of Oklahoma Press, 1991).

25. On early slaving expeditions into New Mexico, see George P. Hammond and Agapito Rey, eds., *The Rediscovery of New Mexico, 1580–1594: The Explorations of Chamuscado, Espejo, Castaño de Sosa, Morlete, and Leyva de Bonilla and Humaña* (Albuquerque: University of New Mexico Press, 1966); and Michael V. Wilcox, *The Pueblo Revolt and the Mythology of Conquest: An Indigenous Archaeology of Contact* (Berkeley: University of California Press, 2009), 105–129. For the case of Diego Pérez de Luxán, see George Hammond and Agapito Rey, eds., *Expedition into New Mexico Made by Antonio de Espejo, 1582–1583, as Revealed in the Journal of Diego Pérez de Luxán, a Member of the Party,* 2 vols. (Los Angeles: Quivira Society, 1929), 1:30–31, 52. His life story and exploits as a slaver can be found in Chantal Cramaussel, "Diego Pérez de Luján: Las desventuras de un cazador de esclavos arrepentido," *Meridiano 107* (Ciudad Juárez: Universidad Autónoma de Ciudad Juárez and Gobierno del Estado de Chihuahua, 1991), 12–45. The slavers of northern Mexico comprised a small, tight circle. Pérez de Luxán cut his teeth in Nuevo León and served under Luis de Carvajal, who also authorized Antonio de Espejo's expedition to New Mexico.

26. On the Castaño de Sosa expedition, see Albert H. Schroeder and Daniel S. Matson, *A Colony on the Move: Gaspar Castaño de Sosa's Journal, 1590–1591* (Santa Fe, NM: School of American Research, 1965); and "Accounts of Captain Juan Morlete," in Naylor and Polzer, *The Presidio,* vol. 1, *1570–1700,* 66–110. See also, more recently, Samuel Temkin, "Gaspar Castaño de Sosa's 'Illegal' Entrada: A Historical Revision," *New Mexico Historical Review* 85 (Summer 2010), 259–280; and Samuel Temkin, "Gaspar Castaño de Sosa: El Primer Fundador de Monterrey," *Revista de Humanidades* 27–28 (October 2010), 321–378.

27. The proceedings against Castaño de Sosa and his men are in "Informaciones: Gaspar Castaño de Sosa," Mexico City, 1592, AGI, Mexico, 220, N. 27; available online at PARES, http://pares.mcu.es/. See also "Real cédula del rey a la audiencia de la Nueva España, sobre que proceda conforme a justicia, contra Gaspar Castaño y los demás culpados por haber hecho una entrada en el Nuevo México y haber dado algunos indios de esclavos sin tener permiso; y que se les ponga en libertad a estos," January 17, 1593, AGN, Reales Cédulas Duplicadas, n.d., vol. 2, exp. 540, fols. 331–332. Temkin dismisses all this evidence of slave taking on the grounds that it was obtained under coercion and focuses instead on the hostility of Viceroys Manrique de Zúñiga and Luis de Velasco II toward Castaño de Sosa. As I have shown in chapter 3, there is very credible information on the slaving activities of Governor Luis de Carvajal, and I see no good reason to dismiss all the evidence against Castaño de Sosa, even though the two viceroys were indeed ill-disposed toward him. Many frontier captains resorted

to Indian slavery, and there is little to suggest that Castaño de Sosa was an exception. In 1593 Castaño de Sosa was found guilty of all charges and sentenced to six years of military service in the Philippines. Although he was acquitted in a later appeal, it came too late, as he was killed during a mutiny on the way to the Moluccas while he was still in military service.

28. Hammond and Rey, *Don Juan de Oñate*, 1:477.

29. Zaldívar inquiry, 1602, in Hammond and Rey, *Don Juan de Oñate*, 2:815; Andrew S. Hernandez III, "The Indian Slave Trade in New Mexico: Escalating Conflicts and the Limits of State Power" (Ph.D. diss., University of New Mexico, 2003), 58. It is easy to locate various prices of haciendas and houses. Oñate's yearly salary was 6,000 ducats, or 7,533 pesos. On Spaniards taking Indians out of New Mexico, see Oñate to Viceroy, n.p., March 2, 1599, in Hammond and Rey, *Don Juan de Oñate*, 1:481. See also Hernandez, "The Indian Slave Trade in New Mexico," 48. On the return to Mexico of Oñate, Zaldívar, and thirty other soldiers and their Natives, see "Conviction of Oñate and His Captains, 1614," in Hammond and Rey, *Don Juan de Oñate*, 2:1111, 1115.

30. Depositions of Friar Pedro de Haro de la Cueba and Friar Pedro de Vergara, August 18, 1621, quoted in France V. Scholes, "Church and State in New Mexico 1610–1650," *New Mexico Historical Review* 11 (1936), 149, 170 n. 21. Governor Eulate's successor, Francisco de la Mora y Ceballos (1632–1635), continued the practice of issuing receipts, "which serve as a just title wherewith the bearer may go to any pueblo he likes and take away a boy or a girl from its father or mother." Friar Esteban de Perea, Curac, October 30, 1633, in Hackett, *Historical Documents*, 3:130. See also *Fray Alonso de Benavides' Revised Memorial of 1634* (Albuquerque: University of New Mexico Press, 1945), 171. On Governor Eulate's activities, see Rick Hendricks and Gerald Mandell, "The Apache Slave Trade in Parral, 1637–1679," *Journal of Big Bend Studies* 16 (2004), 61–62; and Zavala, *Los esclavos indios en Nueva España*, 223, 325 n. 422.

31. This well-known anecdote can be found in Alonso de Benavides's memorial of 1630, which has been translated and edited by Baker H. Morrow, *A Harvest of Reluctant Souls* (Niwot: University Press of Colorado, 1996), 76–78. Trade relations between New Mexico and Chihuahua were sporadic in the early seventeenth century, but the pace picked up considerably after the founding of the mines in Parral in 1631. Even though Parral was the northernmost silver-mining center, it still lay some seven hundred miles south of Santa Fe. New Mexican traders had to travel two months to get there. Yet once in Parral, they found a bustling market and a seemingly endless demand for items such as clothes and salt, as well as workers. Unlike the other large silver mines, such as those at Zacatecas or Guanajuato, Parral was too far north to be supplied easily from central Mexico. New Mexico thus became integrated into the silver economy as a net exporter of slave-made goods and slaves. See Jack D. Forbes, *Apache, Navaho, and Spaniard* (Norman: University of Oklahoma Press, 1960), 120; and Hernandez, "The Indian Slave Trade in New Mexico," 52–54.

32. Scholes, "Church and State in New Mexico," 300, 326 n. 7; Hernandez, "The Indian Slave Trade in New Mexico," 55; Blackhawk, *Violence over the Land*, 25. Governor Luis de Rosas exported buffalo hides and hundreds of textiles woven and decorated

by Indians in his sweatshop in Santa Fe. Lansing B. Bloom, "A Trade Invoice from 1638," *New Mexico Historical Review* 10 (October 1935), 242–248.

33. Certificate issued by Captain Juan Manso, Santa Fe, October 12, 1658, AHMP, Parral, microfilm reel 1660C, frames 1375–1387. For more background on this entrepreneurial governor, see Rick Hendricks and Gerald J. Mandell, "Juan Manso, Frontier Entrepreneur," *New Mexico Historical Review* 75:3 (July 2000), 339–365. Hendricks and Mandell rightly comment on the strangeness of this broad sentence against "the entire Apache nation" and conclude that Manso's certificates were "essentially legal gibberish designed to legitimize and simplify the commerce in Apaches." Hendricks and Mandell, "The Apache Slave Trade in Parral," 67–68. Such legal fig leaves were actually quite common. In 1676 the governor of Chile employed virtually the same legal terminology to abet the traffic of Mapuche slaves.

34. Captain Andrés Hurtado, Santa Fe, September 1661, in Hackett, *Historical Documents*, 3:186–188. The physical labor extracted from the Pueblo Indians of the Salinas area during the seventeenth century can be detected through analyses of musculoskeletal stress marker (MSM) scores. During the colonial period, MSM scores increased for adult men in ways that are consistent with bearing loads. MSM scores also increased notably for older adult women, who seemed to have been drawn more heavily into the labor pool than in pre-colonial times. Katherine A. Spielmann, Tiffany Clark, Diane Hawkey, Katharine Rainey, and Suzanne K. Fish, "'. . . Being Weary, They Had Rebelled': Pueblo Subsistence and Labor Under Spanish Colonialism," *Journal of Anthropological Archaeology* 28 (2009), 102–125.

35. Rick Hendricks and Gerald Mandell have compiled a list of New Mexican trade goods available in Parral. Drawn from dozens of estate inventories, the list includes Apache, Ute, and Pawnee slaves, who sold for 50 to 125 pesos apiece, easily the most expensive "item" one could purchase. Hendricks and Mandell, "Francisco de Lima," 277.

36. The quote is from Fray Alonso de Benavides, who specifically wrote "a petition regarding tribute and personal service by the Indians." *Fray Alonso de Benavides' Revised Memorial of 1634,* 169. Encomienda studies in various parts of colonial Latin America have gone from institutional and legalistic in the past to more nuanced examinations of the day-to-day workings of this institution today. Unfortunately, this scholarly revolution has not yet reached New Mexico. The few studies available leave an incomplete and contradictory picture. H. Allen Anderson's study contains important information, but the analysis is thin. Anderson, "The Encomienda in New Mexico, 1598–1680," *New Mexico Historical Review* 60:4 (1985), 353–377. Based on a purely statistical analysis, David H. Snow concludes that the encomienda was not especially burdensome on the Pueblo Indians. Snow, "Note on Encomienda Economics in Seventeenth-Century New Mexico," in Martha Weigle, ed., *Hispanic Arts and Ethnohistory in the Southwest, A.D. 1450–1700* (Tempe: Arizona State University Anthropological Research Papers, 1981), 347–357. Anecdotal information points to some abuses, however, especially encomenderos demanding labor instead of goods, a practice that was against the law. See John L. Kessell, *Kiva, Cross, and Crown: The Pecos*

*Indians and New Mexico, 1540–1840* (Albuquerque: University of New Mexico Press, 1987), 186–188; Cheryl J. Foote and Sandra K. Schackel, "Indian Women of New Mexico, 1535–1680," in Joan M. Jensen and Darlis A. Miller, eds., *New Mexico Women: Intercultural Perspectives* (Albuquerque: University of New Mexico Press, 1986), 17–40; David J. Weber, *The Spanish Frontier in North America* (New Haven, CT: Yale University Press, 1992), 124–125, 411 nn. 13 and 15; Baker H. Morrow, ed. and trans., *A Harvest of Reluctant Souls: The Memorial of Fray Alonso de Benavides, 1630* (Niwot, CO: University Press of Colorado, 1996), 25–27; and *Fray Alonso de Benavides' Revised Memorial of 1634*, 23–24. Osteological evidence also shows increased workloads for Pueblo Indians under the Spaniards. See Spielmann et al., "'. . . Being Weary, They Had Rebelled,'" 102–125.

37. The entries come from Parral, baptismal records, Church of Jesus Christ of Latter-day Saints, Los Angeles Family History Library, microfilm 162634, Bautismos 1662–1686, 1692–1744.

38. "Informaciones sobre los del Nuevo México y la saca que hacen de ganados en detrimento de los diezmos y venta de indios. Año de 1679," Archivo Histórico del Arzobispado de Durango, Archives and Special Collections Department, New Mexico State University Library, Las Cruces, New Mexico (hereafter cited as AHAD), reel 3, frame 429. The quote is from the deposition of Antonio García, San Juan Bautista de Sonora, January 12, 1679, AHAD, reel 3, frame 430. Parral's power to attract free as well as coerced workers was hardly unique or unprecedented. Mexico's silver economy expanded at a torrid pace through the sixteenth, seventeenth, and eighteenth centuries, spawning mining centers small and large. Treasure seekers, merchants, and entrepreneurs of all stripes descended on all of these mining operations, bringing their own workers and turning to the surrounding Indians as a convenient source of additional labor. Local Indians were the first to be inducted into the mining economy, whether as encomiendas, repartimientos, servants of various kinds, convicts serving out their sentences, or salaried workers. When enough local Indians were not available to pull the silver from the ground, mine owners and labor recruiters simply extended their reach to more distant regions. Mines such as Zacatecas, Mazapil, Indé, Sombrerete, and many others tell the same basic story, as they drew men, women, and children, willingly or unwillingly, from large catchment areas. See Sempat Assadourian, *Zacatecas;* Bakewell, *Silver Mining and Society in Colonial Mexico;* Valentina Garza Marínez and Juan Manuel Pérez Zevallos, *El real y minas de San Gregorio de Mazapil, 1568–1700* (Mazapil: Instituto Zacatecano de Cultura Ramón López Velarde, 2004); and Erasmo Sáenz Carrete, *Indé en la historia: 1563–2000* (Indé: Presidencia Municipal de Indé, 2004).

39. The *mita* system has been extensively studied. See Enrique Tandeter, *Coercion and Market: Silver Mining in Colonial Potosí, 1692–1826* (Albuquerque: University of New Mexico Press, 1993); Jeffrey A. Cole, *The Potosí Mita, 1573–1700: Compulsory Indian Labor in the Andes* (Stanford, CA: Stanford University Press, 1985); and, more recently, Melissa Dell, "The Persistent Effects of Peru's Mining Mita," *Econometrica* 78:6 (2010), 1863–1903. For a broader consideration of labor arrangements in the mines of Latin America, see Brown, *A History of Mining in Latin America,* especially chaps. 3 and 4.

## 5. THE SPANISH CAMPAIGN

1. An antislavery crusade of this scope and ambition in the seventeenth century fits poorly with our current understanding of the history of human rights. The dominant view today is that human rights were a product of the Enlightenment. They were "invented" only in the eighteenth century, in time to spark the great Atlantic upheavals of the 1770s, when the French revolutionaries insisted that all men were "equal" and "born free" and the Founding Fathers in the United States were given to write about "self-evident" and "inalienable" rights. And yet the Spanish crusade of the previous century forces us to reexamine this pervasive narrative. At the very least, its existence suggests that perhaps we've drawn too straight a line between the French and American Revolutions, the end of transatlantic slavery, and the rise of human rights around the world. Just as peoples other than Africans suffered from enslavement, so the history of emancipation is more diverse than we generally assume. For the traditional narrative, see Lynn Hunt, *Inventing Human Rights: A History* (New York: Norton, 2007). Indeed, the antislavery movement of the eighteenth century was remarkably modern in its tactics, including sugar boycotts, lobbying campaigns, and tell-all memoirs. For an example of such a memoir, see Vincent Carretta, *Equiano the African: Biography of a Self-Made Man* (Athens: University of Georgia Press, 2005). See also Adam Hochschild, *Bury the Chains: Prophets and Rebels in the Fight to Free an Empire's Slaves* (Boston: Houghton Mifflin, 2005).

2. For Philip's early art education and his collection, see Jonathan Brown, "Philip IV as Patron and Collector," in Andrés Ubeda de los Cobos, ed., *Paintings for the Planet King: Philip IV and the Buen Retiro Palace* (Madrid: Museo Nacional del Prado, 2005), 45–62. For a few telling pages on Philip and the theater, see Martín Andrew Sharp Hume, *The Court of Philip IV: Spain in Decadence* (New York: G. P. Putnam's Sons, 1907), 201–207.

3. I was initially drawn to the life of Philip IV by Joaquín Sánchez de Toca's *Felipe IV y Sor María de Ágreda* (Madrid: Tipografía de los Huérfanos, 1887), and the more accessible but no less vicarious treatment by John Langdon-Davis, *Carlos: The King Who Would Not Die* (Englewood Cliffs, NJ: Prentice-Hall, 1962), 35–57. For more serious works, see John Elliott, *The Count-Duke of Olivares: The Statesman in an Age of Decline* (New Haven, CT: Yale University Press, 1988); Henry Kamen, *Spain in the Later Seventeenth Century, 1665–1700* (London: Longman, 1980); and R. A. Stradling, *Philip IV and the Government of Spain, 1621–1665* (Cambridge: Cambridge University Press, 1988).

4. Philip was especially devoted to a painting titled *Nuestra Señora del Milagro* (Our Lady of the Miracle), housed in a nearby Franciscan convent. In front of this powerful image, he conducted fervent ceremonies in which he placed his family and the entire empire under the Virgin of Miracles' protection. The king even had a banner made of silk and gold, displaying the royal coat of arms on one side and her on the other. Eleanor Goodman, "Conspicuous in Her Absence: Mariana of Austria, Juan José of Austria, and the Representation of Her Power," in Theresa Earenfight, ed., *Queenship and Political Power in Medieval and Early Modern Spain* (Hampshire,

UK: Ashgate, 2005), 170. The quote about taking over the oar is from John Elliott, "Philip IV: A Portrait of a Reign," in Andrés Ubeda de los Cobos, ed., *Paintings for the Planet King: Philip IV and the Buen Retiro Palace* (Madrid: Museo Nacional del Prado, 2005), 38. For Philip's mysticism, see Stephen Haliczer, *Between Exaltation and Infamy: Female Mystics in the Golden Age of Spain* (New York: Oxford University Press, 2002), 27. The gathering took place in the spring of 1643 in the city of Zaragoza. The most important source for this conclave is Fray Francisco Montaron, "Historia apologetica donde se cuenta el beneficio singular que ha hecho Dios en estos tiempos del año 1643 al rey D. Felipe IV en haverse enviado a muchos siervos suyos con el espiritu profetico desde diversas partes de la christianidad," cited in Haliczer, *Between Exaltation and Infamy*, 26. For the correspondence with Sor María, see Carlos Seco Serrano, ed., *Cartas de Sor María de Jesús de Ágreda y de Felipe IV*, vols. 108 and 109 of *Epistolario español: Colección de cartas de españoles ilustres antiguos y modernos* (Madrid: Ediciones Atlas, 1958), passim.

5. The quotes are from King Philip IV to Sor María de Jesús de Ágreda, Zaragoza, October 4, 1643, and Sor María to Philip, Ágreda, November 25, 1661, both in Seco Serrano, *Cartas de Sor María de Jesús de Ágreda y de Felipe IV*. Time and again, the king promised to heed Sor María's advice and appease God with sound policies. See, for instance, Philip to Sor María, Madrid, June 12, 1652, or Philip to Sor María, Madrid, January 9, 1664, in ibid.

6. Philip III's royal decree legalizing Indian slavery in Chile, May 26, 1608, AGI, Chile, 57. For Philip IV's involvement, see "Real cédula al virrey del Perú," Aranjuez, April 13, 1625, in Álvaro Jara and Sonia Pinto, *Fuentes para la historia del trabajo en el reino de Chile* (Santiago: Editorial Andrés Bello, 1982), 276. See also José Bengoa, *Historia de los antiguos mapuches del sur: Desde antes de la llegada de los españoles hasta las paces de Quilín* (Santiago: Catalonia, 2007), 317–348; José Bengoa, *Conquista y barbarie: Ensayo crítico acerca de la conquista de Chile* (Santiago: Ediciones Sur, 1992); Jara, *Guerra y sociedad en Chile;* and Eugene Clark Berger, "Permanent War on Peru's Periphery: Frontier Identity and the Politics of Conflict in 17th Century Chile" (Ph.D. diss., Vanderbilt University, 2006).

7. This progression can be neatly followed in the 1648 real cédula on the need to keep paying the royal fifth (a royal tax consisting of one-fifth the value of the transaction) on Indian slaves; the 1656 real cédula prohibiting customary slavery, whereby Indians sold their children into slavery; the 1660 real cédula curtailing *obrajes,* or textile sweatshops, in which Indians labored as virtual slaves; the three reales cédulas issued in 1662 prohibiting the exportation of Chilean Indian slaves and curbing their mistreatment; the 1663 real cédula urging authorities to fully comply with the real cédula of 1656 prohibiting customary slavery; the 1664 real cédula reiterating the prohibition to export Indians out of Chile; and the 1665 real cédula reducing the amount of work required of slaves so that they could attend their *doctrinas,* classes where they learned the mysteries of the Catholic faith. The real cédula of April 9, 1662, directed the governor of Chile, the bishop of Santiago, and other ecclesiastical authorities to get together to discuss and avoid the abuses caused by the taking of Indian slaves.

8. Early on, Mariana was a giggling adolescent amused by the dwarfs and fools of Phil-

ip's court. With the passage of time, however, her spontaneity withered away, and she became withdrawn. As a mature woman, she often dressed with the severity of a nun. According to the stipulations of Philip's will, Queen Mariana was to rule the empire until her son Carlos (who would rule as Charles II) came of age. Her power was limited by a governing committee handpicked by Philip, whose advice she was forced to heed. On the terms of Mariana's regency, see *Testamento de Felipe IV* (Madrid: Editora Nacional, 1982), especially clauses 22 and 33. The quote is from the Duke of Maura, *Vida y reinado de Carlos II y su Corte*, 2 vols. (Madrid: Espasa-Calpe, 1954), 1:55. For more on Mariana, see Kamen, *Spain in the Later Seventeenth Century*, 27, 330–331.

9. The quote is from Langdon-Davis, *Carlos*, 62.

10. The quote is from a letter from Sor María to Father Manero reproduced in the prologue to Seco Serrano, *Cartas de Sor María de Jesús de Ágreda y de Felipe IV*, xxxviii. More generally, see John Kessell, "Miracle or Mystery: María de Ágreda's Ministry to the Jumano Indians of the Southwest in the 1620s," in Ferenc Morton Szasz, ed., *Great Mysteries of the West* (Golden, CO: Fulcrum, 1993). For the most complete English-language treatment of Sor María today, see Marilyn H. Fedewa, *María of Ágreda: Mystical Lady in Blue* (Albuquerque: University of New Mexico Press, 2009). Alonso de Benavides, head of the Franciscan order in New Mexico, became so intrigued by the spontaneous conversions of Indians in his province that he went through the trouble of traveling first to Mexico City and then to Madrid to report on these occurrences. He wrote a report for the king in August 1630. While Benavides waited at court, the minister-general of the Franciscans assured him that the mysterious "lady in blue" could only be a young nun he had met years earlier named Sor María. An expectant Benavides made his way to Ágreda to interview María and was able to match some of the details he had heard from the Jumanos with what she told him. Sor María said that she had traveled in spirit to the Americas no less than five hundred times. Benavides no longer had doubt that this young nun was indeed the lady in blue. The news traveled fast to the court, and it caused a great sensation. See the prologue to Seco Serrano, *Cartas de Sor María de Jesús de Ágreda y de Felipe IV*, xxxix. Eduardo Royo cites valuable sources in *Autenticidad de la Mística Ciudad de Dios* (Barcelona: Herederos de Juan Gili Editores, 1914). See also Juliana Barr, *Peace Came in the Form of a Woman: Indians and Spaniards in the Texas Borderlands* (Chapel Hill: University of North Carolina Press, 2007), especially chap. 1.

11. Fedewa, *María of Ágreda*, 242, 247.

12. Although scholars working on colonial Chile, New Spain, Trinidad, the Philippines, and elsewhere are aware of some of these royal initiatives, it is only with the recent digitization of Spain's most important colonial archives that one can finally grasp the full extent of this movement. All but the Chilean and Ecuadorean documents are digitized at PARES, http://pares.mcu.es/.

13. The first two quotes are from "Memoria de los caciques de paz que degolló el Capitán Pedro de Ripete y de las piezas de paz que cautivó . . . by Chaplain Diego de Rosales," Concepción, July 25, 1672, and "Memoria de los caciques e indios que vinieron a dar la paz con todas sus familias, ganados y alahas al capitán Bartolomé de Villagrán . . . ," n.p., n.d., both in AGI, Chile, 57. The next two quotes are from Governor

Juan Enríquez to King Charles II, Santiago, October 8, 1676, AGI, Chile, 57. The last two quotes are from Miguel de Miranda Escobar, cited in Jara, *Guerra y sociedad en Chile*, 149. The research on Indian slavery in Chile is extensive. For excellent introductions, see Jaime Valenzuela Márquez, "Esclavos Mapuches: Para una historia del secuestro y deportación de indígenas en la colonia," in Rafael Gaune and Martín Lara, eds., *Historias de racismo y discriminación en Chile* (Santiago: Uqbar Editores, 2009), 38–59; and Walter Hanisch Espíndula, "Esclavitud y libertad de los indios de Chile, 1608–1696," *Historia* 16 (1981), 65.

14. For Spanish slaving in Paraguay and Tucumán, see Governor Ángelo de Peredo of Tucumán, September 13, 1671, describing how his predecessor, Governor Antonio Mercado, had captured and distributed among his soldiers many Indians from the Calchaquí Valleys, who were then taken to other provinces, AGI, Chile, 57. Royal decrees on behalf of the Natives from Tucumán and Paraguay can be found in *Libros registros-cedularios del Tucumán y Paraguay, 1573–1716* (Buenos Aires: Instituto de Investigaciones de Historia del Derecho, 2000). For the best introduction to the subject, see Gaston Gabriel Doucet, "Sobre cautivos de guerra y esclavos indios en el Tucumán," *Revista de Historia del Derecho* 16 (1988), 59–152; and Christophe Giudicelli, "'Identidades' rebeldes: Soberanía colonial y poder de clasificación; sobre la categoría calchaquí (Tucumán, Santa Fe, siglos XVI–XVII)," in Alejandra Araya Espinoza and Jaime Valenzuela Márquez, eds., *América colonial: Denominaciones, clasificaciones e identidades* (Santiago: Ril Editores, 2010), 137–172. See also Juan Carlos Garavaglia, "Invaded Societies: La Plata Basin, 1535–1650," and James Schofield Saeger, "The Chaco and Paraguay, 1573–1822," both in Frank Salomon and Stuart B. Schwartz, eds., *The Cambridge History of the Native Peoples of the Americas*, vol. 3, part 2 (New York: Cambridge University Press, 1999), 1–58 and 257–286, respectively. A reasonable discussion of the number of slaves taken by *bandeirantes* can be found in John M. Monteiro, *Negros da terra: Índios e bandeirantes nas origens de São Paulo* (São Paulo: Companhia das Letras, 1994), 73–74. And as Hal Langfur reminds us, the *bandeira* did not end in the seventeenth century. Langfur, "The Return of the *Bandeira*: Economic Calamity, Historical Memory, and Armed Expeditions to the Sertão in Minas Gerais, Brazil, 1750–1808," *The Americas* 61:3 (January 2005), 429–461.

15. The Spanish report is quoted in Whitehead, *Lords of the Tiger Spirit*, 186–187. See also Jiménez G., *La esclavitud indígena en Venezuela*; Nancy C. Morey and Robert V. Morey, "Foragers and Farmers: Differential Consequences of Spanish Contact," *Ethnohistory* 20:3 (Summer 1973), 229–246; Joseph Gumilla, *El Orinoco Ilustrado* (Madrid: M. Aguilar Editor); and Juan Rivero, *Historia de las misiones de los llanos de Casanare y los ríos Orinoco y Meta* (Bogotá: Imprenta de Silvestre y Compañía, 1883).

16. The quote is from Fernando de Haro y Monterroso to Queen Mariana, Guadalajara, March 20, 1672, in Arizona State Museum, Tucson, MF 02-A-09. See also Zavala, *Los esclavos indios en Nueva España*, 225–228; and Deeds, *Defiance and Deference in Mexico's Colonial North*, 74.

17. "Carta de Guido de Lavezaris sobre los esclavos de Filipinas," n.p., n.d. (circa 1573), AGI, Filipinas, 6, R. 2, N. 16. For an English translation, see Emma Helen Blair, ed., *The Philippine Islands, 1493–1803*, vol. 3 (New York: Bibliolife, 2008), 204–205. For

this traffic in slaves, see, more generally, Seijas, *Asian Slaves in Colonial Mexico,* chap. 2. All along the crown's policies toward the slaves of the Philippines had been ambiguous at best. Although in theory the enslavement of native Filipinos was forbidden by the New Laws of 1542 and expressly forbidden in the Philippines by a decree in 1574, in practice such prohibitions did not apply to Filipino elites, who continued to hold slaves and indirectly allowed Spaniards to benefit from slave labor through encomiendas and repartimientos. Seijas, *Asian Slaves in Colonial Mexico,* 36–45. Moreover, the Spanish crown allowed the enslavement of Muslims, and the Spaniards understood such royal permission broadly. See the discussion in Patricio Hidalgo Nuchera, "¿Esclavitud o liberación? El fracaso de las actitudes esclavistas de los conquistadores de Filipinas," *Revista Complutense de Historia de América* 20 (1994), 61–74; and Scott, *Slavery in the Spanish Philippines,* 23. For their part, the Portuguese delivered slaves from all over the Indian Ocean to Manila. See Tatiana Seijas, "The Portuguese Slave Trade to Spanish Manila, 1580–1640," *Itinerario* 32:1 (2008), 19–38. For slave raids on Muslims, see "*Autos* (records) of the Audiencia of Manila," Manila, July 9, 1682, AGI, Mexico, 59, R. 3, N. 24. The information is too fragmentary to make even a rough estimate of the number of slaves in the Philippines. Markus Vink has estimated that in the Dutch urban centers of the Indian Ocean — such as Batavia (Java), Colombo (Ceylon), and Malacca — between one-third and two-thirds of the population consisted of Native slaves. There is no reason to assume that the Spanish settlements in the Philippines were significantly different. See Vink, "'The World's Oldest Trade': Dutch Slavery and Slave Trade in the Indian Ocean in the Seventeenth Century," *Journal of World History* 14:2 (June 2003), 131–177. On the various shades of slavery/servitude in the Philippines, see John Leddy Phelan, "Free Versus Compulsory Labor: Mexico and the Philippines, 1540–1648," *Comparative Studies in Society and History* 1:2 (January 1959), especially 197–198; and Scott, *Slavery in the Spanish Philippines,* chap. 2.

18. Neil L. Whitehead, "Indigenous Slavery in South America, 1492–1820," in David Eltis and Stanley L. Engerman, eds., *The Cambridge World History of Slavery* (New York: Cambridge University Press, 2011), 248–271.

19. Both the contents of the real cédula of 1667 and the reactions to it are discussed in Viceroy Pedro Antonio Fernández de Castro, Count Lemos, to Queen Mariana, Lima, January 24, 1670, AGI, Chile, 57.

20. Memorial, Madrid, October 24, 1674; "Extracto de consulta del Consejo," Madrid, November 6, 1674; and "Informe del relator, licenciado Angulo, de lo contenido en las cartas, autos, y papeles tocantes al punto de la esclavitud de los indios de Chile," Madrid, November 6, 1674, all in AGI, Chile, 57. See also Ernesto Schäfer, *El Consejo Real y Supremo de las Indias: Su historia, organización y labor administrativa hasta la terminación de la Casa de Austria,* 2 vols. (Madrid: Marcial Pons Historia, 2003), 1:359.

21. Queen Mariana to the viceroy of Mexico, Madrid, May 9, 1672, AGN, Reales Cédulas Duplicadas, vol. 30, exp. 93, fol. 131; Queen Mariana to the viceroy and Audiencia of Mexico, Madrid, December 23, 1672, AGN, Reales Cédulas Duplicadas, vol. 30, exp. 45, fol. 79; real cédula freeing the Indians of Chile, Madrid, December 20, 1674, AGI,

Chile, 57; real cédula to Governor of Tucumán José de Garro, Madrid, December 20, 1674, AGI, Buenos Aires, 5, L. 3, F. 18v–19v; real cédula freeing the slaves of Paraguay, Madrid, July 25, 1679, AGI, Buenos Aires, 6, L. 1, F. 20r–20v; real cédula freeing all Indian slaves of the hemisphere, Madrid, June 12, 1679, AGN, Reales Cédulas Originales, vol. 17, exp. 18, fol. 39; real cédula freeing the slaves of the Philippines, Madrid, June 12, 1679, AGI, Filipinas, 25, R. 1, N. 46. The Spanish orders of the 1670s in effect closed all the loopholes and exceptions introduced during the reigns of Philip II and Philip III, as well as the early part of the reign of Philip IV. They signaled the crown's commitment to "disavow harsh means like slavery and instead use love and good treatment to preserve and reduce the Indians to the Catholic fold." Real cédula freeing all Indian slaves of the hemisphere, Madrid, June 12, 1679, AGN, Reales Cédulas Originales, vol. 17, exp. 18, fol. 39. It is only fitting that in 1680 the crown was finally able to publish a vast compendium of all the laws related to the Spanish colonies, known as the *Recopilación de las leyes de Indias*. Book 6, title 2 of the *Recopilación* was devoted to the Indians and explicitly referred back to the New Laws of 1542 (and even earlier legislation), emphatically prohibiting the enslavement of Indians "except when expressly permitted in that same legal compendium." A digital copy of the *Recopilación de las leyes de Indias* can be found at http://fondosdigitales.us.es/fondos /libros/752/1030/recopilacion-de-leyes-de-los-reynos-de-las-indias/. All of the quotes in this section are from this version.

22. The most obvious antecedent of the *Recopilación de las leyes de Indias* was the effort undertaken by Juan de Ovando between 1571 and 1575. However, this so-called Código Ovandino remained incomplete.

23. Governor Sebastián de Roteta to Charles II, San José de Oruña, Trinidad, August 1, 1688, AGI, Santo Domingo, 179, R. 1, N. 34.

24. The first quote is from a letter written by Fernando de Haro y Monterroso, June 1, 1675, quoted in King Charles II to the members of the Audiencia of Guadalajara, Madrid, April 2, 1676, in Hackett, *Historical Documents*, 2:32–33, 204–208. The second quote is from Haro y Monterroso to Queen Mariana, Guadalajara, March 20, 1672. For Haro y Monterroso's biography, see "Relación de méritos y servicios del licenciado Don Fernando de Haro y Monterroso," Mexico City, November 18, 1686, AGI, Indiferente, 132, N. 22.

25. Report by Captain Miguel Calderón y Oxeda, Villa de San Felipe y Santiago, April 18, 1673; report by Captain Calderón, pueblo of Nío, April 23, 1673; and report by Captain Calderón, Guasave, April 23, 1673, all in "Libertad y servicio personal de indios: Sonora y Sinaloa," AGI, Patronato, 231, R. 1. On slaving in Sinaloa, see "Autos sobre los presos que hizo don Gaspar de Quejada," Sinaloa, January 1654, Main Library, University of Arizona, Tucson, microfilm 0318, reel 1654A, frames 0374–0394. On the cruelty of the Jesuit priests of Sinaloa, see the depositions of Juan Bautista and Martín Juárez, Mocorito Indians from San Miguel, December 10 and 12, 1672, in "Libertad y servicio personal de indios: Sonora y Sinaloa." Victor Adrián González Pérez has transcribed and edited Juan Bautista's deposition. See "Declaración del indio nombrado Juan Bautista acerca de los maltratos . . . ," *Clío* 1:28 (2002), 171–179. See also

Luis Navarro García, *Sonora y Sinaloa en el siglo XVII* (Mexico City: Siglo Veintiuno Editores, 1992), 158.

26. Letters of Chaplain Jacinto Cortés, n.p., February 8, 1673, and Pedro de Maya, Villa de San Felipe y Santiago, April 26, 1673, both in "Libertad y servicio personal de indios: Sonora y Sinaloa." The *apoderado* (lawyer) of the missions of Sinaloa, Father Gutiérrez, presented a petition denouncing Luque. Members of the Audiencia of Guadalajara discussed the accusations against him on June 23, 1673. See "Libertad y servicio personal de indios: Sonora y Sinaloa." For a more in-depth discussion of the legal proceedings, see Navarro García, *Sonora y Sinaloa en el siglo XVII*, 169–173.

27. Deposition of Pedro Francisco Santillón, San Miguel Arcángel, October 3, 1679, and deposition of Juan de Encinas, San Miguel Arcángel de Sonora, October 3, 1679, both in AHAD, reel 3, frames 433–434.

28. For an even earlier crackdown, see the royal order regarding the manumission of Apache slaves, Guadalajara, October 31, 1659, cited in Hendricks and Mandell, "The Apache Slave Trade in Parral," 68–69, 79.

29. Haro y Monterroso to Queen Mariana, Guadalajara, March 20, 1672. See also Zavala, *Los esclavos indios en Nueva España*, 225–228; and Deeds, *Defiance and Deference in Mexico's Colonial North*, 74. The chart of New Mexican Indians baptized in Parral in appendix 5 shows clear dips in the early 1660s and early 1670s, which almost certainly reflect the impact of the antislavery initiatives. The use of royal carriages to traffic Indians is well documented in the AHMP. See, for example, "Información del capitán Juan Manso," Parral, December 21, 1653, AHMP.FC.A08.001.012; "Mandato de Juan de Aguileta," Parral, December 6, 1656, AHMP.FC.A16.001.019; and "Auto del doctor Juan de Gárate y Francia," Parral, December 27, 1669, AHMP.FC.A16.001.032.

30. "Memorial del capitán Juan Bautista de Ynarra, vecino de Lima, poseedor de varios indios esclavos procedentes del reino de Chile … presentado en el Concejo de Indias," Madrid, December 7, 1677, AGI, Chile, 57. See especially the title of ownership on behalf of Captain Juan de Ynarra, Concepción, September 6, 1669, AGI, Chile, 57. The Mapuches overran the area south of the Bío-Bío River in the late 1500s, but the Spaniards regained control of the area and refounded the city of Valdivia in 1645, fearing that the Dutch would establish a beachhead there. The governorship of Valdivia was dependent on the viceroyalty of Peru.

31. Governor Enríquez to Charles II, Santiago, October 8, 1676.

32. Ibid. J. H. Elliott succinctly discusses this formula, and more generally the matter of resistance to royal authority, in *Empires of the Atlantic World: Britain and Spain in America, 1492–1830* (New Haven, CT: Yale University Press, 2006), 130–132.

33. Don Juan de la Peña y Salazar, licenciado Don Diego Portales, and other audiencia members to Charles II, Santiago, March 18, 1678, AGI, Chile, 57.

34. Governor Enríquez to Charles II, Santiago, December 6, 1680, AGI, Chile, 57.

35. "*Autos* of the Audiencia of Manila," Manila, July 9, 1682.

36. Audiencia report on slavery, Manila, June 22, 1684, transcribed and translated in Scott, *Slavery in the Spanish Philippines*, 38; Archbishop of Manila Fray Felipe Pardo to Charles II, Manila, April 5, 1689, AGI, Mexico, 59, R. 3, N. 24.

37. Audiencia report on slavery, Manila, June 22, 1684, 38, 45; Archbishop Felipe Pardo to Charles II, Manila, April 5, 1689.

38. Antonio de Morga, *Sucesos de las Islas Filipinas* (Mexico City: Fondo de Cultura Económica, 2007), 224. This book was originally published in 1609, much earlier than the Spanish campaign, but evidence that emerged during the campaign, as well as other sources, make it clear that Native Filipinos continued to hold slaves throughout the seventeenth century and later. Nicolás García, Baltazar Balurot, Juan García, Don Tomás Manalang, Don Agustín Bernal Yumol, Nicolás Pangan, Don Juan Alvarado Sumang, and others, n.p., n.d. (circa 1688), AGI, Mexico, 59, R. 3, N. 24. Unfortunately, the scope of this book makes it impossible to say but a few words about this interesting episode. The file "Cartas del Virrey Conde de Galve" (AGI, Mexico, 59, R. 3, N. 24) contains more than a thousand pages of documents related to it. Additional documents can be found in "Carta de Curucelaegui sobre libertad de los indios," AGI, Filipinas, 12, R. 1, N. 8.

39. For the difficulties involved in ending Native slavery in the Philippines, see Scott, *Slavery in the Spanish Philippines*, chap. 7. Tatiana Seijas emphasizes the importance of formal abolition in *Asian Slaves in Colonial Mexico*, chap. 7.

40. Governor Enríquez to Charles II, Santiago, October 8, 1676; Don Juan de la Peña y Salazar et al. to Charles II, Santiago, March 18, 1678; "Traslado de autos del acuerdo de la Audiencia de Manila en cumplimiento de la cédula sobre que no se esclavice a los indios," Manila, June 11, 1683, AGI, Filipinas, 13, N. 17.

41. On the pronouncement against the enslavement of Indians by Carolina's proprietors, see Gallay, *The Indian Slave Trade*, 66–67. See also Francis Daniel Pastorius and others, "Quaker Protest Against Slavery in the New World, Germantown (Pa.), 1688," http://triptych.brynmawr.edu/cdm/ref/collection/HC_QuakSlav/id/8; Samuel Sewall, "The Selling of Joseph: A Memorial (1700)," http://digitalcommons.unl.edu/cgi/viewcontent.cgi?article=1026&context=etas; and Epifanio de Moirans, *A Just Defense of the Natural Freedom of Slaves: All Slaves Should Be Free (1682)*, ed. and trans. Edward R. Sunshine (Lewiston, NY: Edwin Mellen Press, 2007), 23. Moirans was one of two Capuchin missionaries to Havana who wrote impassioned tracts against the African slave trade using religious and moral arguments. The other was Francisco José de Jaca (1645–1688). Both were tried for sedition in Havana and subjected to lengthy legal proceedings. José Tomás López García, *Dos defensores de los esclavos negros en el siglo XVII* (Caracas: Universidad Católica Andrés Bello, 1982).

## 6. THE GREATEST INSURRECTION AGAINST THE OTHER SLAVERY

1. Testimony of Juan Unsuti, Tiwa of Alameda, encampment and *plaza de armas* of the house of Captain Francisco de Ortega, December 27, 1681, in Barbara De Marco, "Voices from the Archives: Testimony of the Pueblo Indians on the 1680 Pueblo Revolt," part 1, *Romance Philology* 53 (Spring 2000), 440.

2. For a rundown of these conspiracies, see, for example, testimony of Pedro Naranjo, December 24, 1681, in De Marco, "Voices from the Archives," part 1, 417; testimony of

the lieutenant general of the cavalry, place on the Río del Norte, December 20, 1681, in Charles W. Hackett, ed., *Revolt of the Pueblo Indians of New Mexico and Otermín's Attempted Reconquest, 1680–1682*, 2 vols. (Albuquerque: University of New Mexico Press, 1942), 2:266; and testimony of Sargento Mayor Luis de Quintana, hacienda of Luis de Carbajal, December 22, 1681, in Hackett, *Revolt of the Pueblo Indians*, 2:278.

3. The quote is from testimony of Juan, Tewa from Tesuque, camp on the Rio Grande within sight of the pueblos of Alameda, Puray, and Sandia, December 18, 1681, in De Marco, "Voices from the Archives," part 1, 392. For the connections between Po'pay, Poseyemu, and the Devil, see especially testimony of Pedro Naranjo, December 24, 1681, 418. Another version has Po'pay in direct contact with Caudi, Tilimi, and Tleume, three spirits who had traveled from the primordial lake of Copala to Taos. For more on Poseyemu and his influence on the Pueblo Revolt, see Richard J. Parmentier, "The Mythological Triangle: Poseyemu, Montezuma, and Jesus in the Pueblos," in Alfonzo Ortiz, ed., *Handbook of North American Indians: Southwest*, vol. 9 (Washington, DC: Smithsonian Institution Press, 1979), 609–622. See also Stefanie Beninato, "Popé, Pose-yemu, and Naranjo: A New Look at Leadership in the Pueblo Revolt of 1680," *New Mexico Historical Review* 65:4 (October 1990), 417–435; and Robert W. Preucel, *Archaeological Semiotics* (Malden, MA: Blackwell, 2006), 218–221.

4. For the killing of Po'pay's son-in-law, see testimony of Juan, Tewa from Tesuque, December 18, 1681, 392. For Governor Treviño's campaign, see testimony of Diego López Sambrano, hacienda of Luis de Carbajal, December 22, 1681, in Hackett, *Revolt of the Pueblo Indians*, 2:330–331. Several scholars refer to this campaign, including Andrew L. Knaut, *The Pueblo Revolt of 1680: Conquest and Resistance in Seventeenth-Century New Mexico* (Norman: University of Oklahoma Press, 1995), 164; and Ramón Gutiérrez, *When Jesus Came, the Corn Mothers Went Away: Marriage, Sexuality, and Power in New Mexico, 1500–1846* (Stanford, CA: Stanford University Press, 1991), 131–132.

5. There is some confusion about the precise date of the uprising. Originally the revolt was to take place on August 13. But according to modern astronomical calculations, the full moon occurred on August 10, which is when the rebellion in fact broke out, after frantic date changes just prior to that date. For the "juntas" of the "old men," see testimonies of Nicolás Catúa and Pedro Omtuá, Santa Fe, August 9, 1680, in Hackett, *Revolt of the Pueblo Indians*, 1:4; and Edward P. Dozier, *The Pueblo Indians of North America* (New York: Holt, Rinehart and Winston, 1970), 56.

6. The quote is from testimony of Pedro Naranjo, December 24, 1681, 418. For a broad introduction to Indian runners, see Peter Nabakov, *Indian Running: Native American History and Tradition* (Santa Fe, NM: Ancient City Press, 1981). The book begins with the runners of the Pueblo Revolt of 1680, placing them in a much larger regional — and sometimes continental — context. In 1980 the three hundredth anniversary of the Pueblo Revolt included a tricentennial run following some of the routes of the original Pueblo couriers. In addition to Nabakov's book, see Herman Agoyo, "The Tricentennial Commemoration," in Joe S. Sando and Herman Agoyo, eds., *Po'pay: Leader of the First American Revolution* (Santa Fe, NM: Clear Light, 2005), 93–106.

7. Fray Silvestre Vélez de Escalante, "Extracto de noticias," Biblioteca Nacional de

México, L. 3, N. 1, transcription in Eleanor B. Adams Papers, box 13, folder 23, Center for Southwest Research and Special Collections, University of New Mexico, Albuquerque.

8. Testimony of Pedro Naranjo, December 24, 1681, 419. Vélez de Escalante, "Extracto de noticias," August 23 and 26, 1680. For a fascinating look into the materiality of the Pueblo interregnum in the Jemez district, see Matthew J. Liebmann, "'Burn the Churches, Break Up the Bells': The Archaeology of the Pueblo Revolt Revitalization Movement in New Mexico, A.D. 1680–1696" (Ph.D. diss., Harvard University, 2006); and Matthew J. Liebmann, *Revolt: An Archaeological History of Pueblo Resistance and Revitalization in 17th Century New Mexico* (Tucson: University of Arizona Press, 2012), passim.

9. J. Manuel Espinosa, ed. and trans., *The Pueblo Indian Revolt of 1696 and the Franciscan Missions in New Mexico: Letters of the Missionaries and Related Documents* (Norman: University of Oklahoma Press, 1988), 35. A partial list of the deceased friars can be found in "Memorial of the Religious Whom the Indians of New Mexico Have Killed," Hackett, *Revolt of the Pueblo Indians*, 1:108–111.

10. Andrew O. Wiget, "Truth and the Hopi: An Historiographic Study of Documented Oral Tradition Concerning the Coming of the Spanish," *Ethnohistory* 29:3 (1982), 181–199.

11. Testimony of Juan, Tewa from Tesuque, December 18, 1681, 393.

12. Vélez de Escalante, "Extracto de noticias," August 14, 1680.

13. David Roberts, *The Pueblo Revolt: The Secret Rebellion that Drove the Spaniards out of the Southwest* (New York: Simon & Schuster, 2004), 20–22.

14. Vélez de Escalante, "Extracto de noticias," August 14–15, 1680. The quotes are from Governor Otermín to Friar Francisco de Ayeta, September 8, 1680, in Hackett, *Revolt of the Pueblo Indians*, 1:99. The same version of the conversation can be found in Friar Francisco de Ayeta's account in Barbara De Marco, "Voices from the Archives: Francisco de Ayeta's 1693 Retrospective on the 1680 Pueblo Revolt," part 2, *Romance Philology* 53 (Spring 2000), 459.

15. As mentioned earlier, Bishop Bartolomé García de Escañuela of Durango launched a formal investigation into this burgeoning business a few months before the outbreak of the Pueblo Revolt. "Informaciones sobre los del Nuevo México y la saca que hacen de ganados en detrimento de los diezmos y venta de indios. Año de 1679," AHAD, reel 3, frame 429. See especially the deposition of Antonio García, San Juan Bautista de Sonora, January 12, 1679, AHAD, reel 3, frame 430.

16. This account comes largely from Vélez de Escalante, "Extracto de noticias," section titled "Gobierno de Otermín." Silvestre Vélez de Escalante was, to put it in terms that are instantly familiar to us, the Indiana Jones of his time. He was a friar and a scholar, having become a "brother philosopher" of the Franciscan order when he was only nineteen. But Vélez de Escalante was also a man of action. Today he is remembered for pioneering an overland route between landlocked New Mexico and the recently established missions of California. Passing through Colorado, Utah, Nevada, and California — some of the most desolate and challenging areas of North America — Vélez de Escalante and his party successfully completed their mission in

1776. But unlike the usual Hollywood version of the scholar-adventurer, Fray Vélez de Escalante paid a heavy price for his exploits. He returned to New Mexico a much-diminished man, afflicted by a chronic illness that would take his life in 1780. Even so, during his prolonged demise he reviewed old documents in the government archives of Santa Fe and composed a history of early New Mexico modestly titled "Extracto de noticias" (Digest of events). Vélez de Escalante was a meticulous historian. Frequently he quotes from documents that are still available to us, but just as often his narrative draws on letters and reports that have since vanished. Because he was writing less than one hundred years after the Pueblo Revolt, it is also likely that he gathered some of his information from oral traditions that were still in circulation.

17. For Xavier's objections to the kachina dances, see Hackett, *Historical Documents,* 3:177. There were two Francisco Xaviers in New Mexico, but the other one would have been barely a boy in 1661. For the campaign of 1675, see testimony of Pedro Naranjo, December 24, 1681, 417; testimony of the lieutenant general of cavalry, December 20, 1681, 2:266; and testimony of Sargento Mayor Luis de Quintana, December 22, 1681, 2:278. See also Knaut, *The Pueblo Revolt of 1680,* 167–168.

18. For Xavier's early involvement in the Indian slave trade, see the copy of the receipt signed by Juan Manso in favor of Governor Villanueva, November 29, 1665, in Hackett, *Historical Documents,* 3:282; and Vélez de Escalante, "Extracto de noticias," section titled "Gobierno de Otermín." See also Kessell, *Kiva, Cross, and Crown,* 231–232; and Brooks, *Captives and Cousins,* 52. Many Indians shared a very negative view of Xavier as indicated later in this chapter.

19. Governor Otermín to Friar Francisco de Ayeta, September 8, 1680, 1:99.

20. The muster was held at a place called La Salineta, just north of present-day Ciudad Juárez, before the survivors left New Mexico and entered Chihuahua. *Auto* for passing muster, La Salineta, September 29 and October 2, 1680, in Hackett, *Revolt of the Pueblo Indians,* 1:134–153, 157–159. Unfortunately, the muster list does not distinguish between those who had been holed up in Santa Fe and the Spanish survivors who came from other places.

21. The exact number of individuals who passed muster is 1,579. It does not include another 317 Christianized Pueblo Indians from Isleta, Sevilleta, Alamillo, Socorro, and Senecú who joined the exodus for one reason or another.

22. The *maestre de campo,* Pedro de Leiva, stated that "of thirty servants whom he had, the enemy left him only three," and Sergeant Major Fernando Durán Sánchez declared that the enemy had "carried off or killed … twenty-eight servants." Unfortunately, the muster list does not always make a clear distinction between family members and servants. For example, Esteban López listed himself "and a family of 23 persons including mother, brothers, and servants," and Ensign Blas Griego passed muster with "seventeen persons including wife, children, mother, and servants." To solve this problem, I did a low estimate of the numbers of servants and Spaniards (512 servants in the hands of 1,067 Spaniards) and a high estimate (611 servants owned by 968 Spaniards). The value of the servants far exceeded that of the 444 horses, 25 mules, 8 mares, and 5 jacks the Spaniards also reported. As for the servants/slaves themselves, they consisted largely of Apaches, some Pueblos, and a sprinkling of

Navajos and other Plains Indians. The muster list offers fleeting glimpses of them. Sergeant Major Diego Lucero de Godoy, for instance, noted that his Indian servant was armed and willing to fight alongside the Spaniards. Evidently not all the Indians were unwilling prisoners of their masters. It also seems clear that the vast majority of them were women and children. Gregorio Valdés identified his servant as "an Indian woman," Pedro de Cuéllar passed muster with "a boy who serves him," Francisco González said that he had "one Indian woman with three children," Captain Esteban de Grazia specified that he had "two Indian servant women and two servant boys," and so on.

23. The quote is from Vélez de Escalante, "Extracto de noticias," section titled "Gobierno de Otermín." My description follows Vélez de Escalante's unless otherwise noted.

24. Roberts, *The Pueblo Revolt*, passim.

25. The quotes are from the report by the Jesuit provincial of Mexico, Francisco Báez, n.p., April 1602, transcribed and translated in Naylor and Polzer, *The Presidio*, vol. 1, *1570–1700*, 160; and Priest Diego de Medrano, "Informe sobre sucesos en Durango," Durango, August 31, 1654, Arizona State Museum, Tucson, MF J-03-A-13 Pastells Col. V. 008, pp. 383–458. The connection between witchcraft in Europe and idolatry in the New World went back to the first bishop of Mexico, Juan de Zumárraga, who received his appointment in part because of his prior experience in battling witchcraft in Spain. Similarly, Friar Andrés de Olmos composed a famous treatise on witchcraft titled *Tratado de hechicerías y sortilegios* (1553) by adapting a European manual on witchcraft to the circumstances of the New World. Patricia Lopes Don, *Bonfires of Culture: Franciscans, Indigenous Leaders, and Inquisition in Early Mexico, 1524–1540* (Norman: University of Oklahoma Press, 2010); Friar Andrés de Olmos, *Tratado de hechicerías y sortilegios* (Mexico City: UNAM, 1990). For northern Mexico, see Daniel T. Reff, "The 'Predicament of Culture' and Spanish Missionary Accounts of the Tepehuan and Pueblo Revolts," *Ethnohistory* 42:1 (Winter 1995), 62–90; and Daniel T. Reff, *Plague, Priests, and Demons: Sacred Narratives and the Rise of Christianity in the Old World and the New* (New York: Cambridge University Press, 2004). In northern Mexico, missionaries always identified rebellion leaders as *hechiceros* (sorcerers), men endowed with supernatural powers and in league with the Devil. Chantal Cramaussel, "La Rebelión Tepehuana de 1616: Análisis de un discurso," in Chantal Cramaussel and Sara Ortelli, eds., *La Sierra Tepehuana: Asentamientos y movimientos de población* (Zamora: El Colegio de Michoacán, 2006), 186. Spanish and English colonists shared a similar demonological discourse. See Jorge Cañizares Esguerra, *Puritan Conquistadors: Iberianizing the Atlantic, 1500–1700* (Stanford, CA: Stanford University Press, 2006). Spanish sources ordinarily named the Devil as the ultimate and true instigator of these insurrections. It is likely that some Christian Europeans sincerely believed these rebellions were the work of the Devil. See, for example, Cramaussel, "La Rebelión Tepehuana de 1616," 186. But we also have to recognize that such explanations conveniently glossed over more earthly and controversial alternatives, such as ill treatment and exploitation of the Natives.

26. L. Bradford Prince, quoted in David J. Weber, *What Caused the Pueblo Revolt of 1680?* (Boston: Bedford/St. Martin's, 1999), 10.

27. My description is entirely based on the excellent biographical treatment of Bancroft by John Walton Caughey, *Hubert Howe Bancroft: Historian of the West* (Berkeley: University of California Press, 1946), passim.

28. Hubert Howe Bancroft, *History of Arizona and New Mexico, 1530–1888* (Albuquerque: Horn and Wallace, 1962), 174–175. To his credit, Bancroft acknowledged that there had been "elements of secular oppression," as he called them, motivating the Pueblos. As David Weber has observed, other historians of that era, such as Ralph Emerson Twitchell, essentially repeated Bancroft's interpretation. Weber, *What Caused the Pueblo Revolt of 1680?*, 17 n. 12.

29. Weber, *What Caused the Pueblo Revolt of 1680?*, 10–11. Daniel T. Reff has argued that the Pueblo Revolt was a millenarian movement triggered by the devastating effects of Old World diseases. Reff, *Disease, Depopulation, and Culture Change in Northwestern New Spain, 1518–1764* (Salt Lake City: University of Utah Press, 1991); Reff, "The 'Predicament of Culture,'" 63–90. Andrew L. Knaut considers a number of factors in his fine book *The Pueblo Revolt of 1680*. In addition to the religious cleavage, he emphasizes Apache raiding, famine, and the disintegration of European authority in seventeenth-century New Mexico. Knaut, *The Pueblo Revolt of 1680*, especially 119–170. The quotes are from Gutiérrez, *When Jesus Came*, 127.

30. Governor Mendizábal's quotes are from his reply to accusations made against him, n.p., March 1664, in Hackett, *Historical Documents*, 3:211–213. It is true that Mendizábal expressed these unflattering opinions out of spite as he tried to defend himself against his religious detractors. And indeed, no evidence has come to light linking New Mexico's friars directly with the Indian slave trade. But there was a kernel of truth in Mendizábal's assertions, as the friars' ambitious building projects and livelihood depended on resources that could be mustered only by tapping deeply into the pool of Native labor. Scholars have long echoed the work of France V. Scholes to the effect that during the seventeenth century, New Mexico was in turmoil due to an ongoing dispute between church and state. There were many reasons for this clash, not the least of which was their competition over Indian labor. Scholes, "Church and State in New Mexico," passim. For the Hopi oral traditions and their documentary support, see Wiget, "Truth and the Hopi," 183–187.

31. Testimony of Juan Domínguez de Mendoza, Mexico City, June 20, 1663, in Hackett, *Historical Documents*, 3:234. See also Wiget, "Truth and the Hopi," 189; and Gutiérrez, *When Jesus Came*, 131–132.

32. Howard Lamar wrote a pioneering and ambitious essay specifically interpreting the Pueblo Revolt as an insurrection against labor coercion. Lamar, "From Bondage to Contract: Ethnic Labor in the American West, 1600–1890," in Steven Hahn and Jonathan Prude, eds., *The Countryside in the Age of Capitalist Transformation* (Chapel Hill: University of North Carolina Press, 1985), 293–324. James Brooks's book *Captives and Cousins* powerfully describes the captive exchange system involving various Indian groups in New Mexico. Chantal Cramaussel has underscored the rising tide of slaves from New Mexico flowing into the mines of Chihuahua in the waning decades of the seventeenth century. Rick Hendricks and Gerald Mandell have shed considerable light on the workings of the Apache slave trade. Most recently,

archaeologist Michael V. Wilcox has cast doubt on the pervasive historical narrative describing the demographic collapse of the Pueblo Indians as being induced by
epidemic disease. Instead, he has emphasized both the high levels of violence that
accompanied the European settlement of New Mexico and the creative responses of
the Pueblo Indians, who resorted to complex strategies of abandonment and reoc-
cupation of various sites and to strengthening their ties with the Athapaskan peoples surrounding them. See Brooks, *Captives and Cousins*, 52; Cramaussel, *Poblar
la frontera*, 186–205; Hendricks and Mandell, "The Apache Slave Trade in Parral,"
59–81; and Wilcox, *The Pueblo Revolt*. Not all the work is so recent. In his pioneering *Apache, Navaho, and Spaniard* (1960), Jack Forbes presents the Pueblo Revolt
of 1680 as a multiethnic movement responding to a long-term history of abuse and
enslavement.

33. As the Spaniards and their dependents began their retreat to the south, they were
able to capture forty-seven Pueblo Indians, who were interrogated more for tactical
information than to learn the underlying causes of the uprising—at least the *auto*
drawn up by Governor Otermín the day after the Indians were captured sheds no
light on these causes. The opening question posed to the nine Pueblo Indians captured at the end of 1681 was as follows: "What was the cause and reasons that led all
the Indians of this kingdom to rise up, reverting to their idolatrous ways, abandon-
ing the law of God, withholding their obedience to His Majesty, burning images and
temples, and committing all the other crimes?" This line of questioning implied an
unmistakable condemnation of the movement couched in religious language. Interestingly, the shrewdest prisoners turned the religious tenor of the questions in their
favor. For example, Alonzo Attuzayo, a widower from the pueblo of Alameda, admitted that he had done wrong in joining the rebels but went on to explain that
"the devil had blinded his heart and tricked him and for this reason he had done
those crazy things." Testimony of Alonzo Attuzayo, December 27, 1681, in De Marco,
"Voices from the Archives," part 1, 436. Juan, a married Indian from Tesuque, remarked that Pop'ay "speaks with the devil and for this reason everyone was terrorized
by him." Testimony of Juan, Tewa from Tesuque, December 18, 1681, 392. There were
nine prisoners but only eight testimonies because two brothers, Juan and Francisco
Lorenzo, declared jointly. See also testimony of Pedro Naranjo, December 24, 1681,
418; and testimony of Joseph, December 19, 1681, 404.

34. On earlier rebellion attempts, see testimony of Pedro Naranjo, December 24, 1681,
417; testimony of the lieutenant general of cavalry, December 20, 1681, 2:266; and
testimony of Sargento Mayor Luis de Quintana, December 22, 1681, 2:278. For
concise considerations of famines and epidemics, see Knaut, *The Pueblo Revolt of
1680*, 155–159; and John P. Wilson, "Before the Pueblo Revolt: Population Trends,
Apache Relations and Pueblo Abandonments in Seventeenth Century New Mexico," in Nancy Fox, ed., *Prehistory and History in the Southwest* (Santa Fe: Ancient
City Press, 1985), 118.

35. West makes clear that the Indian slaves of Parral came from New Mexico, Sonora,
and the region of the eastern Tobosos. West, *The Mining Community in Northern
New Spain*, 50 (map), 51–56. Deeds reaches the same conclusion when she writes,

"Slaving expeditions . . . continued to commandeer Apaches and Navajos from New Mexico, Pimas from Sonora, and hunter-gatherers, especially Tobosos, from the east." Deeds, *Defiance and Deference in Mexico's Colonial North,* 71.

36. Revolts broke out among the Acaxees in 1601–1603; the Xiximes in 1610; the Tepehuanes in 1616–1620; the Tobosos, Conchos, Salineros, and others in 1644–1645; and the Tarahumaras in 1648–1652. Yet the Great Northern Rebellion of the 1680s and 1690s dwarfed all previous resistance movements and changed the balance of power in significant ways. In effect, these rebels forced the colonists to rely less on slave labor. The composition of the workforce in the mines offers the best evidence of this transformation. Whereas in a seventeenth-century mine such as Parral, ten percent or more of all indigenous workers were slaves, by the end of that century labor arrangements had evolved. In an eighteenth-century mine such as Santa Eulalia, in the vicinity of Chihuahua City (which in many ways succeeded Parral as a regional magnet), there were few Indian slaves and almost no encomienda Indians. Santa Eulalia's workforce consisted primarily of salaried workers and repartimiento Indians coming from nearby missions to fulfill their labor obligations. To attract laborers, eighteenth-century miners were forced to rely on market incentives to a greater extent than their predecessors. See Roberto Baca, "La esclavitud y otras formas de servidumbre en Chihuahua: Una visión desde los archivos coloniales," in Jesús Vargas Valdés, ed., *Chihuahua: Horizontes de su historia y su cultura,* 2 vols. (Chihuahua: Milenio, 2010), 1:118–145; Cramaussel, "Encomiendas, repartimientos y conquista en Nueva Vizcaya"; Cheryl Martin, "El trabajo minero en Chihuahua, siglo XVIII," in *Actas del primero congreso de historia regional comparada 1989* (Ciudad Juárez: Universidad Autónoma de Ciudad Juárez, 1990), 185–196; Salvador Álvarez, "Agricultural Colonization and Mining Colonization: The Area of Chihuahua During the First Half of the Eighteenth Century," in Alan K. Craig and Robert C. West, eds., *In Quest of Mineral Wealth: Aboriginal and Colonial Mining and Metallurgy in Spanish America* (Baton Rouge: Geoscience Publications, 1994), 171–204; Deeds, "Rural Work in Nueva Vizcaya," 425–449; Deeds, *Defiance and Deference in Mexico's Colonial North,* chaps. 3, 4, and 5; Cheryl Martin, *Governance and Society in Colonial Mexico: Chihuahua in the Eighteenth Century* (Stanford, CA: Stanford University Press, 1996), chap. 3; and Philip L. Hadley, *Minería y sociedad en el centro minero de Santa Eulalia, Chihuahua, 1709–1750* (Mexico City: Fondo de Cultural Económica, 1979), 190–201.

## 7. POWERFUL NOMADS

1. For a pioneering study of Indian slavery in colonial America, see Almon Wheeler Lauber, *Indian Slavery in Colonial Times Within the Present Limits of the United States* (New York: Columbia University, 1913). For a more recent survey, see Barbara J. Olexer, *The Enslavement of the American Indian in Colonial Times* (Columbia, MD: Joyous, 2005). For the Carolinas and Florida, see Gallay, *The Indian Slave Trade;* Snyder, *Slavery in Indian Country;* and Krauthamer, *Black Slaves, Indian Masters.* Robbie Ethridge draws on the ideas of Ferguson and Whitehead, *War in the Tribal Zone.* As she writes, "In coining the term *militaristic slaving society* I hope to emphasize that

an Indian group's involvement in the commercial slave trade in eastern North America required that a society become militarized and that this militarization informed much about how a group acted and reacted to the events and opportunities that arose with the Indian slave trade." Ethridge, "Creating the Shatter Zone," 208. For the role of the Westo Indians, see Eric E. Bowne, *The Westo Indians: Slave Traders of the Early Colonial South* (Tuscaloosa: University of Alabama Press, 2005). For French Canada, see Rushforth, *Bonds of Alliance*.

2. Cecilia Sheridan, *Anónimos y Desterrados: La contienda por el "sitio que llaman de Quauyla," siglos XVI–XVIII* (Mexico City: CIESAS, 2000); Cecilia Sheridan, "Social Control and Native Territoriality in Northeastern New Spain," in Jesús F. de la Teja and Ross Frank, eds., *Choice, Persuasion, and Coercion: Social Control on Spain's North American Frontiers* (Albuquerque: University of New Mexico Press, 2005), 121–148. Sheridan elaborates on cases such as the Tobosos and Alazapas. Similarly, Carlos Manuel Valdés has written about the lives of two adolescents, Negrito and Miguelillo, who were caught stealing horses in 1666. Their trial reveals that they were part of a mixed Native community that operated in a gigantic quadrangle extending two hundred miles south from the Texas border and that they traded horses and captives with no less than twenty-five different Indian nations. Negrito was the son of an African slave who grew up around the mining towns of San Luis Potosí. He was later kidnapped by an Indian group known as the Momones and traded to another group called the Bobosirigames for a white horse. Miguelillo was an Indian from the Tusare nation who had been baptized in Parras but ultimately chose a roving existence. Valdés, *La gente del mezquite: Los nómadas del noreste de la Colonia* (Mexico City: CIESAS-INI, 1995), 199–201.

3. The quotes are from Diego de Vargas, letters of July 13 and October 4, 1692, in Forbes, *Apache, Navaho, and Spaniard*, 237–241; his diary entry for November 22, 1692, in John L. Kessell and Rick Hendricks, eds., *By Force of Arms: The Journals of Don Diego de Vargas, 1691–1693* (Albuquerque: University of New Mexico Press, 1992), 208; and J. Manuel Espinosa, *Crusaders of the Río Grande* (Salisbury, NC: Documentary Publications, 1977), 100. See also Charles L. Kenner, *The Comanchero Frontier: A History of New Mexican–Plains Indian Relations* (Norman: University of Oklahoma Press, 1994), 19, 26–27. Matthew Liebmann reminds us that these relationships were complex. For example, relations between Jemez and the Utes actually deteriorated during the interregnum of 1680–1692. Liebmann, *Revolt*, 42, 97–98. On the instability and violence that characterized Pueblo-Ute relations more broadly, see Blackhawk, *Violence over the Land*, especially 32–33.

4. For the background of this trade, see Katherine A. Spielmann, "Late Prehistoric Exchange Between the Southwest and Southern Plains," *Plains Anthropologist* 28:101 (1983), 257–272; Katherine A. Spielmann, "Colonists, Hunters, and Farmers: Plains-Pueblo Interaction in the Seventeenth Century," in D. H. Thomas, ed., *Columbian Consequences*, vol. 1, *Archaeological and Historical Perspectives on the Spanish Borderlands West* (Washington, DC: Smithsonian Institution Press, 1989), 101–113; and Spielmann et al., "'. . . Being Weary, They Had Rebelled,'" 101–125.

5. Francis Haines, "The Northward Spread of Horses Among the Plains Indians," *American Anthropologist* 40:3 (July–September 1938), 430–431; Pekka Hämäläinen, "The Rise and Fall of Plains Indian Horse Cultures," *Journal of American History* 90 (December 2003), 836–837.

6. The anti-Spanish Pueblo–Plains Indian movement of 1704–1705 has received very little attention from historians. One of the reasons is that the records are scattered. For Juan Páez Hurtado's investigation, see "Diligencias sobre haber contraído amistad los pueblos con los infieles," Santa Fe, 1704–1705. This was one of the items gathered by the Hemenway Southwestern Archaeological Expedition and now housed at the Peabody Museum, Harvard University. I consulted the microfilm version: Hemenway Expedition, New Mexico State Records Center and Archives, roll 2, vols. 8–13. Correspondence and testimonies pertaining to Páez Hurtado's investigation can also be found in "Record of Proceedings re Reported Conspiracy Between Pueblo Indians and Apaches and Utes," Santa Fe, December 12, 1704, to February 28, 1705, Spanish Archives of New Mexico, roll 3, frames 927–963. To be sure, these closer Pueblo-Plains Indian associations could be volatile, shifting from peaceful barter to mutual predation and enslavement. It was an unstable embrace between agriculturalists and nomads based on economic convenience, nutritional complementarity, and bonds of enslavement and kinship.

7. Hämäläinen, *The Comanche Empire*, chap. 1; Thomas W. Kavanagh, *The Comanches: A History, 1706–1875* (Lincoln: University of Nebraska Press, 1996), 28–132; Rivaya-Martínez, "Captivity and Adoption Among the Comanche Indians," chap. 2; Blackhawk, *Violence over the Land*, chap. 1; Elizabeth A. John, *Storms Brewed in Other Men's Worlds: The Confrontation of Indians, Spanish, and French in the Southwest, 1540–1795* (College Station: Texas A&M University Press, 1975), 117–121.

8. Friar Miguel de Menchero, apostolic preacher and officer of the Inquisition, Santa Bárbara, May 10, 1744, in Hackett, *Historical Documents*, 3:401–402. The exact ethnicity of this individual will remain ambiguous forever not only because it is not clear whether "Ponna" really means Pawnee but also because French trappers often referred to Indian slaves as "Pawnees" without necessarily implying a specific ethnic affiliation. See Richard White, *The Roots of Dependency: Subsistence, Environment, and Social Change Among the Choctaws, Pawnees, and Navajos* (Lincoln: University of Nebraska Press, 1983), 152.

9. Friar Pedro Serrano to the viceroy of Mexico, n.p., 1761, in Hackett, *Historical Documents,* 3:486–487.

10. In 1639 Governor Rosas sent a force against a band of Utes who had entered New Mexico not as assertive traders, but as slaves bound for the silver mines of Chihuahua. Had Comanches lived closer to New Mexico at that time, they may well have suffered the same fate. See Blackhawk, *Violence over the Land*, 47. This does not mean that the Spaniards stopped raiding the surrounding nomads in the eighteenth century. In 1716 a Spanish detachment attacked a group of Utes, taking dozens of captives. Ibid., 38.

11. The beheading incident is narrated in Alfred Barnaby Thomas, *After Coronado: Spanish Exploration Northeast of New Mexico, 1696–1727; Documents from the Archives of*

*Spain, Mexico, and New Mexico* (Norman: University of Oklahoma Press, 1935), 13–14. This episode is also discussed in Russell M. Magnaghi, "Plains Indians in New Mexico: The Genízaro Experience," *Great Plains Quarterly* 10:2 (Spring 1990), 87–88. Magnaghi writes that the "utopian-minded" New Laws of 1542 were "all but ignored," that the principle of "just wars" justified the enslavement of non-Christian Indians, and that the *Recopilación de las leyes de Indias* "carefully spelled out the Christian obligation to ransom captive Indians enslaved by other Indian tribes." I was unable to find any such regulation for ransoming Indians in book 7, title 7, laws 2 and 17, cited by Magnaghi. Book 7 actually deals with royal officials. In book 6, title 2, law 1, the *Recopilación* explicitly refers back to the New Laws of 1542 and prohibits the enslavement of Indians under all circumstances, even slaves taken in "just wars" or ransomed from other Indians, as stated in chapter 5 of this book. As noted earlier, the general tenor of book 6, title 2 is to prohibit any enslavement of Indians "except when expressly permitted by the crown." In the following laws, only the enslavement of the cannibalistic Carib Indians and the Muslim inhabitants of Mindanao, in the Philippines, is permitted. *Recopilación de las leyes de Indias,* http://fondosdigitales.us.es/fondos /libros/752/1030/recopilacion-de-leyes-de-los-reynos-de-las-indias/.

12. For a sound overview of trade relations between the New Mexicans and the Comanches and Utes in the 1700s, see Cheryl Foote, "Spanish-Indian Trade Along New Mexico's Northern Frontier in the Eighteenth Century," *Journal of the West* 24:2 (April 1985), 22–33.

13. Instructions left by Governor Cachupín to his successor, Francisco Marín del Valle, Santa Fe, August 12, 1754, in Alfred Barnaby Thomas, *The Plains Indians and New Mexico, 1751–1778* (Albuquerque: University of New Mexico Press, 1940), 129–143. On the treaty with the Comanches and Utes, see also Hämäläinen, *The Comanche Empire,* 47–48; and Blackhawk, *Violence over the Land,* 63–64.

14. Friar Menchero, Santa Bárbara, May 10, 1744. The genízaro settlement of Tomé was built on the site of an earlier community. In the 1660s, Tomé Dominguez de Mendoza had established a hacienda in the area and given his name to the place. On the 1733 genízaro petition, see Malcolm Ebright and Rick Hendricks, *The Witches of Abiquiu: The Governor, the Priest, the Genízaro Indians, and the Devil* (Albuquerque: University of New Mexico Press, 2006), 28–29. For a broader consideration of the captive exchange in New Mexico, see Brooks, *Captives and Cousins.* See also Doris Swann Avery, "Into the Den of Evils: The Genízaros of Colonial New Mexico" (master's thesis, University of Montana, 2008); Joaquín Rivaya-Martínez, "Reflexión historiográfica sobre los genízaros de Nuevo México, una comunidad pluriétnica del septentrión novohispano," in David Carbajal López, ed., *Familias pluriétnicas y mestizaje en la Nueva España y el Río de la Plata* (Guadalajara: Universidad de Guadalajara, 2014); Hämäläinen, *The Comanche Empire,* 38–39; and James F. Brooks, "'We Betray Our Own Nation': Indian Slavery and Multi-ethnic Communities in the Southwest Borderlands," in Alan Gallay, ed., *Indian Slavery in Colonial America* (Lincoln: University of Nebraska Press, 2009), 319–351.

15. Gary Anderson, *The Indian Southwest, 1580–1830* (Norman: University of Oklahoma Press, 1999), chaps. 4 and 5; Hämäläinen, *The Comanche Empire,* 28–29.

16. For the Apache settlements known to archaeologists as the Dismal River Culture, see Waldo R. Wedel, *Central Plains Prehistory: Holocene Environments and Culture Change in the Republican River Basin* (Lincoln: University of Nebraska Press, 1986), chap. 8. Expeditions led by Juan de Ulibarri, Antonio de Valverde, and Pedro de Villasur visited these Apache settlements. See Thomas, *After Coronado,* passim.

17. Hämäläinen, *The Comanche Empire,* 28–32; Pekka Hämäläinen, "The Western Comanche Trade Center: Rethinking the Plains Indian Trade System," *Western Historical Quarterly* 29:4 (Winter 1998), 485–513; Kavanagh, *The Comanches,* 66. The quote is from Pedro de Rivera to Casa Fuerte, Presidio del Paso del Norte, September 26, 1727, in Thomas, *After Coronado,* 211.

18. The quotes are from Governor Antonio de Valverde, La Cieneguilla, September 21, 1719, and General Juan Domingo de Bustamante, Santa Fe, November 8, 1723, both in Thomas, *After Coronado,* 112–113 and 194, respectively.

19. On pre-contact Cherokee slaving practices, see Theda Perdue, *Slavery and the Evolution of Cherokee Society, 1540–1866* (Knoxville: University of Tennessee Press, 1979), 3–18. On the early Iroquois, see Richter, "War and Culture," 528–559; and Parmenter, *The Edge of the Woods,* xliii–xliv, 45–51. Joaquín Rivaya-Martínez has recently argued that the Comanche practice of adopting outsiders was primarily driven by their desire to appropriate these captives' labor rather than to replace lost population, as other scholars have assumed. He has shown that Comanche raiding expeditions often resulted in more deaths of Comanches than captives assimilated into their society. Rivaya-Martínez, "A Different Look at Native American Depopulation: Comanche Raiding, Captive Taking, and Population Decline," *Ethnohistory* 61:3 (Summer 2014), 391–418.

20. The quote is from Rivaya-Martínez, "Captivity and Adoption Among the Comanche Indians," 47–48. For the importance of the hide trade, see Hämäläinen, *The Comanche Empire,* 247–249. For a good description of women's work among the Comanches, see Rister, *Border Captives,* 14–16. Rister's book was published in 1940. More recently, Joaquín Rivaya-Martínez has de-emphasized the physical challenges of Comanche captives and stressed instead other psychological, cultural, and reproductive factors that shaped their lives. See Rivaya-Martínez, "Becoming Comanches: Patterns of Captive Incorporation into Comanche Kinship Networks, 1820–1875," in David Adams and Crista DeLuzio, eds., *On the Borders of Love and Power: Families and Kinship in the Intercultural American Southwest* (Berkeley: University of California Press, 2012), 47–70.

21. Rivaya-Martínez, "Captivity and Adoption Among the Comanche Indians," especially chap. 2; Brian DeLay, *War of a Thousand Deserts,* 92. The testimonies of Mexican captives taken by Comanches in the nineteenth century attest to this dynamic more clearly. See Cuauhtémoc Velasco Ávila, *En manos de los bárbaros: Testimonios de la guerra india en el noreste* (Mexico City: Breve Fondo Editorial, 1996), 18.

22. On the extent of the Comanchería, see Hämäläinen, *The Comanche Empire,* 59, 66. For a demographic discussion of the Comanches in the eighteenth century, see Rivaya Martínez, "Captivity and Adoption Among the Comanche Indians," chap. 3; and Rivaya-Martínez, "A Different Look at Native American Depopulation," 393–394.

23. John, *Storms Brewed in Other Men's Worlds;* Kavanagh, *The Comanches;* Hämäläinen, *The Comanche Empire;* DeLay, *War of a Thousand Deserts,* 105; Rushforth, *Bonds of Alliance,* 239–242.

24. For estimates of the proportion of slaves held by the Comanches, see Hämäläinen, *The Comanche Empire,* 250. Hämäläinen calls Comanche captives an "evaporating resource," because many of them were either traded away or assimilated into Comanche society. Rivaya-Martínez also makes the interesting point that in his sample, only a small proportion (around eleven percent) remained with their captors for the balance of their lives. A majority escaped or were killed or traded away. Rivaya-Martínez, "A Different Look at Native American Depopulation," 405–406. For a critique of the distinction between "societies with slaves" and "slave societies" first proposed by Moses Finley, see Rivaya-Martínez, "Captivity and Adoption Among the Comanche Indians," 335–336. Fernando Santos-Granero has studied the proportion of slaves in various early Native American societies and concluded that the ratio fluctuated between five and nineteen percent of the total population. The Comanches fit into this range fairly well. Santos-Granero, *Vital Enemies,* conclusions.

25. Blackhawk, *Violence over the Land,* passim.

26. For information on Ute seasonal movements, see the report of Governor Fernando de la Conacha, quoted in Blackhawk, *Violence over the Land,* 65.

27. Knack, *Boundaries Between,* 20–31.

28. This lifestyle characterized not only Paiutes but also other peoples of the Great Basin. See Steven J. Crum, *The Road on Which We Came: A History of the Western Shoshone* (Salt Lake City: University of Utah Press, 1994), 1–5.

29. William Wolfskill, quoted in J. Cecil Alter, ed., "Journal of Orange Clark and George Yount," *California Historical Quarterly* 2 (April 1923), 13; Mark Twain, quoted in Blackhawk, *Violence over the Land,* 11.

30. Knack, *Boundaries Between,* 30–36; Leroy R. Hafen and Ann W. Hafen, *Old Spanish Trail: Santa Fe to Los Angeles* (Lincoln: University of Nebraska Press, 1993), 261–273. For a broader consideration of the autonomous world created by Natives, see Natale A. Zappia, "Indigenous Borderlands: Livestock, Captivity, and Power in the Far West," *Pacific Historical Review* 81:2 (May 2012), 193–220; and Natale A. Zappia, *Traders and Raiders: The Indigenous World of the Colorado Basin, 1540–1859* (Chapel Hill: University of North Carolina Press, 2014), passim.

31. Ted J. Warner and Fray Angelico Chavez, eds., *The Dominguez-Escalante Journal: Their Expedition Through Colorado, Utah, Arizona, and New Mexico in 1776* (Salt Lake City: University of Utah Press, 1995), 91–92, 101–102.

32. For the parish records, see Thomas D. Martínez, *Abiquiu Baptisms, 1754–1870: Baptism Database of Archives Held by the Archdiocese of Santa Fe and the State Archive of New Mexico* (San Jose, CA: published by author, 1993). These records are organized by last name and in chronological order. At least 152 "Ute" boys and girls were baptized between 1754 and 1870, not counting scores of others identified simply as "Indian." For a broader discussion of the role of Abiquiu and the distribution of these entries, see Blackhawk, *Violence over the Land,* 71–75.

33. For the meaning of "yuta" and the broader patterns of the enslavement of Indians

in New Mexico as revealed by parish records, see Brugge, *Navajos in the Catholic Church Records of New Mexico,* 18–19; and Blackhawk, *Violence over the Land,* 71–75. On the 1752 peace agreement between the New Mexicans and Utes, see Joseph Lobato to Governor Tomás Vélez Cachupín, San Juan de los Caballeros, August 17, 1752, in Thomas, *The Plains Indians and New Mexico,* 117–118.

34. On the opening of the trail and the role of Spanish slavers, see Joseph P. Sánchez, *Explorers, Traders, and Slavers: Forging the Old Spanish Trail, 1678–1850* (Salt Lake City: University of Utah Press, 1997). For a more detailed look at the case of one slaver, see Sondra Jones, *The Trial of Don Pedro León Luján* (Salt Lake City: University of Utah Press, 2000). For the broader context, see Bailey, *Indian Slave Trade in the Southwest,* especially section 3 on the Great Basin; and Estévan Rael-Gálvez, "Identifying Captivity and Capturing Identity: Narratives of American Indian Slavery, Colorado and New Mexico, 1776–1934" (Ph.D. diss., University of Michigan, 2002), especially chap. 1.

35. On the Arze-García case, see Leland Hargrave Creer, "Spanish American Slave Trade in the Great Basin, 1800–1853," *New Mexico Historical Review* 24:3 (July 1949), 171–182; Bailey, *Indian Slave Trade in the Southwest,* 136–137; and Hafen and Hafen, *Old Spanish Trail,* 264–266.

36. The quotes from Wootton and Farnham are cited in Hafen and Hafen, *Old Spanish Trail,* 267.

37. For the Jones quote, see Daniel W. Jones, *Forty Years Among the Indians* (Los Angeles: Westernlore Press, 1960), chap. 7. For a brief recapitulation of the trade in Utes and Paiutes, as well as excellent quotations from nineteenth-century Americans, see Carling Malouf and A. Arline Malouf, "The Effects of Spanish Slavery on the Indians of the Intermountain West," *Southwestern Journal of Anthropology* 1:3 (Autumn 1945), 378–391.

38. The evidence for slaves among pre-Columbian agricultural societies in monuments, vessels, Indian languages, and early European documents is quite abundant. Some of the sources of this information include Redmond and Spencer, "From Raiding to Conquest"; Clendinnen, *Aztecs;* Richter, "War and Culture"; Parmenter, *The Edge of the Woods,* xliii–xliv and 45–51; Fox, "Events as Seen from the North"; and Donald, *Aboriginal Slavery on the Northwest Coast of North America.* I learned that some nomadic societies on the coast of Texas refused to accept castaways who willingly offered themselves as slaves while I was researching a previous book about the Pánfilo de Narváez expedition to Florida. See Andrés Reséndez, *A Land So Strange: The Epic Journey of Cabeza de Vaca* (New York: Basic, 2007), passim.

## 8. MISSIONS, PRESIDIOS, AND SLAVES

1. Among the works that emphasize Native power, see Kathleen Duval, *The Native Ground: Indians and Colonists in the Heart of the Continent* (Philadelphia: University of Pennsylvania Press, 2007); Hämäläinen, *The Comanche Empire;* and Blackhawk, *Violence over the Land.* The information on silver production comes from TePaske, *A New World of Gold and Silver,* 110–113. For a brief discussion of the reasons behind

this boom, see Brown, *A History of Mining in Latin America,* 29–35. The works of Thomas Sheridan and Paul Conrad, "Captive Fates," have been especially influential in shaping my thinking for this chapter. For an overview of the mass deportation of Apaches, see Mark Santiago, *The Jar of Severed Hands: Spanish Deportation of Apache Prisoners of War, 1770–1810* (Norman: University of Oklahoma Press, 2011).

2. Herbert E. Bolton, "The Mission as a Frontier Institution in the Spanish American Colonies," *American Historical Review* 23:1 (October 1917), 42–43, 46, 61. For an intellectual biography of Bolton, see Albert Hurtado, *Herbert Eugene Bolton: Historian of the American Borderlands* (Berkeley: University of California Press, 2012).

3. Bolton was extremely influential both as a scholar and as a teacher of a subsequent generation of frontier historians. See especially David J. Weber, "Turner, the Boltonians, and the Borderlands," *American Historical Review* 91 (February 1986), 313–323; and Hurtado, *Herbert Eugene Bolton,* passim. For a more recent appraisal, see Samuel Truett, "Epics of Greater America: Herbert Eugene Bolton's Quest for a Transnational American History," in Christopher Schmidt-Nowara and John Nieto-Phillips, eds., *Interpreting Spanish Colonialism* (Albuquerque: University of New Mexico Press, 2005), 213–247. On Bolton's one-sidedness, see Albert H. Hurtado, "Herbert E. Bolton, Racism, and American History," *Pacific Historical Review* 62 (May 1993), 127–142; and Hurtado, *Herbert Eugene Bolton,* 91, 102. The mission literature is vast. See Susan M. Deeds, "Indigenous Responses to Mission Settlement in Nueva Vizcaya," in Erick Langer and Robert H. Jackson, eds., *The New Latin American Mission History* (Lincoln: University of Nebraska Press, 1995), 77–108; Cecilia Sheridan, *Anónimos y Desterrados;* Ignacio Almada Bay, José Marcos Median Bustos, and María del Valle Borrero, "Hacia una nueva interpretación del régimen colonial en Sonora: Descubriendo a los indios y redimensionando a los misioneros," *Región y Sociedad* 19 (2007), 237–265; Matthew M. Babcock, "Turning Apaches into Spaniards: North America's Forgotten Indian Reservations" (Ph.D. diss., Southern Methodist University, 2008); Cynthia Radding, *Wandering Peoples: Colonialism, Ethnic Spaces, and Ecological Frontiers in Northwestern Mexico, 1700–1850* (Durham, NC: Duke University Press, 1997); and José Refugio De la Torre Curiel, *Twilight of the Mission Frontier: Shifting Interethnic Alliances and Social Organization in Sonora, 1768–1855* (Stanford, CA: Stanford University Press, 2012), 17–28.

4. On the expansion of presidios, see Max L. Moorhead, *The Presidio: Bastion of the Spanish Borderlands* (Norman: University of Oklahoma Press, 1975), 54–55; Weber, *The Spanish Frontier in North America,* 204–235; Charles W. Polzer and Thomas E. Sheridan, eds., *The Presidio and Militia on the Northern Frontier of New Spain: A Documentary History,* vol. 2, part 1, *The Californias and Sinaloa-Sonora, 1700–1765* (Tucson: University of Arizona Press, 1997); and Thomas H. Naylor and Charles W. Polzer, eds., *Pedro de Rivera and the Military Regulations for Northern New Spain, 1724–1729* (Tucson: University of Arizona Press, 1988), passim.

5. For the best early description of the Seris, see Jesuit Adam Gilg to the Jesuits of Brünn, Sonora, February 1692, in Julio César Montané Martí, "Una Carta del Padre Adam Gilg S.J. sobre los Seris, 1692," *Revista de El Colegio de Sonora* 7:12 (1996), 431. On turtle hunting, see Richard Felger and Mary Beck Moser, *People of the Desert and Sea:*

*Ethnobotany of the Seri Indians* (Tucson: University of Arizona Press, 1985), 42–50; and Gary Paul Nabhan, *Singing the Turtles to Sea: The Comcáac (Seri) Art and Science of Reptiles* (Berkeley: University of California Press, 2003). On eelgrass, see Thomas E. Sheridan and Richard Stephen Felger, "Indian Utilization of Eelgrass (*Zostera Marina L.*) in Northwestern Mexico: The Spanish Colonial Record," *Kiva* 43:2 (1977), 89–104; and Felger and Moser, *People of the Desert and Sea*, 376–382. Molecular anthropologist Brian Kemp provided information about the haplogroup distribution of Seri Indians' mtDNA. Kemp, personal communication. For the Y-chromosome information, see Ripan Mahli et al., "Distribution of Y Chromosomes Among Native North Americans: A Study of Athapaskan Population History," *American Journal of Physical Anthropology* 137 (2008), 412–424. Up until a few years ago, some linguists still believed that Seri was part of the Hokan stock. However, this connection is elusive and nearly impossible to prove. See S. A. Marlett, "The Seri and Salinan Connection Revisited," *International Journal of American Linguistics* 74:3 (2008), 393–399.

6. Gilg to the Jesuits of Brünn, February 1692, 144–151.

7. The quote is from Father Juan Fernández, transcribed and translated in Thomas E. Sheridan, ed., *Empire of Sand: The Seri Indians and the Struggle for Spanish Sonora, 1645–1803* (Tucson: University of Arizona Press, 1999), 31–33. Evidence of large yields is plentiful. See, for example, María Soledad Arbelaez, "The Sonoran Missions and Indian Raids of the Eighteenth Century," *Journal of the Southwest* 33:3 (Autumn 1991), 371. For the most detailed information about surplus production at the Sonoran missions, see Radding, *Wandering Peoples*, 75–99.

8. On the origins of Pópulo, see Gilg to the Jesuits of Brünn, February 1692, 149; and Edward H. Spicer, *Cycles of Conquest: The Impact of Spain, Mexico, and the United States on the Indians of the Southwest, 1533–1960* (Tucson: University of Arizona Press, 1962), 105. On the 1700 incursions into the lands of the Seris, see Juan M. Manje, *Unknown Arizona and Sonora, 1693–1701* (Tucson: Arizona Silhouettes, 1954), 146–149; and Bautista de Escalante's diary, cited in Sheridan, *Empire of Sand*, 37–70. See also George B. Eckhart, "The Seri Indian Missions," *Kiva* 25:3 (February 1960), 39–40.

9. On estimates of the number of Seris living in the missions and the difficulties of reaching Tiburón and San Esteban, see Sheridan, *Empire of Sand*, 8–10, 97–99. For a classic work on the regions of refuge, see Gonzalo Aguirre Beltrán, *Regions of Refuge* (Washington, DC: Society for Applied Anthropology, 1979), passim.

10. On the different bands of Seris, see Sheridan, *Empire of Sand*, 9–10, 19–20. María Soledad Arbelaez shows that Indians focused their raids primarily on horses and cattle. Arbelaez, "The Sonoran Missions and Indian Raids of the Eighteenth Century," 366–385. On the back-and-forth movement of Seris between missions and zones of refuge, see Thomas E. Sheridan, "Cross or Arrow?: The Breakdown in Spanish-Seri Relations, 1729–1750," *Arizona and the West* 21:4 (Winter 1979), 317–334.

11. On presidios as garrisons and prisons, see Norwood Andrews, "Muros de prisiones, espacios carcelarios y fronteras" (presentation in Ciudad Real, Spain, June 13, 2013).

12. The first quote is from article 190 of the regulations of 1729, cited in Naylor and Polzer, *Pedro de Rivera*, 279. The second quote is from Jack Jackson, ed., *Imaginary Kingdom: Texas as Seen by the Rivera and Rubí Military Expeditions, 1727 and 1767*

(Austin: Texas State Historical Association, 1995), 205. See also Santiago, *The Jar of Severed Hands,* 36–37.

13. This entire section is based on "Averiguación sobre los indios presos en el presidio de San Pedro de la Conquista del Pitic," conducted by José Rafael Rodríguez Gallardo, July–August 1748, Presidio de San Pedro de la Conquista, Sonora, AGN, Inquisición, L. 1282, pp. 366–432. For the larger context, see Rafael Rodríguez Gallardo, *Informe sobre Sinaloa y Sonora, año de 1750* (Mexico City: Archivo General de la Nación, 1975); and Polzer and Sheridan, *The Presidio,* vol. 2, part 1, *The Californias and Sinaloa-Sonora, 1700–1765,* 253–408. For the larger context, see Radding, *Wandering Peoples,* 40–43; and De la Torre Curiel, *Twilight of the Mission Frontier,* 17–28.

14. "Averiguación sobre los indios presos en el presidio de San Pedro de la Conquista del Pitic" contains very graphic testimony of the tortures and provides unusually detailed information about the circumstances surrounding the imprisonment and deaths of these three individuals. See also Flavio Molina Molina, "Instrumentos de hechicería usados por pimas de Onavas, 1743," in *Memorias del IV simposio de historia de Sonora* (Hermosillo: Instituto de Investigaciones Históricas, 1979).

15. Rodríguez Gallardo himself wrote in his *averiguación* that "even when Indians receive wages their service is still involuntary."

16. In addition to Rodríguez Gallardo's, see "Investigación by Juez Pesquisidor Rodríguez Gallardo of Indian Prisoners at Pitic," in Polzer and Sheridan, *The Presidio,* vol. 2, part 1, *The Californias and Sinaloa-Sonora, 1700–1765,* 353–370; and Sheridan, "Cross or Arrow?," 317–334.

17. "Father Miranda on the Impact of Horcasitas Presidio on the Mission Seris, 1749," in Sheridan, *Empire of Sand,* 148. See also Sheridan, "Cross or Arrow?," 323–325; and "Protest of Father Provincial Andrés García on the Transfer of Pitic, 1749," and "On the Building of Horcasitas, 1750," both in Polzer and Sheridan, *The Presidio,* vol. 2, part 1, *The Californias and Sinaloa-Sonora, 1700–1765,* 371–380 and 381–393, respectively. For additional context, see "Relación of Father Nicolás Perera, 1750," in Sheridan, *Empire of Sand,* 161–162; and Radding, *Wandering Peoples,* 155–156. On the presidio of Janos, see Blyth, *Chiricahua and Janos.*

18. The quotes are from "Relación of Father Nicolás Perera," 161–162.

19. Rodríguez Gallardo, *Informe sobre Sinaloa y Sonora,* 10–11, 102–103; Juan Nentvig, *Rudo Ensayo* (Tucson: University of Arizona Press, 1980), 134.

20. Rodríguez Gallardo, *Informe sobre Sinaloa y Sonora,* 10–11, 102–103. Sheridan provides additional details about the collera of Seris dispatched by Rodríguez Gallardo in "Cross or Arrow?," 324. The two Seri escapees were almost certainly Manuel el queretano—thus nicknamed after his stint in an *obraje* (sweatshop) in Querétaro—and his son Marcos. "Ortiz Parrilla and the Jesuits Propose to Deport the Seris, 1750," in Sheridan, *Empire of Sand,* 171.

21. The quote is from "Decree of Governor Ortiz Parrilla Ordering the Expedition to Tiburón Island, 1750," in Sheridan, *Empire of Sand,* 165–168. On the expulsion plan, see also Nentvig, *Rudo Ensayo,* 133–134; and "Ortiz Parrilla and the Jesuits Propose to Deport the Seris," 169–176. For the Tobosos and Apaches, see Conrad, "Captive Fates,"

and Santiago, *The Jar of Severed Hands*. For the banishment of vagrants to the Philippines, see Eva Maria Mehl, "Vagrants, Idlers and Troublemakers in the Philippines, 1765–1861" (Ph.D. diss., University of California, Davis, 2011).

22. "Ortiz Parrilla and the Jesuits Propose to Deport the Seris," 171–172.

23. The chaplain of the expedition, Father Francisco Antonio Pimentel, kept a diary of his experiences. See "Pimentel's Diary of the Expedition to Tiburón Island, 1750," in Sheridan, *Empire of Sand*, 177–231. For a blow-by-blow account, see Sheridan, "Cross or Arrow?," 327–333.

24. The quote is from Nentvig, *Rudo Ensayo*, 75–76. The mission records of Tumacácori contain fifty-one references to Seri Indians. "Mission 2000: Searchable Spanish Mission Records," Tumacácori National Historical Park, http://home.nps.gov /applications/tuma/search.cfm. Some of the other Indians included under the rubric "nijoras" or "nixoras" were Seris.

25. Several scholars have shed light on various aspects of the presidial frontier. One place to start is the classic work by Max Moorhead, *The Presidio: Bastion of the Spanish Borderlands*. See also the following compilations of documents: Naylor and Polzer, *The Presidio*, vol. 1, *1570–1700*; Polzer and Sheridan, *The Presidio*, vol. 2, part 1, *The Californias and Sinaloa-Sonora, 1700–1765*; and Diana Hadley, Thomas H. Naylor, and Mardith K. Schuetz-Miller, eds., *The Presidio and Militia on the Northern Frontier of New Spain: A Documentary History*, vol. 2, part 2, *The Central Corridor and the Texas Corridor, 1700–1765* (Tucson: University of Arizona Press, 1997). Another key work is William B. Griffen, *Apaches at War and Peace: The Janos Presidio, 1750–1858* (Norman: University of Oklahoma Press, 1988). The most recent and suggestive works include Conrad, "Captive Fates"; Santiago, *The Jar of Severed Hands*; Babcock, "Turning Apaches into Spaniards"; and Blyth, *Chiricahua and Janos*.

26. For figures and other statistical information on Apache prisoners, see Santiago, *The Jar of Severed Hands*, 201–202. Conrad includes non-Apache captives in his estimates, which are the ones I have used here. Conrad, "Captive Fates," 212–213. For a suggestive interpretation of the start of the Apache wars, see Sara Ortelli, *Trama de una Guerra conveniente: Nueva Vizcaya y la sombra de los apaches, 1748–1790* (Mexico City: El Colegio de México, 2007).

27. Advice of Marquis of Croix copied in San Carlos, July 9, 1770, AGN, Provincias Internas, 31, fols. 332–342. The escape while the soldiers were occupied with the Indian women took place at a much earlier time. See judicial proceedings, Parras, September 1723–January 1724, Main Library, University of Arizona, Tucson, microfilm 318, reel 1723A, frames 72–81. For a brief biographical sketch of Viceroy Croix, see Herbert Ingram Priestley, *José de Gálvez: Visitor-General of New Spain, 1765–1771* (Berkeley: University of California Press, 1916), 164 n. 70.

28. Pedro de Nava to Marquis of Branciforte, Chihuahua, November 14, 1797, AGN, Provincias Internas, vol. 208, exp. 13, fols. 482–528.

29. Report of Juan Antonio de Araujo, Hospicio de Pobres, January 17, 1798; second report of Juan Antonio de Araujo, January 22, 1798; report of Manuel de Villerias, Mexico City, February 1, 1798; and third report of Juan Antonio de Araujo, February 13,

1798, all in AGN, Provincias Internas, vol. 208, exp. 13, fols. 482–528. For the larger context of the illness, see the excellent book by Elizabeth Fenn, *Pox Americana: The Great Smallpox Epidemic of 1775–82.*

30. Report of Manuel de Villerias, Mexico City, February 1, 1798. On the Acordada, see Teresa Lozano Armendares, "Recinto de maldades y lamentos: La cárcel de la Acordada," *Estudios de Historia Novohispana* 13 (1993), 149–157.

31. For how yellow fever and malaria have shaped the history of tropical and subtropical America, see J. R. McNeill, *Mosquito Empires: Ecology and War in the Greater Caribbean, 1620–1914* (New York: Cambridge University Press, 2010).

32. The aggregate demographic information is still somewhat fragmentary, so it is hard to determine with precision the incidence of epidemics in these drives. Santiago's *Jar of Severed Hands* includes an appendix listing each collera, including the number of men, women, children; individuals who managed to escape, were left behind, or were "deposited" with Christian families along the way; and, most important for our purposes, those who died or were killed before reaching their final destination. Santiago, *The Jar of Severed Hands,* 203. Conrad's "Captive Fates" has a more extensive appendix with aggregate demographic information that includes not only Apaches but other Indians of northern Mexico. It does not, however, distinguish between prisoners who escaped, who were deposited, or who died along the way. In aggregate numbers, out of 3,317 who started out, only 1,627 — less than half — reached their final destination. Conrad, "Captive Fates," 256–258. For a discussion of the spread of epidemic disease, see Ann F. Ramenofsky, "The Problem of Introduced Infectious Diseases in New Mexico, A.D. 1540–1680," *Journal of Anthropological Research* 52:2 (Summer 1996), 161–184.

33. Donald B. Cooper, *Epidemic Disease in Mexico City, 1761–1813: An Administrative, Social, and Medical Study* (Austin: University of Texas Press, 1965), 56–69; Fenn, *Pox Americana,* 138–166. For the colleras of 1778, see Conrad, "Captive Fates," 256.

34. Conrad, "Captive Fates," 256.

## 9. CONTRACTIONS AND EXPANSIONS

1. Gallay, *The Indian Slave Trade;* Rushforth, *Bonds of Alliance;* Snyder, *Slavery in Indian Country;* Krauthamer, *Black Slaves, Indian Masters.*

2. In 1813 the rebel priest José María Morelos presented a plan to the Constituent Congress known as the Sentiments of the Nation. It called for "the abolition of slavery forever" and the elimination of "all distinctions of caste so we shall all be equal, and only vice or virtue will distinguish one from another." By "slavery" Morelos really meant African slavery. Although African slaves constituted a small percentage of Mexico's overall workforce in 1813, they were highly concentrated in southern Mexico, where Morelos was from. But he also had in mind other forms of labor coercion that affected Indians throughout the emerging nation. Three weeks after the publication of the Sentiments of the Nation, Morelos, as the main insurgent leader, specifically instructed officials "not to enslave the Indians from the communities through personal services." Article 15 of the Sentiments of the Nation, Chilpancingo, September 14, 1813, and or-

ders by Morelos reaffirming the abolition of slavery, Chilpancingo, October 5, 1813, both in Carlos Herrejón, ed., *Morelos Antología Documental* (Mexico City: SEP, 1985), 134 and 136, respectively. Nonwhites also took part in various independence movements in South America and often did so in the hope of obtaining freedom. See Peter Blanchard, *Under the Flags of Freedom: Slave Soldiers and the Wars of Independence in Spanish South America* (Pittsburgh: University of Pittsburgh Press, 2008).

3. For this expansion, see especially DeLay, *War of a Thousand Deserts,* and Babcock, "Turning Apaches into Spaniards." See also specific citations in the following notes.

4. Miguel Ramos Arizpe to Lucas Alamán, Puebla, August 1, 1830, Herbert E. Bolton Papers (hereafter cited as BP), carton 40, no. 673, Bancroft Library, University of California, Berkeley. This presidial line included Laredo, Rio Grande, Aguaverde, and the old presidio of Monclova. The Spanish government closed down the strategic presidio of Aguaverde and relocated it in Villa de Rosas farther south. It also relocated the old presidio of Monclova — which had once stood close to the Rio Grande — back to the town of Monclova. To retain a presence on the Rio Grande, the government tried to set up a new presidio called Palafox in 1810–1811 but could not maintain it.

5. Given what we know about specific Indian raids, these numbers seem exaggerated and almost certainly are. According to estimates by knowledgeable witnesses such as José Francisco Ruiz and Jean Francois Berlandier, the Comanches held about 500 to 600 captives in the 1820s. Brian DeLay counted around 270 captives successfully taken by the Comanches in the period between 1831 and 1848. It is hard to imagine that the Comanches and other Indians of the frontier would have been able to capture nine times as many people in just a handful of years and in less territory. For the estimates by Ruiz and Berlandier, see Rivaya-Martínez, "A Different Look at Native American Depopulation," 397–398 and n. 29. For the number of captives taken by Comanches between 1831 and 1848, see DeLay, *War of a Thousand Deserts,* 320–340. In personal communications, Joaquín Rivaya-Martínez and Brian DeLay assessed the validity of Ramos Arizpe's estimates of the number of Mexican captives, for which I am grateful. In the 1820s, Ramos Arizpe was arguably the most powerful politician in Mexico, and he decided to expend some of his political capital by prodding the national government to restore the abandoned presidios. In 1830 he suggested moving the presidio of Lampazos, located in the middle of the state of Nuevo León, to the Rio Grande and proposed that the presidio of Monclova be relocated to the ruined presidio of Aguaverde. He even offered to donate the land for it. But not even Ramos Arizpe's clout could overcome the fact that Mexico's treasury was depleted. "What will the sad fate of Coahuila, Nuevo León, and Tamaulipas be," the Coahuilan politician asked, "states that have their principal population centers and wealth not far from the banks of the Rio Grande, which will suffer an even more destructive invasion than the previous one [of 1816–1821], this time encouraged and directed by more exalted [Anglo-American] leaders and by even greater and more deliberate interests?" José María Díaz de Noriega, Monclova, June 23, 1834; Ramos Arizpe to Alamán, Puebla, August 1, 1830; and Ramos Arizpe's petition to the state government of Coahuila and Texas, Saltillo, November 12, 1828, all in BP, carton 40, no. 673.

6. Some of the structural factors that impelled Comanches and Apaches to send raiding parties into Mexico are discussed in Pekka Hämäläinen, "The Politics of Grass:

European Expansion, Ecological Change, and Indigenous Power in the Southwest Borderlands," *William and Mary Quarterly* 67:2 (April 2010), 173–208; and Babcock, "Turning Apaches into Spaniards," especially chap. 5. These Indian incursions occurred in discrete bursts and in coordinated fashion. The raids of 1816–1821, which had resulted in so many captives and deaths, ceased immediately after Mexico's independence in the autumn of 1821. At first Apache and Comanche leaders took time to meet with Mexico's new leaders. Some of them, such as Chiefs Cuelgas de Castro and Yolcna Pocarropa (Scant Clothes) of the Lipan Apaches and Guonique of the Comanches, even journeyed to Mexico City to negotiate treaties. The fact that nearly all incursions stopped so suddenly implies coordination and shows that some Indian leaders exercised control over a multiplicity of bands. See DeLay, *War of a Thousand Deserts*, 17–20, 61–62, 115–118, 317–340; Andrés Reséndez, *Changing National Identities at the Frontier: Texas and New Mexico, 1800–1850* (New York: Cambridge University Press, 2005), 57–58; and Ramos Arizpe to Alamán, Puebla, August 1, 1830. See also Kavanagh, *The Comanches*, 196, 199–205; and the diary of governor of New Mexico José Antonio Chávez, Santa Fe, August 2, 1829, Mexican Archives of New Mexico (hereafter cited as MANM), reel 9, frames 871–877.

7. Chief Esakeep's remark about his sons is from Rister, *Border Captives*, 32. For further context on the Comanches and horses, see DeLay, *War of a Thousand Deserts*, 86–113; Rivaya-Martínez, "Captivity and Adoption Among the Comanche Indians," chap. 2; and Rivaya-Martínez, "A Different Look at Native American Depopulation," 391–398. See also Thomas W. Kavanagh, ed., *Comanche Ethnography: Field Notes of E. Adamson Hoebel, Waldo R. Wedel, Gustav G. Carlson, and Robert H. Lowie* (Lincoln: University of Nebraska Press, 2008), 152.

8. DeLay, *War of a Thousand Deserts*, 90–95.

9. The trades were reported by James S. Calhoun, the U.S. Indian agent in the territory of New Mexico, based on what the captives themselves told him. Calhoun specifically said that he gave "full credit" to such statements and that "the Mexicans from whom I received these captives will claim to have paid more." In other words, the prices quoted here are probably quite realistic. Indian Agent in New Mexico James S. Calhoun to Orlando Brown, Esq., Commissioner of Indian Affairs in Washington, D.C., Santa Fe, March 31, 1850, in U.S. Congress, House Documents, 31st Cong., 2nd sess., Executive Document no. 1, 136.

10. Niyah, July 6, 1933, and Post Oak Jim, July 12, 1933, in Kavanagh, *Comanche Ethnography*, 59, 63, 137–138.

11. The quote is from Post Oak Jim, July 12, 1933, 153–155.

12. Ibid.

13. On the 1840–1841 raid, see Isidro Vizcaya Canales, *La invasion de los indios bárbaros al noreste de México en los años de 1840 y 1841* (Monterrey: Publicaciones del Instituto Tecnológico y de Estudios Superiores de Monterrey, 1968), 51–52, 181–185; and DeLay, *War of a Thousand Deserts*, 114–118. On the 1846 raid, see George F. Ruxton, *Adventures in Mexico and the Rocky Mountains* (Glorieta, TX: Rio Grande Press, 1973), especially chap. 14. See also Rister, *Border Captives*, 43–45.

14. Testimony of Abelino Fuentes, Monclova, Coahuila, September 27, 1873, in Velasco Ávila, *En manos de los bárbaros*, 50–51.

15. I want to thank Joaquín Rivaya-Martínez for elucidating the term "Saritɯhka," which was used by the Comanches to refer to other Plains nomads and which literally means "dog eater." Rivaya-Martínez, personal communication. See also testimonies of Juan Vela Benavides, Ciudad Guerrero, Tamaulipas, August 2, 1873, and José Ángel Villarreal, Salinas Victoria, Nuevo León, June 6, 1873, both in Velasco Ávila, *En manos de los bárbaros*, 68–69 and 91–92, respectively. The level of involvement of each band could even depend on the temperament of its leader. Mexican captive Benito Martínez, for example, observed that the leader of the band that held him was very keen on launching campaigns against Mexico. See testimonies of Benito Martínez, Lampazos, Nuevo León, July 5, 1873, and Fernando González, Lampazos, Nuevo León, July 7, 1873, both in Velasco Ávila, *En manos de los bárbaros*, 76–77 and 35–36, respectively. For the Kiowas, see James Mooney, *Calendar History of the Kiowa Indians* (Washington, DC: Smithsonian Institution Press, 1979), 236–237. One of Mooney's Kiowa interviewees was a man with a goatee and an incredible life story named José Andrés Martínez, better known to his fellow band members as Än'Dali (Andele). See J. J. Methvin, ed., *Andele, the Mexican-Kiowa Captive: A Story of Real Life Among the Indians* (Albuquerque: University of New Mexico Press, 1996), passim. The 1902 census of Comanche families is discussed in Rivaya-Martínez, "Captivity and Adoption Among the Comanche Indians," 134–135.

16. George E. Hyde, *A Life of George Bent Written from His Letters* (Norman: University of Oklahoma Press, 1968), 68–69.

17. The data are from Rivaya-Martínez, "Captivity and Adoption Among the Comanche Indians," 410. For the description of Matilda Lockhart by Mary Maverick, see Rena Maverick Green, ed., *Memoirs of Mary A. Maverick* (Lincoln: University of Nebraska Press, 1989), 38. For a broader consideration of captivity texts, see Richard Van Der Beets, *The Indian Captivity Narrative: An American Genre* (Lanham, MD: University Press of America, 1984).

18. Jesús María Guzmán, Villaldama, Nuevo León, June 20, 1873, in Velasco Ávila, *En manos de los bárbaros*, 60–63. The witness provided additional deals that are of interest: "And he saw some going and others coming every month and understood that the campaigns were directed against Mexico because the brands on the horses that they stole were all Mexican and, most especially, because he saw the scalps that they brought which were all Mexican." (Presumably he could tell by the type of hair.)

19. Josiah Gregg, *Diary and Letters of Josiah Gregg* (Norman: University of Oklahoma Press, 1941), 57; Kenner, *The Comanchero Frontier*, 94–95. On the abduction of Mrs. White and her daughter, see *The Official Correspondence of James S. Calhoun*, 63–65.

20. Governor of New Mexico Manuel Armijo to the Ministry of Foreign Relations, Santa Fe, January 10, 1846, AGN, Gobernación [without section], 1845, caja 292, exp. 8, fols. 1–6.

21. On San Carlos, see Joaquín Rivaya-Martínez, "The Captivity of Macario Leal: A Tejano Among the Comanches, 1847–1854," *Southwestern Historical Quarterly* 117:4 (2014), 384–385.

22. The precise timing of the presidial decline in the early decades of the nineteenth century is a matter of debate. The response to this decline varied from group to group among the Apaches. It started as early as the 1790s and continued until the 1830s. See Babcock, "Turning Apaches into Spaniards," 250–305.

23. On the Apache peace settlements, see Babcock, "Turning Apaches into Spaniards." On Mahco, see Eve Ball, *Indeh: An Apache Odyssey* (Norman: University of Oklahoma Press, 1980), 14–15; Edwin R. Sweeney, *Mangas Coloradas: Chief of the Chiricahua Apaches* (Norman: University of Oklahoma Press, 1998), 31; and Robert M. Utley, *Geronimo* (New Haven, CT: Yale University Press, 2012), 6–7. The quotes are from Jason Betzinez, *I Fought with Geronimo* (Lincoln: University of Nebraska Press, 1959), 14.

24. The data on expenditures and men at Janos are from Babcock, "Turning Apaches into Spaniards," tables 4.2 and 5.1. The information about the decline of the civilian population of Janos is from Griffen, *Apaches at War and Peace,* 120. For an in-depth, long-term look at the relationship between Janos and the Apaches, see Blyth, *Chiricahua and Janos,* passim. Geronimo himself gave the year of his birth as 1829 and the place as the Gila River in Arizona, but other evidence suggests the time and place indicated in the text. See Utley, *Geronimo,* 6.

25. For an extremely detailed and illuminating biography of Mangas Coloradas, see Sweeney, *Mangas Coloradas.* On his appearance and Carmen, see ibid., 33, 90.

26. Frederick Turner, ed., *Geronimo: His Own Story; The Autobiography of a Great Patriot Warrior* (New York: Penguin, 1996), 70–71; Utley, *Geronimo,* 15. On the so-called novice complex, as young Apaches trained for raiding, see Morris Edward Opler, *An Apache Life-Way: The Economic, Social, and Religious Institutions of the Chiricahua Indians* (Lincoln: University of Nebraska Press, 1941), 332–353; and Keith H. Basso, ed., *Western Apache Raiding and Warfare: From the Notes of Grenville Goodwin* (Tucson: University of Arizona Press, 1998), 288–298.

27. For an excellent analysis of the Treaty of Guadalupe Hidalgo, see DeLay, *War of a Thousand Deserts,* xiii–xxi. On how the newly redrawn international border provided sanctuary for the Apache camps, see Betzinez, *I Fought with Geronimo,* 19. On Mangas Coloradas, Cochise, and Miguel Narbona (named after the Mexican military leader Antonio Narbona, who captured Miguel), see Sweeney, *Mangas Coloradas,* especially chap. 9; and Edwin R. Sweeney, *Cochise: Chiricahua Apache Chief* (Norman: University of Oklahoma Press, 1995), 406–407. On Juh, see Dan L. Thrapp, *The Conquest of Apacheria* (Norman: University of Oklahoma Press, 1975); and above all Dan L. Thrapp, *Juh: An Incredible Indian* (El Paso: Texas Western Press, 1992), passim. For telling descriptions of Juh, Geronimo, and some other leaders by fellow Apaches, see Ball, *Indeh,* passim. The use of captives as bargaining chips was widespread. By the start of 1850, for instance, Sonoran and Chihuahuan authorities together held at least thirty-three Chiricahuas. Among them were both the mother and mother-in-law of an important war leader of the Chokonen band named Demos, as well as some relatives of Arvizo and Galindo of the Nednhi band. All of these captives had relatives and friends eager to sue for peace and negotiate their release. From the Mexican perspective, it seemed like a good strategy to force the Chiricahuas back to the negoti-

ating table. However, the practice of using prisoners as bargaining chips also gave the Apaches an incentive to acquire prisoners of their own in order to gain leverage in such negotiations. The Apaches captured Mexican women and children to incorporate them into their bands but also to exchange them for their relatives when the time came to broker a deal. On the Chiricahua prisoners in 1850, see Sweeney, *Mangas Coloradas*, 188–204. On the long-standing practice of exchanging prisoners, see Blyth, *Chiricahua and Janos*, especially chaps. 4 and 5.

28. The most detailed reconstruction of these raids can be found in Sweeney, *Mangas Coloradas*, 209–219, 235, 502 n. 50. See also Sweeney, *Cochise*, 83–87. Geronimo's own account is demonstrably inaccurate and needs to be used with caution. Even after the Pozo Hediondo episode, Mangas Coloradas and his warriors were not done. Aware that Sonora lay momentarily unprotected, the war party headed back home by way of the presidio of Bacoachi, striking it on the morning of January 21, 1851. The attackers easily overwhelmed the undermanned garrison and killed six residents (one of whom was the alcalde). They also took five prisoners, intending to use them as bargaining chips to open peace negotiations with Mexican authorities. One of the five captives was an eight- or nine-year-old boy named Jesús Arvizu (probably Alviso), who remained in Mangas Coloradas's extended family for some time before he was sold to the Navajos. While with the Navajos, he was in the family of a chief named Kla. Apparently Jesús became quite fluent in Navajo and acted as an interpreter until late in life. See Frank McNitt, *Navajo Wars: Military Campaigns, Slave Raids, and Reprisals* (Albuquerque: University of New Mexico Press, 1990), 406–408. Another one of the captives was a thirteen-year-old boy named Saverro Heradia (probably Severo Heredia), spotted six months after his capture by members of the U.S. Boundary Commission, who on occasion received visits from Apache bands and that day were visited by Mangas Coloradas's group. The Boundary Commission took Saverro/Severo, along with another Mexican captive, and refused to return them, proclaiming that they were bound by the terms of the Treaty of Guadalupe Hidalgo. See John Russell Bartlett, *Personal Narrative of Explorations and Incidents in Texas, New Mexico, California, Sonora, and Chihuahua, 1850–1853*, 2 vols. (Chicago: Rio Grande Press, 1965), 1:310–312.

29. For an insightful discussion of this episode, see Sweeney, "'I Had Lost All': Geronimo and the Carrasco Massacre of 1851," *Journal of Arizona History* 27:1 (Spring 1986), 35–52. The principal works on Janos include Blyth, *Chiricahua and Janos*; Babcock, "Turning Apaches into Spaniards"; William B. Griffen, "The Chiricahua Apache Population Resident at the Janos Presidio, 1792 to 1858," *Journal of the Southwest* 33:2 (Summer 1991), 151–199; William B. Griffen, "The Compás: A Chiricahua Apache Family of the Late 18th and Early 19th Centuries," *American Indian Quarterly* 7:2 (Spring 1983), 21–49; and Moorhead, *The Presidio: Bastion of the Spanish Borderlands*, 259–261. See also Sweeney, *Mangas Coloradas*, 218–219; and Turner, *Geronimo: His Own Story*, 75–78.

30. Turner, *Geronimo: His Own Story*, 90–91, 102.

31. Petition of Indian Juan Vázquez, Turicato, Michoacán, August 31, 1587, AGN, Instituciones Coloniales, Indiferente Virreinal, caja 2094, exp. 13. For clues about the spread

of debt peonage, see the classic works of François Chevalier, *Land and Society in Colonial Mexico: The Great Hacienda* (Berkeley: University of California Press, 1970); and Taylor, *Landlord and Peasant*. For a regional discussion, see Cuello, "The Persistence of Indian Slavery," 683–700. The New Laws abolished Indian slavery in 1542. The Spanish crown abolished encomiendas in northern Mexico in 1673 and repartimientos after 1777. For a discussion of this last date, see Cramaussel, "Encomiendas, repartimientos y conquista en Nueva Vizcaya," 73–89. For brief introductions to the topic of debt peonage, see Moisés González Navarro, "El trabajo forzoso en México, 1821–1917," *Historia Mexicana* 27 (1977–1978), 588–615; and Alan Knight, "Mexican Peonage: What Was It and Why Was It?," *Journal of Latin American Studies* 18:1 (May 1986), 41–74. Debtor-lender relationships are complex. For instance, in early Mexico the mere existence of a worker's debt in an employer's account book did not necessarily imply a coercive relationship. Sometimes such debts reflected exactly the opposite: the worker's ability to extract credit from his employer. Far from being subservient or coerced, such workers used their bargaining power to get this concession, which gave them immediate access to a variety of goods. Serious scholars trying to form an accurate idea of conditions in a given time and place are forced to wade through the minutiae of hundreds or even thousands of individual cases generally running the gamut from benevolent patron-client relationships to abject bondage. We are far from having such extensive research for any region of Mexico in the nineteenth century. At present we must rely on studies of labor conditions at individual haciendas, textile mills, or other businesses and extrapolate to an entire industry, state, or region. Needless to say, this approach is risky and potentially quite misleading. And yet it is vital to chart the spread of debt peonage and understand its dynamics across time and space.

32. For debt peonage in Yucatán, see Moisés González Navarro, *Raza y tierra: La guerra de castas y el henequén* (Mexico City: El Colegio de México, 1970), 58. For Oaxaca, see González Navarro, "El trabajo forzoso en México," 590. For Chiapas, see Mercedes Olivera Bustamante and María Dolores Palomo Infante, eds., *Chiapas: De la Independencia a la Revolución* (Mexico City: CIESAS, 2005), 78–79. The state of Tabasco exported precious woods such as mahogany and desperately needed workers in the logging camps. Thus the 1825 state constitution refused to grant citizenship rights to those who had "no fixed address, employment, trade, or visible means to support themselves," which applied to many of those on logging crews. The constitution is available online at http://biblio.juridicas.unam.mx/libros/6/2870/10.pdf. For Coahuila, see Charles H. Harris III, *A Mexican Family Empire: The Latifundio of the Sánchez Navarro Family, 1765–1867* (Austin: University of Texas Press, 1975), passim. The state constitution of Sonora specifically stated that individuals classified as servants did not enjoy full citizenship rights. Officials routinely tracked down runaway servants and returned them to their masters, while adding the costs of capture to their accounts. See Miguel Tinker Salas, *In the Shadow of the Eagles: Sonora and the Transformation of the Border During the Porfiriato* (Berkeley: University of California Press, 1997), chap. 2. For Chihuahua, see law number seven in *Nueva colección de leyes del estado de Chihuahua* (Chihuahua City: Imprenta de Horcasitas, 1880), 528–

535. It goes without saying that conditions varied from place to place. Historian Alan Knight has argued for the existence of at least two distinct forms of debt peonage in Mexico: one that was not coercive and was based entirely on market incentives, in which workers were free to come and go (as documented in parts of Zacatecas and San Luis Potosí), and another that relied on corporal punishment, the restriction of workers' movements, and the assiduous pursuit of runaway workers (which spread throughout southern and northern Mexico). Knight, "Mexican Peonage," 45. For Mexico's far north, which became the American Southwest, see William S. Kiser, "Debt Peonage and Judicial Empowerment in Territorial New Mexico" (paper presented at the Western History Association Conference, Tucson, AZ, October 2013); and William S. Kiser, "A 'Charming Name for a Species of Slavery': Political Debate on Debt Peonage in the Southwest, 1840s–1860s," *Western Historical Quarterly* 45:2 (Summer 2014), 169–189. For Texas, see James David Nichols, "The Line of Liberty: Runaway Slaves and Fugitive Peons in the Texas-Mexico Borderlands," *Western Historical Quarterly* 44 (Winter 2013), 413–433.

33. John Kenneth Turner, *Barbarous Mexico* (Chicago, C. H. Kerr, 1911), 5–6. Alan Knight discusses other sources that corroborate Turner's account of labor conditions in Yucatán. Knight, "Mexican Peonage," 52–53. For the most recent and enlightening examination of this journey, see Claudio Lomnitz, *The Return of Comrade Ricardo Flores Magón* (New York: Zone, 2014), 146–171.

34. Turner, *Barbarous Mexico*, 7–10.

35. Ibid., 10–15. For the Mayan community perspective of this era, see Paul K. Eiss, *In the Name of El Pueblo: Place, Community, and the Politics of History in Yucatán* (Durham, NC: Duke University Press, 2010), 50–54, 107–110.

36. Turner, *Barbarous Mexico*, 6–8.

## 10. AMERICANS AND THE OTHER SLAVERY

1. On these demographics, see D. W. Meinig, *The Shaping of America: A Geographical Perspective on 500 Years of History*, vol. 2 (New Haven, CT: Yale University Press, 1993), 222–223. As we have seen, although Indian slavery had existed in the East in colonial times, it had nearly disappeared or been eclipsed by African slavery by the nineteenth century. It is no wonder that easterners making their way across the continent experienced Indian slavery as something of a novelty.

2. Calhoun's most relevant experience prior to his appointment as Indian agent was his tour of duty during the U.S.-Mexican War. He was captain of the Crawford Guards and Georgia Light Infantry of Muscogee County. Although the Georgia volunteers saw no military action (scores of volunteers died of dysentery but none by bullets), Calhoun traveled widely through Tamaulipas, Coahuila, and Nuevo León and as far as Veracruz. Wilbur G. Kurtz Jr., "The First Regiment of Georgia Volunteers in the Mexican War," *Georgia Historical Quarterly* 27:4 (December 1948), 307. The quotes are from Commissioner of Indian Affairs William Medill to Indian Agent Calhoun, Office of Indian Affairs, April 7, 1849, and Governor Charles Bent to Medill, Santa Fe, November 10, 1846, both in *The Official Correspondence of James S. Calhoun*, 3–4

and 6–9, respectively. According to the memorandum, all of these Indian groups were involved in human trafficking. The Utes had been at war with the New Mexicans for two years and had taken many captives; the Comanches were at peace with New Mexico but were waging an incessant war against Chihuahua, Durango, and Coahuila, "from which they have carried off and still hold as slaves a large number of women and children"; and the Navajos had in their possession "many New Mexicans whom they hold and treat as slaves."

3. Calhoun to Medill, camp near Santa Fe, July 29, 1849; Calhoun to Medill, Santa Fe, August 15, 1849; and Calhoun to Medill, Santa Fe, October 1, 1849, all in *The Official Correspondence of James S. Calhoun*, 17–37. See also McNitt, *Navajo Wars*, 136–154; and Brugge, *Navajos in the Catholic Church Records of New Mexico*, 75–107.

4. The quotes are from Calhoun to Medill, October 1, 1849, 29–30.

5. Ibid., 26–29. For earlier treaties and agreements in which the Navajos surrendered or exchanged captives, see "Paz celebrada con los Navajos," signed by Governor José Antonio Vizcarra, Santa Fe, February 14, 1824, MANM, reel 2, frame 558; "Tratado de paz con la nación Navajo," Jemez, July 15, 1839, MANM, reel 26, frames 540–542; and "Manifiesto a los habitantes de la frontera de Jemez," n.d. (circa March 10, 1841), n.p., MANM, reel 28, frames 1704–1707. For an excellent discussion of the Navajos and their captives, see Brooks, *Captives and Cousins*, 241–250.

6. Calhoun to Orlando Brown, Commissioner of Indian Affairs, Santa Fe, February 12, 1850, in *The Official Correspondence of James S. Calhoun*, 148–150.

7. Calhoun to Brown, Santa Fe, March 15, 1850, in *The Official Correspondence of James S. Calhoun*, 161–162.

8. The quote is from ibid., 162.

9. After all, this southern gentleman was not especially interested in upholding the rights of Indians or blacks. Among other things, Calhoun persuaded the Pueblo Indians to give up their citizenship rights under the Treaty of Guadalupe Hidalgo and instead put themselves "under the protection of the laws regulating trade and intercourse with the various tribes of the United States," a move that in effect resulted in their disenfranchisement. He also proposed "penning up" the Comanches and Apaches to solve the problem of Indian depredations in New Mexico. And after becoming territorial governor, Calhoun attempted to restrict the movement of "free negroes" into New Mexico. It is not surprising, then, that his attitude toward captivity/peonage was to allow it to thrive. He broached the subject of the rights of the Pueblo Indians in several letters, such as Calhoun to Brown, Santa Fe, November 16, 1849, and Calhoun to Brown, Santa Fe, February 2, 1850, both in *The Official Correspondence of James S. Calhoun*, 79–80 and 133–134, respectively. For a general discussion of this topic, see Anthony P. Mora, *Border Dilemmas: Racial and National Uncertainties in New Mexico, 1848–1912* (Durham, NC: Duke University Press, 2011), 60–63. On having the Comanches and Apaches "penned up," see Calhoun to Medill, Santa Fe, October 15, 1849, in *The Official Correspondence of James S. Calhoun*, 55. For Calhoun's attempts to exclude free blacks from New Mexico, see Brooks, *Captives and Cousins*, 309–310. For his duty to return Mexican captives, see Calhoun to Brown, March 15, 1850, 162.

10. Already on September 13, 1813, the Spanish Cortes (an assembly consisting of representatives from all parts of the Spanish empire) had ordered the secularization of all missions in the New World, but the order was not carried out in California. During the Mexican era, the secularization of the California missions became a bone of contention between liberals and conservatives in Mexico. Finally, during a period when the notoriously liberal Valentín Gómez Farías ran the executive branch as the sitting vice president while President Antonio López de Santa Anna spent time at his haciendas in Veracruz, the order to secularize the California missions sailed through the Mexican Congress in August 1833. For an excellent discussion of this process, see Louise Pubols, *The Father of All: The de la Guerra Family, Power, and Patriarchy in Mexican California* (Berkeley: University of California Press, 2009), chap. 4. For a full listing of the largest ranches in California in the 1830s and 1840s, see Martha Ortega Soto, *Alta California: Una frontera olvidada del noroeste de México, 1769–1846* (Mexico City: UAM, 2001), tables 56–58.

11. Numerous works on the life of Mariano Guadalupe Vallejo or based on his extensive correspondence are preserved in the Bancroft Library at the University of California, Berkeley. For a flavor of life on the ranch, see Harry D. Hubbard, *Vallejo* (Boston: Meador, 1941), especially chap. 2. One Swedish visitor was G. M. Waseurtz af Sandels, *A Sojourn in California by the King's Orphan* (San Francisco: Grabhorn Press, 1945), 37.

12. Zephyrin Engelhardt, *Upper California*, vol. 4 (San Francisco: James H. Barry, 1915), 136. In addition to the Vallejos, other prominent Mexican families adopted the custom of setting aside one servant for each child. James J. Rawls, *Indians of California: The Changing Image* (Norman: University of Oklahoma Press, 1984), 71; Myrtle M. McKittrick, "Salvador Vallejo: Last of the Conquistadores" (manuscript, UCLA, n.d.). The quote is from Salvador Vallejo, "Notas Históricas sobre California," Sonoma, 1874, Biographical Manuscripts, C-D 22, p. 46, Bancroft Library, University of California, Berkeley.

13. Salvador Vallejo, "Notas Históricas," p. 46. The most insightful recent study of life at Rancho Petaluma is Stephen W. Silliman, *Lost Laborers in Colonial California: Native Americans and the Archaeology of Rancho Petaluma* (Tucson: University of Arizona Press, 2004), especially chap. 3.

14. On the origins of the Native laborers at Rancho Petaluma, see Silliman, *Lost Laborers in Colonial California*, 61–66. On Mexican Californians conducting raids on nearby Indian settlements, see Cook, *The Conflict Between the California Indian and White Civilization*, 197–251. Sandels reported the return of one of these expeditions led by Salvador Vallejo in 1843. Sandels, *A Sojourn in California by the King's Orphan*, 36.

15. On Vallejo's Native Hawaiians, see Silliman, *Lost Laborers in Colonial California*, 54. Sinclair's Pacific Islanders are mentioned in Sandels, *A Sojourn in California by the King's Orphan*, 61. More generally, see Sucheng Chan, *This Bittersweet Soil: The Chinese in California Agriculture, 1860–1910* (Berkeley: University of California Press, 1986), 16–26. For a very stimulating discussion of the rise of debt peonage in a transnational framework, see Edward D. Melillo, "The First Green Revolution: Debt Peonage and the Making of the Nitrogen Fertilizer Trade, 1840–1930," *American*

*Historical Review* 117:4 (2012), 1028–1060. I rely on Cook's work for Indian population estimates. Sherburne F. Cook, *The Population of the California Indians, 1769–1970* (Berkeley: University of California Press, 1976), passim.

16. Josiah Belden, *1841 California Overland Pioneer: His Memoir and Early Letters*; John Bidwell, *A Journey to California*; and John Marsh, "Letter of Dr. John Marsh to Hon. Lewis Cass," all quoted in Rawls, *Indians of California*, 60–61, 74–80.

17. Lansford W. Hastings, *The Emigrants' Guide to Oregon and California*, quoted in Rawls, *Indians of California*, 74–80.

18. Rockwell D. Hunt knew Bidwell in his old age and wrote a sympathetic biography that nonetheless contains useful firsthand information. Hunt, *John Bidwell* (Caldwell, ID: Caxton, 1942), chap. 7. For a more scholarly treatment, see Michael J. Gillis and Michael F. Magliari, *John Bidwell and California: The Life and Writings of a Pioneer, 1841–1900* (Spokane, WA: Arthur H. Clark, 2003), passim.

19. According to Bidwell's most recent biographers, his attitude toward the California Indians remained "a blend of curiosity, humanitarianism, and pragmatic self-interest." Gillis and Magliari, *John Bidwell and California*, 250.

20. This section is based entirely on Hunt, *John Bidwell*, 140–142; Gillis and Magliari, *John Bidwell and California*, 249–310; and Rawls, *Indians of California*, 94–95, where the original quotes can also be found.

21. A rendition of the massacre of the Lewis children can be found in Theodora Kroeber, *Ishi in Two Worlds: A Biography of the Last Wild Indian in North America* (Berkeley: University of California Press, 1961), 70–71.

22. Hunt, *John Bidwell*, 141, 142; Gillis and Magliari, *John Bidwell and California*, 279–282.

23. I rely heavily on Albert Hurtado's luminous biography of Sutter, *John Sutter: A Life on the North American Frontier* (Norman: University of Oklahoma Press, 2006). The quotes are from Sandels, *A Sojourn in California by the King's Orphan*, 58.

24. Sandels, *A Sojourn in California by the King's Orphan*, 58.

25. For Sutter's proclivity to take on debt and Bancroft's quote, see Hurtado, *John Sutter*, 98.

26. Ibid., 97–99.

27. Ibid., especially chap. 6 and pp. 152–153; Rawls, *Indians of California*, 78–79.

28. William Joseph's quote is from Hurtado, *John Sutter*, 80.

29. Sutter, "Personal Reminiscences," 1877, quoted in Cook, *The Conflict Between the California Indian and White Civilization*, 457. For the incident with the Indian traffickers, see Hurtado, *John Sutter*, 74–75.

30. Sutter to Pierson B. Reading, May 8, 1845, quoted in Hurtado, *John Sutter*, 154. See also Albert L. Hurtado, *Indian Survival on the California Frontier* (New Haven, CT: Yale University Press, 1988), 59–61.

31. Sutter to Antonio Suñol, May 19, 1845, and John Marsh to Antonio Suñol, June 16, 1845, both quoted in Hurtado, *John Sutter*, 154 and 115–116, respectively.

32. Ibid.; Hubert Howe Bancroft, *History of California*, vol. 4 (Santa Barbara, CA: Wallace Hibberd, 1883), 138, 344.

33. Not all the Kelseys settled in California immediately. Samuel and David Kelsey apparently spent two years in Oregon before rejoining Benjamin and Andrew in Cali-

fornia. On the Kelseys settling in Napa, see Minnie B. Heath, "Nancy Kelsey: The First Pioneer Woman to Cross the Plains," *Grizzly Bear Magazine* 40 (1937), 3–7.

34. On the Clear Lake Indians right before the arrival of whites, see Frederick John Simoons, "The Settlement of the Clear Lake Upland of California" (master's thesis, University of California, Davis, 1949), especially chap. 5; and Lyman L. Palmer, *History of Napa and Lake Counties . . .* (San Francisco: Slocum, Bowen, 1881), 23–40. The latter source contains especially valuable information provided to the author by Augustine, a Pomo chief working as overseer of a cattle operation at Clear Lake, as well as other firsthand sources.

35. Palmer, *History of Napa and Lake Counties,* 49. Again the information provided by Augustine is the most valuable and jibes well with other sources.

36. Mariano Guadalupe Vallejo told this story to Major Edwin A. Sherman around 1851–1853, and it was confirmed by Salvador Vallejo. Sherman, "Clear Lake Expedition of 1850," *Grizzly Bear Magazine* 12:2 (December 1912), 15. Juan Bojorges, a member of the expedition, gave the same account in 1877 to historian Hubert Howe Bancroft, who was in the process of compiling information for a projected history of California. A transcription can be found in Robert F. Heizer, *The Collected Documents on the Causes and Events in the Bloody Island Massacre of 1850* (Berkeley: Archaeological Research Facility, Department of Anthropology, University of California, Berkeley, 1973), 67–69.

37. For the wanton lashings and killings, see Palmer, *History of Napa and Lake Counties,* 56. Thomas Knight gave a statement of these events to Bancroft in 1879. The original testimony remains in the Bancroft Library, but it was also published in Heizer, *The Collected Documents,* 77–78. The statement about the partners' "unbridled lusts" was made by George Yount, quoted in Benjamin Logan Madley, "American Genocide: The California Indian Catastrophe, 1846–1873" (Ph.D. diss., Yale University, 2009), 110.

38. Palmer, *History of Napa and Lake Counties,* 54–55.

39. Chief Augustine's testimony is included in its entirety in Palmer, *History of Napa and Lake Counties,* 58–62. For other versions of the Kelsey and Stone massacre, see unidentified Pomo informants, 1903–1906, and William Benson (his Pomo name was Ralganal), an informant and interpreter for later American anthropologists who visited Lake County, both in Heizer, *The Collected Documents,* 42–45 and 49–53, respectively.

40. Henry Clay Bailey, *Indians of the Sacramento Valley* (Bloomington, CA: San Bernardino County Museum Association, 1959), 3–4, 17–18. See also Cook, *The Conflict Between the California Indian and White Civilization,* 314.

41. For Captain John B. Montgomery's proclamation and its context, see Madley, "American Genocide," 167–169.

42. The quotes are from Madley, "American Genocide," 169–171. For excellent analyses of the certificate and pass system, see also Hurtado, *Indian Survival on the California Frontier,* 94–96; and Rawls, *Indians of California,* 85.

43. J. Ross Browne, *Report of the Debates in the Convention of California on the Formation of the State Constitution* (Washington, DC: John T. Tower, 1850), 64–65, 70.

44. The Indian Act of 1850 has received considerable scholarly attention. See, for example, Richard Steven Street, *Beasts of the Field: A Narrative History of California Farmworkers, 1769–1913* (Stanford, CA: Stanford University Press, 2004), 119–121; Kimberly Johnston-Dodds, "Early California Laws and Policies Related to California Indians" (report prepared for the California Research Bureau, Sacramento, 2002), 5–15; Magliari, "Free Soil, Unfree Labor," 349–390; Hurtado, *Indian Survival on the California Frontier,* 129–131; Rawls, *Indians of California,* 85–105; and Madley, "American Genocide," 189–197.

45. In 1860 the state legislature expanded the "apprenticeship" component of the 1850 act, allowing male Indians younger than fourteen to be indentured until they turned twenty-five, and females younger than fourteen to be indentured until they turned twenty-one.

46. In 1855 section 6 of the 1850 act was amended to allow Indians to serve as competent witnesses in court. Yet even in the 1860s, California legal treatises continued to cite laws prohibiting Indians from being witnesses as valid law. Johnston-Dodds, "Early California Laws and Policies Related to California Indians," 8. For slaving activities in the 1850s, see Bailey, *Indians of the Sacramento Valley,* 17; and Michael F. Magliari, "Free State Slavery: Bound Indian Labor and Slave Trafficking in California's Sacramento Valley, 1850–1864," *Pacific Historical Review* 81:2 (May 2012), 155–192. For how petitioners laying claim to Indian children got around the law, see Smith, *Freedom's Frontier,* 119–121.

## 11. A NEW ERA OF INDIAN BONDAGE

1. "Brigham Young's Speech on Slavery, Blacks, and the Priesthood," Salt Lake City, February 5, 1852, http://www.utlm.org/onlineresources/sermons_talks_interviews/brigham 1852feb5_priesthoodandblacks.htm. Not only Mormons but also Protestants believed in Cain's mark and its identification with black skin.

2. Andrew Love Neff, *History of Utah, 1847 to 1869* (Salt Lake City: Deseret News Press, 1940), 364–365. The Woodruff quote is from Floyd A. O'Neil and Stanford J. Layton, "Of Pride and Politics: Brigham Young as Indian Superintendent," *Utah Historical Quarterly* 46:3 (1978), 239–241. For an excellent introduction to this subject, see Juanita Brooks, "Indian Relations on the Mormon Frontier," *Utah State Historical Society* 12:1–2 (January–April 1944), 2–4; and Michael K. Bennion, "Captivity, Adoption, Marriage and Identity: Native American Children in Mormon Homes, 1847–1900" (master's thesis, University of Nevada, Las Vegas, 2012).

3. The story of Charles Decker and his captive is based on the 1847 journal of Mary Ellen Kimball and the recollections of John R. Young, both quoted in Peter Gottfredson, *History of Indian Depredations in Utah* (Salt Lake City: Press of Skeleton, 1919), 16–17. The details of the story vary from one source to another, but the general gist is the same. For the wider context, see Bailey, *Indian Slave Trade in the Southwest,* 148–149; Malouf and Malouf, "The Effects of Spanish Slavery on the Indians of the Intermountain West," 384–385; Knack, *Boundaries Between,* chap. 4; Jones, *The Trial*

*of Don Pedro León Luján,* 42–52; and Blackhawk, *Violence over the Land,* especially chap. 7.

4. The first quote is from Brigham Young's testimony, cited in Jones, *The Trial of Don Pedro León Luján,* 49–50. The second quote is from Solomon Nunes Carvalho, *Incidents of Travel and Adventure in the Far West with Colonel Frémont's Last Expedition,* in Kate B. Carter, ed., *Heart Throbs of the West,* vol. 1 (Salt Lake City: Daughters of the Utah Pioneers, 1947), 147–148. See also Jones, *Forty Years Among the Indians,* 53. Euro-Americans reported such selling techniques not only in Utah but also in New Mexico, Wyoming, and Idaho and at least since the eighteenth century. See Malouf and Malouf, "The Effects of Spanish Slavery on the Indians of the Intermountain West," 384–385; and Jones, *The Trial of Don Pedro León Luján,* 44–52. See also chapter 7 of this book.

5. Quoted in Eugene E. Campbell, *Establishing Zion: The Mormon Church in the American West, 1847–1869* (Salt Lake City: Signature, 1988), 79.

6. The first quote is from ibid., n. 9. The second quote is from Orson Pratt, July 15, 1855, *Journal of Discourses,* cited in Jones, *The Trial of Don Pedro León Luján,* 44. For an excellent discussion of Indian slavery among the Mormons, see Jennifer Lindell, "Mormons and Native Americans in the Antebellum West" (master's thesis, San Diego State University, 2011).

7. See *Acts, Resolutions and Memorials, Passed at the Several Annual Sessions of the Legislative Assembly of the Territory of Utah* (Salt Lake City: Joseph Cain, 1855), 173–174.

8. Daniel W. Jones acted as interpreter. The quote is from Jones, *Forty Years Among the Indians,* 151. On this episode, the best source by far is Jones, *The Trial of Don Pedro León Luján,* especially chaps. 4 and 5.

9. Jones, *The Trial of Don Pedro León Luján,* 95.

10. The Frémont quote is from Jones, *The Trial of Don Pedro León Luján,* 46. For a reasonable sketch of Walkara (also spelled Wakara), see Conway B. Sonne, *The World of Wakara* (San Antonio: Naylor, 1962), chap. 6. Peter Gottfredson claims that the cause of Chief Walkara's raids in southern California was "bad treatment by certain ranchers." Gottfredson, *History of Indian Depredations in Utah,* 22. See also Blackhawk, *Violence over the Land,* 139–141, 234–245; and Bailey, *Indian Slave Trade in the Southwest,* 156–161.

11. Jones, *Forty Years Among the Indians,* 31. The brewing conflict between the Mormons and Utes eventually exploded in the so-called Walker War of 1853. (Walker was the Mormons' name for Walkara.)

12. See "Brigham Young's Address to the Council and House of Representatives of the Legislature of Utah, Great Salt Lake City, Utah, January 5, 1852," in Carter, *Heart Throbs of the West,* 152–153. The most relevant parts of the Act for the Relief of Indian Slaves and Prisoners are sections 1 and 4. For a direct comparison of the terms in the Utah and California servitude laws, see Bennion, "Captivity, Adoption, Marriage and Identity," 89–92. See also Bruce Q. Cannon, "Adopted or Indentured, 1850–1870: Native Children in Mormon Households," in Ronald W. Walker and Doris R. Dant, eds., *Nearly Everything Imaginable: The Everyday Life of Utah's Mormon Pioneers* (Provo,

UT: Brigham Young University Press, 1999), 351. I want to thank Dale Topham for steering me toward this reference.

13. Richard D. Kitchen, "Mormon-Indian Relations in Deseret: Intermarriage and Indenture, 1847–1877" (Ph.D. diss., Arizona State University, 2002, apps. C and D); Bennion, "Captivity, Adoption, Marriage and Identity," app. 4. For a discussion of Utah's demography, see Pamela S. Perlich, "Utah Minorities: The Story Told by 150 Years of Census Data" (report, Bureau of Economic and Business Research, David Eccles School of Business, University of Utah, Salt Lake City, 2002). See also Brooks, "Indian Relations on the Mormon Frontier," 33–34; and Carter, *Heart Throbs of the West*, 159–164. Indian slavery was not evenly distributed throughout Utah but was instead concentrated in certain districts. For example, according to Martha Knack each of the one hundred households in the town of Parowan had one or more Paiute children. Knack, *Boundaries Between*, 57.

14. These vignettes and many others appear in Carter, *Heart Throbs of the West*, 159–164. See also Brooks, "Indian Relations on the Mormon Frontier," 33–34.

15. Carter, *Heart Throbs of the West*, 159–164; Brooks, "Indian Relations on the Mormon Frontier," 33–34; Bennion, "Captivity, Adoption, Marriage and Identity," 80–81. For work as a central aspect of the Indians' redemption, including the quotes, see O'Neil and Layton, "Of Pride and Politics," 240; and Lindell, "Mormons and Native Americans in the Antebellum West," 64. See also Sondra Jones, "'Redeeming' the Indian: The Enslavement of Indian Children in New Mexico and Utah," *Utah Historical Quarterly* 67:3 (Summer 1999), 220–241.

16. The first quote is from Brigham Young and Herbert C. Kimball, "Fourteenth General Epistle," *Deseret News*, December 13, 1851, in Lindell, "Mormons and Native Americans in the Antebellum West," 62–63. The second quote is from "Address of Elder E. T. Benson, Provo, July 13, 1855," in Carter, *Heart Throbs of the West*, 148.

17. See the discussion of marriage in Juanita Brooks, "Indian Relations on the Mormon Frontier," 33–48; and Bennion, "Captivity, Adoption, Marriage and Identity," 156–157 and app. 1, table 10.

18. Darlis A. Miller, *The California Column in New Mexico* (Albuquerque: University of New Mexico Press, 1982), 4–11.

19. For a relevant biographical sketch, see Adam Kane, "James H. Carleton," in Paul Andrew Hutton and Durwood Ball, eds., *Soldiers West: Biographies from the Military Frontier* (Norman: University of Oklahoma Press, 2009), 122–148. See also Gerald Thompson, *The Army and the Navajo: The Bosque Redondo Reservation Experiment, 1863–1868* (Tucson: University of Arizona Press, 1976), chap. 2. For antecedents, see William S. Kiser, *Dragoons in Apacheland: Conquest and Resistance in Southern New Mexico, 1846–1861* (Norman: University of Oklahoma Press, 2012), especially chaps. 8 and 9.

20. For a blow-by-blow account of the Navajo attack on Fort Defiance, see McNitt, *Navajo Wars*, 382–384. See also Brugge, *Navajos in the Catholic Church Records of New Mexico*, 87–88. The newspaper is the *Santa Fe Gazette*, November 10, 1860, quoted in McNitt, *Navajo Wars*, 385.

21. To correlate Navajo baptisms with events during the eighteenth century, I have relied primarily on J. Lee Correll, *Through White Men's Eyes: A Contribution to Navajo History; A Chronological Record of the Navajo People from Earliest Times to the Treaty of June 1, 1868*, 6 vols. (Tucson: University of Arizona Press, 1988), 1:25–52; Hackett, *Historical Documents*, 1:268; Frank D. Reeve, "Navaho-Spanish Wars, 1680–1720," *New Mexico Historical Review* 33:3 (1958), 20–33; and Frank D. Reeve, "The Navajo-Spanish Peace, 1720–1770," *New Mexico Historical Review* 34:1 (1959), 28–43.

22. "Exchange Between Armijo and Agent Greiner," Santa Fe, January 1852, in Brugge, *Navajos in the Catholic Church Records of New Mexico*, 80–81. The exchange is also described in Brian DeLay, "Blood Talk: Violence and Belonging in the Navajo–New Mexican Borderland," in Juliana Barr and Edward Countryman, eds., *Contested Spaces of Early America* (Philadelphia: University of Pennsylvania Press, 2014), 229–256. For additional information about this dynamic, see McNitt, *Navajo Wars*, 140–143; and Brugge, *Navajos in the Catholic Church Records of New Mexico*, 82.

23. Manuelito to General O. O. Howard, 1872, in Brugge, *Navajos in the Catholic Church Records of New Mexico*, 103–104. For a more extensive biographical sketch of Manuelito and his wife, Juanita, see Jennifer Nez Denetdale, *Reclaiming Diné History: The Legacies of Navajo Chief Manuelito and Juanita* (Tucson: University of Arizona Press, 2007), passim.

24. Not everyone was in favor of this policy. New Mexico's military commander, Colonel Thomas T. Fauntleroy, was reluctant to arm such groups, which, as he put it, "were the freebooting, plundering parties which I understood from hearsay." Colonel Fauntleroy's suspicions were well-founded. Article 38 of New Mexico's Militia Law, July 10, 1851, and its later amendments are discussed in McNitt, *Navajo Wars*, 385–386 n. 2.

25. Ibid., 388–389; Bailey, *Indian Slave Trade in the Southwest*, 97; Brooks, *Captives and Cousins*, 250–257.

26. A brief diary kept by Chaves's adjutant general, the Marquis Lafayette Cotton, gives us a rare glimpse into the battalion's activities. See McNitt, *Navajo Wars*, 393–394. The campaign against the Navajos continued into the winter. The Diné had become so weakened by the pounding of these militias and by U.S. military forces (which eventually became involved as well) that they sued for peace and signed a treaty in February 1861. The American officers were quite satisfied with these results and decided to abandon Fort Defiance. Not so the militias. Once engaged, these volunteer forces remained a constant threat to the fragile peace. Less than a month after the peace treaty was signed, a unit from Taos was caught holding six Navajo women. They "openly avowed their intentions to disregard the treaty," wrote the U.S. officer who apprehended them, "and on their return home, to organize a new expedition to capture Navajos and sell them [on the Rio Grande]." Edward Canby to A.A.G. [Assistant Adjutant General], Department of New Mexico, February 27, March 11, and March 18, 1861, cited in Bailey, *Indian Slave Trade in the Southwest*, 98.

27. Ann Oldham, *Albert H. Pfeiffer: Indian Agent, Soldier and Mountain Man* (Washington, DC: published by author, 2003), 50–52; Thomas W. Dunlay, *Kit Carson and the*

*Indians* (Lincoln: University of Nebraska Press, 2000), 217; Blackhawk, *Violence over the Land,* 208–210; McNitt, *Navajo Wars,* 402–403.

28. Strictly speaking, Colonel Edward Canby made the decision to launch a new campaign against the Navajos before General Carleton replaced him. For additional background on this as well as the quote by Canby, see Dunlay, *Kit Carson and the Indians,* 261–262, 316. Indian subagent Pfeiffer specifically referred to the division among the Navajos: "The rich Navajoes, who are few want peace, but all the poor who live in Chelle Tehasca & Tchacca want War and they say they want to steal all the Animals from the Mexicans as soon as they get in good condition. Tehasca is only five days easy travel from here & Tchacca from two to three days & a tolerable road." Pfeiffer to Collins, May 15, 1859, in Oldham, *Albert H. Pfeiffer,* 50–51. See, more generally, Brooks, *Captives and Cousins,* 241–250 and app. A; and DeLay, "Blood Talk," 229–236.

29. General Carleton to Colonel Edwin A. Rigg, Santa Fe, August 6, 1863, in U.S. Congress, *Condition of the Indian Tribes: Report of the Joint Special Committee, Appointed Under Joint Resolution of March 3, 1865* (Washington, DC: Government Printing Office, 1867), 124.

30. Carleton to Rigg, August 6, 1863, 124; Dunlay, *Kit Carson and the Indians,* chaps. 5 and 6.

31. On the number of soldiers, see General Carleton to Brigadier General Lorenzo Thomas, Santa Fe, August 6, 1863, in U.S. Congress, *Condition of the Indian Tribes,* 124. On requesting a weekly report, see Carleton to Carson, Santa Fe, August 7, 1863, in ibid., 125–126. The emphasis is in the original. On campaigning through the Canyon de Chelly, see Carleton to Carson, Santa Fe, December 5, 1863, in ibid., 146. On killing adult males and taking women and children prisoner, see Carleton to Captain Peter W. L. Plympton at Fort Union, Santa Fe, July 29, 1863, or Carleton to Major Joseph Smith at Fort Stanton, Santa Fe, July 29, 1863, both in ibid., 120–121.

32. The description of how Carson organized the Navajo campaign comes from H. R. Tilton, the surgeon who attended Carson five years later and reportedly heard it from Carson himself. Dunlay, *Kit Carson and the Indians,* 277–278.

33. Carson to Carleton, July 24, 1863, quoted in full in Dunlay, *Kit Carson and the Indians,* 283.

34. The first quote is from Carleton to Carson, Santa Fe, August 18, 1863, in U.S. Congress, *Condition of the Indian Tribes,* 128. The italics are in the original. The second quote is from Carson to Cutler, August 19, 1863, cited in Dunlay, *Kit Carson and the Indians,* 280–281.

35. For the plan to raise volunteer forces in each county, see Carleton to Thomas, Santa Fe, August 23, 1863, in U.S. Congress, *Condition of the Indian Tribes,* 129–130.

36. Baca's quote comes from Baca to Cutler, December 7, 1863, General Orders No. 3, in Correll, *Through White Men's Eyes,* 3:413. The report about Baca taking hundreds of captives is from Nathan Bibo, "Reminiscences of Early Days in New Mexico," *Albuquerque Evening Herald,* June 11, 1922. Subagent Bibo claimed that he knew "hundreds" of Indian prisoners who "married or mixed with the frontier population . . .

always content and applying themselves to their housework or in the open just the same as the balance of the people."

37. Dunlay, *Kit Carson and the Indians,* 289–300; Oldham, *Albert H. Pfeiffer,* 95–99. The quotes are from Pfeiffer to Lawce G. Murphey, January 20, 1864, in Lawrence C. Kelly, ed., *Navajo Roundup: Selected Correspondence of Kit Carson's Expedition Against the Navajo, 1863–1865* (Boulder, CO: Pruett, 1970), 102–104; and Kit Carson's report, in Dunlay, *Kit Carson and the Indians,* 296.

38. Carleton to Thomas, Santa Fe, February 7, 1864, in Oldham, *Albert H. Pfeiffer,* 102.

39. The quotes are from Dunlay, *Kit Carson and the Indians,* 296, 300.

40. On the number of Navajos who surrendered in March 1864, see Carleton to Major Henry Wallen, Commander at Fort Sumner, Santa Fe, March 11, 1864, in U.S. Congress, *Condition of the Indian Tribes,* 165.

41. On the attack against the Navajos walking toward Fort Canby, see Carey to Asst. Adj. General, Fort Canby, April 29, 1864, in Correll, *Through White Men's Eyes,* 4:152. Similar attacks had occurred at other posts. E. W. Eaton, who was in command at Fort Wingate in Navajo country, declared that when the first large party of Navajos were on their way to Fort Wingate to surrender, "they were pursued by a party of Mexicans who ran after them to take their flocks and herds . . . The Mexicans killed some of the Navajoes and captured some captives and stock . . . The Indians were in sufficient force to have resisted them, but were coming in to surrender themselves, and made no resistance for fear that the troops would attack them. There were not over fifty or sixty in the party." Deposition of Commander Eaton, n.p., 1865, in U.S. Congress, *Condition of the Indian Tribes,* 336.

42. On the attack near Albuquerque, see Brotherton to Asst. Adj. Gen., May 2, 1864, in Correll, *Through White Men's Eyes,* 4:148–159. Captain McCabe offered a different version of events, which also involved the taking of captives. See Correll, *Through White Men's Eyes,* 4:159–161.

43. On Baca's activities, see McFerran to Carey, Albuquerque, May 5, 1864, in Correll, *Through White Men's Eyes,* 4:164–165. For the tribulations of Herrero's niece, see Brugge, *Navajos in the Catholic Church Records of New Mexico,* 98–100; and Bailey, *Indian Slave Trade in the Southwest,* 110–111. The report of Navajos held in bondage in Cebolleta and some other neighboring communities appears in Campbell to Carleton, March 3, 1864, in Brugge, *Navajos in the Catholic Church Records of New Mexico,* 97.

44. The lists of Indian peons in Costilla and Conejos Counties are included in their entirety in McNitt, *Navajo Wars,* 441–446.

45. On Carson's complaints about the "independent campaigns" and Connelly's proclamation, see Carson to A.A.G., April 13, 1864, and Governor Henry Connelly's proclamation, Santa Fe, May 4, 1864, both in Bailey, *Indian Slave Trade in the Southwest,* 106 and 107–109, respectively. For the larger story of removal and beyond, see L. R. Bailey, *The Long Walk: A History of the Navajo Wars, 1846–68* (Tucson: Westernlore Press, 1988); and Peter Iverson, *Diné: A History of the Navajos* (Albuquerque: University of New Mexico Press, 2002), passim.

46. The census of the Navajos at Bosque Redondo appears in General Orders No. 4, Santa Fe, February 18, 1865, in U.S. Congress, *Condition of the Indian Tribes,* 264.

47. Testimony of Chief Justice Kirby Benedict, Santa Fe, July 4, 1865, in U.S. Congress, *Condition of the Indian Tribes,* 325–327. The italics are mine.

48. The quotes are from testimony of Chief Justice Kirby Benedict, July 4, 1865.

## 12. THE OTHER SLAVERY
## AND THE OTHER EMANCIPATION

1. John Greenleaf Whittier, editorial, *Pennsylvania Freeman,* Philadelphia, May 10, 1838, and James G. Birney, open letter to the *Liberator,* Boston, January 18, 1839, both quoted in Linda K. Kerber, "The Abolitionist Perception of the Indian," *Journal of American History* 62:2 (September 1975), 273–274. The possibilities and limitations of eastern abolitionist thinking about Indians are clear in the writings of novelist, women's rights activist, and abolitionist Lydia Maria Child. After the Civil War, she wrote "An Appeal for the Indians," her most ambitious text about the condition of Native Americans. Child began her essay with a reference to the recent sectional dispute: "There was too much excitement and anxiety to admit of attention to any other topic, but I think the time has now come when, without intermitting our vigilant watch over the rights of black men, it is our duty to arouse the nation to a sense of its guilt concerning the red men." In twenty-four pages, Child offered a clear-eyed narrative of abuse perpetrated against Indians through much of the nineteenth century, including passages about lawless bands of Georgia slaveholders "going into Florida, capturing whomsoever they pleased, and selling them into slavery"; John C. Frémont's pathfinders pushing into California and shooting Indians "in mere sport"; and Oregon gold hunters burning wigwams simply to take possession of Indian lands. Child's text is quite typical of the abolitionist perspective in that it touched on a multiplicity of ills that affected Indians but at the same time prevented concrete action to be taken on a single issue on behalf of Natives. The quotes are from Lydia Maria Child, "An Appeal for the Indians," in *A Lydia Maria Child Reader,* ed. Carolyn L. Karcher (Durham, NC: Duke University Press, 1997), 84, 86, 88. Child's interest in Indians spanned her entire life, beginning with her first novel, *Hobomok,* published in 1824, about an upper-class white woman who married and had a child with an Indian chief. For a brief but insightful discussion of *Hobomok,* see Karen L. Kilcup, ed., *Soft Canons: American Women Writers and Masculine Tradition* (Iowa City: University of Iowa Press, 1999), 31–38. When the Cherokee removal controversy erupted in the late 1820s, Child was already getting involved in political journalism. She wrote a revisionist history of the Cherokees and argued that they should be allowed to retain what was left of "their native inheritance." Child, "An Appeal for the Indians," 85–90.

2. When New Mexico became organized as a territory as a result of a federal act passed on September 9, 1850, another statute provided that "all the laws passed by the Legislative Assembly and Governor shall be submitted to the Congress of the United States and if disapproved shall be null and void." The New Mexican laws regulating servitude can be found in John Codman Hurd, *The Law of Freedom and Bondage in*

*the United States,* 2 vols. (New York: Little, Brown, 1862), 2:209–210; and *Laws of the Territory of New Mexico Passed by the Legislative Assembly, Session of 1858–9* (Santa Fe: A. De Marle, 1859), 24–25. Information about the preliminary discussions and bill in Congress nullifying New Mexico's indenture codes can be found in John Armor Bingham, *Bill and Report of John A. Bingham, and Vote on Its Passage . . .* (1858; repr., Ann Arbor: University of Michigan Library, 2005); available online at http://name .umdl.umich.edu/ABJ5148.0001.001. For the legal history of these debates stretching back to the 1840s, see the excellent article by Kiser, "A 'Charming Name for a Species of Slavery,'" 169–189.

3. The quote is from An Act to Secure Freedom to All Persons Within the Territories of the United States, House of Representatives, Washington, D.C., June 19, 1862, http://www.freedmen.umd.edu/freeterr.htm.

4. William Frederick Doolittle, comp., *The Doolittle Family in America,* quoted in Francis Paul Prucha, *The Great Father: The United States Government and the American Indians,* 2 vols. (Lincoln: University of Nebraska Press, 1984), 1:479–480, 485–486. C. Joseph Genetin-Pilawa has shown that U.S. Indian policy did not necessarily have to result in Indian dispossession and forced assimilation. Genetin-Pilawa, *Crooked Paths to Allotment: The Fight over Federal Indian Policy After the Civil War* (Chapel Hill: University of North Carolina Press, 2012), 56, 76.

5. The quote is from U.S. Congress, *Condition of the Indian Tribes,* 4. The other committee members were Senators Lafayette S. Foster of Connecticut and James W. Nesmith of Oregon and Representatives William Windom of Minnesota, Asahel W. Hubbard of Iowa, William Higby of California, and Lewis W. Ross of Illinois. The 531-page report is a gold mine of information, especially for New Mexico. The report contains many factual errors and unsubstantiated claims, and, of course, it was in part motivated by politics. See Prucha, *The Great Father,* 1:486–487; and Harry Kelsey, "The Doolittle Report of 1867: Its Preparation and Shortcomings," *Arizona and the West* 17 (Summer 1975), 107–120. Even so, it provided a wealth of firsthand information.

6. *Santa Fe Gazette,* August 5, 1865, quoted in Bailey, *Indian Slave Trade in the Southwest,* 175. Secretary Harlan instructed the commissioner of Indian affairs, William Dole, to "prepare a letter to the President, advising him that the law abolishing slavery in New Mexico is disregarded, and that there is evidence in your office that the practice of selling Indian children still continues." These instructions are quoted in Rael-Gálvez, "Identifying Captivity and Capturing Identity," 221–222.

7. The quotes are from "Report of Special Agent Julius K. Graves, No. 40, New Mexico Superintendency," in *Annual Report of the Commissioner of Indian Affairs for the Year 1866* (Washington, DC: Government Printing Office, 1866), 131–134. See also Bailey, *Indian Slave Trade in the Southwest,* 172–173; William A. Keleher, *Turmoil in New Mexico, 1846–1868* (Santa Fe: Rydal Press, 1952), 364–368.

8. The quotes are from "Report of Special Agent Julius K. Graves, No. 40," 132–134.

9. Michael Vorenberg, *Final Freedom: The Civil War, the Abolition of Slavery, and the Thirteenth Amendment* (New York: Cambridge University Press, 2001), passim. Justice Samuel Miller's reasoning appears in the Slaughter-House Cases, 83 U.S. 36 (1873). See also Baher Azmy, "Modern Slavery and a Reconstructed Civil Rights

Agenda," *Fordham Law Review* 71:3 (2002), 981–1061; and Eric Foner, *Free Soil, Free Labor, Free Men: The Ideology of the Republican Party Before the Civil War* (New York: Oxford University Press, 1995), 37. Foner's book remains the most insightful investigation into the ideology of free labor in the 1850s and 1860s.

10. The quotes are from Foner, *Free Soil*, chap. 1. See also Vorenberg, *Final Freedom*, especially chaps. 2 and 3; and Alexander Tsesis, "The Thirteenth Amendment's Revolutionary Aims," in Alexander Tsesis, ed., *The Promises of Liberty: The History and Contemporary Relevance of the Thirteenth Amendment* (New York: Columbia University Press, 2010), 1–23.

11. Journal of George W. Julian, quoted in James M. McPherson, *Battle Cry of Freedom: The Civil War Era* (New York: Oxford University Press, 1988), 839–840.

12. The quotes are from David M. Oshinsky, "Convict Labor in the Post–Civil War South: Involuntary Servitude After the Thirteenth Amendment," in Alexander Tsesis, ed., *The Promises of Liberty: The History and Contemporary Relevance of the Thirteenth Amendment* (New York: Columbia University Press, 2010), 100–118. See also Daniel A. Novak, *The Wheel of Servitude: Black Forced Labor After Slavery* (Lexington: University Press of Kentucky, 1978), passim.

13. The quote is from "The 1866 Civil Rights Act," *Reconstruction: The Second Civil War,* PBS, December 19, 2003, http://www.pbs.org/wgbh/amex/reconstruction/activism/ps_1866.html. For Justice Miller's opinion, see Slaughter-House Cases, 83 U.S. 36 (1873). As examples of such usage, he mentioned long-term apprenticeships and former slaves reduced "to the condition of serfs attached to the plantation." Although the Thirteenth Amendment prohibited these practices, the Civil Rights Act of 1866 offered a practical remedy by extending the rights and protections of whites to all former slaves. See the analysis in Jacobus tenBroek, "Thirteenth Amendment to the Constitution of the United States: Consummation to Abolition and Key to the Fourteenth Amendment," *California Law Review* 39 (1951), 199–200.

14. The quotes are from Slaughter-House Cases, 83 U.S. 36 (1873). Dissenting justice Stephen Field preferred a more expansive understanding of the term "involuntary servitude." It is worth quoting him at length: "The words 'involuntary servitude' . . . include something more than slavery in the strict sense of the term; they include also serfage, vassalage, villenage, peonage, and all other forms of compulsory service for the mere benefit or pleasure of others. Nor is this the full import of the terms. The abolition of slavery and involuntary servitude was intended to make everyone born in this country a freeman, and, as such, to give to him the right to pursue the ordinary avocations of life without other restraint than such as affects all others, and to enjoy equally with them the fruits of his labor . . . A person allowed to pursue only one trade or calling, and only in one locality of the country, would not be, in the strict sense of the term, in a condition of slavery, but probably none would deny that he would be in a condition of servitude. He certainly would not possess the liberties nor enjoy the privileges of a freeman. The compulsion which would force him to labor even for his own benefit only in one direction, or in one place, would be almost as oppressive and nearly as great an invasion of his liberty as the compulsion which

would force him to labor for the benefit or pleasure of another, and would equally constitute an element of servitude."

15. For an excellent introduction to the legal debates surrounding the Thirteenth Amendment, see tenBroek, "Thirteenth Amendment to the Constitution of the United States," 171, 199–200; Risa L. Goluboff, "The Thirteenth Amendment and the Lost Origins of Civil Rights," *Duke Law Journal* 50 (2001), 1609–1685; and Azmy, "Modern Slavery and a Reconstructed Civil Rights Agenda," 981–1061.

16. Both the Civil Rights Act of 1866 and the Fourteenth Amendment contained the clause quoted and excluded Indians. For a brief but sound discussion of the legislation surrounding Indian citizenship, see Bryan H. Wildenthal, *Native American Sovereignty on Trial: A Handbook with Cases, Laws, and Documents* (Santa Barbara, CA: ABC-CLIO, 2003), 27–29. For census information, see James P. Collins, "Native Americans in the Census, 1860–1890," *Prologue* 38:2 (Summer 2006); available online at http://www.archives.gov/publications/prologue/2006/summer/indian-census.html.

17. The quote is from Elk v. Wilkins, 112 U.S. 94 (1884). For a broader analysis, see Stephen D. Bodayla, "'Can an Indian Vote?': *Elk v Wilkins*, a Setback for Indian Citizenship," *Nebraska History* 67 (1986), 372–380. On the interesting connections between community freedom and citizenship among African Americans, see Steven Hahn, *A Nation Under Our Feet: Black Political Struggles in the Rural South from Slavery to the Great Migration* (Cambridge: Harvard University Press, 2003); and Stephen Kantrowitz, *More Than Freedom: Fighting for Black Citizenship in a White Republic, 1829–1889* (New York: Penguin, 2012).

18. The quotes are from Smith, *Freedom's Frontier*, 185–186.

19. Woodman's letter and Hanson's reply appeared in the *Marysville (CA) Daily Appeal*, June 18, 1862. For additional context, see Smith, *Freedom's Frontier*, 186–187.

20. Smith, *Freedom's Frontier*, 188–190; Brendan C. Lindsay, *Murder State: California's Native American Genocide* (Lincoln: University of Nebraska Press, 2012), chap. 6.

21. Charles Sumner, resolution and remarks in the Senate, January 3, 1867; and Peonage Act of 1867, March 2, 1867, both cited in Aviam Soifer, "Federal Protection, Paternalism, and the Virtually Forgotten Prohibition of Voluntary Peonage," *Columbia Law Review* 112 (2012), 1607–1640. Senator Sumner's correspondence with New Mexicans included a very revealing letter from the acting governor, W.F.M. Arny, which reads as follows: "The House of Representatives has first passed a law entirely repealing all Peon and involuntary servitude laws of this Territory and it has also been read twice in the Council and as soon as it passes I will sign and approve it. But my dear sir: it appears to me that the repeal of laws and the declaration of Congress will not be sufficient to correct the evil so long as we have military officers who will deliberately encourage the enslavement of Indians and Mexicans, and will give away Indians to be held in servitude." W.F.M. Arny to Sumner, Santa Fe, January 21, 1867, MS AmW 13, Houghton Library, Harvard University. Governor Robert B. Mitchell's proclamation is quoted in Keleher, *Turmoil in New Mexico*, 471. See also Rael-Gálvez, "Identifying Captivity and Capturing Identity," chap. 6; and Kiser, "A 'Charming Name for a Species of Slavery,'" 169–189.

22. William T. Sherman to Ulysses Grant, June 7, 1868, quoted in Thompson, *The Army and the Navajo*, 151–152. For a relevant biography of Sherman, see Robert G. Athearn, *William Tecumseh Sherman and the Settlement of the West* (Norman: University of Oklahoma Press, 1956), 15–16. See also Keleher, *Turmoil in New Mexico*, 472–474; and Bailey, *Indian Slave Trade in the Southwest*, 177–178.

23. Council Proceedings, Fort Sumner, May 29, 1868, in Brugge, *Navajos in the Catholic Church Records of New Mexico*, 100–105.

24. "Joint Resolution No. 65," U.S. Congress, Washington, D.C., July 27, 1868," and William T. Sherman to George W. Getty, St. Louis, September 8, 1868, both in Keleher, *Turmoil in New Mexico*, 470–471 and 471–472, respectively. See also Bailey, *Indian Slave Trade in the Southwest*, 176–178.

25. Both quotes are from Commissioner William W. Griffin to S. B. Elkins, September 28, 1868, cited in Rael-Gálvez, "Identifying Captivity and Capturing Identity," 292.

26. Descriptions of these proceedings and the newspaper editorial appear in Keleher, *Turmoil in New Mexico*, 471–472. Additional details can be found in Rael-Gálvez, "Identifying Captivity and Capturing Identity," 295–296; and Brooks, *Captives and Cousins*, 351–353 and app. C.

27. The numbers of Navajos appearing in baptismal records are from Brugge, *Navajos in the Catholic Church Records of New Mexico*, 102–103.

28. tenBroek, "Thirteenth Amendment to the Constitution of the United States," 171–172. Present-day legal scholars continue to highlight the inadequacy of the Thirteenth Amendment to counter the rise of modern forms of human trafficking, servitude, and enslavement. As Baher Azmy observed in 2002, modern victims of slavery generally have no recognized Thirteenth Amendment remedy for what are quite obviously Thirteenth Amendment violations. More recently, Americans and people around the world are paying more attention to this problem. In 2000 the United Nations adopted the Convention Against Transnational Organized Crime, which included protocols on human trafficking and smuggling. That same year, the U.S. Congress promulgated the Trafficking Victims Protection Act. Although it is still too soon to tell whether these initiatives will make a difference, at least they address some of the deficiencies of the previous legal framework. On the continuing relevance and potential of the Thirteenth Amendment, see Azmy, "Modern Slavery and a Reconstructed Civil Rights Agenda," 981–1061; Tobias Barrington Wolff, "The Thirteenth Amendment and Slavery in the Global Economy," *Columbia Law Review* 973 (2002); and Neal Kumar Katyal, "Men Who Own Women: A Thirteenth Amendment Critique of Forced Prostitution," *Yale Law Journal* 103:3 (1993), 817–820.

29. The quotes are from *Albuquerque Journal*, April 26, 1967, and *Albuquerque Tribune*, March 29, 1967.

## EPILOGUE

1. Gunther Peck, *Reinventing Free Labor: Padrones and Immigrant Workers in the North American West, 1880–1930* (New York: Cambridge University Press, 2000), especially

chaps. 2 and 3. Peck repeatedly locates this relationship as somewhere in a continuum between free and unfree labor.

2. See Kevin Bales, *Disposable People: New Slavery in the Global Economy* (Berkeley: University of California Press, 1999); and Kevin Bales, *The Slave Next Door: Human Trafficking and Slavery in America Today* (New York: Cambridge University Press, 2010). The Global Slavery Index for 2014 can be found at http://www.globalslavery index.org/findings/#rankings.

3. Shelley, *Human Trafficking,* passim.

## APPENDIXES

1. All of these figures are quite speculative, but I offer them in the hope that they will generate competing estimates and significant adjustments. To paraphrase one prominent economic historian, all of these numbers are, without exception, inaccurate. However, this is not a valid argument against their use. One needs to begin somewhere.

2. This region includes the plains of Colombia and Venezuela.

3. Indians from Florida were traded all across the Caribbean and some as far as Spain. Swagerty, "Beyond Bimini," 38–74; Mira Caballos, *El indio antillano;* and Hoffman, *A New Andalucia,* 41–47. I propose a range of 2,000 to 10,000 subject to revision. I do not include Indian captives held by other Indians in any of these estimates not only because of lack of sources but also to be consistent with the methodology used for counting African slaves that considers only those who crossed the Atlantic but not the ones held by other Africans.

4. I discard Las Casas's estimate of "more than three million slaves" in Mexico, Central America, and Venezuela. Instead, I use Motolonía's numbers, which added all the slaves taken in the various provinces of Mexico up to 1555 and arrived at a range between 100,000 and 200,000. See Berthe, "Aspectos de la esclavitud de los indios," 66–67. I then added the number of Indian slaves taken in Central America as discussed in William L. Sherman, *Forced Native Labor,* chap. 6; David R. Radell, "The Indian Slave Trade and Population of Nicaragua during the Sixteenth Century," in William M. Denevan ed., *The Native Population of the Americas in 1492* (Madison: The University of Wisconsin Press, 1976), 67–76; Linda A. Newson, *The Cost of Conquest: Indian Decline in Honduras Under Spanish Rule* (Boulder: Westview Press, 1986), 110–111 and 127; and Linda A. Newson, "The Depopulation of Nicaragua in the Sixteenth Century," *Journal of Latin American Studies* 14:2 (November 1982), 271–275. Their estimates range between 150,000 and 500,000.

5. The total population of the Caribbean at the time of contact is hotly debated. I discard the "'High Counters'" figures of 8 or 10 million (see discussion in chapter 1) and instead assume a total initial population of around half a million. Considering that early Caribbean labor institutions like naborías, repartimientos, and encomiendas were quite coercive (see discussion in chapters 1 and 2), I further assume that all of these Indians were enslaved broadly speaking. This would yield an estimate of

between 100,000 and 150,000. See Livi Bacci, *Conquest*, 67–88; Livi Bacci, "Return to Hispaniola," 3–51; and Mira Caballos, *El indio antillano*, passim. To this figure we must add the slaves of the plains of Venezuela and Colombia. Slave-takers were very active in this large region, so an estimate of 30,000 to 50,000, while speculative, is reasonable. See Jiménez G., *La esclavitud indígena en Venezuela*, chap. 6; and Mena García, *El oro del Darién*. Nancy E. van Deusen estimates the total number of enslaved Indians in the sixteenth century at 650,000 or more in van Deusen, *Global Indios*, 2.

6. The late conquest of places like Peru, Chile, Río de la Plata, and Ecuador left little time for the acquisition of slaves during this period. Some Indians sold others into slavery and Spaniards acquired them readily. See "Real Provisión de D. Carlos por la que manda que ni los caciques, ni los indios principales puedan hacer esclavos, ni venderlos, ni rescatarlos, entre los indios de la provincia del Perú," Toledo, January 31, 1539, AGI, Lima, 565, L. 3, F. 71. A related category of coerced Indians known as *yanaconas* may have also been significant. The first encomiendas are awarded. Many more Indians were pressed into military service by Spanish conquistadors. See Karen Spalding, "The Crises and Transformations of Invaded Societies: Andean Area (1500–1580)," in Frank Salomon and Stuart B. Schwartz eds., *The Cambridge History of the Native Peoples of the Americas*, vol. 3, part 1 (New York: Cambridge University Press, 1999), 904–972. A range of 40,000 to 80,000 is speculative.

7. The figures for early Brazil remain quite speculative. The Portuguese (and fleetingly the French) initially bartered for brazilwood with the Natives of coastal Brazil but ultimately enslaved them. This was especially the case after the development of sugar plantations starting in the 1540s. See Stuart B. Schwartz, *Sugar Plantations in the Formation of Brazilian Society: Bahia, 1550–1835* (New York: Cambridge University Press, 1985), 37–38; John Hemming, *Red Gold: The Conquest of the Brazilian Indians, 1500–1760* (Cambridge: Harvard University Press, 1978), chap. 2; Monteiro, *Negros da terra*; John M. Monteiro, "The Crises and Transformations of Invaded Societies: Coastal Brazil in the Sixteenth Century," in Frank Salomon and Stuart B. Schwartz eds., *The Cambridge History of the Native Peoples of the Americas*, vol. 3, part 1 (New York: Cambridge University Press, 1999), 973–1023; Stuart B. Schwartz, "Indian Labor and New World Plantations: European Demands and Indian Responses in Northeastern Brazil," *The American Historical Review* 83:1 (February 1978), 44–79; and Alida C. Metcalf, "The Entradas of Bahia of the Sixteenth Century," *The Americas* 61:3 (2005), 373–428.

8. During this period Spaniards started making incursions into Texas, New Mexico, and the coast of California. However, the number of Indian slaves taken in these areas was still relatively small. Florida was almost certainly a more important slaving ground at this time. See the "expediente promovido por el general Pedro Menéndez de Avilés, sobre los grandes daños y muertes que hacían ciertos indios de la costa de la Florida, y que en su virtud se declarasen por esclavos, pues así podría continuarse la conquista y población de aquellas provincias," Madrid, 1574, AGI, Patronato, 257, N. 1, R. 20. A provisional range of 5,000 to 15,000 seems appropriate.

9. Mexico was mired in the Chichimec Wars until the end of the sixteenth century. At the same time the fantastic silver discoveries of this period created great demand for Indian labor. I do not include the encomienda Indians of central Mexico who were generally able to pay in goods rather than service. This, however, was not the case for the encomienda Indians of northern Mexico who were enslaved for all practical purposes. See del Hoyo, *Esclavitud y Encomiendas de indios en el nuevo reino de León*. Although speculative, I also include Indians in repartimientos, debt peonage, and other coercive arrangements but not the slaves coming from the Philippines and the Indian subcontinent. I propose a very provisional range of 80,000 to 140,000. To this we must add the Indian slaves of Central America. In spite of the Cerrato reforms, Spaniards reverted to holding Indians in bondage after Cerrato's death, partly motivated by a boom in cacao. A range of 30,000 to 50,000 is speculative but possible.

10. Although the Indian population of the Caribbean experienced a near collapse, Spaniards continued to organize slaving raids. See "Real Provisión por la cual se da licencia a los vecinos de la isla Española para que los indios caribes que vinieren a infestar a los vecinos de ella y a los ellos comarcanos, puedan armar contra ellos y hacerles guerra . . . y se permite que a los indios caribes que se cautivaren en la dicha guerra y fueren presentados ante la audiencia y a ella le constare que se cautivaron en ella y siendo adjudicados por ella los puedan tener por esclavos," Valladolid, June 22, 1558, AGI, Santo Domingo, 899, L. 1, F. 111. A range of 5,000 to 15,000 is possible for this period. Slaving continued in coastal Venezuela and Colombia in spite of royal prohibitions. Jiménez G., *La esclavitud indígena en Venezuela*, chap. 8. Moreover, the encomienda in Colombia and Venezuela was based on personal services. See Juan A. and Judith E. Villamarin, *Indian Labor in Mainland Colonial Spanish America* (Newark: University of Delaware, 1975), 114. I propose a range of 25,000 to 60,000, subject to revision.

11. For Peru and Bolivia in this period it is necessary to consider that over 200 Indian villages located in a contiguous region around the mines of Potosí and Huancavelica were required to provide one-seventh of their adult male population as a rotating draft or mita beginning in 1573. This system continued for 250 years. Scholars have long debated the degree of coercion involved in the mita system. See Peter Bakewell, *Miners of the Red Mountain: Indian Labor in Potosí, 1545–1650* (Albuquerque: University of New Mexico Press, 1984); Cole, *The Potosí Mita 1573–1700*; and Tandeter, *Coercion and Market*. Moreover, the number of conscripted workers fluctuated: in 1573 it was 9,500; in 1575 it was 11,500; and so on. Yananconaje continued to exist. A rough estimate of the forced laborers in Peru and Bolivia during this period would hover between 100,000 and 150,000. Chile also experienced a mining boom at this time and consequently the enslavement of Indians as well as other forms of labor coercion increased. According to one contemporary report, in 1594 the number of "indios de servicio" in Chile had "dwindled" to 37,000. A total enslaved population of between 50,000 and 90,000 is plausible. For the report see Jara, *Guerra y sociedad en Chile*, 31. For Ecuador and the Río de la Plata region, the numbers are more speculative but there is still abundant evidence of enslavement. For example, see the "real cédula al presidente y oidores de la Audiencia de Quito para que hagan cumplir lo

que está mandado de que los indios puedan libremente vivir y trabajar sin que se les obligue ni esclavice," Madrid, November 11, 1566, AGI, Quito, 211, L. 1, F. 122v; and the "real cédula al marqués de Cañete . . . acerca de la relación hecha por el cacique principal de los pueblos de Soconcho y Manogasta, de la provincia de Tucumán, respecto de que de los indios de aquellos pueblos se sirven los gobernadores de aquella provincia como de esclavos y los sacan de su natural para trabajar en charcas y otras labores . . ." Madrid, March 16, 1594, in *Libro registros-cedularios del Tucumán y Paraguay, 1573–1716* (Buenos Aires: Instituto de Investigaciones de Historia del Derecho, 2000), 36. Ecuador also experienced a gold boom at this time. Although speculative, I propose a range of 15,000 to 30,000.

12. The Tenure of Governor Mem de Sá marked a turning point in the enslavement of the Natives of coastal Brazil. According to the Jesuit missionary Anchieta, over 50,000 captives were taken within a few months in the early 1560s. He also reported that slaving raids in 1577 yielded 20,000 Indian slaves. Sugar production expanded rapidly at this time and the Indian slaves were replaced by African slaves over a lengthy period. A range of 120,000 to 200,000 is speculative but not inconceivable.

13. In this period Spaniards colonized New Mexico and incorporated it to the silver mining economy. Indian slavery in Florida continued, although here Spanish colonists relied more readily on African slaves imported from the Caribbean. French exploration and colonization ventures along the Saint Lawrence River as well as English settlements in the mid-Atlantic coast resulted in the capture of Natives, although these were still few in number. I propose a preliminary range of 15,000 to 45,000 including Indian slaves, servants, criminals serving out sentences of forced labor, and encomienda Indians who were forced to render personal services.

14. The Chichimec Wars came to an end but the silver mining economy expanded during this period. Significant uprisings by Xiximes, Tepehuanes, and other indigenous groups in northern Mexico resulted in Spanish military campaigns and slave-taking. Plenty of evidence of Indian enslavement exists for Nuevo León, Coahuila, Sinaloa, and Sonora. I propose a very speculative range of 20,000 to 60,000. In Central America debt peonage proliferated as the encomienda system came to an end. The cacao boom continued for two or three decades. See Murdo J. MacLeod, *Spanish Central America: A Socioeconomic History 1520–1720* (Berkeley: University of California Press, 1973). A range of 15,000 to 30,000 is speculative.

15. The main area of enslavement in this period was centered on the northeastern portion of South America as far as the Guianas. Here Spain, England, and Holland competed against each other, forged indigenous allies, and created networks of enslavement. The Carib Indians emerged as important suppliers of slaves at this time. One later Spanish source estimated that the Carib Indians made around 300 prisoners a year. Quoted in Whitehead, *Lords of the Tiger Spirit*, 186–187. A range of 15,000 to 30,000 is possible. In addition, Colombia and Venezuela continued to have encomiendas based primarily on personal services, although in Colombia it was gradually converted into an institution based on the collection of tribute. The Indian population thus subjected may have ranged from 15,000 to 25,000.

16. The mita continued in Peru although in decreasing numbers. A range of 150,000

to 250,000 is therefore plausible. In Chile Indian slavery flourished in the wake of a major Indian insurrection. In 1608 Philip III stripped the Mapuche Indians of the customary royal protection against enslavement thus making Chile one of the very few zones of the empire where slave-taking was entirely legal. Although speculative, I propose I range of 30,000 to 70,000. In this period Spaniards also intensified their raids into the Calchaquí Valleys and more generally Tucumán and Paraguay. See Doucet, "Sobre cautivos de guerra y esclavos indios en el Tucumán," 59–152; Giudicelli, "'Identidades' rebeldes: Soberanía colonial y poder de clasificación," 137–172; Garavaglia, "Invaded Societies: La Plata Basin, 1535–1650," and Saeger, "The Chaco and Paraguay, 1573–1822," both in Frank Salomon and Stuart B. Schwartz, eds., *The Cambridge History of the Native Peoples of the Americas* vol. 3, part 2 (New York: Cambridge University Press, 1999), 1–58 and 257–286, respectively. A range of 10,000 to 30,000 is subject to discussion.

17. The *bandeirantes* took upwards of 60,000 captives in the middle decades of the seventeenth century from Jesuit missions in Paraguay. For a reasonable discussion of these numbers see Monteiro, *Negros da terra,* 73–74. *Bandeirantes* also took an unknowable number of captives from Indians at large. A range of 80,000 to 150,000 is quite speculative.

18. In this period Indian slavery was widespread in the Carolinas and Florida. Alan Gallay proposes a range between 25,000 and 40,000 from the 1670s through 1700. Gallay, *The Indian Slave Trade,* 298–299. In New England King Philip's War (1675–1678) resulted in hundreds of enslaved Indians many of whom were shipped to the Caribbean. French colonists and their Native allies developed an extensive network of enslavement in New France that reached into the Great Lakes region and resulted in the capture of hundreds or even thousands of victims. The Spanish province of New Mexico was rocked by the Pueblo Revolt of 1680, which was largely a response to widespread enslavement (chapter 6). A range of 40,000 to 90,000 for this period is subject to debate.

19. This was a tumultuous period of some stagnation in the silver mines, a massive Indian rebellion in northern Mexico, and an empire-wide Spanish campaign to free all Indian slaves (see chapter 5). In addition, Honduras experienced a mining boom but against the background of a dwindling Native population. The decline of encomiendas meant a greater reliance on repartimientos and also a transition toward debt servitude and other forms of labor extraction. See Newson, *Indian Survival in Colonial Nicaragua,* 150–167. A range of 45,000 to 90,000 is possible but subject to discussion.

20. Slaving in coastal Colombia and Venezuela continued as well as imperial competition in the Guianas. At this time Venezuela became the primary supplier of cocoa to Europe and also developed some gold mining. Although plantation and mine owners relied primarily on African slaves, they also had coerced Native laborers as encomiendas and repartimientos. The range of 20,000 to 35,000 is highly speculative.

21. In Peru and Bolivia the mita continued but in decreasing numbers. A range of 90,000 to 180,000 is subject to debate. In Chile Indian slavery remained legal and flourished. Governor Juan Enríquez affirmed categorically in 1676 that "in Chile there are many more Indian slaves than Spaniards" at a time when the Spanish population in Chile

had reached 100,000. Governor Juan Enríquez to King Carlos II, Santiago, October 8, 1676, in AGI Chile, 57. Slaves were so plentiful that merchants also shipped them to Peru. See contemporary description by Miguel de Miranda Escobar, cited in Jara, *Guerra y sociedad en Chile*, 149. A range of 80,000 to 140,000 is subject to discussion. Across the Andes, in Paraguay and Tucumán slavery also proliferated. A very speculative range would be between 15,000 and 35,000.

22. Raiding by *bandeirantes* continued as they explored the interior of Brazil. A range of 60,000 to 100,000 is possible.

23. Indian slavery continued to be widespread in the Carolinas and Florida. Inferring from Gallay's study, in the first two decades of the eighteenth century perhaps 5,000 to 12,000 Natives were taken. Indian slaves also continued in New France, New England, and the mid-Atlantic colonies. New York under Dutch and English control has left a copious paper trail about Indian slaves. Farther south Comanches sold Plains Indians both in Louisiana and New Mexico. These captives (and others sold by Utes, Navajos, and Apaches) became known as genízaros in New Mexico and were so plentiful that they formed their own communities. It is hard to make an accurate assessment, but a range of 20,000 to 40,000 may serve as a starting point.

24. In Mexico encomiendas declined or disappeared in this period and mine owners relied more on repartimiento Indians and salaried workers. At the same time silver production more than doubled during this fifty-year period. I rely on the silver production figures provided by TePaske, *A New World of Gold and Silver*, 23. In Central America encomiendas remained in use much longer than in other Spanish colonies and were only abolished in 1718. The repartimientos continued. I propose a range of 20,000 to 50,000 subject to debate.

25. The Spanish crown still sanctioned the enslavement of Carib Indians because they were reputedly cannibals. At the same time the cacao boom continued in Venezuela and gold production rose in Nueva Granada. See TePaske, *A New World of Gold and Silver*, 39. Thus the demand for labor was great at a time when the Indian population was declining. I propose a very speculative range of 15,000 to 25,000.

26. In Peru and Bolivia the mita continued but with ever-dwindling conscripts. I propose a range of 120,000 to 190,000, subject to revision. In Chile Indian slavery was no longer legal after the 1680s but other forms of coerced labor persisted. I propose a very speculative range of 15,000 to 50,000. The Spanish crown also cracked down on slaving activities in Paraguay and Tucumán with mixed results. A range of 10,000 to 20,000 is merely an informed guess based on very fragmentary information.

27. A range of 50,000 to 130,000 is speculative but not unreasonable. Only in the seven-year period between 1738 and 1745 in Pará, the Junta das Missões approved petitions for 10,250 Indian slaves. See Barbara A. Sommer, "Colony of the Sertão: Amazonian Expeditions and the Indian Slave Trade," *The Americas* 61:3 (January 2005), 413. I want to thank Barbara for drawing my attention to this information. According to Jonathan D. Hill, Portuguese slave trading and warfare against indigenous groups reached its zenith in the 1740s–1750s when approximately 20,000 indigenous slaves were taken only from the upper Rio Negro region. See Jonathan D. Hill, "Indigenous Peoples and the Rise of Independent Nation-States in Lowland South America," in

Frank Salomon and Stuart B. Schwartz, eds., *The Cambridge History of the Native Peoples of the Americas* vol. 3, part 2 (New York: Cambridge University Press, 1999), 709. See also David G. Sweet, "A Rich Realm of Nature Destroyed: The Middle Amazon Valley, 1640-1750" (Ph.D. diss., University of Wisconsin, 1974).

28. Indian slavery declined through much of the eastern seaboard and was largely replaced by African slavery or by free labor. Yet, west of the Mississippi it continued. Utes, Navajos, and Comanches continued to sell captives in New Mexico. A brisk trade for Coahuiltecan Indians developed along the Rio Grande Valley. Missionaries in the Pimería Alta acquired Indians offered by other Indians. The occupation of Alta California created new markets for Indians. At the same time Hispanic New Mexicans and Texans held individuals on account of debts thus adopting the system that was prevalent farther south. A very speculative range of 15,000 to 30,000 is subject to debate.

29. The Mexican military launched "deportation" campaigns against the Seri Indians in the 1750s and Apaches beginning in the 1770s. The colonization of Nuevo Santander by José de Escandon led to enslavement and servitude. See Patricia Osante, ed., *Testimonio acerca de la causa formada en la colonial del Nuevo Santander al coronel Don José de Escandón* (Mexico City: UNAM, 2000). More broadly, debt peonage increased at this time. In Central America the repartimientos continued. The range of 30,000 to 60,000 is speculative particularly because of the difficulties of estimating the number of debt peons and servants.

30. Carib Indians can still be legally enslaved even in this very late period. See "cédula real para que no se considere esclavo a ningún indio que no sea Caribe," Madrid, February 7, 1756, Archivo General de la Nación, Reales Cédulas Originales, vol. 76, file 13. The gold boom in Colombia and Venezuela peaked at this time. Although prospectors and miners relied increasingly on African slaves, coercive practices imposed on Indians persisted. The Indian population began recovering at this time. I propose a very speculative range of 10,000 to 20,000, subject to revision.

31. In Peru and Bolivia the mita continued with fewer conscripts. A range of 90,000 to 120,000 is speculative. In Chile encomiendas persisted until 1791. In Paraguay encomiendas continued in this period. Forms of servitude persisted throughout the region. A very speculative range of 10,000 to 25,000 is subject to revision.

32. Hal Langfur reminds us that the *bandeira* did not end in the seventeenth century. Langfur, "The Return of the *Bandeira*," 429–461. Moreover, formal abolition of Indian slavery led to forms of servitude and peonage that characterized many other parts of Latin America. The range of 40,000 to 100,000 is quite speculative.

33. Comanches, Apaches, Navajos, and Utes continued to trade captives in New Mexico. In California the destruction of the mission system and the emergence of a ranchero class led to the peonization of the former mission Indians and the proliferation of raids to capture Indian servants. Utah became a crossroads for the caravans going from New Mexico to California and back. Utes captured Paiute Indians and sold them to the passing merchants. They also began selling captives to the Mormon pioneers (see chapter 11). A very speculative range would be 10,000 to 20,000.

34. Deportation campaigns against Apaches and other Indians ceased at this time. On

the other hand, there is a great deal of evidence of debt peonage in the south, the center, and the north of Mexico. See González Navarro, "El trabajo forzoso en México," 588–615. In the north and in the south various state legislatures regulated various aspects of servitude. Similar conditions existed in Central America. For the case of Guatemala, see Severo Martínez Peláez, *La patria del criollo: Ensayo de interpretación de la realidad colonial guatemalteca* (Guatemala: EDUCA, 1979). A very speculative range of 30,000 to 80,000 may serve as a point of departure.

35. There is scant information about this period. Indian population all along the circum-Caribbean region experienced a marked rebound. Debt peonage and other coercive methods of labor extraction persisted, although it is very hard to determine how common these practices were. The wars of independence in Colombia and Venezuela led to military conscription but the scale remains unclear. I propose a highly speculative range of 15,000 to 45,000 as a starting point.

36. In Peru and Bolivia the mita ended. However the wars of independence that ranged all over the region, including Uruguay, Argentina, Chile, Peru, and Bolivia, resulted in forced conscription of indigenous peoples. Debt peonage and other forms of labor coercion persisted. I propose a very speculative range of 40,000 to 90,000.

37. Forms of servitude and peonage continued in this period. This range is decidedly speculative.

38. Indian slavery increased when millions of American settlers moved to the West. Indian servitude laws were implemented in California, Utah, and New Mexico (see chapters 10, 11, and 12). A range of 40,000 to 90,000 is speculative but a starting point.

39. In Mexico debt peonage and other forms of labor coercion continued in the 1850s and 1860s and increased markedly during the Porfirian period as export booms of henequen, coffee, sugar, mining, and other commodities required more labor. Central America experienced a similar transformation with coffee, bananas, and other products. For a broad overview, see Steven C. Topik and Allen Wells, eds., *The Second Conquest of Latin America: Coffee, Henequen, and Oil during the Export Boom, 1850–1930* (Austin: University of Texas Press, 1998). For Guatemala see David McCreery, "Debt Servitude in Rural Guatemala, 1876–1936," *Hispanic American Historical Review* 63:4 (1983), 735–759; and McCreery, "'An Odious Feudalism': *Mandamiento* Labor and Commercial Agriculture in Guatemala, 1858–1920," *Latin American Perspectives* 13:1 (1986), 99–117. As noted, American journalist John Kenneth Turner estimated that Mexico had 750,000 slaves by 1908. A range of 70,000 to 150,000 is speculative.

40. Export booms in the circum-Caribbean region also resulted in more servants and peons at a time when African slavery was abolished. A range of 20,000 to 70,000 is very speculative.

41. Peru, Bolivia, Ecuador, Chile, Argentina, Uruguay, and Paraguay also experienced a "second conquest" as described by Topik and Wells and against the background of the abolition of African slavery. Booms in guano, copper, rubber, and various other products increased demand for coerced and slave labor. For just a glimpse of the surprising transformations that occurred at this time see Melillo, "The First Green Rev-

olution," 1028–1060; and Nara Milanich, "Women, Children, and Domestic Labor in Nineteenth-Century Chile," *Hispanic American Historical Review* 91:1 (February 2011), 29–62. A range 100,000 to 180,000 is highly speculative.

42. Like other Latin American nations, Brazil experienced export-led booms at this time. The rubber boom, for instance, had a tremendous impact on Brazil's indigenous population in the Amazon basin. The range of 70,000 to 150,000 is highly speculative.

43. Extensive lists of slaving expeditions and licenses appear in Mira Caballos, *El indio antillano*, 391–399.

44. Price information comes from ibid., 288–289.

45. The data on silver and gold production come from TePaske, *A New World of Gold and Silver*, 113; and Craig and Rimstidt, "Gold Production History of the United States," 407–464. For the conversions, I assume that 1 troy ounce equals 31.1035 grams.

46. William B. Griffen has compiled a table of the Indians from New Mexico baptized in Parral. These figures tell us little about the absolute number of New Mexican slaves because many were sold in places other than Parral or were never baptized in the first place. But the numbers do indicate that the flow of slaves increased in the 1650s, continued to grow in the 1660s, and reached a record high in the 1670s. Griffen, *Culture Change and Shifting Populations in Central Northern Mexico* (Tucson: University of Arizona Press, 1969), 102. The years shown in the chart are as they appear in the original. Many slaves went unreported. Rick Hendricks and Gerald Mandell observe that in 1646, only two Apaches were baptized, even though between seventeen and twenty-four Apaches arrived in Parral in the spring of that year. Hendricks and Mandell, "The Apache Slave Trade in Parral," 73.

47. This graph is derived from the information in appendix 1.

48. This chart is based entirely on data from Brugge, *Navajos in the Catholic Church Records of New Mexico*, 22–23.

# Index